SELF-DISCOVERY

SELF-DISCOVERY

The Illustrated Guide to Your Personality and Potential

Edited by Glenn Wilson

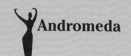Andromeda

CONTRIBUTORS

VOLUME EDITOR

Dr Glenn Wilson
Senior Lecturer in Psychology,
Institute of Psychiatry,
University of London, UK

DISTINGUISHED
CONSULTANTS

Professor Seymour Feshbach
Professor of Psychology, University
of California, Los Angeles, USA

Professor Hans J Eysenck
Professor Emeritus,
University of London, UK

ADVISORY EDITORS

Dr Irene Martin
Reader in Physiological Psychology,
Institute of Psychiatry,
University of London, UK

Professor Richard Lynn
Professor of Psychology,
University of Ulster, Coleraine,
Northern Ireland

KEY TO AUTHORS

AH **Anna C Higgitt**
Senior Registrar, Kings College and
Dulwich Hospitals, London, UK

AER **Dr A E Reading**
Associate Clinical Professor,
School of Medicine, University of
California, Los Angeles, USA

AZ **Professor Avner Ziv**
Professor of Psychology,
Tel Aviv University, Israel

BWPW **Professor Brian W P Wells**
Professor of Psychology, Newport
University, California, USA

DKBN **Dr David K B Nias**
Lecturer in Psychopathology,
City of London Polytechnic, UK

GM **Dr Gerry Mulhern**
Lecturer in Psychology,
University of Ulster,
Coleraine, Northern Ireland

GW **Dr Glenn Wilson**
Senior Lecturer in Psychology,
Institute of Psychiatry,
University of London, UK

HWR **Dr Helen Warren Ross**
Associate Professor of Family
Studies and Consumer Sciences,
San Diego State University, USA

JJC **Dr James J Conley**
Psychologist, Department of Mental
Retardation, Connecticut, USA

JM **Jessica Madge**
Lecturer in Nursing, University
College, Swansea, UK

JMGW **Dr John Mark G Williams**
Research Scientist, Medical
Research Council, Applied
Psychology Unit, Cambridge, UK

JPF **Dr Joseph P Forgas**
Associate Professor of Psychology,
University of New South Wales,
Australia

KPO **Dr Kieron P O'Connor**
Research Fellow, Hôpital Louis-
Hippolite Lafontaine and University
of Montreal, Canada

KTS **Professor K T Strongman**
Professor of Psychology and
Head of Department,
University of Canterbury,
New Zealand

MC **Dr Mark Cook**
Lecturer in Psychology,
University College, Swansea, UK

PF **Dr Peter Fonagy** ·
Lecturer in Psychology,
University College, London, UK

PK **Professor Paul Kline**
Professor of Psychometrics,
University of Exeter, UK

PMI **Dr Paul M Insel**
Associate Professor, Department of
Psychiatry, Stanford University, USA

PW **Dr Pamela Wells**
Senior Lecturer, Department of
Psychology, Goldsmiths' College,
London, UK

RLS **Professor Robert L Solso**
Professor of Psychology,
University of Nevada, USA

RP **Professor Robert Plutchik**
Professor of Psychiatry and
Psychology, Bronx Municipal
Hospital Center, USA

RM **Dr Robert Maurer**
Director of Behavioral Sciences,
Santa Monica Hospital Medical
Center, USA

RW **Dr Ronnie Wilson**
Senior Lecturer in Psychology,
University of Ulster, Coleraine,
Northern Ireland

SMH **Dr Stephen M Hudson**
Lecturer in Psychology,
University of Canterbury,
New Zealand

WPdS **Dr W P de Silva**
Senior Lecturer in Psychology,
Institute of Psychiatry,
University of London, UK

PROJECT EDITOR
Stuart McCready

TEXT

Copy editors
David Blomfield
Nancy Duin
Joanne Lightfoot
Shirley McCready
Michael March
Nick Russell

Indexer
Fiona Barr

Word-processing
Reina Foster-de Wit
Regina Barakauskas

PICTURES

Research coordinator
Thérèse Maitland

Researchers
Celia Dearing
Suzanne Williams
Sue Williams

ART

Art editor and layout
designer
Chris Munday

Additional layout
designers
Martin Anderson
Michael Grendon

Artists
Martin Anderson
Simon Driver
Mary Ann Le May

First published in the UK by
Andromeda Oxford Ltd, 1989

 Devised and produced by
Andromeda Oxford Ltd
Dorchester-on-Thames
Oxford OX9 8JU, UK

Typeset by Opus, Oxford, UK

Originated by Scantrans,
Singapore

Printed by G Canale Co, Italy

SUMMARY CONTENTS

CONTENTS PART 1

4 By noticing the way you form impressions of others, you can become more conscious of how they form impressions of you.

5 Skillful self-presentation helps reinforce the impression you wish to have of yourself.

8 We instinctively help each other to meet basic needs and find progressively more fulfilling pursuits as basic needs are met.

of environmental influences shape our personalities.

13 Psychologists have devised various techniques for measuring personality. Some of these may help you to assess and understand your own personality.

able to express them, and how sensitive you are to the needs of others.

CONTENTS PART 2

likely to be victimized by our bad moods.

20 Knowing how to express your feelings appropriately and adequately can make all the difference to your social life and psychological well-being.

25 Can you develop a more relaxed lifestyle and learn to keep calm in tense situations?

26 Why it is worth making a habit of explaining events to yourself in a more positive way, thinking of things that are pleasant to remember and doing things that cheer you up.

30 There are searching questions that you should ask yourself before allowing a sense of guilt to dominate your life. A misplaced sense of guilt can be harbored unconsciously.

the world, and you need to know how to find more enjoyment in the present.

PROBABLY, like most other people, you are aware of missing opportunities for greater self-fulfillment. You have thought of trying to express your personality more effectively, make your relationships more satisfying, manage your emotions better, be more in control of your life – and, like most people, you have probably found these ideas difficult to pin down in any precise, practical way. How *do* people put them into effect? How can *I*, in particular, do so?

At least part of the answer lies in access to expert knowledge, for the experience of both those who succeed and those who fail to live as they would wish has been intensively studied. In the pages that follow, a distinguished international panel of 25 experts attempts to answer your questions, applying their own research and experience and the accumulated wisdom of fellow workers in their fields.

They have written a book that will help you clarify in your own mind the self that you are and the self you would like to be. There is a recurrent theme: if you allow your images of these two selves to drift too far apart, you will undermine your potential to change in ways that can bring you genuine satisfaction and fulfillment. This is not a book, therefore, that aims to fire you at once with overambition. If your road to a better life involves taking an impossibly big first step you are likely to do nothing to change, and a sense of achievement will continue to elude you.

The contributors to the book all adhere to the simple principle that you will find happiness and contentment by setting goals that you can attain. They agree, too, that the sense of vitality we gain from small successes does much more than overambitious goal-setting can do to spur us on.

For example, several chapters give practical advice about dividing big emotional problems into smaller ones, grading them by difficulty and overcoming the easy ones first. You can apply a similar divide-and-conquer strategy to almost any problem you face.

Another way of limiting the gap between your real self and your ideal self is to avoid underestimating your potential and overestimating the obstacles and limitations that lie within you. Several chapters are concerned with showing how people's understanding of themselves can become more sympathetic, and often much more realistic, when they learn to appreciate that they are already closer than they thought to being the people they want to be. We need encouragement, not only from others but from ourselves, and if we allow ourselves to feel more attractive and more competent, other people are much more likely to form a favorable impression of us, and so reinforce our self-esteem.

Your understanding of yourself can become more sympathetic and realistic, too, if you can recognize and come to accept your personality as it is. The very idea of identifying your personality may seem objectionable, for this means putting labels on yourself – seeing yourself in terms of a set of personality stereotypes. As you will probably have been warned already, sorting people into types can be very harmful; we tend to exaggerate the similarities between those within a category and exaggerate the ways in which they are different from others. Individual qualities can easily be overlooked. However, stereotypes are inevitable and indispensable. We cannot form impressions of people, not even of ourselves, without comparing and generalizing.

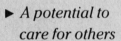

▶ *A potential to care for others*

In several chapters you are invited to test aspects of your own personality. It is hoped that this may give you greater insight into your temperament – your emotional makeup – as well as insight into your style of dealing with social situations and problems. But you should not take the picture that emerges as final. Personality tests are more reliable when they are administered directly by experts and when you are less conscious of their purpose than you will be as you read this book. Also, not everything about your personality is unchangeable. The expression of personality develops throughout life; people can learn to be less anxious, more versatile, more resilient, more assertive or less assertive, as may be appropriate. The advantage of personality self-assessment is that it can give you a starting point – a sense of the goals for personal growth that are most likely to be possible and worthwhile for you.

Understanding your personality, of course, goes far beyond finding a set of categories that apply to you. We each have a unique personal history that has helped to give us a pattern of needs and desires that may seek expression without our consciously recognizing them. The details of Sigmund Freud's famous theory of human motivation may be unconvincing (see Chapter 9), but you might still find it useful to apply some of the techniques in Chapter 31 that have sprung from Freud's methods. They may help you to become more aware of the psychological defense mechanisms you use to hide your own motives from yourself.

The most important message of this book is that *you* should be the one to identify possibilities and set goals. Often people fail to see their potential because they wait for someone else to define it for them and say what goals they should pursue. Sometimes people are deterred from doing what they would find fulfilling because they feel guilty about pursuing personal satisfaction or feeling good about themselves. Several chapters emphasize the importance of taking it upon yourself to map your own life, to make your own needs and expectations known, and to be unashamed about making the most of the self that you, more intimately than anyone else, perceive.

11

▲ *A potential to be and feel attractive*
▶ *A potential to be creative*

USE this alphabetical guide to find the main subjects in Part One, *Your Personality and Potential*. A single reference is given for each, indicating the page or beginning page of its fullest treatment. For a guide to Part Two see page 14. For a wider reference to a subject and for a more extensive list of subjects, see the index at the end of the book.

◀ *A potential to triumph over disabilities*

13

▲ *A potential to take delight in natural things*

◄ *A potential to take a pride in achievement*

USE this alphabetical guide to find the main subjects in Part Two, *Your Emotional Well-Being*. A single reference is given for each, indicating the page or beginning page of its fullest treatment. For a guide to Part One see page 12. For a wider reference to a subject and for a more extensive list of subjects, see the index at the end of the book.

14

◄ *A potential to love and be loved*

15

▲ *A potential to see the humorous side of life*

▶ *A potential to enjoy simple pleasures*

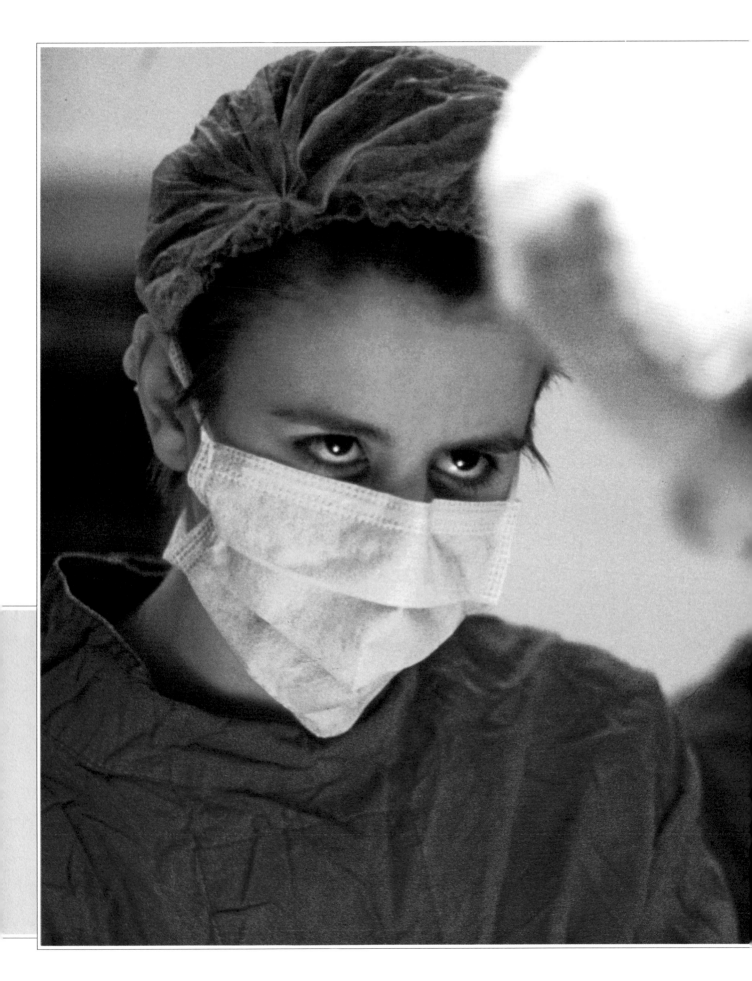

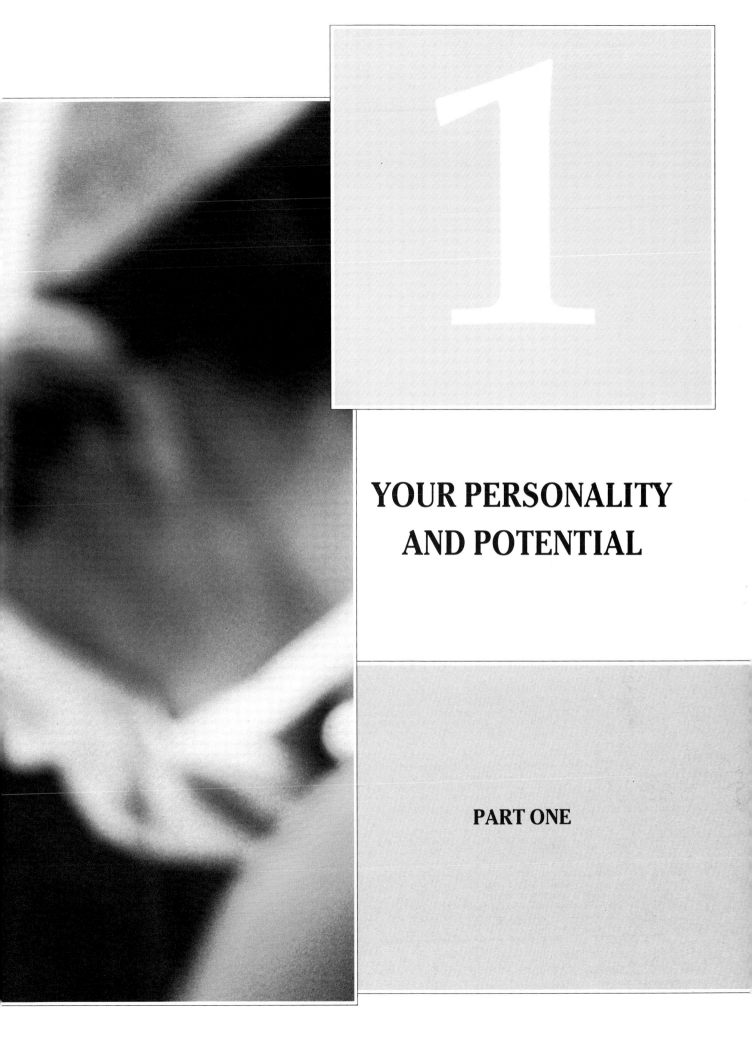

1

YOUR PERSONALITY
AND POTENTIAL

PART ONE

Self-Fulfillment

MOST of us would like to discover our inner nature, make the most of everything we are capable of being and doing, and live life to the full. Some psychologists believe that this urge to achieve the upper limits of our potential is inherent in human nature. They believe that the ultimate goal of life is the expression and full development of each person's unique qualities which, in those who achieve an ideal self-fulfillment, are blended into a harmonious whole.

What kind of person can realistically pursue this ideal? It is not in fact a goal only for exceptional people and those who achieve it *can* reconcile their dreams and wishes with the needs of others.

Becoming a self-actualizer

Studies of human behavior often strike a pessimistic note. Psychologists who emphasize the environmental forces that shape our personalities can create the impression that we have no part to play in making ourselves. Others emphasize our drive to express an inborn nature, but many – Freudian psychoanalysts, especially – seem to have a negative view of this nature: we are seen as products of a conflict between unruly instincts and the restraints that society is forced to impose (see *Ch 9*).

The "humanistic" style of psychology, pioneered by Carl Rogers and Abraham Maslow, takes a more positive view.

Maslow, in particular, constructs a hierarchy of increasingly human natural needs (see *Ch 8*). We begin by being strongly motivated to fulfill basic deficiencies (of nourishment, security, love and acceptance, self-esteem). Our struggle to overcome these deficiencies may sometimes create an unattractive picture of humanity, but, in Maslow's view, when deficiency needs are mastered, "self-actualizing" needs begin to express the best in us. Maslow's studies provide a summary of typical characteristics of self-actualizers (see p20).

Whether or not it is possible to be self-actualizing does, of course, depend on an element of luck. A broken or violent

■ **Achieving and enjoying self-fulfillment**. *The passive pleasures of contentment* LEFT *are a relatively minor part of living a fulfilled life. Many psychologists prefer to focus their study on the active part, to which they give such names as "self-realization" and "self-actualization." It is normal and healthy to actively seek fulfillment through competitive achievement, like this log-roll winner* RIGHT *in Wisconsin. Everyone, however, not just those who come out on top, has a self to actualize – a set of goals that it would be realistic for them to choose and satisfying for them to achieve. People who overcome obstacles and handicaps in order to do what fulfills them are worth thinking of*

*People who become what they want to be know
their own potentials and limitations. They set
their goals for themselves and achieve them by
their own energy and creative insight. Success
increases rather than absorbs their vitality.*

home, poverty, unemployment, limited mental or physical
attributes, and ill health are only some of the many things
likely to diminish anyone's potential for personal growth.
It takes a rare individual to overcome these disadvantages,
although a few do.

Inevitably, some people become so bitter, resigned or
pessimistic as a result of their present or past circumstances
that they may never feel positive or confident enough to respond to self-actualizing urges.

In addition, self-actualization is not necessarily a constant and permanent state. Ill health, job loss, powers
waning with age, and the loss of friends and family can all
make it difficult to prevent a shrinking in personality.

However, it is unusual for those who have become self-
actualized to any extent to regress completely. Once
established, self-actualizers' positive self-regard and
acceptance of themselves as worthwhile human beings is
very hard to shake.

As long as their basic survival needs are met to a minimal
degree, and valued purposes remain, a previously healthy
personality usually manages to adapt and persist. In fact,
adversity and even suffering can often provide a rich soil for
further growth.

Disadvantages or disabilities may be advantageous if they
are experienced as challenges. Perhaps even a sense of
inferiority (see *Ch 6*) will cause some to stretch to the limits
of their potential. The danger is, though, that the impetus to
overcome deficiencies may lead to an underdevelopment of
other qualities.

By the same token, special aptitudes and other apparent
advantages can become liabilities if easy successes lead to
the neglect of other, even more suitable options. Just as
particular disadvantages or disabilities may have the greatest influence on what we make of ourselves, marked artistic,
intellectual or physical gifts may overshadow and diminish
the development of other potentialities.

Family life and personal growth

Compromises are inevitable and, in some circumstances
and at certain stages in life, our freedom or opportunities to
pursue personal development may be severely restricted,
with any one choice tending to preclude or curtail another.

19

*when the limitations in our lives
make it seem that there are no
worthwhile objectives open to
us. CENTER, Mike Spring sailing
solo between Britain and the
Azores during a vacation from
his job in a computer company,
in spite of lacking the use of his
legs.*

For example, raising a family can be a profoundly fulfilling experience, but it cannot be done without cost – not only in terms of time and money, but also in the loss of opportunities to do other, highly valued, things.

For a woman, the dilemma of whether to have children or pursue a career more fully is often a very painful one. Either she remains childless or she does have children but has to delegate much of their upbringing to others. Whichever decision she makes is likely to result in her feeling unfulfilled.

If she has decided that her career is much more important than having children, she may later feel that she has missed out on one of the most significant experiences a woman can have. If, however, she has compromised and has opted for both a career and children, she may find herself thinking that not only would she have achieved far more had she given her job first priority, but also that, by continuing to

SIX ASPECTS OF SELF-ACTUALIZATION

GENERATING VITALITY
■ *When self-actualizers apply energy and a creative attitude to occupations that match their capabilities and potential, the resulting successes and satisfactions tend to increase rather than absorb their vitality. Some of this energy spills over into their outside interests and relationships, giving them dynamic and magnetic personalities.*

INSIGHT AND REALISM
■ *There is a thoughtful and reflective side to the self-actualizing personality. Insightful and realistic about themselves, self-actualizers are more alert to self-deception than most. However, their tendency to be introspective seldom leads to egocentricity or self-absorption. Although inclined to enjoy privacy and to limit their close personal relationships to a few people, it is typical of self-actualizing people that their appetite for new experiences and their interest in others always remains fresh.*

▶ *Personal vitality is both a cause and an effect of the satisfactions that self-actualizers achieve. By working hard and playing hard they produce results that generate an enthusiasm and exuberance that they easily communicate to other people. ABOVE RIGHT Organizing a breakfast meeting for business executives. RIGHT An environmentalist devotes herself to her labors.*

A ZEST FOR LIVING
■ *Perhaps the most marked quality of self-actualizers is their spontaneous and zestful attitude toward life. Having satisfied their basic needs, they have more energy available to pursue other interests, exercise their imagination, and entertain a much wider range of original solutions to problems. Discarding preconceptions and habitual modes of thinking, self-actualizers tend to live more in the present. Not careless of the future, or less able to draw lessons from the past, they nevertheless give most of their energy to the here and now.*

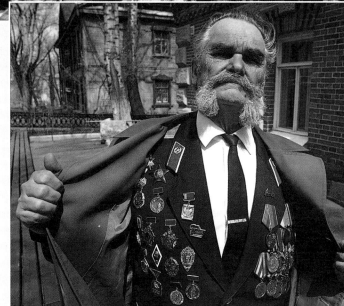

Self-actualizers' closest personal relationships are likely to be very intense. Being sensitive to their own needs and feelings helps them to come to terms with another's. Their self-awareness helps them to make intimate personal contact.

work, she has missed a great deal of the precious years of her offspring's childhood.

A great deal of emphasis is today placed on how marriage and family life can restrict the personal growth of both sexes. While a woman's family responsibilities are usually more onerous than a man's, each must surrender some of their time and much of their freedom to creating and maintaining a home. In addition, each must somehow manage to achieve the necessary compromises needed to balance the conflicting claims of career, relationships and home. This is a problem which, if not faced and equably settled by both partners, may rob either of significant opportunities for growth, create feelings of resentment and result in the loss of much love and esteem – both vital in achieving a satisfy-

ing and self-actualizing life. Of course, marriage and family life may not suit everyone, but it is one of the more important and natural ways of achieving our potential as caring and responsible adults.

After all, maturity is not only a matter of gratifying personal goals and achieving independence. Becoming fully adult inevitably means accepting restraints and moving beyond independence to acknowledging and adopting some degree of interdependence. What matters is that you must clearly see the choice to take on a set of responsibilities as a choice of your own: the tasks that fall to you must be part of what *you* are trying to achieve in your life.

Self-actualization and achievement

Unfortunately, an even development of all potentialities is not always possible. In addition to whatever constraints may be involved in marriage or other important relationships,

INDIVIDUALITY

■ *Self-actualizers may or may not conform to social norms and customs, but to the extent they are at odds with convention, it is probably because whatever social rules they reject limit their own (or other people's) freedom of action and self-determination. Their morality may not be conformist, but it follows a strongly held system of values. They allow others the freedom they claim for themselves, and so tend to hold highly democratic views, responding to other people in an open, positive and constructive way. Consequently, they tend to get along well with others, even though they may have serious problems with authority figures and groups who try to impose their own norms or codes.*

◄ **Past glories and present vitality.** *A World War II veteran from Khaborovsk in the Soviet Union displays his medals. Looking back with satisfaction helps us to unlock energies for the here and now.*

SENSITIVITY TO OTHERS

■ *Self-actualizers' close personal relationships are usually very intense, and they are often characterized by trust and openness. Sensitive and responsive to their own needs and feelings, they find it easier*

to recognize those of others. Empathetic rather than competitive or demanding, they are prepared to reveal more of their inner selves, and enjoy the mutual explorations of true intimacy.

PEAK EXPERIENCES

■ *Having met their primary needs to a sufficient degree, self-actualizers tend to become more directly motivated by the most enduring human concerns – for example, truth, wisdom, freedom, and beauty. Such interests are capable of producing states of mind far more satisfying than the usual forms of happiness we experience every day. They make self-actualizers much more likely than others to have what Maslow calls "peak experiences." These are highly charged moments of joy and wonder which are unexpectedly triggered by events such as hearing an evocative piece of music or seeing an exquisite work of art. Such psychological highlights occur on a random basis and, when they do, create an intense sense of wonder, delight and perfection. They can seem like mystical events – vivid and somehow meaningful to an extent far beyond the ordinary perception and enjoyment of things.*

21

most of us also have a diverse and unequal balance of needs and assets which we must prune into a workable and satisfying shape. Sooner or later, decisions have to be taken as to which things have to be renounced or given a lesser prominence, and which should be given a higher priority. Of these, career decisions involve some of the most far-reaching consequences, and are particularly difficult to make when many appealing options are attainable.

With more things possible than can be achieved, there is always the tantalizing prospect of "might-have-beens" to introduce a sense of dissatisfaction into a life that might actually be very rich. However, while self-actualizing people are usually achievers, achievement is not the same as self-actualization. Even the most interesting, worthwhile and self-initiated attainments may yet fail to produce much in the way of happiness or contentment. For example, if you were, through a great deal of effort and ability, to succeed in politics, writing a best-selling novel or building up a profitable business, this ought to bring with it great personal satisfaction. But although such an achievement usually does, this by no means guarantees fulfillment in the wider sense. In fact, such time- and energy-consuming ambitions are often only realized at the expense of other things. And, whether a particular achievement, or the road toward it, is fulfilling depends very much on what has had to be sacrificed. More importantly, it depends on how highly you value

EXCEPTIONAL SELF-ACTUALIZERS

■ *You do not have to be great and famous to achieve your full potential, and many of the people Abraham Maslow, the psychologist of self-actualization, presents as examples are people he knew personally. But most were famous or historical figures – such as the humanitarian Albert Schweitzer, the American Civil War president Abraham Lincoln, and the naturalist and philosopher Henry David Thoreau – whose biographies and written testaments are available for minute scrutiny.*

The fame and the self-actualization of many famous people can be attributed in part to the advantages to which they are born. Others are famous for the way they have overcome disadvantages. Helen Keller, for example, had first to overcome the blindness, deafness and consequent muteness she experienced as an infant. She was fortunate in having her teacher Anne Sullivan to show her how to sign and speak and use alternative means of reading and writing, and to provide her with the love and positive regard that made possible her great upward struggle. She justified the faith, support and encouragement she received, graduating with honors from Radcliffe College in Boston, and going on to become a major figure in the education of children, including the disadvantaged.

Helen Keller and others who become self-actualized in spite of disadvantages share many qualities. They are realistic about the obstacles in their way, but they continue to be problem- rather than self-centered.

Their ideas are imaginative, and their goals important to others. Working toward these goals they reject the stereotyped roles and expectations that are usually applied to those with the same disadvantages.

In private, their emotional lives are intense and shared by very few, although their lifework shows them to be interested in humanity in a broad sense. They are at a great disadvantage pursuing their own particular objectives, but they do more than cope with their circumstances: they transcend them.

▲ **One of the great women of the 20th century,** *Helen Keller, seen here running her sensitive fingers across the face of US President Dwight Eisenhower on meeting him in 1953. Born blind and deaf, she was mute for much of her childhood but eventually graduated from university and became an authority on education.*

Many famous self-actualizers achieve their goals in spite of striking disadvantages. Being problem-oriented rather than self-centered, they do much more than cope with their difficult circumstances. They learn to transcend them.

(or have come to value) whatever was given up. Nevertheless, achievement of worthwhile and personally important goals is the normal outcome of self-actualizing impulses, and some form of creativity is its natural accompaniment. The arts, of course, are only one of many ways in which imagination and inventiveness can be applied to things which interest us.

Maslow's summary of the typical characteristics of self-actualizers shows that this creative element can be expressed in an almost infinite number of ways – from science, technology, commerce and politics to imaginative lifestyles such as setting up a self-sufficiency farm or becoming an explorer or a freelance photographer. The most creative focus of your life may equally be a nonoccupational activity that you pursue in your free time.

Are self-actualizers saints?

The characteristics used by Maslow to describe self-actualization are, as he was the first to agree, inclined to seem more like the criteria for sainthood than the model for a healthy personality. In fact, they are simply an ideal distilled from the many self-actualizers he studied. Few, if any, individuals are likely to be such paragons of all the virtues.

Like anyone else, even highly self-actualized people can sometimes be boring or vain, ruthless in pursuit of their aims or unpleasant and thoughtless in their behavior. Naturally, they will have many counterbalancing qualities, but in the real world there is always room for improvement. And self-actualization should be considered a continuous process of becoming, not an elevated plateau of being.

Obviously, no one and nothing can be perfect, but self-actualizers do live a fuller and richer life than most. This does not necessarily mean they will always be the life of the party, universally popular or great achievers. In fact, their attainments and successes may be quite modest, with prospects which extend very little beyond their family, friends and job. They may or may not have any special talents, but what distinguishes them from the majority of people is their determination and ability to get the best out of whatever assets and opportunities they have.

Achievements, social status, and prosperity may come as by-products, but irrespective of whether they do or not, the essence and primary gain of self-actualization is living to the full, discovering our inner nature and being all that it is in us to be. **BWPW**

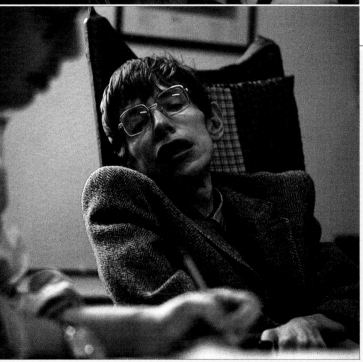

◄ **Family man, teacher and brilliant researcher**, *Professor Stephen Hawking of Cambridge University* TOP *with two of his three children and* BOTTOM *at work. He was still a young man when he experienced the first symptoms of a degenerative neurological illness (amyotrophic lateral sclerosis) that soon confined him to a wheelchair and eventually forced him to use a voice synthesizer. He and his fiancée chose to marry in full knowledge of what the disease would do, and he pursued his career energetically. His special interest became the physics of astronomical "black holes." The genius that he brought to the study of physics has been compared to Albert Einstein's. When unable to jot down ideas by his own hand or even to dictate them, he continued working with complex formulae that he held in his memory.*

HOW SELF-ACTUALIZED ARE YOU?

■ *Your answers to this questionnaire will give some idea of how self-actualized you are. It is best to work through fairly quickly, jotting down each question number and either an "a" choice or the "b." If you seem to fall somewhere between the "a" choice and the "b" choice, leave that item and continue to the end. When you have finished, go back to any you have left and try again. One of the two opposites will usually prove to be more characteristic than the other. When you are ready, look for an interpretation of your score on p25.*

If you have already read the main text, you can probably work out how someone who is highly self-actualized might answer the questionnaire, and you might be tempted to fit

yourself into that desirable image. If so, try to resist this very natural impulse. The questionnaire is not a test: there are no "right" or "wrong" answers, and the only prize to be won – increased self-awareness – depends entirely upon your objectivity.

1 **a** *Most of my spare time is spent usefully or enjoyably.*
   b *My spare time is generally wasted or dull.*
2 **a** *I find life empty and meaningless.*
   b *My life is full and has meaning.*
3 **a** *I spend much of the present concerned about the future.*
   b *I let the future take care of itself.*
4 **a** *I like my work.*

   b *My work is not interesting or enjoyable.*
5 **a** *The prospect of failure often worries me.*
   b *I seldom worry about failure.*
6 **a** *I make use of good things as soon as I can.*
   b *I generally save good things for later.*
7 **a** *In most respects I control the course of my life.*
   b *The course of my life is largely controlled by other people.*
8 **a** *I tend to give up easily.*
   b *I am tenacious and determined.*
9 **a** *Although not wanting to, I generally adapt to please others.*
   b *I am more inclined to please myself than adapt to what others want.*

10 **a** *I sometimes lack confidence in my worth.*
   b *Even if others do, I do not doubt my worth.*
11 **a** *I have clear moral standards of my own.*
   b *I usually adopt society's view of morality.*
12 **a** *I have important goals.*
   b *I have no important personal goals.*
13 **a** *I am inclined to feel guilty when pleasing myself.*
   b *I seldom feel guilty about pleasing myself.*
14 **a** *I frequently do things on the spur of the moment.*
   b *I am usually cautious in the things I do.*
15 **a** *I am often self-conscious about the impression I may be giving others.*
   b *I do not worry about saying or doing the wrong thing.*

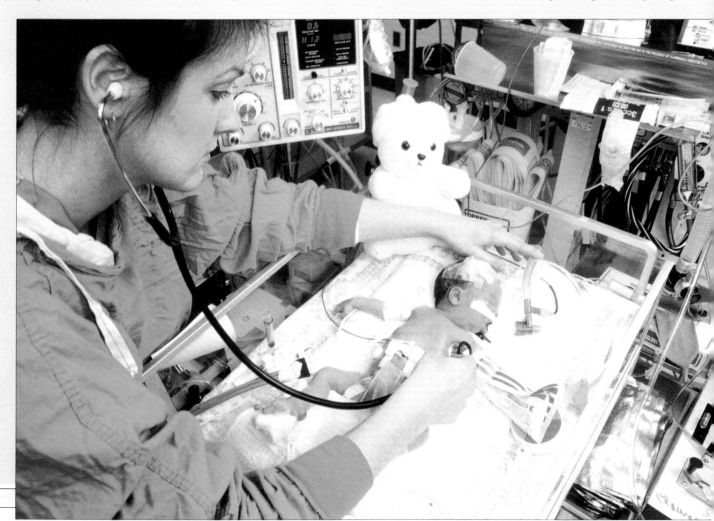

Most people answering questionnaires like this one score in the medium range. Checking back through your answers can help you to identify areas for improvement – such as problems with relationships, or lack of purpose.

16 **a** *I usually manage to do things I want to do.*
b *I am seldom able to get my own way.*

17 **a** *I seldom feel the need to justify my actions.*
b *I frequently feel the need to justify my behavior to others.*

18 **a** *I seldom rely on my feelings and intuitions as guides to action.*
b *I trust my feelings and intuitions, and usually act on them.*

19 **a** *I tend to be rather morose and pessimistic.*
b *My mood is usually buoyant and optimistic.*

20 **a** *Natural or beautiful things can sometimes lift me into a state of rapture or ecstasy.*
b *I never respond to natural or beautiful things with rapture or ecstasy.*

21 **a** *I am never troubled by inferiority feelings.*
b *Feelings of inferiority sometimes trouble me.*

22 **a** *My sex-life is thoroughly enjoyable and satisfying.*
b *I would not describe my sex-life as either enjoyable or satisfying.*

23 **a** *Other people's values and beliefs are no barrier to my getting on with them.*
b *I find it hard to get along with people whose values and beliefs differ from mine.*

24 **a** *I have a real sense of belonging.*
b *I lack any real sense of belonging.*

◄ **Self-fulfillment through work** is easiest when the work is challenging and gives us recognition for our special skills, especially when the work is meaningful as well – giving us an outlet for caring instincts.

INTERPRETING YOUR SELF-ACTUALIZATION SCORE

■ When you have completed the questionnaire, count a point for each of your answers which corresponds with these: 1a, 2b, 3b, 4a, 5b, 6a, 7a, 8b, 9b, 10b, 11a, 12a, 13b, 14a, 15b, 16a, 17a, 18b, 19b, 20a, 21a, 22a, 23a, 24a, 25a, 26b, 27a, 28b, 29a, 30b, 31b, 32a, 33a, 34a.

It is worth rereading all of these answers, because they are characteristic of self-actualizers and can help you to define the concept.

LOW SCORERS (0-11)

You will almost certainly need to review your relationships very carefully, and see what can be done to improve them. Check back over the questions to verify this, but it is highly probable that your affiliative needs for friendship, love, the esteem of others and a sense of belonging are so unsatisfied that you lack a sufficiently secure psychological base to express much of your potential.

MEDIUM SCORERS (12-24)

Most people score somewhere within this range, though individual patterns will vary a great deal. Consider each of your replies carefully and try to establish which aspects of your life seem to have most room for improvement. If your relationships with other people are satisfying, it may well be that you lack any clear sense of purpose or feelings of achievement. Another handicap in the way of self-actualization for otherwise socially and occupationally successful people is guilt. Frequently, this is due to an early implantation of strict moral or religious ideas which consider sensual enjoyment and personal gratification inherently immoral or selfish. It is always worth back-tracking and asking why you feel guilt in circumstances where unalloyed pleasure might be appropriate. Even if the answer is not very obvious, a careful and objective reappraisal of your feelings and behavior may be the first step toward changing them.

HIGH SCORERS (25-34)

If you score toward the lower end of this range, you are well on the road toward genuine self-actualization. Your life is likely to be highly satisfying, though you may yet feel unfulfilled. Looking back over your replies, you may find the clue to what is missing.

It may be that you have acquired a basic mistrust of human nature, or have adopted authoritarian attitudes which can make spontaneity of thought and action difficult. If so, you may need to take more chances with people, being prepared for painful as well as rewarding outcomes.

It may be that you lack sufficient resilience and persistence for these experiments, or that these missing qualities undermine your ability to achieve personally important goals. Whatever problems there are in your otherwise well-developed personality, they can be rectified.

If you have scored high in this range and, in addition, been able to choose "a" for questions 20 and 34, you are not only a highly self-actualized person, but a very rare and fortunate one also.

25 **a** *I can love completely and unreservedly.*
b *I am not able to give myself completely and unreservedly in loving relationships.*

26 **a** *Fear of being hurt or rejected sometimes makes it impossible for me to show affection.*
b *I am not at all apprehensive about expressing affection.*

27 **a** *There are people with whom I can exchange innermost thoughts and feelings.*
b *There is no one with whom I can exchange innermost thoughts and feelings.*

28 **a** *I have no feeling of being needed.*
b *I feel myself needed by someone or some group.*

29 **a** *A number of people like and admire me.*
b *No one seems to like or admire me.*

30 **a** *I generally find it hard to admit it when I make a mistake.*
b *I usually find I can admit mistakes without too much difficulty.*

31 **a** *People only do things for personal gain.*
b *People often do things without expecting anything back in return.*

32 **a** *If they harm no one, people should be allowed to do as they please.*
b *Society has the right to expect people to behave according to its rules.*

33 **a** *Everyone should participate in making political decisions.*
b *Political decisions should be left to those with demonstrable knowledge or political expertise.*

34 **a** *I am sometimes overwhelmed by a sense of joy and wonder.*
b *I never experience overwhelming feelings of joy and wonder.*

Origins of Self-Awareness

WHAT ARE you conscious of when you are conscious of yourself? What *is* this self and where did it come from? How can you make it more like the one you want it to be? Asking questions like these may seem to invite an unhealthy self-preoccupation. Is it not better simply to forget about ourselves and get on with living? If the alternative is excessive self-absorption, then the answer of course would be yes. But not paying attention to what you are like is often simply impractical. After all, a high level of self-awareness is the greatest strength of our highly successful species. It has its origins in our evolution – and the normal development of an effective personality is impossible without cultivating it.

What is a self?

Psychologists distinguish four elements of the self. Almost any creature could be argued to have three of them. First, we each have our own bodies and their automatic processes, such as the beating of the heart and the drawing of breath. Second, we each have our own experience of sensory stimuli – we see, smell, hear, taste and feel. These two elements together are classed as parts of a *passive self*. You are also, third, an *active self*, an agent responding to your environment. Beings of little complexity are more difficult to think of as "selves," yet even a slug or an insect is a passive self, with some kind of sensory "experience," and it is an active self when it moves away from danger or toward food. Your pet dog is probably easier to think of in terms of selfhood, because mental life (something we find in our own selves) is so much easier to see in its behavior. You can tell when it sees you coming because it acts in recognition, standing up and wagging its tail when you come into view.

You probably have less evidence, however, that your dog experiences the fourth element of selfhood: the self-awareness and reflection about self that makes a human a *reflexive self*. Does the fact that a dog answers to the name "Fido" mean that it is conscious of *being* Fido? Do the facts that it

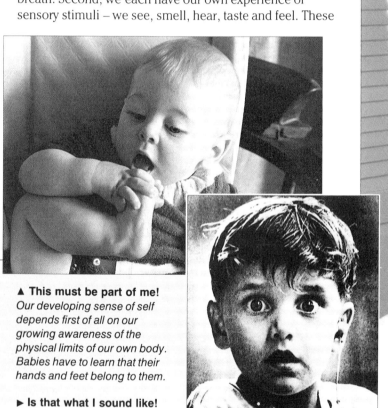

▲ **This must be part of me!** *Our developing sense of self depends first of all on our growing awareness of the physical limits of our own body. Babies have to learn that their hands and feet belong to them.*

▶ **Is that what I sound like!** *Born deaf, but now fitted with a special hearing aid, this young boy reacts with amazement as he hears his own (prerecorded) voice for the first time. His discovery of the world of sound brings a new dimension to his awareness of self.*

▶ **I can influence events!** *Just as selfhood presupposes an ability to respond actively to one's surroundings, so self-awareness entails a sense of interacting not only physically but also socially.*

26

Although self-absorption is something we need to guard against, our capacity for self-awareness is our species' greatest asset. It develops naturally in infancy – but can be cultivated to advantage throughout life.

feels pain when it bites its tail and that it judges which way it must jump to avoid a falling object mean that it is aware of its body as its own? In some sense perhaps the answer is yes, but members of only three species – humans, chimpanzees and orangutans – appear to have enough sense of physical self to recognize themselves in a mirror. Many animals simply ignore a mirror image, and others react as though their reflection were another member of their species. Macaques, gibbons and gorillas, for example, court, challenge or play with their mirror images.

It is hard to imagine how animals could be aware of their *experiences* as the experiences of a self – lacking language, they cannot compare them and distinguish them. They cannot think about experiences, they can only have them.

They could not notice in the way the first humans could, for example, that a certain distant shape looked like a gazelle to one (he *said* that is how it looked) but not to another (he looked and found that he could not see it that way).

Do animals have a *sense of agency* or do they simply act – responding instinctively to stimuli, like automatons? Pet owners believe that their dogs look proud of themselves when they do something right – like fetching a stick when told to. But excitedly carrying a stick or some other object to other members of the pack (or to the humans they substitute for their own kind) is a standard part of the social behavior that dogs have inherited from their wolf ancestors. This behavior helps to bond the group, but we have no evidence that wolves or dogs perform it self-consciously – for example, picturing how they must look and considering whether other members of the group will judge their performance successful.

27

▲ **Is that really me** reflected in the mirror? I wonder what sort of person I am and how my life will unfold? The ability to ask searching questions about ourselves and to see ourselves as beings with a past and a future – a future that could depend crucially on what we decide to do next – is central to human self-awareness.

Dogs sometimes look guilty when they have done something wrong, but any social animal will cringe and cower in postures of appeasement if it senses that a dominant animal (such as its human master) has become menacing. This behavior does not necessarily mean that the animal identifies a wrong action with itself.

Why do we need a sense of self?

What is the evolutionary advantage of self-awareness? It seems that the answer to this question lies partly in the complex nature of the social life of the creatures who have it. In experiments, it has been shown that considerable social interaction is necessary before a chimpanzee can recognize itself in a mirror. Those reared in isolation never learn that the reflection is an image of themselves. Apparently, chimpanzee socialization helps an individual to form a self-image.

Chimpanzees have been closely studied in the wild, and certain features of their social life offer hints of what might cause them to form self-images. Their communities are very loosely organized, and individuals have to create a place for themselves in order to survive and maximize their reproductive success. A male who does not make himself accepted by a male group – by making submissive gestures to dominant members, by ingratiating himself through grooming others and by displaying a physical prowess that the group needs in its members – is at a disadvantage. The male group, especially its most dominant members, may prevent his access to females, and if a group from a neighboring community finds him alone near their border, they will kill him. A male thus faces a problem of *self-presentation* in order to win an essential group membership.

Another arena for self-presentation in the lives of chimpanzees is in male-female relationships. Although mating is promiscuous, most pregnancies probably result from "consortships" in which a chosen male and a fertile female avoid the rest of the community for several days or weeks. The male later acts as one of the female's protectors when her offspring is still vulnerable to attack from other females anxious to reserve resources for their own young. To estab-

28

▲ **It was his fault!** *The young boy who bumped the arm of the girl who spilt the milk may learn to be more careful in future. The sense of agency that is part of being self-aware gives rise to the idea of a self that is responsible and whose performance is assessable. Without this, flexible social cooperation and coordinated social action would be impossible.*

Why did we evolve the ability to be aware of ourselves? Almost certainly because of the competitive advantage of being able to visualize where and who we are and mentally rehearse our possible future actions.

lish a consortship, the male and the female have to present themselves to each other and find each other appealing.

Human self-awareness, certainly, is typically triggered by situations of self-presentation. To form the strikingly co-operative working, defensive and reproductive relationships that are characteristic of our species, we have had to develop the ability to judge character and personality, to know in whom to invest as a leader, follower, friend, mate, co-parent. This in turn has meant a personal survival and reproductive advantage for any individual who could consciously cultivate a self that would be seen by others as desirable and useful.

Another kind of situation in which we typically become self-aware is when we are in danger. As a bear lumbers into

view when you are walking in the mountains, your first thought is "Has it seen me?" Once again, the image of self comes to mind because of the image that might be in the mind of another.

Of course, many creatures experience danger and present themselves socially, especially in courtship – consider the colorful displays of peacocks. The difference between those which are self-conscious and those which are not is an aspect of intelligence. The less intelligent an animal is, the more it must rely on sheer instinct in winning social acceptance and avoiding danger. It can respond instinctively to a complex range of reaction cues in others (and so can we) but it cannot use the idea of how it looks to others to help it invent new ways of looking and so adapt itself individually to particular situations. A wolf, for example, cannot form the idea of putting on sheep's clothing in order to stalk sheep more effectively, but a human can.

Our intelligence makes us aware of our bodies not simply in the sense that we know instinctively how to avoid bumping into things. We are also sometimes inventively – imaginatively – aware of how we might use our bodies in new ways – we picture how we might extend the power of an arm by furnishing it with a club. We are self-consciously aware of our *experiences* especially when we are considering what knowledge we can claim usefully to offer to others (the hunter wonders if he can rightly claim to his partners that he *did* see a gazelle). Our sense of agency allows human communities to achieve extremely complex and subtle forms of cooperation. Individuals can claim responsibility for actions and their consequences, and so there can be a system of assessing individual contributions to and compliance with the needs of the group.

▲ **Can they see me?** *The same sense of body-location that enables this little girl to play hide-and-seek enables a hunter stalking his quarry or a fugitive evading pursuers to do so with great ingenuity.*

▶ **More power to the elbow.** *Being able to put our bodies to new uses by extending them in various ways is another advantage of self-awareness. Originally this led to the discovery and improvement of hunting weapons. Here it is reflected in arm-extending devices for striking and catching a "quarry" in the shape of a baseball.*

As part of our sense of agency, we also reflect on entire patterns of behavior. We consider what attitudes and other behavioral traits are attractive to others and useful for satisfying our own needs, and we consider whether we have them and how to make others aware of them in us.

The development of self-awareness

The emergence of self-awareness in a developing human is a fascinating process to observe. At birth we have the first three of the four elements of self – body, experience and activity, each very underdeveloped – but at this point we seem to lack any hint of the fourth: there is no discrimination between a "me" and the rest of what exists. For example, the newborn's cry seems to startle the baby itself.

At four months there will still be a look of shock and horror when the infant bites itself. Between four and seven months, when it achieves mobility and begins to learn that it occupies space, it bangs into things and looks surprised. You may have seen a baby crawl under a low table and try to sit up only to be stunned by pain when it knocks its head.

During this time, however, a process of separation and individuation is under way. During the first two months every infant lacks involvement with the world and most of its responses are innate reflexes. A serious condition known as "early infantile autism" results if, between them, the child and its caregiver cannot break this barrier to interaction. This condition, often masked as severe mental retardation, is characterized by a lack of response to external stimuli.

Between two and five months, the normal child develops an attachment to its primary caregiver. Unless this intense sense of connectedness is successfully established, a strong and independent sense of self is difficult to find later. The infant must be involved in the experience of someone for whom it is an object of consistent and reassuring attention before it sees itself as an individual.

Modern laboratory technology has determined that around six months of age most infants will respond to their

HOW EARLY CAN WE RECOGNIZE OURSELVES?

■ In studies beginning shortly after birth, infants have been observed in front of a mirror with a rouge spot on the face. They are considered to have recognized themselves in the mirror when they touch the rouge spot on their own face while looking at the reflected one.

One study reports a sequence of mirror behavior. From three to five months, babies respond with "mirror" movement. In the second half of the first year, they begin to react to a sociable "playmate." A one-year-old begins to "search" for the "other." During the second year, infants begin to withdraw and become wary of the mirror image. Between 18 months and two years they show self-recognition.

Any organism that can see anything can see itself in a mirror, but research suggests that only humans, chimpanzees and orangutans clearly demonstrate self-recognition.

► **Consistent and reassuring attention** *from a primary caregiver during infancy seems to* be an important factor in developing a strong and independent sense of self.

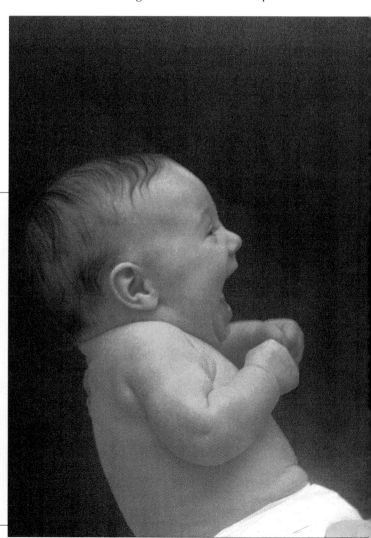

Nature usually sees to it that we are fully conscious of ourselves as distinct individuals by the time we are two; but the quality of our sense of self at this stage depends heavily on the nature of our earlier experience.

names with a deceleration of heart rate or momentary cessation of activity and dilation of the pupil of the eye. This is also the time when the baby's actions begin to affect the environment directly. It affects the world not simply through the intermediary action of its caregivers, but by kicking and pushing at toys and other objects. The repetitive experiments in agency that now occur prompted the Swiss researcher Jean Piaget to call this the age "for making interesting experiences last."

When the baby is 8 to 12 months old, it enters another stage, beginning to grasp that objects have a life of their own and exist when not seen. This is a major step as it provides the cornerstone for memory, and without a memory, there is no basis for self-awareness. The baby now takes up the discovery of the world in earnest. The time from about a year to 18 months is known as the period of "experiments in order to see." The infant's world is literally experimented upon to see what it can do with objects. It forages through the world of objects – banging, pulling, throwing, tasting, taking things apart to see what can be done. The parent often mis-

takes this experimentation for destructiveness, but the baby is only beginning to work on concepts of cause and effect: "If I do this, then what happens?" Peekaboo becomes a favorite pastime.

Between 18 months and two years, the infant can picture internally actions that previously could only be accomplished by physically completing them. Prior to this it used trial and error to find solutions. A missing toy was sought by random searching. Now it can remember and look for the toy where it was last seen. It is now that a baby can recognize itself in a mirror. It also has a new tool, one that enriches and extends the self – language.

Until the child learns to speak, we have to make assumptions about the development of the self. With language the child tells us about it. "Me do," it says. The self-awareness is there for all to hear.

With the acquisition of language, the child moves beyond the establishment of an "existential self" – the sense of what is "me" and what is "not me" – to the establishment of a "categorical self" – it learns how to describe itself in terms of socially recognized categories and attributes, beginning perhaps with "I am a girl" and "I am tall." This self finds its origins in a bewildering variety of sources – see *Ch3*. **HWR**

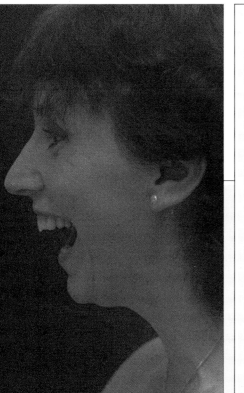

PROMOTING SELF-AWARENESS THROUGH PLAY

■ *A developing infant constantly seeks opportunities to test ways of effecting change in its environment. The growth of a sense of agency is crucial for a child, but it may prove a frustrating experience. The infant often lacks the necessary skills yet feels compelled to try to achieve the desired result. Thus the parents should make every effort to arrange the play area in such a way that the infant enjoys the maximum degree of success in effecting change, with the minimum of frustration. The infant's actions should have realistic consequences – it should be allowed to take some risks, such as falling over when it tries to walk – but the consequences should never be dire or so frustrating that desired goals seem impossible to attain. Regularly confining a child to the safety of a play pen without toys is a potentially serious form of understimulation.*

Your Self-Image

PERSONAL counselors and self-help manuals often urge you to "assert yourself" or to "express yourself." But what exactly is it that you are supposed to be asserting or expressing? The answer is not nearly as easy as you might at first imagine. This is because the information we gain about ourselves comes from a range of different and potentially conflicting sources. Part of the business of knowing who you are involves choosing which sources to believe and which to ignore – deciding for yourself who to *be*.

This is a complex and ongoing process. To construct and revise our "self-image," we interpret reflections of ourselves, very often in real mirrors but mainly and more importantly in "human mirrors": the reactions and opinions of other people. Our self-image is the complex impression we have not only of our appearance but also of our personality traits, our personal history and the profusion of social roles and group affiliations on which our sense of personal identity further depends.

Acquiring a physical self-image

Development of a self-image begins when a baby bites its own toes and discovers that it hurts. The infant goes on to learn the bounds of its own body by touch, pain and pleasure. It hears its own voice when it cries and gets visual

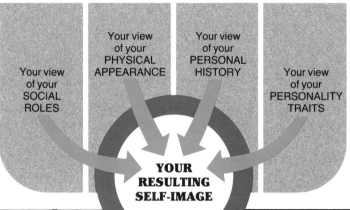

Your view of your SOCIAL ROLES

Your view of your PHYSICAL APPEARANCE

Your view of your PERSONAL HISTORY

Your view of your PERSONALITY TRAITS

YOUR RESULTING SELF-IMAGE

■ **Mirrors deal in half-truths.** *The face we see in the mirror is not the face that others see. It can be examined from one angle only, is usually reversed left to right, and has a less three-dimensional appearance than the real thing. Even the very best mirrors subtly distort its shapes and colors. Mirrors are often less sympathetic than most of us realize. Try comparing the face of a friend with its reflection in a mirror. You could be better looking than you think!*

▲ **"Never so beautiful** *as on her wedding day," a bride does her best to live up to folkloric expectations. If she likes what she sees, it will help her to cope that much more confidently with the pressures of the day ahead.*

▶ **Painting your self-portrait** *is one way of acquiring a more detailed mental picture of your own face. The limitations of second-hand images still apply, however.*

The sort of person you really think you are – your self-image – profoundly affects your chances of happiness. Much depends on how you interpret the often unreliable feedback you receive from outside sources. Are you being fair to yourself?

feedback by watching the movements of its limbs. As it grows older, mirrors and family photographs provide a more complete picture, giving the child a physical self-image – a sense of its size, shape, sex, coloring and physical attractiveness.

Throughout life these continue to be our most direct sources of information about our physical appearance. What we see and hear is never quite what others see and hear: we are not in a position to look at or listen to ourselves as directly as they can or as often as they do. The image in the mirror is reversed and we are limited to frontal views, unless two or three mirrors are arranged to reflect each other. A recording of what your own voice sounds like to others can seem like the voice of a stranger.

Photographs are only two-dimensional, and therefore unreal, but sometimes they startle us with their revelations. Having lost track of changes, we may find it hard to identify with this so much fatter, thinner or older person than we expect to see posing with *our* friends or family. In this sense, at any given moment, most people's physical self-image is obsolete.

However fragmented, recorded images and direct observations of parts of your body powerfully influence your impression of the kind of person you are. The judgments you consequently form about how attractive you are, what sort of character you have and how like or unlike other people you are – all have an effect on your behavior.

For example, research shows that most of us date and marry people who are on a similar level of attractiveness as ourselves. We avoid "flying too high" and do not attempt to appeal to those who are out of our league – presumably

▲ **Human mirrors** – *the people with whom we interact – tell us, through their remarks and other reactions, about the image of ourselves we project publicly. For most of us, the regard of others is the mainstay of our self-image.*

▶ **The photographic record** *of past and more recent selves – nowadays often supplemented by family videorecordings – helps reinforce the historical dimension of our self-image.*

Age 9

Age 21

Age 78

Age 54

Age 40

Age 29

**ONE WOMAN'S LIFE
A SUCCESSION
OF SELVES**

33

because of the likelihood of a rebuff. On the one hand, a positive physical self-image is a useful boost to self-esteem, but, on the other hand, even a small misconception about yourself can sometimes lead to painful corrective feedback.

Interpreting those human mirrors

Parents, connecting our names with words like "pretty," "clever," "bad" or "good," give us our first awareness of how other people see and think of us. We internalize their view and make it our own, and for the rest of our lives, we tend to see ourselves as we think others see us.

Even at pre-school age, playmates are influential. Child-ren are more likely to list other children than parents as people who like them. When a parent is listed, it is more likely to be the mother than the father. As we grow up, our peers become progressively more influential in telling us what we should think about ourselves. First, it is our same-sex friends, as we learn our gender role and place within the social hierarchy. Later on, we are particularly sensitive to the comments of prospective sexual and marriage partners. Maintaining confidence as a novice in the love-stakes is a major task in growing to mature adulthood.

Self-image absorbs not only comments but other reac-

SELF-IMAGE AND YOUR SELF-ESTEEM

■ *Even the mildest situations in which you are caught at a disadvantage often prompt a smile or laugh of dissociation. "This is not the real me," is the message being signaled, just in case anyone should think or be thought to think otherwise, even for a moment. However slight the risk of distortion to their self-image, people who are even momentarily embarrassed seem to feel a need to indicate that whatever the observer has seen is "of course not to be* taken seriously!" This very common reaction underscores the dependence of our self-esteem on our self-image. It reveals how sensitive most of us are to anything which could possibly (1) detract (in our own eyes) from our prevailing self-image or (2) widen the gap between the prevailing self-image and our ideal self-image – the gap between how we do and how we would really like to think of ourselves. The thicker skinned among us are less affected.*

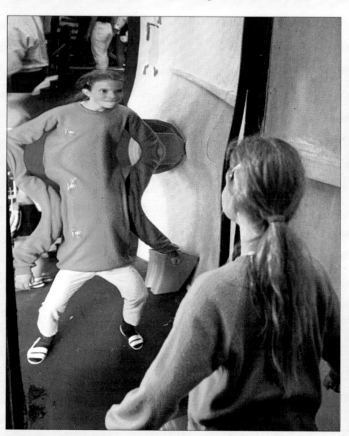

For practical purposes it is important that the image we have of ourselves should be tolerably in line with the image others have of us. We are helped in this by the fact that our self-image is largely a product of their reactions to us.

tions too. When we make conversation, we learn from our listeners' postures and facial expressions whether we are boring or interesting. We feel attractive or unattractive depending on whether we do or do not attract others. Self-image also helps to *determine* these reactions. Confidence in your own attractiveness or conversational skill creates self-fulfilling expectations that others will find you attractive or interesting.

Not everyone necessarily views us in the same way. Some react more favorably than others. We are attracted to people who see us as we want to see ourselves. Friends and romantic partners are selected partly for their capacity to reinforce or improve our self-image. But not all close relationships are chosen. The family you are born into, or the in-laws you acquire on marrying, may not reinforce a desired self-image. And even chosen relationships, once established, permit closer looks and frank disclosures. It is often those nearest to us who tell us the worst, who let slip the "home truths."

When criticism is motivated only by the other person's malice, jealousy or insecurity, even the most constructive response – for example, making yourself into a tidier person to please a jealous mother-in-law – may fail to bring harmony between your self-image and one of the "human mirrors" in your life. It is important to identify such negative

feedback for what it is, and disregard it, for falling victim to the unreasonably negative views of others can be a serious danger. If enough thoughtless people tell you often enough that you are untalented, unattractive or irresponsible, you are likely to take the same view.

Another way we come to know ourselves is by observing our own behavior and drawing conclusions from it. Having helped an old lady across the road, we say to ourselves, "That was a kind thing to do; therefore I am a kind person." After passing a difficult examination, we conclude that we are clever; if we fail, we infer our own limitations. In other words, we "identify" our personality traits in much the same way as we do with other people – by observing behavior, in this case our own.

Of course, we are able to observe ourselves in a much broader range of situations than other people. Only we can be aware of the extent to which we present different faces to different people – each of whom is likely to develop a somewhat different, one-sided view of our character. In consequence, we usually have a more complex, less consistent image of our own personality than the version each of our acquaintances has of it. To the extent that this is so, we all have to cope with a personality that is at least mildly "split" (see box on next page).

When the world refuses to reflect back the kinds of image we want, however, it appears that undue resistance or indifference to the tide of external opinion is not helpful. People who react in this way are well known to clinical

HOW MUCH IN CONTROL DO YOU FEEL?

■ *An important variable in your self-image is your view of how the events in your life are controlled. In terms introduced by the psychologist Julian B Rotter, people who believe that it is in their own power to influence what happens to them (Internals) are said to have an internal locus of control, while people who generally see things as the outcome of fate or the actions of other people (Externals) are said to have an external locus of control.*

Rotter's Locus of Control Scale measures these tendencies by scoring answers to questions such as these:

▲ **Internals** *have the conviction and the confidence to feel that they can shape their own lives. Adverse circumstances are there to be faced up to and changed.*

▲ **Externals** *are inhibited by the pressure of events which they take to be beyond their control. They are inclined to see themselves as victims of circumstance.*

Asked to jot down a few descriptive words about themselves, Externals are more likely to list social categories and physical characteristics. Internals mention more positive personality traits, especially those implying competence.

Internals have been found to fall ill less often than Externals, and they recover more quickly when they do. In one study of hospital patients, it was found that the Internals among them asked their doctors more questions and took more interest.

Internals report greater happiness than Externals. This reflects the fact that seeing ourselves as masters of our own fate is an important step toward the actual control of rewards: believing in your own competence increases your competence. In addition, a sense of being in control seems to be part of what happiness is.

1 *As a general rule, do you think of yourself as*
a *being the victim of powerful people?*
b *controlling your own destiny?*

2 *Success in a job depends mainly on*
a *one's own efforts*
b *being in the right place at the right time*

3 *Passing an examination is a matter of*
a *being lucky with the questions*
b *preparing thoroughly*

psychologists. Their symptoms range from "Walter Mitty" style daydreaming to the full-blown delusions of the paranoid schizophrenic.

Social labels and our sense of identity

A particularly important part of our self-image is the catalog of social roles we see ourselves as performing. A role may be consciously chosen, as when parenthood results from family planning, or when you join a distinctive subculture because you like its ideals and lifestyle. Many of our social roles, however, are simply handed to us, such as being male or female, a born Catholic or a born Protestant, black or white. And the behavior expected for each role, whether chosen or not, receives its definition from other people: society at large or a particular religion, subculture, club or clique.

Throughout life we are called upon to categorize ourselves – by, for example, neighbors, schoolteachers, employers and market researchers. We are forced to acknowledge or reject membership of one role-category after another, and acknowledgment reinforces commitment to the way society, or a narrower group, expects a role to be lived. Answering to the label "mother," for example, increases the likelihood that a person will see herself as concerned and caring.

Sometimes, self-definition includes an element of role-rejection (for example, "I am sort of a Catholic," said by someone born and baptized a Catholic but not confirmed). More often, we apply labels to ourselves without qualification, and accept the implications this may have for a more detailed description: "I am a Catholic, therefore I attend mass, will educate my children in a Catholic school, etc."

DIFFERENT SELVES FOR DIFFERENT AUDIENCES

■ *In some degree we all have "split" personalities. Not everyone and not every situation brings out the same behavior in us. Our lives have compartments – there may be an at-home self and an at-work self, a with-good-friends self and a with-chance-acquaintances self.*

You often have to forget what you are like in one familiar set of circumstances in order to be the self that you are expected to be in another. For example, children and family have little need of the conscientious employee who has been at the office all day. They are happier if you change clothes as soon as you can on arriving home – taking on your "proper" appearance – and start behaving in ways you never would at work, fathers being expected perhaps to clown and play, mothers to get down to preparing the meal and tending needs. It can be an awkward strain to play to more than one of your established audiences at once, as when entertaining visitors who have little in common.

Sometimes, forgetting is literally what happens, for we find it easier to remember things about ourselves that are consistent with the identity we are acting out at any given moment. When telling intimate friends the story of a job you left, you are more likely to remember details that imply your leaving was an act of daring and defiance.

Explaining the same situation to a new employer, it is often not a matter of hiding these details – they simply do not come to mind. This is a reflection of the general principle that we tend to remember situations in ways that reinforce our self-image. This is also reflected, for example, in psychological experiments in which volunteers almost always overstate their own contributions when asked to say how much they contributed toward a joint task just completed.

In extreme cases, people who cannot accept what they are sometimes like may "dissociate" from themselves, exhibiting a split personality in a dramatic way. One such split is called "fugue." A person may disappear from family, friends and job to be discovered some time later living a totally new life, with complete amnesia regarding the old one. More dramatic still are rare cases (only about 100 have been reported) in which two or more personalities compete to dominate one person's behavior. These alternative selves are often strongly contrasting, with one highly virtuous self being unaware of another, miscreant self. This condition is associated with childhood experiences of being set an impossibly high standard of good behavior to live up to while being painted a vivid picture of the unworthy person it is all too easy to become if you fail.

Also important in shaping our self-image is our consciousness of identifying with certain social roles and the purposes of certain social groups. A casual act in sympathy with some cause may engender a sense of commitment and belonging.

Our self-categorizations, and the behavior that goes with them, are sometimes selected to advertise an identification that impresses us and, we hope, others as well. Researchers interviewing adolescent smokers have found that they view themselves as tougher, more mature and more sexually sophisticated than nonsmokers. They also see themselves as academic failures, relative to nonsmokers, suggesting that smoking may bolster an "adult" self-image adopted by young people to compensate for lack of success in school.

Meanwhile, adults forced to describe themselves as smokers or nonsmokers – at airline check-in counters, in job applications, on life-insurance forms – find in the modern health-conscious world that smoking makes an increasingly negative contribution to their self-esteem. Yet, for many, this classification is central enough to their self-concept to make it difficult to shed.

The challenge of learning to live the life of a nonsmoker includes more than simply enduring the unpleasant physical effects as your body chemistry readjusts. You have to behave like a different person, unable to relate in old familiar ways to the friends and acquaintances who shared matches, cigarettes and the mystique and comfort of smoking. This threat to continued identification with friends is enough to defeat some people's attempts to stop, and successful quitters often report how much it helps to spend the hardest time in a new environment, away from constant cues to play the smoker's role.

A change in social role (for example, through marriage, divorce, graduation or promotion) is likely to result in a change of self-perception, affecting feelings and behavior across a wide front. It may be the focus of a stressful life-changing event, especially if many other aspects of our life, such as home, friends and style of dress, also have to change.

One source of stress may be a confusion of identity caused by role-conflict. Being promoted to supervisor, for example, makes it impossible to continue sharing identity and attitudes with old workmates. Some conflicts may endure without ever being resolved. Women who continue working after marriage, for example, often find great difficulty meeting domestic as well as career expectations,

COMMITMENT AND SELF-IMAGE

■ *Common sense says that we buy a Ford because we like the car, and that we vote for one political party rather than another because we support the party. There is of course much truth in this, but it is also true that buying a Ford increases our liking for the car, and that voting for a certain party makes us think of ourselves as the kind of person who supports it. We often gain a sense of commitment, after the fact, from the things we have done. When other people form their impressions of us, they too are influenced by this "behavioral commitment."*

◄ **What you do** *or do not do helps you to judge what you are like. Whatever your initial motives, if you act in a way that is labeled "socially concerned," you are likely to think of yourself as a socially concerned person. Protest marches may or may not influence the uncommitted, but the convictions of those who do participate are undoubtedly strengthened.*

Benjamin Franklin maintained that the best way of making somebody like you is to get them to do you a favor, like lending you a book. Assuming themselves to be consistent, they reason (unconsciously): "I must like that person – after all, I lent them a book." A great many studies in social psychology laboratories have confirmed this effect.

Studies of the "foot-in-the-door" technique practiced by door-to-door salesmen confirm the power of commitment to influence self-image. Researchers found that suburban home-owners could more easily be persuaded to give permission for a very large, ugly "DRIVE CAREFULLY" billboard to be erected in their garden if they had first placed a tiny sticker in their window advocating auto safety. Placing the window sticker apparently caused the people to classify themselves as concerned, campaigning citizens. Since they were not forced to display the window sticker, they thought they must

have done so because of their own convictions. Agreeing to the billboard was compatible with this altruistic self-image.

This research makes it seem that things we do are causes of the way we think and feel as much as they are effects. Arbitrary and insignificant acts may result in a restructuring of our self-perception. For example, when you sign a petition against the death penalty because a friend asks you to, you may be led to think of yourself as an abolitionist, and future opinions and behavior will be influenced by a desire to be consistent with that way of thinking.

▲ **Our self-image** *is constantly subject to superficial change, but there are times in our lives when it needs to undergo some very radical readjustments. The transition from childhood to adulthood is just such a time. Teenagers must start experimenting with adult patterns of behavior and cultivate an increasingly adult view of themselves. Which adult patterns attract their attention first will usually depend on the peer group they associate with.*

especially when their children are still dependent. People sometimes shed old roles to resolve an identity conflict, or lose them for other reasons: dismissal from a job, retirement, children leaving the family nest. Such role-loss in its turn undermines the sense of identity: to a large degree, living up to expectations is what gives us our sense of worth. When a particular set of expectations no longer applies to you, it is hard not to feel that you are less of a person, unless other opportunities to fuel self-esteem are at hand.

Adolescents are particularly vulnerable to identity confusion as they go through the process of separating from the family and establishing themselves as adults. Each faces a bewildering set of choices and several years of uncertainty before settling in any concerted way on the expectations it will be the main task of adult life to fulfill. This achievement is more difficult for people who have had a less successful childhood experience of constructing and maintaining a sense of identity.

It is sometimes suggested that actors may experience identity confusion as an occupational hazard. Being required to assume one role after another, perhaps portraying very contrasting personalities, there is a danger that they may lose track of who they really are. Character actors interviewed on "chat shows" often move through so many different characterizations that it is hard for viewers to glean what is their natural self or what they would be like to live with. The actor Peter Sellers, renowned for his radio and movie characterizations, once complained that he never knew exactly who he was until he had adopted a false

From time to time, our self-image is liable to be altered uncomfortably by events. "Life-changes" such as losing a spouse or a job, or failing an important examination, can severely undermine our sense of identity and disorientate us.

mustache, a strange accent and a funny way of walking.

Even if performers know themselves, audiences may be unwilling to think of them apart from the roles they play. This problem is especially acute for the stars of long-running "soaps." Those who play the villains are sometimes abused – or even assaulted in the street – by viewers who resent their acts of wickedness on the screen.

However, acting itself may not be the root of actors' identity problems. A study of the self-images of professional actors did encounter more identity confusion than was found among housewives and executives, but the degree of confusion decreased when they began rehearsing a role. Acting, rather than causing confusion, may be an adaptation to the performer's need for a clear identity.

Self-image and personal choice

People sometimes worry that they may have been assigned social roles which do not really suit them, that life may be passing them by. The bored housewife imagines herself in the role of a famous novelist; the accountant suspects he would really have liked to be an arctic explorer. Is it just a fantasy, they wonder, or the drowning cry of a submerged self? Rescuing yourself from such a predicament to become your true self can seem impossible: guilt and insecurity stand in the way of any attempt to pit yourself against social expectations and shrug off the responsibilities that seem to block genuine self-expression.

STABLE AND UNSTABLE SURROUNDINGS

■ *We derive our self-image mainly from others. As a consequence, children raised in very stable circumstances – without frequent moves and frequent changes of teachers, neighbors and school friends – have a clearer self-image than those who are more mobile.*

The stay-at-homes are surer about which social categories apply to them, and they have a stronger sense of being a person from a particular place, eligible to share in all of the reflected glory that people there will claim for themselves.

Children who find themselves repeatedly in new surroundings, however, spend more of their lives with people who do not know them well enough to reflect a clear image, and there are fewer group identities that they can readily claim. A study

of children whose parents were in the military and moved house frequently, revealed that they felt less sure of their parents' affection and less certain of social success outside school.

Some sociologists even attri- bute the unusually high incidence of religious cults, fads and crazes in California to the fact that the population is unusually mobile and relationships are often transient. Faced with change and confusion,

◄ **The process of separating from the family** *and establishing themselves as adults can render teenagers particularly vulnerable to identity confusion as they compare their existing self-image with that demanded by the new circumstances. Setting up a home away from home – or (as here) moving into residence at a university – may for some be easier if they continue to be surrounded by familiar possessions.*

people cling to fashionable ideologies and movements in an eager search for identity. Any satisfactions so gained seem short-lived, however, for people seem equally unstable in their attachment to the sects and cults that they create for themselves.

However, most lives leave room for adjustments to self-image that do not entail such conflict. In particular, it is possible to feel less trapped by circumstances by adopting an image of yourself as being more in control of events. Steps in this direction may include reviewing the roles that have fallen to you in life and taking it consciously upon yourself to judge which cannot reasonably be abandoned, and judging for yourself what is a fair-minded expectation of how these roles should be lived. When these decisions are your own, it is easier to find a sense of self-fulfillment in meeting the demands of life.

Roles that we enjoy and select freely also enhance self-image and clarify our identity. They should be actively sought. But they should not become avenues of escape. We all need to feel we have a place in society and people who depend upon us – we derive our social rewards and our identity from others.

Acting in a spirit of free choice, not compulsion, can help to resolve the seeming conflict between self and social expectations. **GW**

■ **Who am I?** *It would seem that identity confusion among actors is an occupational hazard. Some studies suggest that many actors' sense of identity strengthens as they assume a new fictional role but weakens when they are resting between parts. The actor Peter Sellers often declared himself affected in this way. Some commentators surmise that actors are typically people who have not developed a strong sense of self in childhood and are attracted to institutionalized role experimentation; other commentators are skeptical.*

IS YOUR NAME AFFECTING YOUR SELF-IMAGE?

■ *There is a widespread popular belief that given names can influence the development of self-image and personality. At the simplest level, it expresses itself in occasional parental concern about nicknames (Will a son turn out to be a "James" or a "Jimmy," a daughter a "Susan" or a "Susie"?); or in a felt need to change a name (Could Marion Morrison and John Wayne really be one and the same person?) As yet, little is known scientifically about name effects in most societies; but the impact of naming on the the Ashanti people of Africa has been studied and is revealing. The Ashanti give their children a "soul name" according to the day of the week they are born on. Although no particular association is attached to girls' names, there is a consensus about the kind of boy who has a particular day name. The most striking contrast is between "Kwadwo" (Monday boys), who are supposed to be quiet, retiring and peaceful, and*

"Kwaku" (Wednesday boys), held to be quick-tempered, aggressive and troublesome.

Juvenile Court records show that Kwadwo are significantly less likely than other boys to be delinquent, while Kwaku are most likely to have committed offenses such as assault, fighting and wounding. Thus, in the Ashanti, there appears to be some truth in the ancient Latin saying "nomen est omen" (name is fate). Although we cannot discount judicial bias, it is likely that Ashanti boys internalize the description of themselves implied by their name and come to think of themselves as well-behaved or as troublesome accordingly. Their behavior reflects their name-affected self-image.

A similar explanation would account for the slight tendency that has been measured in Western society for the personalities of people who believe in astrology to conform to expectations based on astrological birth signs.

39

Your Impressions of Others

WE FORM impressions of other people's personalities, and much else about them, all the time, usually without realizing that we are doing it. To understand how automatically you do this, try the following experiment: when sitting in a crowded place, look at a stranger for a few seconds, then close your eyes and reflect on what you have seen. You will find that in those few seconds you have formed impressions not only of sex, age and build but also of nationality, profession and social class and of how warm, friendly, assertive, neat and even of how trustworthy the person is. How do we form these impressions? How accurate are they? And how can we improve their accuracy?

The impact of appearance

First impressions are of crucial importance. Not only can they determine whether we decide to form a relationship with someone or not, but they can persist and color our attitude toward a person long after we have come to know them better. The first impression we form of someone depends on the first information we receive. This might be physical appearance, behavior or a name. It might be the person's social or professional role, their friends or family,

or something someone has said about them. From what we observe we may make further assumptions that go far beyond what we can actually know and these can, as we shall see, sometimes be quite inaccurate.

As often as not, our first information about someone is their appearance. We are likely to notice sex, height, build, facial expression, clothes, their general manner and who they are with. Some features are especially likely to lead us to further assumptions – in particular, height and attractiveness. Research has shown that if someone is physically attractive we will get the impression that they also have an attractive personality and possess a wide range of desirable attributes. They are expected to be kind, interesting, sensitive, responsive and modest, for example. We also make predictions about intelligence, but these are sex-biased. In one study subjects expected attractive men to be less intelligent than unattractive ones but attractive women were expected to be more intelligent than unattractive ones.

How distinctive someone is has a strong impact on our impression of them. When observing two people, we tend to see the more distinctive one as being in control. In a series of experiments, one of two people in a videotaped conver-

FIRST IMPRESSIONS

■ *When we meet someone new, our natural impulse is to size them up at once. Our survival could depend on it. If we did not follow this impulse, we would risk misreading the immediate intentions of the other person or fail to interact with them as we might need to. To help us decide quickly, we try to see the newcomer in terms of one of the mental images we have of different types of person. But because these* mental images (or stereotypes) *are built on limited past experience, they are imperfect tools and easily misapplied.*

▶ **The three key steps** *we take in forming a rapid impression of someone. A quick glance is all it usually takes to trigger an automatic assessment.*

▼ **Thrown together for the first time,** *schoolgirls size one another up spontaneously.*

1
Our first glance takes in selected features of appearance and manner. Voice, smell and context are other factors likely to influence us

2
We match these features against stereotypes – mental pictures of different sorts of person – and choose the one that seems to fit best

3
The stereotype at once prompts us to assume the existence of other characteristics, often mistakenly (eg: confident, therefore competent)

▲ **Try the experiment** *suggested in the opening paragraph of the chapter. Which stereotype do you think fits this man best? Pop star, seaman, farmer, religious revivalist, bar bum, soap actor? Is he any of these things?*

Knowing how to avoid forming inaccurate impressions of others is an invaluable social skill. It can also help you to communicate your own personality more effectively. How do we decide quickly what someone else is like?

sation was either illuminated by a bright light, dressed in a boldly patterned black-and-white shirt or else was seated in a rocking chair that he kept in continuous motion. Observers of the videotapes were asked which they thought affected each actor's behavior more – the situation the actor was in or the actor's personality. Observers thought that the distinctive actor was in control, displaying his own personal talkativeness, friendliness etc; and they thought that the nondistinctive actor was simply responding to the circumstances.

However, in a further series of experiments only one of a group of four actors was made distinctive. This time it was the three nondistinctive actors who were seen to be in control. They formed a unit to which observers thought the other would try to conform. Our impressions of people can depend to a large degree on the circumstances that surround them.

This was shown too in a study of how we form an impression of mental prowess. Volunteers were randomly given

the role of questioner or contestant in a quiz game. The questioners could ask questions to which they themselves knew the answer. After the quiz, a group of observers was asked to assess the contestants and the questioners on their general knowledge and competence. In spite of realizing that the quiz situation had given the questioners a better opportunity to display their knowledge, these observers consistently rated the questioners as superior.

Whether or not we wear glasses affects the first impression we create quite strikingly. People who wear glasses are judged to be more intelligent than people who do not. The difference is large – 15 IQ points – the difference between average and bright or bright and very bright. Interestingly,

◀ **At first glance**, *what struck you most forcibly about this woman: the fact that she is highly attractive and smartly dressed; or the fact that she is black? Racial stereotypes are notoriously unreliable guides to individual qualities.*

▲ **What caught your eye first?** *The level gaze of this good-looking young man, his hair-style, his necktie, or his business suit and buttoned-down collar? Do you find any aspect of his appearance reassuring or disconcerting?*

this difference is not entirely imaginary. Research has shown that people who wear glasses are, on average, slightly more intelligent than those who do not, but only by five IQ points. Wearers of glasses may also come to think of themselves as more academically minded than nonwearers.

The importance of reputation

We often receive our first impression of someone before we actually meet them, for example by their reputation or from a job application form or a letter. The impression

We sometimes base our impressions of people on things we have previously heard or read about them, even if these conflict with the evidence of our own eyes. When we eventually meet them, we may persist in seeing what is not there.

created may affect how we act when we encounter the person and what further impression we form.

This is illustrated by an experiment in which two descriptions of a new lecturer were distributed at random among a group of American students. The descriptions were identical, giving details of the lecturer's background and personality, except that in one he was described as "a very warm person" and in the other as "rather cold." These descriptions affected the behavior of the students (who were unaware that two different descriptions had been circulated) when the lecturer led a 20-minute discussion. Those expecting him to be "very warm" actually contributed more to the discussion and afterwards described him as more informal, sociable and humorous than did the others, in spite of the fact that all the students experienced the same encounter with him. The personality traits "warm" and "cold" have been shown to have a particularly strong impact on impression formation. They have been described as central traits in impression formation.

Other means by which we gain our first impression of someone's personality might be a person's name – Sebastian or Chancey can create quite a different impression from Joe or Al (and it will probably affect its owner's self-image as well – see *Ch3*). Or, our first impression might be of their handwriting – a forward-sloping style might suggest a hurried, impetuous manner, while a neat, legible, upright hand might indicate a calm, methodical and careful person. Our impressions might be influenced by a firm or limp handshake, garish or somber clothing, a relaxed smile or a tense expression.

▲ **Women forming impressions of men.** TOP The open, forward posture of the woman here confirms what her sympathetically attentive expression suggests: that a favorable impression is forming in her mind. BOTTOM In contrast, the back-

ward lean, barrier-like arm position and skeptical expression of the woman here indicate the opposite.
 Are women generally better than men at forming accurate impressions of others? Popular reference to "women's intui-

tion" often seems to imply this. Women do indeed show more empathy than men – they are more likely to cry if they see someone else crying, or wince if they see someone hurt themselves. Research has also shown that women are better at interpreting emotions from facial expressions, body language and vocal cues. What is more, these differences appear very early in life, so may be a true sex difference rather than a result of social conditioning. In other respects, however, women have not been shown to be any better – or worse – than men at forming accurate impressions of others.

▲ **People who wear glasses** look more studious than people who do not and are also commonly supposed to be more intelligent. Research finds that wearers of glasses seem as a group only to be slightly more intelligent than nonwearers.

But why should these individual features often seem so significant and lead us to make wider assumptions about a person's character and personality?

How we organize information

What determines which features we notice and which we do not? One factor that can influence this is the order in which we receive information. There is evidence that what we observe first about someone can have a greater impact than what we learn later. In one laboratory study, subjects were shown to form a more positive impression of someone described as:

intelligent – industrious – impulsive – critical – stubborn – envious

than of someone described as:

envious – stubborn – critical – impulsive – industrious – intelligent.

This is called a *primacy* effect. It does not always determine our impressions, however. In some instances quite the opposite can occur and we are more influenced by what we have learned more recently – a *recency* effect. This is likely to occur if later information is more forceful, or if it makes more sense to us or if it is what we prefer to believe.

Having taken in specific features we then relate them to

HOW INTERVIEWERS CAN BE LED ASTRAY

■ *A recent study of the job interview illustrates how job interviewers often form wrong impressions of candidates. In one experiment, interviewers had the task of assessing the social skill of candidates and their motivation for the job. All they had to go on was the candidates' behavior during the interview – facial expressions, gestures, body posture, sex, dress, what they said, length of time spent talking, and so forth. Their assessments were then compared with each candidate's "actual" social skill and motivation, as measured by other, more searching psychological tests.*

It emerged that the interviewers had little difficulty making accurate assessments of social skill. They had based their impressions mainly on gestures, how much the candidate said, and the candidate's dress – which, considered together, are good predictors of social skill.

However, their impressions of a candidate's motivation turned out to be highly unreliable. The reason for this was that they continued to concentrate on factors indicating social skill rather than motivation. Had they concentrated instead on dress, sex and body posture (how far back they leaned) – together found to be good indicators of motivation – they would have been much more successful.

There are, too, some aspects of personality that are not reflected at all in the way people behave at interviews. Psychological adjustment, for example, cannot be reliably assessed by a job interviewer.

However, research also shows that the same person is likely to be rated by most people as much higher in intelligence when wearing glasses than when not wearing them.

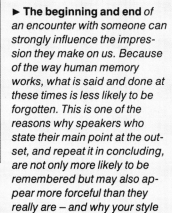

▶ **The beginning and end** *of an encounter with someone can strongly influence the impression they make on us. Because of the way human memory works, what is said and done at these times is less likely to be forgotten. This is one of the reasons why speakers who state their main point at the outset, and repeat it in concluding, are not only more likely to be remembered but may also appear more forceful than they really are – and why your style of handshake can be important.*

Watch your first words...

Watch your final words...

our previous experience. Our brains cannot efficiently hold a large jumble of unrelated facts and observations, so in order to remember and store information in a coherent way we arrange individual items in groups and patterns. Some of these groups consist of character traits that we have learned often go together to form a composite picture of a particular kind of person – the typically warm person, the typically domineering person, the typically lazy person. Such pictures, as mentioned earlier, are called *stereotypes*. We build up stereotypes from the time when we are children by watching people, by listening to our parents and from books and television.

If our impression of an individual includes several traits that fit a certain stereotype we tend to assume that other traits that we have not yet observed will also fit. This is how we are able to form impressions so quickly.

How accurate are our impressions?

People often have great faith in the accuracy of their impressions of others. Being a "good judge of people" is something they pride themselves on. But is their confidence justified? Experiments, in fact, show that when we judge strangers on the basis of the kind of information we usually *have* about strangers, our accuracy is poor. People generally fail to do better than guessing when shown photographs

or videotapes of, for example, two men in tennis gear with the question "Who won the match?" or of two men and a boy with the question "Which is the boy's father?" The same is true even when people asked to predict how someone will act at a turning point in their life are given information about how the same person reacted at 20 key points previously.

Nor do people who have known each other for a long time necessarily have entirely accurate impressions of each other. Married couples asked to predict how their spouses would respond to a series of questions about how they feel, act and think are often mistaken. The commonest source of error is for husband or wife to assume their partner will think or act as they would themselves when, in fact, their opinions and inclinations differ.

People who form impressions of others for a living do not necessarily do it very well either. As long ago as 1919 research showed that different interviewers formed quite different views of the same candidates for employment. A large body of research carried out since then has shown that there is very often little or no correlation between an interviewer's impression of a candidate and how well that candidate will do if offered the job.

The stereotypes we build up and the associations we make between personality traits are usually based on exper-

44

THE HALO EFFECT

■ *This often distorts our impressions of other people. For example, if you are told that a stranger being introduced is a doctor, and you tend to think of doctors as being kind and considerate, you may mistakenly infer that this doctor is kind and considerate. If he is attractive and personable, you may also find yourself believing, for no better reason, that he is also a good doctor. In its extreme form the Halo Effect shows itself as a tendency to see people as "all good" or "all bad."*

We are much poorer judges of character and future behavior than most of us suppose. Even husbands and wives will often have each other guessing. Watch out for the "thought traps" that spring us to premature conclusions.

ience, and so they are better than nothing, and they can improve with experience. However, there are a number of stumbling blocks that have been identified by psychologists and it is as well to understand these if we are to avoid them.

We have a strong tendency to associate positive attributes with other positive attributes and negative ones with each other. Some of us, as a result, gain an overall impression of people as either all good or all bad, making further assumptions on this basis. This is what psychologists refer to as the *halo effect*. An example of this is the assumption some

patients make that doctors with a good "bedside manner" are also more technically competent than others who do not relate as well to their patients.

Research has highlighted another source of inaccuracy – the tendency to think that people who are like us will think and behave in the same way that we do. For example, one survey showed that teenagers who smoke estimate a larger proportion of teenagers to be smokers than do other teenagers. In another study, students were asked questions on topics as diverse as whether they would prefer to pay a fine or contest a traffic charge in court or whether they would like to see more funds allocated for space research. Others were asked whether they would be willing to carry around

THE LIKENESS EFFECT

■ This is another trap for the unwary. It can take various forms. If you recognize one of your own character traits in another person or find them shar-ing a strongly held view of yours, you may jump too swiftly to the conclusion that they are like you and will think and behave as you do. If you like someone, you may also imag-ine that they are more like you than they really are – that they share your values, would vote like you, and would approach a job much as you would. And if you are at a social gathering where all present are linked by an active common interest, as above, it is especially easy to be beguiled by the Likeness Effect. To judge an attribute in another you need more precise information.

an advertiser's sandwich board for 30 minutes. They were then asked what proportion of other students they expected to respond in the same way as they did. In all cases they overestimated the number who would.

Whether or not we like someone has been shown in a number of studies to depend on how many of our own traits they share. This, again, can lead us to an error of judgment, since we may wrongly assume that someone will think or behave in a certain way because we like them, as we saw in the case of married couples. This is illustrated, too, in the novel *First Among Equals* by Jeffrey Archer. Sir Duncan

Fraser is delighted when his son decides to contest a seat in the British parliamentary election, but not so delighted when he realizes that the son plans to stand as a Labour candidate. "But you've been a Conservative all your life," he says incredulously. "No, Father," replies the son, "it's you who have been a Conservative all my life."

Stereotypes, too, can cause wrong assumptions. Vital though they are to the way we remember and interpret the world around us, they are generalizations and so are error-prone. The more limited our experience the more over-simplified our stereotypes are likely to be.

READYMADE AND BLINKERED IMPRESSIONS

■ *To interact effectively with other people we need to match individuals to one or more of the readymade mental images we have of particular categories of person – eg "man," "woman," "eccentric," "ordinary." Such images, or stereotypes, strongly influence our impressions of other people. We tend to exaggerate similarities with other people we place in the same category, and differences from people we do not.*

Stereotypes also guide our attention: we notice what we expect to see, and tend to overlook traits that do not belong to the stereotype we happen to be applying.

It is often our tendency to attach too much importance to a conspicuous or unusual feature of a person that causes us to misapply a stereotype in the first place. Having noticed the feature, we instantly put on blinkers and allow it to distract us from attending to other relevant information. Just as a person carrying a trombone is not necessarily a jazz soloist or even a musician at all, so it is dangerous to suppose that a man with an earring in one ear is a homosexual, whereas a man wearing a macho neck-chain is a heterosexual – or that someone who speaks rapidly is highly intelligent, while someone with a speech impediment is slow-witted. We all, too often, fall into this trap, closing our minds to more reliable, corrective evidence.

▶ **What is the teddy doing** *on the back of this Englishman's bicycle? Is this the case of an eccentric who even as an adult is still inseparably attached to his childhood teddy bear? Or is he simply taking the teddy bear back home to his infant son or daughter?*

▲ **To be tattooed from neck to ankle** *– what motivated this woman's original decision, with its painful and permanent consequences? Exhibitionism? Exceptional modesty? A wish to belong to a special group?*

▶ **What impressions are forming** *in the minds of the tourists eyeing the woman in the black dress as she walks down the Champs Elysées? Parisian shopper? Office manager?*

Forming impressions of others is a responsible business – especially if you are in a position of authority: the label you carelessly put on another person could restrict the realization of their potential for self-expression and achievement.

The other important source of error is one we saw illustrated again and again in the first sections of this chapter. It is the tendency to neglect or ignore some pieces of information either because they are not brought prominently to our attention or because other things are noticed first or because we cannot make sense of them in terms of the stereotypes we work with. This can reinforce wrong impressions because the more inaccurate our impression the less likely we are to be able to make new information fit and the more likely we are to ignore it.

The self-fulfilling prophecy

There is a large body of research that shows that our impressions of someone can actually alter the way they behave. They tend to modify their behavior according to our expectations of them. This effect was shown very clearly in a study of how people reacted in a telephone conversation with someone they thought was physically attractive compared to someone they thought was not. In questionnaires men revealed that they expected attractive women to possess specific personality traits – sociability, poise and humor. They were then asked to have a telephone conversation with a women whom they could not see. They were given a photograph of a woman, either attractive or unattractive, and told that this was the person they would be speaking to. The conversations were taped and afterward a group of independent observers, male and female, were asked to estimate, simply from listening either to the woman's voice or the man's, how much they thought each participant was enjoying the conversation, how enthusiastic they were and how intimate they thought the conversation was. The men who thought that they were speaking to attractive women scored high in all respects. The women they spoke to seemed to observers to be more poised, humorous and sociable. These women were clearly responding to the expectation betrayed by the men's manner.

Physical deformity is commonly included in the stereotype of a criminal person. To test the effect of this, a group of disfigured offenders in a New York jail were given plastic surgery on their release. Their crime rate one year later was 36 percent lower than a control group who had not undergone surgery. While isolated studies of this sort are not conclusive, it seems possible that improved physical appearance enabled these people to find jobs more easily or in other ways altered people's impression of them.

In schools, too, the impression teachers have of their pupils can be influenced by personality and appearance, and higher expectations can lead to reinforcement and higher standards of performance.

Since our impressions of people's personalities can have such important effects on them, it is important to be clear in our own minds which of our judgments are really justified. How many cues do we ignore because they fail to fit in with our expectations? How many indications of personality do we simply fail to notice? We should also be aware of how our behavior can bring out and reinforce positive personality traits like sociability, self-confidence and enthusiasm in other people and perhaps try to cultivate such reinforcing behavior as much as possible. **MC**

THE PYGMALION EFFECT

■ Teachers are not immune to the tendency to form inaccurate impressions - including impressions of children's potential and aptitudes - and their expectations may affect children's performance. In one classic study, children picked out at random by researchers and presented to teachers as likely to show accelerated progress in the following year actually did make more progress than their classmates. Other studies have shown that high-achieving children receive more reinforcement from their teachers than low-achieving children. The teachers' expectations influence the children's expectations of themselves, so the children are likely to work harder,

with more confidence, and perform better.

Low-achieving children whom teachers and classmates clearly regard as inferior performers often come to see themselves in the same light,

and typically respond with substandard behavior. One researcher, investigating why some children labeled as "less able" develop aggressive and rowdy behavior, suggests that this is their self-defensive way

of reacting against a social framework in which they feel low self-esteem. In their "alternative culture," where fighting and group solidarity are valued, they regain a sense of self-worth and achievement.

◄ **These three young children** sitting next to their teacher are all reacting to him in subtly different ways – bored, attentive, and otherwise preoccupied. Many teachers overlook the fact that their different assessments of responsive and unresponsive pupils may sometimes say more about their own personality and teaching style than about their pupils' potential.

Self-Presentation

MOST OF US care deeply about the way other people see us. The desire to create a positive impression, to present ourselves to advantage is almost universal. If we present ourselves successfully, not only will others think more positively of us, but ultimately, our self-image and self-esteem will also improve. Successful self-presentation will almost always be incorporated into our self-image: we become the people we make others think we are.

Self-presentation is a particularly important skill in modern industrialized societies. For most of our history, human beings have lived their entire lives within the confines of small, familiar groups, such as the extended family, the tribe or the village. There was little mobility, and most relationships lasted a lifetime. The emergence of industrialized mass societies during the past few hundred years, however, has created a very different social setting. In this "society of strangers" frequent, short and superficial encounters between people of no shared past or future are increasingly the norm. The ability to create a positive impression on strangers is thus of particular importance in this age, and is likely to play a growing role both in our working, and in our private lives.

Actors on a stage

Just as professional actors prepare for their performances, learn their roles and use "props," people in everyday life seem to use similar skills to stage their self-presentations. This is suggested by the so-called "dramaturgical" model that has become influential in the study of self-presentation. According to this model, we prepare for our performances backstage (in our bathroom and in front of the mirror in the bedroom) the same way as actors do. We select our costumes for the day with no less care, and seek to convince our audience, be they friends or strangers, of our authenticity. Selecting a wallpaper, office decor or furniture for our house is similar to stagecraft: we aim to construct a stage for our social life. People also use a "mask" or "face," different from their private selves, to present themselves in public. Accent, dress, mannerisms, vocabulary can all be part of the "face" we present to the world.

The skill of self-presentation

To fail in a performance leads to loss of face, which upsets the pattern of social intercourse. When somebody acts out of role, we no longer know what to expect. Tension and embarrassment result, and the painful silence, feeble joke or nervous laughter warn us that the predictable social order has broken down. Fortunately, most people learn their scripts well, and rarely act out of role. Psychologists call this skill "impression management." But we are not all equally good at presenting ourselves to advantage.

What does it take to be good at self-presentation? There are many people who seem never to lose their self-confi-

PUTTING ON A FACE FOR THE WORLD

■ *The face we present to the world is carefully managed.* RIGHT *Like actors, we costume and groom ourselves to have desired effects on hoped-for audiences. A mime artist in his dressing room preparing for a performance is little different from any of us in front of the mirror before a party.* LEFT *By personalizing the exteriors of our houses, we encourage first impressions of the selves we will try to express more intimately to those we invite into the even more personalized settings within.*

The desire to create a positive impression – one that presents us to advantage – is almost universal. If you present yourself successfully, not only will others think more positively of you, but your self-image and self-esteem will also benefit.

dence, are always sociable and cheerful – but are they good impression managers? Not necessarily. In some situations, losing your temper or appearing helpless may be the most suitable strategy. Just like a skilled actor on stage, the expert impression manager must know his or her audience, be sensitive to the requirements of various social situations, and be able to judge a performance with some degree of detachment.

There are a number of psychological tests that measure these characteristics – the Self-Monitoring Scale, for example. People with high scores on this scale are better at assessing how others see their performances and are more skilled in changing their behavior to suit a particular audience or situation. For example, in one study some members of a discussion group were told that videotapes of their per-

formances would be shown to members of the group, while others were told outsiders would see them. People who scored high on self-monitoring changed their performances to suit the expected audience, appearing friendly and likable for the in-group audience, and independent and nonconformist when expecting an outside audience. Low self-monitoring individuals failed to change their behavior to suit the situation.

Concern with effective self-presentation is by no means a recent phenomenon. In his classic work, *The Prince*, the Renaissance scholar Niccolo Machiavelli (1469-1527) offers detailed advice on how to develop strategic skills to influence people. Based on Machiavelli's ideas, modern psychologists have constructed a Machiavellianism scale to discriminate between good and bad impression managers. The scale measures the extent to which a person views others and social situations with a degree of cool intellectual detachment and even skepticism.

High scorers on this test were found to get the best deal for themselves when bargaining with others over the distribution of money, and were more successful in persuading a potential partner to go to a party with them. In one study, high and low scorers were given the task of disturbing a person allegedly taking a test, without appearing to do so. High scoring Machiavellians produced an ingenuous series of distractions, including whistling, pencil tapping, dissecting a ball-point pen, and "accidentally" knocking over

The ability to see ourselves as others will helps us adapt our behavior to changes in the social situation – to new roles, new aims and new people. It is an important skill to acquire for successful impression management.

a table, followed by loud and lengthy apologies. Machiavellianism can also be measured in children: for a financial reward, 10-year-old Machiavellians did far better than low scorers in convincing other children to eat several bitter-tasting cookies soaked in quinine, while appearing more innocent in doing so.

It seems that detachment, the ability to see ourselves as others will, is an important characteristic of the good impression manager. Most of the time, we are preoccupied with our environment and are not consciously aware of ourselves as others might see us.

In some situations, however, we are forced to become aware of ourselves in a different way: we come to think of ourselves as we appear to others – for example, when somebody points a camera at us, when we see ourselves on a videotape, or when we see our image in a mirror. Several studies have shown that when people are made to look at themselves in this way their thinking and actions change. They become more dependent on the "outside" view of themselves. Clearly, self-presentation should be more effective when we are consciously aware of how we appear to others.

Playing for an audience

Generally, people tend to like people who are similar to themselves, particularly in the early stages of a relationship. A good manager can create a more positive image by adjusting self-presentation to match the characteristics of the audience. We tend to present a more modest, quiet image to a person who is an introvert, and will appear more

---

HOW CLOSELY DO YOU MONITOR YOURSELF?

■ *Read the following statements carefully. They deal with possible personal reactions to social situations. In each case, decide whether the statement is true or mostly true of you. There are no right or wrong answers – try to be as honest as possible.*

● *1 I can usually pretend that I am happy even if I am not enjoying myself.*
● *2 I am not very good at imitating the behavior of others.*
● *3 If I am unsure about how to behave, I take my cues from others.*
● *4 I am quite happy for other people to be the center of attention at social gatherings.*
● *5 My behavior often depends on the kind of people I am with.*
● *6 I never change my opinions to suit another.*

● *7 I think I would probably make quite a good actor.*
● *8 I find it difficult to make other people like me.*
● *9 I have no difficulty appearing friendly to people I do not really like.*
● *10 I am not very good at changing my behavior to suit different situations.*

To score your answers, count one point for each "true" answer you gave to an odd-numbered statement and each "not true" answer you gave to an even-numbered item. The closer your score is to 10, the more you are likely to be a highly self-monitoring person. High self-monitors are particularly good at judging how they appear to others, are very aware of the requirements of social situations and are good at adapting their actions to suit a particular occasion.

► **Judging how we appear** *and what effect we have on others involves watching in particular their faces, but also their postures and gestures. From these we note – often unconsciously – reactions to what we say and to how we use our own body language. In this scene, each participant can feel sure of the appropriateness of her own performance, and she is led on to contribute more of herself, because the others show interest and acceptance by leaning forward with interest, gesturing and exchanging frequent eye contact with her.*

▲ **Rituals of self-presentation** help us to interact in impersonal situations. TOP LEFT A strong and warm handshake gives strangers a more convincing way than mere words can of expressing good will and agreement. This gesture and the facial expressions and postures that go with it imitate more spontaneous displays that occur in closer relationships. TOP RIGHT Japanese businessmen in Tokyo bow in courteous greeting. Two are of relatively high status and they carefully watch the others to be sure of not misrepresenting themselves by bowing too high or too low. BOTTOM Before buying a car from George Davis, we can feel assured of his experience and success in the business and of his credentials as a family man. In our homes too, although usually with more restraint, we display trophies and personal objects that show the people and the places we are connected with.

confident and assertive to an extroverted and dominant partner. Research has shown that people will even modify deeply held political convictions to fit in with the expected attitudes of an audience.

The extent to which we match a person's opinions in our self-presentations largely depends on how much interest we have in our partner. In an interesting experiment, single, female, unattached university students matched the opinions of a male conversation partner on such issues as women's roles only if the partner was highly desirable (a tall, older, unattached student from a prestigious university). In identical conditions, no opinion matching occurred when the partner was less desirable (a younger, small student from a lesser university, with a girlfriend). Indeed, if we positively dislike a person who happens to express opinions and ideas similar to our own, we may end up changing our existing attitudes just to distance ourselves.

In general, skilled impression management involves behaving in ways that match the actions and attitudes of people we like, and esteem, but contrast with those of people we dislike. The commercial implications of this common strategy are not lost on advertisers. Images of very popular people such as sportsmen or film stars drinking a particular brand of beer or using a certain brand of shampoo are expected to create a consumer desire.

The need for consistency

A very important requirement for successful self-presentation is that we project a consistent image over time. Once we have established a public "face," there is a strong tendency to live up to that image. Indeed, people will often go to extraordinary lengths to remain consistent with their projected image, a need that is sometimes exploited by salesmen and advertisers.

A good example is the well-known "foot-in-the-door" technique. Once a salesman persuades you to do him a small and reasonable favor (for example, give him a glass of water or allow the use of your telephone), you have been

SOCIAL SITUATIONS

■ *In order to successfully present ourselves to others, we must have a good understanding of the social situations we are participating in. In recent years, psychologists have done considerable work on the way various social situations are perceived and understood by people. They found that most of our interactions with others occur as part of a very limited number of recurring social settings. Most people can only report about 20 to 30 such typical settings – for example shopping, having an evening meal at home, visiting a doctor, meeting friends for a drink, going to a movie.*

Is there a difference between skilled and unskilled impression managers in how they see such common situations? Research shows that people with low social skill concentrate on one single feature: how much self-confidence they feel. People who are highly skilled socially and particularly competent in presenting themselves tend to perceive social situations in a more sensitive and detailed way. *They evaluate the success of the encounter in achieving its purposes. They measure their own involvement in the encounter and its importance or seriousness to them. Studies such as these strongly suggest that a clear and unbiased understanding of the characteristics of various social situations is an important prerequisite for skilled self-presentation.*

▲ **Performers and spectators** *in the ritual arrival of celebrities at an event in the Cannes Film Festival. The stars and the policeman on ceremonial duty are all on display, each striking a pose appropriate to a different role. Policemen with traffic and crowd-control duties look where they like and stand as they please, counting them-* selves among the spectators. In most social interactions, however, we are each other's spectators and we are all performers.

"Self-conscious" people are conscious mainly of their anxious feelings when meeting strangers. Skilled self-presenters are aware of themselves too, but in more constructive ways – calmly assessing how well they play their role.

manipulated into presenting yourself as a helpful and friendly person. It will now be much more difficult to refuse a later and less reasonable request like buying an expensive encyclopedia than it would be without the initial small favor. The deeply felt need to remain consistent with a previous self-presentation, to live up to what others expect of us is a powerful factor in impression management (see also *Ch 3*).

Another commercial ploy capitalizing on the need for consistency in self-presentation is the so-called "low-ball" technique, much beloved by used car dealers. This involves manipulating a potential customer into a commitment to purchase – for example, by making an unrealistically good trade-in offer. Once the commitment to buy is made, the terms are renegotiated. For example, the salesman comes back with the news that the trade-in was not approved by the boss.

There will now be a powerful need to remain consistent with the initial decision, even though you would not have made a deal on the terms now offered. To be seen by others as vacillating, inconsistent and unpredictable is perhaps the most damaging impression one can create. Few things are as threatening in social life.

Ingratiation

Although the term ingratiation is often used in a rather pejorative sense, most self-presentation and impression management strategies involve some degree of it. It simply means consciously trying to win favor, and we do it because we need to be liked and accepted, because we hope to gain

something by it or as a protection against harm or danger. To avoid our motives being too transparent, complex and subtle methods of impression management are required. For example, it may be effective to criticize someone on minor points and to praise them on major issues; this is less suspect than indiscriminately praising them and flattering them.

Four basic strategies are used in ingratiation. These are: flattery; conforming to the other person's opinion; making

LET YOURSELF GO OR WATCH YOUR MANNERS?

■ *We are all capable of both and understand the situations where each is appropriate.* TOP *A girl finds an opportunity for uninhibited exuberance as individual identity becomes submerged in crowd excitement at a rock concert.* LEFT *The diners at table 14 at a formal Christmas party in Hong Kong are relaxed but poised, and conscious of what to wear, do and say.*

sure that they see your good points; doing favors. Both high- and low-status people use ingratiating strategies – often seeking no more than to be liked. Low-status people are likely to flatter another. High-status people put forward their good points and conform to the other's opinions.

The need for esteem and approval

People differ greatly in how much they need and seek the approval of others. Our basic attitudes toward other people are formed in childhood and adolescence, and tend to remain with us for most of our lives. Firstborn children tend to remain more dependent on others for social support throughout their lives than do later-born children. The extent to which a person needs approval from others can be measured, using the Social Desirability Scale.

Two kinds of statement make up the scale: those about highly desirable characteristics which in fact are rarely lived up to by most people (eg "I never tell a lie") and those about undesirable characteristics which are nevertheless quite common ("I sometimes get angry and resentful when I don't get my way"). People who have a high need for approval tend to agree with the first kind of statement, and not with the second. In effect, they claim for themselves socially desirable characteristics even when the likelihood of this being truthful is rather low.

Is there a relationship between a person's need for approval and their ability to present themselves in a favorable light? Not necessarily. In fact, it seems that people with a high need for approval are usually also more afraid of being rejected. They tend not to initiate interaction with others, and are quiet and conformist in groups.

Public and private selves: are they linked?

By definition, self-presentation means trying to influence public perceptions. Does it also have an effect on the way we see ourselves? What exactly is the relationship between the images we present to others, and our self-image?

People often assume that their self-image is a stable, enduring entity. In reality, self-perception is intricately related to how *others* see us. Our self-image is a social creation important to the extent that it differentiates us from others, and is accepted by others.

Even other primates seem to possess a rudimentary self-image, which can only emerge as a result of intensive exposure to others (see *Ch2*).

In the course of our encounters with others, we try out various ways of presenting ourselves. The most successful presentations will eventually become part of our self-image – we slowly become what others think we are, the role turns into reality. Self-presentation thus determines not only how others will see us, but ultimately, also influences how we come to see ourselves.

Several experiments illustrate the way successful self-presentations are incorporated into our self-image. In one study, subjects were told to try to make a positive public impression of themselves on a partner, who was in fact a confederate of the experimenter.

The impressions were accepted and reinforced in half of the cases but rejected in the other half. Afterwards, subjects who were "successful" in making a good impression were much more likely than unsuccessful subjects to claim that their public presentation was consistent with their true self-image.

▲ **Between performances** in our social lives we have the privacy, like this mime artist between performances on the stage, to ask who we really are. Am I really the person I have been presenting? Most of our private impressions of ourselves, however, will be based on observations of the selves, sometimes public, sometimes more intimate, that we present to others, and on the impressions that others relay back to us (see Ch3).

By disclosing personal information you open the way to closer relationships, in which a limited circle of friends and loved ones can know and give emotional support to the "real you," the self that is too vulnerable for public show.

Other evidence suggests that people who see themselves as having a particular characteristic as part of their self-image also believe that others see them in this way, and in fact they do receive high ratings from their friends and acquaintances on precisely these traits.

Nor is self-image very stable over time. Our perceptions of ourselves can change quite rapidly, depending on the social situation we find ourselves in, and the characteristics of others we compare ourselves with. One intriguing study showed that a person's self-esteem can undergo a major change within the span of less than an hour.

Subjects in this study first completed a self-assessment questionnaire, allegedly as part of an interview for a part-time job. Soon after, a second "applicant" for the job (in fact, a confederate of the experimenter) arrived, who had either very desirable qualities (well dressed, carrying books on philosophy and science, well prepared with sharpened pencils for the test), or had very undesirable qualities (wearing worn and dirty clothes, no socks, disoriented and unprepared for the test).

After the arrival of the second applicant the subjects' self-esteem was again assessed as part of a second questionnaire. Those who met the desirable candidate now rated their self-esteem significantly lower, while subjects who met the undesirable candidate now thought much more highly of themselves.

This study illustrates that our self-image is relatively volatile, and largely depends on the qualities of others with whom we compare ourselves. Positive self-presentation increases our standing compared to others, and thus improves our relative self-image as well. **JPF**

TALKING ABOUT YOURSELF

■ *Telling someone about yourself is one of the most powerful and direct methods of self-presentation. It is a far more complicated process than it first appears. Who can say what, to whom and at what stage of the relationship? These matters are regulated by finely tuned and complex rules.*

Studies show that there is considerable agreement between people about the order in which various topics can be disclosed. Some, such as tastes, interests, attitudes and work are quite readily disclosed even to relative strangers. Other topics, mainly to do with our self-image, personality, family, sexuality or finances, are usually only disclosed to intimate partners.

An important rule of self-disclosure is that it has to be reciprocal. We reveal ourselves to each other at a mutually regulated pace. When one conversation partner says something slightly intimate about themselves, the other may encourage more intimacy by following suit or discourage it by remaining impersonal. Disclosing increasingly personal information about yourself can be a powerful method of self-presentation, and a major contribution to the development of a relationship. However, this works only if your

self-disclosure progresses by small steps, and is at every step reciprocated by similarly personal disclosures by your partner.

For any given relationship, there appears to be an optimal level of intimacy in self-disclosure. In most relationships, there seems to be a tacit agreement that the level and rate of mutual self-disclosure is managed by one of the partners. It is the "manager" who regularly initiates increasingly

intimate topics for discussion as the relationship progresses, with the partner reciprocating with disclosures of his or her own.

Too much self-disclosure too soon can be a disastrous self-

presentation strategy. For example, disclosing highly personal information to relative strangers will not develop the relationship, but may lead to anxiety and rejection by the partner. In one study, passengers approached in an airport waiting room were asked to make judgments about a person on the basis of a sample of their handwriting. In fact, the handwriting was always the same, but the content of the passage was varied, disclosing highly intimate information (eg about family), moderately intimate information (eg about work and place of residence) or nonintimate information (eg about the weather). Highly intimate self-disclosure was just as

counterproductive to creating a good impression as impersonal information. Waiting passengers formed the most positive impressions about the person when assessing handwriting that presented intermediate levels of self-disclosure.

There are also cultural and individual differences between people in how much they like to disclose about themselves. In some cultures intimate disclosure about a person's emotional life, family background or financial affairs is generally frowned upon, while in others it is more readily tolerated, and even expected. There is a clear difference between Northern European and Southern European cultures.

There are also important differences between men and women in how they use self-disclosure. Women generally tend to be more prepared to disclose information about themselves than men and are better at accepting and reciprocating intimate disclosures from others.

The ability to disclose personal information is extremely important for our social adjustment and mental health. It is through self-disclosure that we can obtain the kind of warm, supportive social contacts which we all need.

Self-Esteem

SELF-ESTEEM is the valuation we place on our own worth. It largely hinges on the extent to which we see ourselves as achieving the goals and standards that *we* feel are important, but the esteem of other people is also an important factor in confirming our worth.

Particular sources of self-esteem are impossible to count and weigh exactly, but clearly some are more important than others. A single failure involving some deeply held personal value or a person of special importance can be far more devastating than a whole host of other failings. And, by the same token, a single success or the approval of some special individual or group can do more for our self-esteem than dozens of less crucial accomplishments.

Inevitably, conflicts of interest occur, and choices have to be made as to who we will try to please most – ourselves, family, friends, employer or whoever else confers the crucial approval. Whatever the choice, and however well we succeed in any particular respect, we can expect shortcomings in other respects and consequent feelings of inadequacy or inferiority.

According to the Austrian psychiatrist Alfred Adler (1870-1937), to be human is to have inferiority feelings, and to be a healthy human being is to strive for superiority. It is a maxim which has, when stated in this way, understandably attracted a good deal of criticism – mostly along the lines "I don't feel inferior, and I certainly don't want to be superior to other people." This, however, is not an accurate interpretation of what Adler meant. He argued that inferiority is a fact in every person's life. From infancy, when we are surrounded by adults who are superior in every imaginable way, to old age, when physical and mental shortcomings again become apparent, our self-esteem never ceases to be challenged by the attributes of others.

How much do early experiences affect us?

As with most aspects of our psychological development, many of the most formative events occur in infancy and during the school years.

Like adults, even young children need to feel they are respected and esteemed by others. Their tears and anguish

SOCIAL CONFIDENCE

■ *Early social failure – such as not being chosen for schoolyard teams or being left out at parties or from the "gangs" that form so naturally in adolescence – can all cut very deeply. We may ascribe our failure to real or imagined flaws in our manner, appearance, abilities or background, but whether these have any basis or not, feelings of aversion connected with social gatherings are readily absorbed and magnified.*

This is particularly true during adolescence. The awkwardness and insecurity created by the inevitable physical and social transitions of that stage can make young people so sensitive that they take offense or retreat into their shells at the slightest provocation. Without sufficient encouragement and support, they may remain trapped there: lacking confidence and the opportunity to acquire further social skills, they may soon become reluctant wallflowers or loners.

Some years ago, a group of American male students decided to try an experiment with just such a young woman in their college. They wanted to

know how far another person's self-confidence and social success could be engineered by surreptitious and systematic manipulation.

For their subject, they chose a shy newcomer whose marked gaucheness they proposed to remedy to such a degree that she would be transformed into a campus belle. The method was simplicity itself: they would give or get her invitations to all the social events going and

always be close at hand to partner her at a dance, listen to her views, laugh at her jokes and generally express friendship and admiration. The girl, however, was to know no more of this plan than the rest of the little society into which they would launch her.

It might have been a very cruel thing to have done had things gone wrong, but by the time the experiment ended, and the girl was no longer being

backed and popularized by her supporters, her metamorphosis was complete. Imperceptibly, she had grown into the role. Meeting new circumstances with positive expectations and social skills acquired along the way, she continued to be a popular and outgoing individual. Her confidence was now as self-sustaining as, in the past, her timidity and self-doubt had been.

Feelings of inferiority are a fact of everyone's life. Others help us in our effort to overcome these feelings by expressing their regard for us. For genuine self-esteem, however, we need also to persuade ourselves of our worth.

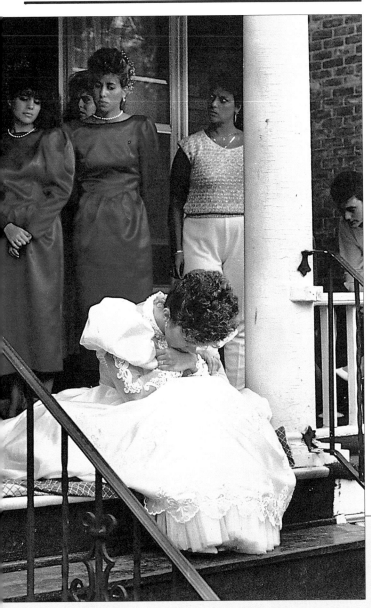

when laughed at, rejected or humiliated make this abundantly clear. Yet, as early as their second year, they and their parents may be expected to manage the vulnerability and the provocations inherent in toilet training. Soiled clothing and beds are undeniably offensive, and it is perfectly natural and necessary that parents should express this view as long as they make it plain that it is the product, not the child, that is offensive. Praise for successful control helps build self-esteem, whereas punishment and scorn cut at its very roots.

Pampering can also undermine children's self-esteem. Overindulgence in meeting their desires, and overprotectiveness – which severely limits the natural course of environmental exploration, risk-taking and decision-making – can seriously impair development of autonomy and self-reliance. Overprotected children are inclined to seek the attention and the care of others, feeling unable or unwilling to trust in their own abilities.

Rejection by parents, however, is the more usual hazard. Sometimes there is an obvious reason – the child may be unattractive or intellectually dull, not the sex that the parents wanted, or not wanted at all. Often, there is no immediately apparent explanation why parents act in harsh or uncaring ways, but when they do, their rejection, neglect and hostile treatment can so depreciate some children's view of themselves that they may never become absolutely confident of their worth.

In one investigation, 1700 boys between the ages of 10 and 12 were studied closely to determine which parental characteristics and home circumstances are associated with the early development of self-esteem. Through a series of tests, interviews, teacher- and self-evaluations, a pattern emerged which, though not unvarying, was very distinctive.

Children with low self-esteem, unlike others with high self-regard, tended to come from homes in which family

WHEN OTHERS VALUE US, WE VALUE OURSELVES

■ *How others value us profoundly affects how much we value ourselves. Positive feedback in social situations LEFT gives us social confidence: to be desired, admired and appreciated are powerful incentives to think well of ourselves. Part of the romantic excitement of intimate relationships RIGHT is the prospect of being idealized.*

A more dependable advantage of lasting close relationships, however, is the knowledge that someone cares for you and feels committed to you in spite of knowing all your shortcomings. The potential benefits to our self-esteem are worth the risks to self-esteem TOP that are part of every relationship.

relationships were poor and marital breakdown or remarriage more common. Parents were more permissive, although occasionally and unpredictably they would inflict harsh punishment. In addition to the effects of having such poor role-models and being treated in such an ambiguous way, these children were shown little respect as individuals and were given less warm attention, and the parents displayed only slight interest or confidence in their abilities.

By contrast, the parents of children with high self-esteem tended to set higher behavioral standards and achievement expectations. Their discipline was less permissive, and although its enforcement was more consistent, punishments were less severe. These parents would display positive interest in the friends and activities of their children, and show encouragement and confidence in their abilities. Clearly, there are lessons as well as conclusions to be drawn from such findings.

From the age of five or so, children usually have a wider circle of people from which to find the esteem that may be lacking at home. If they are talented in some way, or have other characteristics that lead them to be accepted and admired by others, lack of parental esteem may be less damaging. Otherwise, they will find it hard to develop positive self-regard.

It is a sad fact, however, that many children's experiences at school are deeply upsetting, irrespective of their home background. Like the children they teach, teachers vary in their competencies and conduct in the classroom. Some are skillful in the way they motivate and control behavior by judiciously giving or withholding signs of esteem, while others are more inclined to use ridicule, sarcasm or disparagement of a child's abilities or personal qualities. However, the opinions and attitudes of other children are often of greatest importance in shaping self-esteem.

For some children, their size, shape and/or appearance may be a particular cause for concern. Being undersized or ill-favored in looks, having some peculiarity or disfigurement, or simply having to wear thick glasses can be very damaging to their self-esteem if others tease or shun them. Even those who are physically average may still have problems with bullying, or assaults on their self-esteem due

▲ **In the parent-child relationship** *it is especially the child whose self-esteem is vulnerable. Pampering and overindulgence of whims can seriously undermine the growing self-reliance on which much of the child's sense of worth will later* *depend. However, harsh or uncaring parental disregard teaches children to think that they are of little worth. Every parent must decide when to be supportive and when to expect children to use and develop their own coping abilities.*

Parents of children with high self-esteem set higher standards of behavior and achievement. They are less permissive, but punishments are less severe. They show interest in the friends and activities of their children.

to their poor academic ability or lack of the social skills needed to make friends.

In some cases, habitual criticism or rejection leads to progressive withdrawal, a sense that their low self-esteem is confirmed by their experiences, and increasing feelings of alienation and depression. In others, the opposite may occur: frustration turns outward and may be expressed as indiscriminate resentment or anger directed toward "society," "the system" or anyone or anything they happen to pick on.

Generally, neither withdrawal nor aggression is a practical solution to the problem of low self-esteem, although social withdrawal may occasionally lead to constructive solitary activities, and violent antisocial behavior may sometimes provide some measure of esteem and status within a street or criminal subculture. Whether either of these confers self-esteem depends upon the extent to which they are compatible with what the person has decided is his or her ideal self.

If our home life has been loving and supportive, and if we

have been successful and well-adjusted and had good friends at school, the transition into adult life will probably be easier than for those who have had more difficulty sustaining their self-confidence and self-esteem. However, although crushing experiences may have serious short- and long-term consequences, too easy a passage is not always an advantage. It may seem paradoxical but, Adler argues, feelings of inferiority are often an important element in attaining our full stature as human beings.

Adult strategies for compensation

Up to and perhaps a little beyond the time we leave school, parents and classmates set most of the benchmarks we use to judge our failure or success. But once away from the inescapable social and intellectual grading process of those years, we become more able to choose the people we want around us and to determine our own criteria of success.

We also have access to a far wider range of indirect methods of compensating for inferiority feelings. Although a hackneyed example, the small man in a big car, relentlessly pursuing commercial power or political stature, captures the essence of many adult compensations.

HOW PARENTS VALUE THEIR CHILDREN

■ *Parents value their children in different ways and at different times, but in whatever way a child is appreciated, it is essential that the appreciation should be shown. Parents benefit from the love, affection and emotional support of their children LEFT, they enjoy playing parental roles, such as that of teacher CENTER, and they bask*

in the reflected glory of their children's achievements RIGHT. Parents also report that they value the companionship and help that children provide. Fear of creating too much youthful self-esteem can cause parents to withhold praise and emphasize criticism in a way that makes it difficult for children to believe that they can be of

value to others. Later, their ability to sustain a sense of self-worth when facing the world alone may be hampered. However, an excessive parental fear of undermining children's self-esteem can equally hamper development. Children who are never criticized and never required to pay attention to the needs of others learn that they

do not really matter. In the absence of opportunities to genuinely please others, we will try to please ourselves, but this is very difficult to achieve in isolation. Both too much and too little negative feedback can have the effect of encouraging an egocentric, or "narcissistic" personality whose self-esteem is in reality very low (see Ch 7).

Successes of this kind do not automatically confer feelings of great self-worth, but as long as the achievements are admired and do not conflict with the individual's own values and standards of morality, they frequently do create a real basis for high self-esteem. Conversely, early advantages and a relative lack of inferiority feelings can undermine self-esteem if they lead to underachievement. As in the race between the tortoise and the hare, advantages that breed complacency can easily lead to failure.

Gambits of the "I could have been/done/had" sort, followed by reference to some more prestigious, interesting or better-paid occupation than the speaker has, are among the most obvious ways of compensating for inferiority feelings.

Whether such things were ever remotely possible varies, but their failure to materialize is usually blamed on bad luck, the incompetence or unkindness of others, or self-sacrifice. Sometimes, of course, such stories are true, or they may contain a grain of truth which has gained much in the telling. Either way, the tellers claim our higher regard, which, if given, enables them to sustain a greater self-esteem than the realities might afford.

Most of us bend the truth to some extent to elicit or retain the esteem of others. However, although this may work admirably, any form of pretense makes it harder to express and develop the authentic self. It is a common dilemma, and one expressed neatly in the title and content of Eugene

OVERCOMING INFERIORITY

■ Even if it is not objectively justified, we may feel mentally, physically, occupationally or socially inferior, and our need for self-esteem requires that we try to overcome this unsatisfactory state of mind. This, according to the Austrian psychiatrist Alfred Adler (1870-1937), is the source of our striving for superiority. Appropriately and constructively channeled, it can lead to achievements capable of creating and sustaining considerable, solidly based self-esteem.

Sometimes there are very real obstacles in the way of attaining personally important goals, and to overcome these may require a great deal of effort. Adler himself was physically disadvantaged as a child and felt keenly inferior to his strong and athletic older brother. It took tremendous effort to develop his own frail body and to strengthen legs bowed by rickets, but he worked at it and ultimately became an agile tennis player and robust mountain walker.

Later, he was to describe this sort of behavior as "compensation." "Striving for superiority" was the motivation necessary to transform feelings of inferiority into those of self-esteem. This is, he argued, a universal tendency, whether or not actual deficiencies are involved.

"Direct compensation," as in Adler's own case, involves overcoming the specific cause of an inferiority feeling. There are, however, some sources of inferiority feelings that no amount of exercise or effort will improve to an acceptable extent. It may therefore be necessary to compensate indirectly, to pursue excellence along other lines and, in this way, attain the approval and satisfaction needed to support self-esteem.

The dull child attempting to build self-esteem on sporting successes, and the puny one who seeks intellectual superiority to offset his feelings of inferiority are by now stock examples of indirect compensation. No doubt both strategies occur often enough to justify their frequent use as examples, but it by no means follows that deficiencies in physical qualities will be balanced by greater intellectual potential or vice versa. Even if they are, it cannot be assumed that such compensations will necessarily be very successful. That depends a great deal on whether the alternatives are accepted and approved by those most influential in shaping and sustaining a person's self-regard. Being good at sports may completely fail to impress parents or even friends if they think far more of academic or occupational achievements.

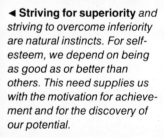

◄ **Striving for superiority** and striving to overcome inferiority are natural instincts. For self-esteem, we depend on being as good as or better than others. This need supplies us with the motivation for achievement and for the discovery of our potential.

Most of us bend the truth about ourselves some-what in order to have the esteem of others. This often works well in winning us advantages and in bolstering our egos, but it can make it harder to develop and express our authentic selves.

Kennedy's book: *If You Really Knew Me, Would You Still Like Me?*

Most of us would probably expect only a qualified "yes" to that question. Our behavior may be quite unexceptional, and we may not be unusually subject to dishonest and aggressive thoughts or to feelings of envy, lust or greed. But, being human, we all have some motives, desires and fantasies that we would not wish others to know.

These undesirable aspects of ourselves may not be particularly great in number or particularly shameful, but whatever we feel necessary to suppress indicates the distance between our actual and ideal selves (see p116), and hints at the state of our self-esteem.

Tailoring ourselves

There are undoubtedly practical advantages to be gained by presenting others with a carefully tailored and expurgated edition of ourselves. However, there is a drawback: fear that we shall be "found out" limits the degree of closeness we can tolerate in our relationships, and means that any feedback we get is to the image we present, rather than to the person within. We are therefore left with doubt and the unanswered question of whether people would like us if they really knew us.

Self-esteem is a fragile and delicately balanced thing. It is, of course, more positive and firmly grounded in some people than in others, but it is only ever as secure as the things upon which it is based. Beauty, vigor and physical skills are highly vulnerable to the effects of illness and aging. Job loss and retirement are particularly threatening to those whose self-esteem largely depends on the status, earnings and influence derived from their employment. And a rash moment can, for those whose self-respect means living up to a strict moral code, transform a high level of self-regard into deepest shame and self-contempt.

Life is filled with events that cause re-evaluations, if not radical changes, in our self-esteem. Being divorced, jilted, or discarded by a friend are also among the more dramatic incidents which may shake our self-esteem, while success in gaining such things as qualifications, expertise, recognition and promotion consolidate it.

Most fluctuations in self-esteem are, however, minor shifts taking place on a day-to-day basis. Small successes or signs of affection or approval help raise it, just as little failures or snubs can lead to a temporary regrouping of psychological forces. Normally, self-esteem is self-righting. However, these small fluctuations may have a more substantial cumulative effect. **BWPW**

▲ **Direct compensation** *for a sense of inferiority means overcoming its specific cause, as in the shot-putting achievements of this committed but wheelchair-bound athlete.*

▶ **Indirect compensation.** *Having a large car at your disposal can help to make up for unrelated feelings of inferiority. Indirect compensation is often a successful strategy for self-esteem: we make up for what we cannot be by focusing efforts on what we can be.*

Individuality and Creativity

SHOULD you make a conscious effort to develop your individuality and creativity rather than conform to social standards? It is not uncommon to hear that someone is "too much of an individualist" for a responsible role or effective membership in a team. Exceptionally creative people often seem like poor models for our own lives, because so many, for all that they achieve, do not achieve personal happiness. However, the persistent pursuit of your own insights and goals can be essential to self-fulfillment.

Are you an individualist?

If you are an individualist you are part of a minority. Experiments have found fewer than 30 percent of us willing to assert our own ideas when they run counter to a majority view. Even when the majority is obviously wrong – for example, if we are placed in a room where everyone else says that lines on a piece of paper look equal in length when in fact they are somewhat unequal – only about one-third of us will disagree, often in a hesitant and doubtful manner.

This minority of people who judge issues for themselves, and assert their judgment, are among the most successful and well-adjusted members of society. We select our leaders – in all areas of life, in industry, fashion, politics and science – from this group: people who resist being easily persuaded and who try to draw out what is best from the sum of the conflicting views that others present to them.

Leaders who stand out from the rest as strong individualists may tend to isolate themselves from the opinions, inter-

62

EXCEPTIONAL INDIVIDUALITY

■ The charisma of exceptional personalities, such as Mao Tse Tung TOP LEFT, John F Kennedy TOP RIGHT and Mikhail Gorbachev BOTTOM derives in part from their ability to make followers sense that they have a very clear vision of their goals and a strong will to pursue them in the face of opposition. Strength of personality is beneficial too in the conduct of our own lives.

For self-fulfillment we need to choose our own standards. This may require considerable insight into our needs and potentials, and it may require us to resist social conventions or the aspirations others have for us. Being individual, however, does not mean rejecting commonly accepted standards simply for the sake of individuality. Questioning may in many cases lead to thoughtful and more confident acceptance.

To fulfill your creative potential and assert your individuality you may need to pursue insights and goals that others do not understand. In laboratory conditions, fewer than 30 percent of us show the necessary independence.

ests and tastes of others even to the point sometimes of being ineffective at organizing support for their views. Many strong individualists have been forced to the margins of political or scientific life as cranks or misfits, only to re-emerge as major figures when circumstances permit. Sir Winston Churchill, Britain's great leader in World War II, was for years considered too eccentric, too unpredictable and too belligerent for high office by key figures among those controlling political power in Britain, and did not become Prime Minister until a charismatic war leader was needed. Charles Darwin, the first major contributor to modern theories of biological evolution, was considered a failure in early life. His reluctance to seek a conventionally successful life in the Church or in medicine, as his family would have wished, was partly due to his being absorbed in unconventional ideas which he kept mostly to himself. He only published them when he was middle-aged, and friends and circum-

stances finally persuaded him that he could no longer delay.

Without such exceptional individualism, it is probable that the human race would make little progress. In the context of self-fulfillment, of course, it is not exceptional individualism that is in question. We are each managers of a life, however, and just as we expect the people who lead countries (not their advisers or critics) to make the final judgment in important matters, to creatively invent solutions to problems and to stand up to social pressures when they have to, so it may be preferable for you – the person who leads your life – to do this.

The creative individual

Everyone is creative in some manner and in some degree – we all experience our greatest sense of agency when we do something in a way that is not simply handed on to us by others but is of our own making. Individual creative expression is a theme of widely different social styles: of the drive in the 1960s to be unconventional, and – contrastingly – of the drive in the 1980s for entrepreneurial

▲ **Expressive creativity** is only one manifestation of the creative impulse that is present to some degree in all of us. Others include the technical creativity of being handy in the workshop or the inventive creativity of finding solutions to problems. Creative people have been found to be energetic, persistent, self-confident, flexible and highly responsive to the feelings of others, but independent in their judgments. Very few of them are geniuses, but they find their creative talents worth cultivating for the satisfaction and increased self-esteem that they bring.

economic success. In the 1980s, such economic individualism even began to be acceptable in the Soviet Union and the People's Republic of China, as a way of channeling energies into greater production of wealth. From the purely psychological standpoint, any social style that encourages a genuinely creative individual expression is to be welcomed, whether this be the creation of a new economic enterprise, an alternative way of life, a song or a rock garden.

Creative genius is confined to a few, such as Albert Einstein or Pablo Picasso. More numerous are those who creatively adapt the insights of the great. Also, without being geniuses, many people are creative in the same ways as the great, but less intensely. Some are able to bring together old ideas and elements in new ways to invent solutions to problems. Many have a talent for creative technical manipulation – they are good at making and fixing things. Expressive creativity is also common – in people with a flair for writing, playing an instrument or singing. In addition, we all to some extent create our own personalities and our own lives as we adjust to the world in which we find ourselves.

The talent that psychologists have most attempted to measure in connection with creativity is *divergent thinking* (also called *lateral thinking*). This is the ability to branch out from a starting point to search for a variety of original possibilities. It is measured by asking such questions as "How many uses can you think of for a brick?" and scoring the answers for *fluency* (how many you come up with) and for *originality* (how different they are from the most common answers). The opposite of divergent thinking is *convergent thinking*, which means bringing information together to formulate a solution to a problem. In fact, both forms of thinking are indispensable to creative activity, but uncreative activity heavily relies on the convergent pattern –

▲ **Creating an individual style**, *a Wodaabe man of northern Nigeria prepares for a courtship festival. We use self-adornment to draw attention to ourselves and to display our power to be distinctive.*

CHOOSING STANDARDS FOR SELF-JUDGMENT

■ *All too often, we try to live according to standards we have never questioned. We may never have considered whether they are realistic or what we really want. The art of living a fulfilled life depends on setting goals that we care about and can attain, yet stretch us. We need to be able to persevere when success is possible, and to consider alternative goals when it is not. Above all, the expectations of others should not dominate our priorities. Of course, the good opinion and affection of other people is always important, but if the* desire to please leads to excessive compromise in adapting our values or aspirations to theirs, the consequent loss of integrity may far exceed the apparent gains. Being "all things to all people" may be a prescription for superficial popularity, but it leads to a confusing and inconsistent sense of self. Its very formlessness will create an ambiguous and flimsy basis for self-esteem, and its uncommitted and changeable nature will probably not be highly valued by the very people whose respect we care about most. **BWPW**

▲ **Making a spectacle of themselves** *is something that even those who are only slightly extroverted find enjoyably stimulating.* ABOVE *A participant tries to outdo the competition with her elaborate costume for the annual Notting Hill Carnival in London.* TOP *Arriving with style to watch lawn tennis at the Wimbledon tournament, a couple express their enthusiasm with individualized headgear. Special occasions bring out creativity by relaxing our sense of conventionality.*

Being independent-minded about your tastes and goals is not the same thing as being egocentric. Very egocentric personalities in fact suffer from an inability to build self-esteem through genuine self-direction and personal achievement.

for example, when we simply follow rules and try to focus on what we are supposed to do.

Related to the idea of divergent thinking is that of *remote association*. Examples of remote associations would be thinking of things in the opposite sense of the obvious (for instance, talking of an old man as if he were a young boy) or drawing a connection between two things because of a

seemingly unimportant quality (for instance, buildings might be compared to blizzards because of their white color).

Some people seem to have an inherited talent for creativity and for particular creative activities, but anyone can cultivate at least some of the traits of personality and the habits of mind that are characteristic of them. All researchers place independence of judgment high on the list. Creative people are also found to have high energy levels, persistence and self-confidence. They are flexible and open to new exper-

EGOCENTRIC PERSONALITIES

■ *Social norms sometimes block self-fulfillment. They may influence us out of guilt or fear to forever postpone becoming the people we want to be, because present obligations seem to stand in the way.*

But is this remark an open invitation to a selfish narcissism? This tendency is named after Narcissus, the character in Greek mythology who pined away after falling in love with his own reflection in the waters of a clear spring. At the extreme,

"pathological narcissists" regard others as mere instruments for their own fulfillment and pleasure. Victims of this personality disorder are boastful, almost grandiose in the way they at times think about themselves. However, their sense of self-importance is a defense against feeling so empty. They have unattainable fantasies involving grossly unrealistic goals, of unlimited power, wealth, brilliance, beauty or ideal love.

Narcissists constantly desire admiration and attention, but they lack empathy and frequently even concern for others. It is not surprising that their interpersonal relationships are rarely if ever satisfactory. They expect special favors from others as entitlements, but the idea that they should offer something in return is absent.

Narcissism seems to be the persistence of an infantile mode of thinking. A baby views itself as all-powerful. A small cry will

conjure up the breast or the bottle. It is not surprising that the infant should view itself as the center of the universe. As babies gradually come to understand their total dependence on others, they usually learn a more realistic attitude.

Sensitive and empathetic parents give their children self-esteem and self-assurance by admiring achievements and meeting needs, but they also give reasonable criticism and make reasonable demands. Inadequate admiration and support, or admiration and support that are not balanced with constructive criticism and demands, will prevent a child from building up a firm, realistic picture of itself. In the absence of this, it is forced to take refuge in the infantile view.

All people are born with a capacity for narcissism, but as we mature, most of us make compromises between self-oriented and social demands – we develop a conscience and accept ethical principles and rules. We are not pathological narcissists, but in some degree we allow our own needs, tastes and even a few of our fantasies to compete with our obligations.

Our sense of self-esteem and our sense of belonging depend greatly on our being what others need us to be. However, this does not mean being dominated by others and their needs. People who achieve self-fulfillment make independent judgments – that are worthy of others' respect – about what it is reasonable for others to demand. **AH PF**

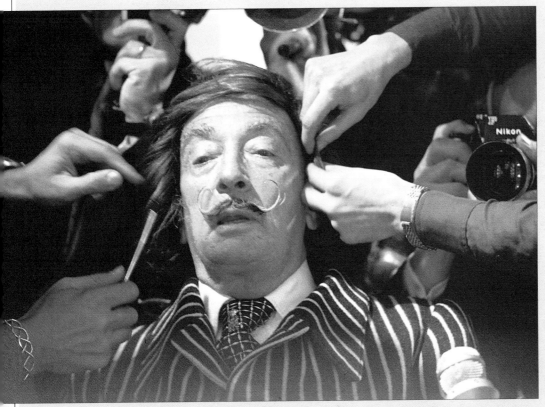

▲ **Famous for being egocentric**, *the Spanish painter Salvador Dali is seen here surround-* *ed by attendants. Far from being the victim of a psychological disorder, however, Dali* *purposely exaggerated the image of eccentricity that was his trademark.*

iences. They tend not to be rigidly sex-typed – not overly concerned about how masculine or feminine they appear. They are spontaneous, have a good sense of humor and a tolerance of ambiguity: it does not always bother them when they do not know how matters will turn out. They have a strong sense of curiosity and of play. They are sensitive to both their own and to other people's feelings and they accept themselves as they are.

In the activities in which they are creative, they do not often rely on sheer luck in order to hit on solutions – usually they form more and more precise ideas of what they are looking for as they explore possibilities, persistently calling up and testing answers to problems they set themselves.

The unruly side of creativity

For some of the most brilliant, creativity has a side that is unruly, unsettling and often unconventional in the extreme. Creative and entrepreneurial talents can be found in conjunction with eccentric or abnormal qualities. The Greek philosopher Plato described the kinds of experiences that lead to poetic, religious or philosophical insights as a kind of "divine madness." Does this count against the idea of creativity as part of the healthy personality?

Poets and some other sorts of creative artists appear to be more susceptible to periods of serious depression than the general population. Some psychologists have suggested that the depth of feeling that characterizes the creative work of the artist may be akin to the rumination and reverie of depression. Ludwig van Beethoven experienced recurrent problems of depression throughout his brilliant musical career. His progressive deafness and his poor relationships with women contributed to his depression in later life, but he also seems to have had a depressive temperament by nature. Beethoven mentioned thoughts of suicide at various

times in his life. His father was a severe alcoholic who was extremely distressed over the young Ludwig's failure to attract attention as a child prodigy. Beethoven's later years were marred by severe disagreements with his nephew and ward which culminated in a dramatic suicide attempt by the nephew. Biographers of Beethoven have generally agreed

CREATIVE GENIUS, CREATIVE INTERPRETATION

■ *Works of genius may need to be interpreted. The scientific theories of Albert Einstein* TOP *have an astonishing creative intensity, but they are expressed almost entirely in mathematical symbols. They would be wholly inaccessible to most of us if no one troubled to interpret their gist in more familiar terms. Great masters* RIGHT *may be better appreciated directly, but even sidewalk artists can reinterpret their works for their own and for our pleasure. The work of interpreters is sometimes almost as creative as the original. Even those who try merely to appreciate works of genius, even at second hand,* *may have to make a creative effort of understanding in order to do this.*

Creative people do not rely on sheer luck to hit on solutions to their problems. They form more and more precise ideas of what they are looking for as they persistently call up and test answers to questions that they pose to themselves.

that this suicide attempt hastened the composer's death the following year. Although Beethoven's personal life was disappointing and sometimes disastrous, his musical productivity was consistently impressive.

Many observers have commented on the high incidence of alcohol abuse among major literary figures. A list of abusers compiled by Upton Sinclair, the American novelist, includes many illustrious writers he knew between 1910 and 1956: Jack London, Stephen Crane, O Henry, Sinclair Lewis, Edna St Vincent Millay, Dylan Thomas, Sherwood Anderson.

Eugene O'Neill, the leading American dramatist of the early 20th century was severely alcoholic in early life, but in his later 20s he achieved a grim but artistically productive sobriety. Another major literary inebriate was James Joyce, whose lifestyle for many years consisted of writing all day and drinking at bars all night. On certain occasions, Joyce was robbed and beaten while drunk.

It has been speculated that there might be a link between creative genius and psychotic madness. Studies of family trees of some outstanding people have indicated high proportions of relatives with serious psychological problems. It has been suggested as an explanation for this that these families have a hereditary tendency toward unusual thought processes. Some family members are able to use these processes in creative work, because they also inherit moderat-

■ **Four kinds of creativity** appear in the work of a composer TOP, an ice sculptor TOP RIGHT and a group of picture restorers RIGHT. An element of invention is involved in any work that presents problems requiring original solutions. Technical creativity is involved in any act of bringing about a desired change with tools, equipment, instruments and materials. Expressive creativity is apparent especially in the invention of something that carries an emotional or other form of message, such as a new piece of music or the image of a snow leopard. The discoveries of science are creatively applied in the work of the restorers.

Scientific creativity

Expressive creativity

Inventive creativity

Technical creativity

ing qualities. On the other hand, those who do not inherit the moderating qualities tend simply to be mad.

The relationship between creative genius and madness is especially close in some individuals. These people have unquestionable talent and equally unquestionable mental illness. Nikola Tesla, for example, was an inventor and applied scientist of the first rank. He was a colleague and rival of Thomas Edison. He developed alternating current electrical generators, discovered plasma electricity and developed the technology of hydroelectric power. Tesla also claimed to be in communication with other planets and to have invented "death rays." Tesla continued to be a highly productive scientist even while making his claims and suffering from several bizarre compulsions.

Wilhelm Reich was a psychoanalyst and psychiatrist who made major theoretical and technical contributions to his field. He was one of the originators of marital and sexual therapy and his theoretical work on sexuality inspired lively professional interest and controversy for decades after his death in 1957. At the same time, however, Reich developed extravagant delusions of persecution, believed that he might represent a special advanced version of the human species, and developed cancer cures based on a theory of the "orgone," a new type of energy that only he and some of his followers were able to detect. Reich died in prison having been convicted of fraudulent use of the United States mail to promote therapies based on his orgone theories. Friedrich Hölderlin was both severely psychotic and one of the finest lyric poets in the German language. His early 30s, however, were a time of advancing madness. On one occasion, he wandered several hundred miles across Europe in a hallucinatory state. His intervals of recovery during this period of his life, were, however, some of his most productive. Some of his finest poetry was produced within months of his final lapse into madness in 1806.

Creativity and personal control

In some respects, great creativity and madness *are* similar. Both are characterized by unconventional thought processes. Both depend on seeing connections which are not obvious to other people. Very creative people are more likely than others to use very remote associations in their thinking. But the two are fundamentally different in other re-

68

GREAT ARTISTS AND ABUSE OF ALCOHOL

■ *Although many renowned creative people are famous for their misuse of alcohol, it seems that far from being something that unlocks and promotes their creativity, drinking destroys it by destroying them.*

▶ **The great French vocalist Edith Piaf** *LEFT in her prime, before alcoholism and a morphine addiction undermined her health.* TOP RIGHT *At 45 years of age, performing during a 1960 concert tour, the last that she ever made. The idolized American singer Elvis Presley suffered a similarly dramatic decline.*

▶ **One of many literary alcoholics**, *the powerfully lyrical Welsh poet Dylan Thomas died of alcohol poisoning in New York City in 1953 at the age of 39 after overdrinking. Many alcoholic artists are remarkable for their interpretation of emotions, but many nonalcoholics are equally accomplished.*

Creativity and madness may both involve ideas that can only remotely, or even bizarrely, stand together. For the mad, these associations are uncontrolled and overwhelming. The creative person is able to control and make use of them.

spects. In the mentally disturbed, remote associations are uncontrolled and unproductive. The victim has little choice about the unconventional thoughts that come to mind and seems overwhelmed by the process. The creative genius, on the other hand, is able to control the overall direction of thought and to use the unusual connections productively.

A conversation between James Joyce and Carl Jung that took place in 1934 illustrates the difference between unconventional thinking and madness. Joyce had placed his 26-year-old severely disturbed daughter Lucia in Jung's care. Jung was the 20th doctor to be consulted on Lucia's deteriorating condition. On a visit to Zurich to see his daughter, Joyce spoke privately with the doctor, expressing his belief that his daughter could not really be mad because her

speech and thought patterns were very similar to his own. Was it not likely, he argued, that Lucia's strange turns of phrase and thought were simply not-yet-appreciated insights? Jung emphatically disagreed with Joyce. He compared father and daughter to two people reaching the bottom of a river. According to Jung, James Joyce had dived there whereas Lucia had fallen in.

Salvador Dali, a leading 20th century painter, actively played up his role as a "madman" both as his inspiration and as a kind of universal language of which he is an interpreter to modern audiences. A close study of Dali's paintings, however, reveals that they are painstakingly planned and executed. Dali's work is powerful and disturbing, but it is very deliberate and craftsmanlike. He controls the disturbing message rather than being controlled by it.

In our more modest degree, creativity for ordinary people too is one aspect of being in control of our lives. **JJC**

▲ **Remote associations** abound in Salvador Dali's "The Metamorphosis of Narcissus" – in the left foreground, for example, a human form is made to look almost like a rock formation. At the same time, the figure resembles a neighboring stone sculpture of a hand, the head corresponding to an egg. However strange the juxtaposition of elements throughout this painting, the viewer cannot fail to recognize that they are all within the firm control of the artist.

Instinct and Human Nature

UNDERSTANDING and accepting ourselves involves understanding and accepting humankind. In spite of striking individual differences, we are all variations on a set of common themes. Each of us has our own personal image of what this common theme is, but we tend to converge in our thinking. Research has shown that most of us are neither *very* optimistic nor *very* pessimistic about issues such as altruism (whether people are in general very selfish or sincerely concerned about others) and trustworthiness (whether we are moral and reliable, or immoral and irresponsible). But many of us are somewhat pessimistic about these issues, and even those who are somewhat optimistic can have their doubts. How much natural kindness and dependability can we reasonably claim? Are we *instinctively* the sort of beings we would wish to be?

Do we have instincts?

Human nature is often viewed as a set of irrational instinctive impulses, in combination with an uncertain potential for rational thought. Most of the impulsive side of our nature tends to be viewed as suspect – this is the unruly "id" of Sigmund Freud (see *Ch 9*), who thought that in order to make civilized society possible, parents and social institutions try to foster the rational part of our nature and repress the irrational.

A more scientific approach to instinct follows from the Darwinian view that instincts are, like other aspects of behavior, a product of natural selection. Experts in animal behavior studying the naturally occurring behavior of birds, fish and other species, have proposed that much of it can be described as *fixed-action patterns* that are characteristic of each species and largely genetically based. These patterns

Our natural tendency is to satisfy our own needs first and to favor relatives and friends at the expense of strangers. This does not mean, however, that all of our instincts are selfish or difficult to reconcile with social ideals.

of behavior are instinctively released by specific triggering events called *sign stimuli*. For example, the red breast of the male robin acts as a sign stimulus that releases aggression in other males. Even a relatively crude model of a red breast provokes a male robin to attack.

In most species of birds and mammals, instinct is heavily supplemented by learning. For example, some songbirds have to hear the song of their species at least once in the throat of another before they can produce it themselves and so have the capacity to fulfill their impulse to communicate. In humans, with their great potential for learning and for developing social systems that teach standards and traditions, it is very difficult to distinguish learned from instinctual behavior. However, no one would maintain that we have no natural urges at all. The cry of a helpless baby or the challenge in another's angry posture and facial expression seem to be powerful sign stimuli for us, and research on the heritability of personality differences (see *Ch12*) points to genetic control of many aspects of motivation and emotional life through determination of the way our nervous system develops and regulation of our body chemistry. Like all inherited traits, instincts exist in a population because they help the population to survive. Thus, to make sense of typical human behavior, it may help to think about how it could have given our ancestors an evolutionary advantage.

The drive for reproductive success

The goal of any species is to maximize reproductive success. There are several different ways of going about this. At one extreme, the *r-strategy* (referring to the *intrinsic rate of increase* of the size of a population) is to produce many offspring but to invest relatively little parental care in each one. Oysters, for example, produce 500 million eggs a year, but engage in no parental care. At the other extreme, the

INSTINCTS ARE FOR SURVIVAL

■ *Fighting to survive and extending a friendly greeting are both instinctive responses. Instincts are tendencies to react in an inborn way to particular situations that commonly affect personal survival and chances of reproduction. In some of the situations that bring out our nature in this way, survival and reproduction are of immediate urgency: FAR LEFT a mother and her children flee from bombing during the Vietnam war. We are instinctively concerned mainly about our own survival and reproduction and that of people who are closely related to us. Those who share at least some* of our genes, especially our own children, matter more to us than strangers. When life is secure and relaxed LEFT, the survival value of our behavior is less obvious, but nevertheless significant. Because we and our kin have evolved to survive and reproduce as members of social groups, we have well-developed social instincts. We feel the urge to form relationships with nonkin and bond with them in groups that provide a framework for mutual help and mutual emotional support in the event that these may be needed.

K-strategy (referring to the *carrying capacity* of the habitat) produces few offspring but invests large amounts of energy in each. The great apes, for example, produce only one offspring every five or six years, but the degree of parental investment is high.

An r-strategist is an opportunist who engages in rapid, prolific breeding to make the most of uncertain and rapidly-changing environments. A K-strategist nurtures each offspring carefully so as to give them the best possible chance in an environment which is at or near the maximum population size that it can support.

Compared with many species, humans are K-strategists. We usually produce just one offspring at a time, with long intervals between each birth, and we nurture each one care-

fully over a period of many years. Even within a population there are differences in the extent to which individuals adopt these strategies. This has been found in species as diverse as dandelions, field mice, fruit flies and fish. Human extroverts tend slightly more toward the r-strategy than introverts do – engaging in intercourse earlier, more frequently and with more different partners. Personality differences may affect parenting styles: introverts are more "careful," "thoughtful" and "reliable," whereas extroverts are "active," "impulsive" and "changeable." There are also individual differences in helping behavior which appear to have some genetic basis. The r-strategy seems to be stronger in families that tend to produce more fraternal (nonidentical) twins and large numbers of children. Compared to mothers of single-

PARENT-OFFSPRING CONFLICT

■ Why should parents and offspring so often be in conflict? Are children so innately bad that the whole of their upbringing has to be devoted to training them to take their place in a civilized society?

One way of looking at this question is from the point of view of the genetic legacy that nature has put in the custody of each party to the conflict. A mother shares some of her genes with her child, but mother and child are not genetically identical. In fact, they are related by only one-half, because the child's remaining genes have been contributed by the father. So, there is no more than an overlap of genetic self-interest between parent and child.

From the point of view of genetic continuation, the benefit of parental investment is that it increases the likelihood of survival of a particular child; but the cost is that high investment in one child may decrease the parent's ability to invest in others. A very demanding child may lower the parent's overall reproductive success. For example, a newborn is more demanding – has more needs that can only be met by others – than a five-year-old. At the extreme, nomads living on the edge of survival have often found it necessary to let a baby die rather than risk the survival of older children by literally carrying an extra burden.

A young baby has no conscious plans based on cost-benefit arguments. Nor does it suffer initially from conflicts about how best to allocate its reproductive resources. But, in evolutionary terms, it has been selected to demand more resources than the parent may be willing to give, because there is only one person to whom it is related 100 percent – itself. This state of affairs holds until it

▲ **Brothers and sisters** are only related to each other by approximately one-half, and so the genetic-survival interest that each represents is not identical and children are naturally adapted to be rivals for their parents' time, energy and material resources.

becomes independent of parental care. When this happens, the child's genetic interests may actually be served by having siblings. Cooperating with a brother or sister may help to perpetuate the genes they share with you, and when you are more independent they are no longer competing as much with you for parental resources.

What can a helpless baby do to commandeer parental resources in the face of possible opposition? One good strategy is to demand frequent feeding – say, every two or three hours instead of the longer intervals that the mother might find more convenient. It might also be a good idea to resist weaning for as long as possible, especially since the burden of continuing

lactation on the mother's physical system reduces the probability of another pregnancy. Another ploy is to become especially demanding at about the time when the mother is likely to become pregnant again. Alternatively, if unwelcome competition in the form of a brother or sister is unavoidable, the child could try reverting to the kinds of behavior that were successful when it was much younger – crying, clinging and bedwetting.

Does this mean that babies are innately selfish? Not really, and certainly no more so than their parents. It is simply the case that the interests of infant and parent may conflict, and whenever such conflict occurs we may expect to see the two parties each attempting to influence the behavior of the other. Temper tantrums, separation anxiety and regression are examples of infant strategies; rigid scheduling of feeds, maternal rejection and enforced early bedtimes are possible examples of adult strategies. The disagreements occurring during adolescence reflect the fact that parental and offspring reproductive strategies may now be in direct conflict: parental reproductive interests may best be served by an older child remaining to help out at home, whereas offspring reproductive interests may best be served by embarking on the process of mate selection.

The most likely beneficiaries of your altruistic impulses are members of your own family. Even organisms as simple as bacteria seem to recognize biological relatives and to help their chances of survival and reproduction.

tons, mothers of fraternal twins have on average a lower age of menarche (first menstruation), a shorter menstrual cycle, a closer spacing of births and greater fecundity.

Men, by comparison with women, are slightly more inclined toward the r-strategy. This is possible, in evolutionary terms, because a man can produce so many more offspring. In a single ejaculation a man can release more than enough sperm to fertilize all the women in North America. Since a woman is limited by the number of nine-month pregnancies that she can accomplish during her reproductive life, her chances of passing her genes on to a future generation may be more dependent than a man's chances are on intensive investment in individual young. It seems to be a feature of our evolutionary history, however, that utterly promiscuous men have succeeded less well in passing on their genes than family men have – those who concentrated their reproductive effort on at most only a small handful of wives,

keeping other men away from them and investing heavily in the welfare of these wives and their children. The K-strategy is far from absent in men.

Sacrificing ourselves for kin

Why should people go out of their way to help each other as much as they do, even sometimes making the ultimate sacrifice – giving their lives to save someone else's? Why should you jump into a river to save another from drowning, when by doing so you might die yourself? Other species do it, too. Why should a bird give an alarm call at the sight of a predator, when giving the call would draw the predator's attention?

An argument for saying there is a genetic tendency toward such altruistic behavior is that it is an extension of the K-strategy – when relatives with shared genes for altruism benefit each other, their genes are more likely to live on in future generations than those of families that do not help each other. It does not matter if an altruist perishes, if relatives benefit enough to survive and reproduce.

▲ **Paternal instincts,** *seen here in a father's affectionate gesture, are less obvious than maternal ones, but research confirms that they are strong. Fathers left alone with their newborn children spend as much if not more time looking at and holding them as mothers in the same situation. Though most direct care and affection is provided by women, both sexes invest intensively in a small number of offspring.*

▶ **Reproductive decisions are a family matter.** *Interest in the choice of a marriage partner for a close relative is universal, and in most cultures marriages are arranged, as in the case of this child bride and child groom in India, enjoying a wedding treat. Our shared genes are more likely to be passed on successfully if the husbands of our female kin and the wives of our male kin are good matches.*

This is a very special definition of altruism: it does not just mean "being nice to people." It means helping someone else to survive and reproduce at the cost of your own reproductive success. It implies that you know who your relatives are.

Of course, we nearly always know this. And we do sometimes risk our lives to save kin in preference to nonkin: anthropologists have recorded that people worldwide are more likely to intervene with help when a relative is in trouble. We also direct material resources toward relatives, for example by leaving them money when we die.

What is more surprising is that many other species seem to know who their relatives are. Monkeys, birds, ground squirrels, tadpoles, bees and even bacteria can distinguish between biological relatives and nonrelatives and adjust their behavior accordingly. In some cases, they even behave as though they could tell the difference between degrees of relatedness, such as full siblings and half-siblings. This tells us that relatedness must be a powerful force throughout much of the animal kingdom, and also that we do not need to assume a high degree of conscious awareness in behaving differently toward our kin.

Understanding the nature of this underlying force can help us to gain insight into some of our own conflicting feelings. For example, many people who become stepparents feel confused and guilty because they cannot conjure up such strong parental feelings toward their stepchildren as toward their biological children, good and loving stepparents though they may be. At worst, stepchildren may actually suffer. American researchers have found children of preschool age living with a stepparent and a natural parent 40 times more at risk of physical abuse than those living with two natural parents.

Murders most commonly occur within the family. But homicide statistics (including murder, manslaughter and infanticide) show that most homicides are carried out by someone who is *not* biologically related to the victim.

▲ **The urge to care for the helpless** *evolved so that our own kin and members of our own communities could better survive. However, when we have resources to spare, the urge can come alive at the sight of helpless strangers and even of helpless members of other species.*

▶ **Creative participation** *in a cooperative effort helps individuals to forge a sense of identity with each other. The urge to make things that did not exist before and to share them with others is an instinct that promotes our technical advancement. More fundamentally, it has for hundreds of thousands of years helped us to establish the emotional foundations of community life.*

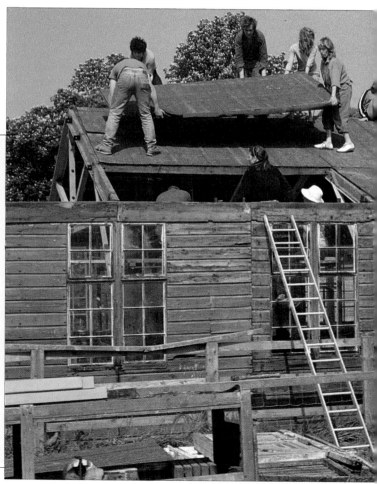

We are most altruistic toward people we like and we like people who are altruistic. Cooperation can therefore become a self-reinforcing cycle in which help and concern promote more help and concern, an essential foundation for friendship.

Marriage partners and acquaintances are at much greater risk than are genetic relatives, and this is not just because husbands and wives generally live in the same household.

Giving help to nonkin

We help and share not only with relatives. Friendship and the emotional bonds that it implies are often all that is needed. Surveys have found that we tend to be more altruistic toward people that we like, and to like people whom we perceive as altruistic.

If people interact with each other on a regular basis, then the chance of receiving some benefit in return is fairly high. An example of this occurred during World War I, when opposing forces were confined for long periods in neighboring trenches. There were few gains to be made from advancing, since the small area of ground so bitterly contested between the trenches and won at such appalling cost was likely to be lost again at the next encounter. Opposing soldiers eventually began to cooperate with each other, putting informal truces into effect at Christmas, deliberately aiming to miss, or firing only at specific and easily predictable times. This continued in the face of furious opposition by the commanders on both sides, who eventually forced

their troops to undertake unpredictable and damaging raids which caused the system of restraint to break down.

Cooperation based on mutual interaction can also be observed in other species. Vampire bats roost in small colonies from which they emerge at night to feed on blood from living animals. They are often unsuccessful, especially when they are young, because it is difficult to take blood from another animal without being detected and brushed off. Since bats that have failed to feed for three days will starve to death, this is a serious matter. As a result, the species has developed a system of mutual support. The bats regularly feed each other by regurgitation to compensate for failed feedings, but they do not feed other individuals at random. They are more likely to feed their relatives, and they are more likely to feed a bat that has previously given them food in the past. They seem to be able to tell each other apart and remember past interactions.

An important aspect of reciprocal altruism is that people associate over long periods. It develops most effectively in stable social groups whose members expect to encounter each other repeatedly.

Can we tame the beast within?

Most of us are probably fairly comfortable with the idea that our personality and behavior depends to some extent on our upbringing and the experiences that we have

HOW TO COOPERATE IN A GROUP

1
Begin by cooperating. Demonstrate that you are prepared to be altruistic.

2
Stop cooperating only if your partner does so. Do not be the first to stop – but do not ignore transgressions.

3
Be forgiving. If your partner begins to cooperate again, do not bear a grudge, but resume your own altruistic behavior.

75

■ Humans are adapted for living in small social groups, and many of the emotions that we experience – such as friendship, gratitude, a sense of fairness – are tailored for social interactions. Some groups seem to function smoothly: people know what is expected of them, and cooperate successfully with each other. In others, there are endless grievances and a general sense of injustice, with everyone trying to score over everyone else.

Some of the possible strategies for group behavior are very simple – for example, "Do what everyone else is doing," or

"Always try and beat the other person." One of the easiest ways to find out which strategies are workable is to play them against each other in a computer tournament. Scientists who invited entries for a tournament of this kind were surprised to find that it was one of these simple rules that was the most successful.

The rule was called "tit for tat," and its strategy was: cooperate on the first interaction, and then do whatever your partner does (whether cooperating or failing to cooperate.) The three principles circled

above summarize this strategy. The success of this simple tactic in the computer tournaments suggests that reciprocal altruism may be quite widespread in nature. It also suggests that its very simplicity may be a virtue: it may be a mistake to be too devious, either in your own behavior or in interpreting other people's.

Furthermore, this form of reciprocal altruism is not blind. The tit-for-tat strategy responds quickly to a lack of cooperation by the withdrawal of its own. Although this may seem like primitive justice, it is at least consistent.

We liberate ourselves from our most basic drives by fulfilling them. This allows distinctively human instincts to emerge, expressed as desires to develop personal potential and apply it to the benefit of the whole community.

undergone. But to suggest that we are also in part the product of our evolutionary heritage seems threatening. Surely, if we have evolved tendencies to favor our relatives and friends at the expense of unrelated people, is this not somehow unfair? If aggression once had some adaptive value, does this mean that aggression is "natural"? And if these tendencies are genetically based, does that not mean that there is nothing that we can do about them?

The idea of "fairness" is obviously an important issue. But consider the implications of the *lack* of the tendency to favor our own relatives. For example, a mother who neglect-

ed her children would tend not to leave any descendants, and so her genes would not continue into the next generation. A tendency not to care for your children would very soon become extinct. Perhaps this is unfair, but the only way of getting round it would be to persuade someone else to bring up your children – and that does not seem very fair either.

It is unduly pessimistic to assume, of course, that, just

MASLOW'S PYRAMID

■ The psychologist of self-actualization, Abraham Maslow, has constructed a deceptively simple-looking hierarchy of needs that is actually the basis for a sophisticated and comprehensive theory of motivation. It is based on the premise that human needs are far more deeply rooted in instinct than in social learning. Of course, Freud also held this view, but while he reduced all human motives to sublimations of the survival and reproductive instincts shared by all animals, Maslow argues that humankind has evolved others.

Our needs, says Maslow, can be ranked in an ascending order. Those higher on the scale can only be given priority once those further down have been met to a sufficient degree. He is never very precise about

the extent to which a given need must be satisfied before a higher one can become a priority. This is hardly surprising in view of the great individual differences which occur in every imaginable attribute from intelligence to appearance. What constitutes a sufficient degree of satisfaction for one person may not be so for another.

The pyramid shape used to represent the hierarchy is doubly apt for, in addition to giving symbolic and graphic form to our evolutionary ascent toward more humanizing needs, it sadly also reflects the diminishing number of people who manage to satisfy them adequately. The pyramid analogy is, however, imperfect, for while a pyramid is static, the human needs and motivations represented are always dynamic and in flux.

"Physiological" needs in particular keep recurring and commanding attention, and "safety" needs are frequently to the fore in some occupations. This may be because a job is inherently dangerous, but it may also be due to a fear of losing it. Safety needs go beyond actual or anticipated danger to include longer-term needs to achieve security, orderliness, and pre-

dictability in any circumstances affecting our lives or livelihoods.

Love-and-belonging needs have an equally wide spectrum, ranging from the need for friends, family and lover to the need for groups or institutions that provide both companionship and a sense of identity. These, in turn, form an important substructure to support our needs for self-respect and self-

■ **Climbing a pyramid of human motives.** LEFT Food is an all-consuming concern for this famine victim, but when such basic questions are settled, relationships and identity become a much more important focus. FAR RIGHT Families in Stratford, New Hampshire, express their attachment to their country. ABOVE Successful relationships in themselves help to sustain our self-esteem, but it is

largely through personal achievement that we earn the respect and admiration that others give us. Self-actualizers, whose self-esteem is secure, still feel the need to maximize their potential to create and do what others will find useful, interesting, enlightening or even life-saving. ABOVE RIGHT Mother Teresa accepts the Nobel Peace Prize for her humanitarian work.

because we have acquired through evolution the tendency to behave in some ways rather than others, there is nothing we can do about it. Even in the case of some genetically transmitted diseases, it is often possible to intervene and improve the patient's chances with, say, a special diet. There are quite large individual differences in certain types of behavior (for example, males are often more aggressive than females), and here we have some clear choices. We can choose, for example, whether to discourage aggression in males, and we can choose whether to encourage assertiveness in females. **PW**

confidence – that is, "esteem" needs. Without the acceptance and love of others, the development of a strong sense of worth is naturally extremely difficult, even when our activities give great satisfaction and we attract the admiration of others.

At the pinnacle of the pyramid are "self-actualizing" needs – the master motives that urge us to realize our potential, do what we are best suited for, and become all it is within us to be. Most of us hardly make the foothills, few reach the summit, and fewer still remain there. But, in making the attempt to scale these heights, we may *achieve some of the qualities of independence, spontaneity, creativity and openness to people and ideas that typify the self-actualizing process (see Ch1).*

In Maslow's scheme of things, we are not only motivated by deficiency needs, we are also urged on toward positive personal growth and fulfillment. The steps from self-preservation to self-actualization may seem very different, but according to Maslow, they all have in common one thing – they are the unfolding of our instinctive aspiration to become fully human. **BWPW**

Self-actualization needs

Self-esteem needs

Need for belonging and love

Safety and security needs

Physiological needs

77

The Psychoanalytic Perspective

PSYCHOANALYSIS embraces both a theory of personality and a method of treating emotional and mental problems developed by Sigmund Freud (1856-1939), an Austrian physician. His theory and methods were later modified by Carl Jung (1875-1961), Alfred Adler (1870-1937) and others. Though the basic theories are now largely rejected by most present-day academic psychologists, the psychoanalytic approach was immensely influential in forming psychological thought and ideas during this century and had a strong impact on the popular view of psychology, contributing such everyday terms to our vocabulary as "the ego" and "the Freudian slip."

Freud spent long hours sitting in his study listening to his patients, mostly middle-class Viennese women, formulating his theories, and developing techniques of psychotherapy. His ideas were based on personal introspection and his interpretations of what he observed. They laid enormous emphasis on the way we cope with hidden sexual and aggressive impulses in order to conform with the demands and expectations of our parents and present an acceptable personality to society.

Id, ego and superego

In psychoanalytic theory there are three mental structures. The infant is all *id*. The id is entirely unconscious and is the home of instincts of sex and aggression. Later in life, material that is unacceptable is repressed into the id by the *ego*. The ego is the conscious self and develops as the child develops. It is the aspect of the mind that is in touch with reality. The ego controls instinctive desires – a strong ego exerts a firm control. A weak ego is characteristic of someone who is impulsive and easily frustrated. The ego is largely conscious but there are unconscious ego processes – the defenses – which will be described later in this chapter. About the age of five, the *superego* appears. Its normal development depends on identification with the same-sex parent, and it represents our acceptance of parents' feelings of right and wrong, their morality.

In adult life there should be a balance between these three components and it is the aim of psychoanalytic therapy to achieve this balance. If the superego is too strong, we feel guilty about all our pleasures. Where the id is too powerful then we see uncontrolled sexuality and aggression. In this account the self is the equilibrium of these three components.

According to the theory of psychoanalysis most of our important motivation is unconscious and beyond our introspection. If a man feels destructively aggressive toward his parents, this will be repressed into his unconscious. He is not aware of it. However, that aggression seeks an outlet, for the Freudian system is a closed-energy system. If a desire or feeling is repressed into the unconscious, it seeks expression all the same.

This is where defense mechanisms can be seen. They protect the ego from unacceptable id-impulses. *Repression* into the unconscious is one defense. We also need others. *Projection* is a defense which releases energy through criticizing, even persecuting, others who appear to have the very faults we repress in ourselves. Projection plays a part in negative racial stereotypes. Another defense is

THE TRIPARTITE MIND

■ *According to Freud's theories, our mind is divided into three parts – the id, the ego and the superego. In a normal, healthy person these three are said to be balanced. But if conflicts between the id and superego are not resolved, then anxiety and mental disturbance result.*

▶ **Aggressive instincts** *help to define the "id" (a Latin word meaning "it"). This is also the home of our sexual impulses, in the Freudian classification of psychological elements. As we develop, our natural impulses are repressed, so that we can adjust to civilized life.*

Sigmund Freud tried to see into the subconscious mind in order to treat unresolved conflicts and release hidden desires. His ideas and techniques have had a powerful influence, but most psychologists believe they cannot be made scientific.

reaction-formation, where the feeling is turned into its opposite, for example, hate becomes love. One other defense should be mentioned: *sublimation*. This allows expression of the impulse but in a changed form. Some psychoanalysts suggest that sadism can be sublimated into surgery, aggression into generalship, the desire to see one's parents copulating ("the primal scene") into scientific curiosity. In Freud's view the arts and sciences are all sublimations of sexuality and aggression.

The importance of sexuality

The development of sexuality is of prime importance in psychoanalytic theory. Freud described the infant as a polymorphous pervert, by which he meant that any form of bodily stimulation is pleasurable to it. Gradually, however, this changes. Up to about one year of age this sexual pleasure is centered on the mouth – this is the oral stage. Later, at around the age of toilet training, the anus becomes the center of excitation – the anal stage. At about the age of five eroticism is centered on the penis and clitoris (the phallic stage). The child then enters the latency period when all sexuality is repressed. At puberty it reawakens, and

THREE DIVISIONS OF THE SELF

ID
The id is the unconscious part of our personality and is concerned solely with the gratification of needs and desires. It is irrational and intent only on pleasure.

SUPEREGO
The superego is the moral force and is concerned with imposing socially acceptable standards of behavior.

EGO
The ego is the conscious self, concerned with reality. It has to reconcile the unconscious desires of the id with the moral requirements of the superego to produce an acceptable balance.

79

◄ **Perceiving and adapting to reality**, *the "ego" (meaning "I" in Latin) reconciles the demands of society with the urges of instinct. A healthy ego is self-accepting, finding satisfying ways of channeling personal drives without coming into excessive conflict with other people.*

▲ **The parent with whom you identify** *gives you your "super-ego" – a set of beliefs about what is right and wrong. Freud sees the superego as tending to be in conflict with the id.*

the adult genital stage is reached, characterized by adult love and sexual satisfaction. This includes oral, anal and phallic components, and is characteristic of a mature healthy person who has passed through all the normal developmental phases.

In Western society anal eroticism is rarely directly expressed, hence it is largely repressed. However, according to Freudian theory it surfaces in defense mechanisms – reaction-formation (ie strongly felt views against anal sex) and sublimations. Thus there is the *anal character* whose repressed anal eroticism emerges as the character traits of rigidity, cleanliness, self-control and stinginess. This latter is supposed to be the sublimation of the refusal to give up the feces. Orality is generally expressed in our culture as love of eating and drinking.

During child development, fixation at any of these stages can occur – for example, when there is sudden weaning or oversevere toilet training. Where fixation occurs there is an undue emphasis on the relevant stage. At times of stress and anxiety many people regress to these earlier stages, for example by resorting to eating and drinking when we feel miserable.

The Oedipus and Electra complexes

Central concepts in Freud's theory were the Oedipus and Electra complexes, castration anxiety and penis envy. He postulated that the male superego develops as a result of a boy's successful resolution of his Oedipus complex. This is the feeling for his mother that develops when he is between 3 and 5 years of age. He begins to want all his mother's love and feels anger toward his father. This anger causes the fear that his father will retaliate. At this phallic stage of development, the child's self-awareness is heavily focused on his penis which makes him feel more complete and valuable than a girl. He conceives of castration as a retaliation which it is in his father's power to effect. The child discovers that he can overcome his castration anxiety, however, by identifying with his father, thus making himself more acceptable to him. The father's moral values now form the boy's superego.

For girls the position is different. A girl already has strong bonds with her mother. When she learns of her lack of a penis, she turns away from her mother, believing that she has been castrated. She experiences penis envy and desires her father. Afraid that her mother will cease to love her,

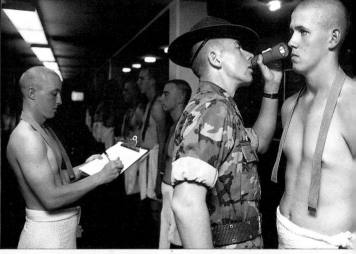

FREUDIAN FIXATIONS

■ *Freud believed that early development occurs in three stages during which the id is satisfied in different ways: orally (from birth to one year), anally (one to three), through phallic pleasure (three to five). If the characteristic needs expressed during these stages are frustrated, this will influence personality in adulthood. We will be fixated on an immature obsession.*

▲ **The oral fixation** *is characterized by activities such as smoking and eating for comfort. In its first year (the "oral stage"), an infant's primary expression of id is to seek fulfillment of its need for nourishment through sucking. Freud said that if the infant's feeding urges are often frustrated, an oral fixation will be seen in the adult personality.*

▲ **The anal fixation** *is said to occur in the "anal retentive" personality, characterized by possessiveness and a superego with an excessive desire for cleanliness and order. After its first year, a child begins to gain the ability to control its bodily functions, and the id experiences pleasure in eliminating feces. According to Freud, an anal fixation results when early toilet training makes a child feel ashamed.*

▶ **The Oedipus complex,** *a natural attraction to the opposite-sex parent, is usually but not always resolved by boys during the "phallic stage" (at about four they become aware of their own genitals as a source of pleasure). Girls experience an Electra complex. Another way of failing to emerge successfully from this stage is to become a "phallic personality," an adult who regards sexual behavior as a display of power.*

The Freudian view sees the instinctive element in our makeup as unavoidably in conflict with our parents' requirements regarding our behavior. Personal development is strongly affected by our earliest experiences of such conflict.

however, the girl identifies with her mother. This is how her female superego comes into being.

Both the Oedipus and Electra complexes are so repressed in childhood that adults have no conscious awareness of them. For Freud these complexes were the key to neurosis, because they affect all personal relationships. How we relate to our parents is essentially how we relate to everyone with whom we become emotionally involved. In psychoanalytic therapy that is how the patient relates to his analyst. This is called *transference*. Analysis of transference allows the bonds of the Oedipus or Electra complex to be broken, and the patient is free at last from his parents. This is the

basic method used by psychoanalysts to treat patients.

Id, ego and superego, mechanisms of defense, pregenital eroticism, Oedipus and castration complexes, Electra complex and penis envy, transference – these are some of the most important concepts in psychoanalysis. Freud believed they enabled him to understand the whole range of human behavior in all cultures, from religion to science, from the arts to neurosis.

Free association, dreams, Freudian slips

An obvious question and difficulty should be prominent in our minds: how could Freud make claims about what is unconscious, when by definition, what is unconscious cannot be known? Freud's answer was that in psychoanalytic theory everything is determined. Thus everything we do and say, however trivial it may seem, bears upon its unconscious determinants, if we have the skills to see it. Freud developed a method of seeing into the unconscious called "free association," which he likened to a mental X-ray. He would ask his patients, who would be lying in a relaxed position on a couch during the one-hour session, to say whatever came into their heads. Any hesitation, was, he

81

▲ **Adult sexuality**. *In the Freudian theory of development a child becomes more and more a conscious agent from five to puberty (the "latency stage"). The ego gains control of the id, and sexual desires are channeled into defense mechanisms. From puberty onward (the "genital stage"), sexual gratification is achieved with a partner. Adult sexual interests and personality were seen by Freud as determined by the experience and resolution of conflicts between id and superego in the earlier stages.*

thought, indicative of something normally kept in the sub-conscious. This free association of ideas was giving clues about unconscious conflicts.

In Freudian theory, dreams are also held to express unfulfilled wishes, in a disguised form. That is why dreams are considered to be an important guide to the unconscious. Symbolism is a well-known disguise, and Freud developed extensive ideas on dream symbolism.

Innumerable other actions can also reveal unconscious aspects of our personality. Freud wrote at length about everyday slips and errors both of speech and action. Indeed the term "Freudian slip" has passed into general usage. In Freudian theory these slips represent breaches of our defenses – the unconscious wish or conflict is coming to the surface. If we lose a wedding ring it means that we wish we were not married. If we forget to mail a letter, it means

that we do not really want its recipient to get the message. Jokes allow expression of otherwise unconscious or repressed impulses. This is why so many jokes are sexual or aggressive in nature.

Psychoanalysis after Freud

Later psychoanalysts felt that Freud laid too much emphasis on sexuality, probably because he and his patients lived in an era of intense sexual repression. Whereas Freud was preoccupied with the id, or the sub-conscious, more recent psychoanalysts have laid greater emphasis on the ego, emphasizing its own importance in perception, memory and thinking, rather than viewing it simply as a force reconciling id and superego.

One of Freud's Swiss colleagues, Carl Jung, differed from him in believing that our inner mental forces and drives are

---

FREUD'S ANALYSIS OF DREAMS

■ Freud believed that desires and impulses hidden in the unconscious self find an outlet in people's dreams. Part of this approach to psychotherapy was to attempt to interpret the symbolism in his patient's dreams, to explore the uncon-scious and identify possible conflicts affecting their personality. He placed great emphasis on sexual imagery because he believed the most important driving forces of our personality and the greater causes of inner conflict to be sexual impulses. Any long or sharp object and any tool or weapon he saw as a symbol of the penis. All hollow objects – boxes and cupboards, for example, he believed, symbol-ized the womb.

Walking up or down stairs or ladders symbolized sexual acts. Rooms represented women. Going through a series of rooms represented a visit to a brothel. Landscapes with bridges or tree-covered hills symbolized the genitals.

For Freud, common slips breach our defenses and allow unconscious wishes and conflicts to come to the surface. A lost wedding ring is a wish that you were not married. If you forget to mail a letter, you do not really want it read.

as much intellectual and spiritual as sexual. He felt that the personality is affected by future goals as much as by childhood experiences. His methods of therapy differed from Freud's – looking at a patient's aspirations, using dreams in particular to discover these and to find a way to achieve future health.

Alfred Adler, an Austrian psychoanalyst, felt that the most important determinant of human personality was the need to overcome inferiority and achieve superiority and so his views focused on how we interact with other people. He developed his concept of the "inferiority complex" (see *Ch 6*) and believed that it was the basis of most abnormal behavior.

A prominent American psychoanalyst was Karen Horney (1885-1952), who believed that our childhood relationships with our parents have the most important influence on our personality. She felt that adult anxieties result from having failed to resolve conflicting feelings of hostility and dependency in childhood. Consistency in love and respect from parents was, therefore, essential to healthy personality development.

Erich Fromm, a German-born American psychoanalyst, like Horney focused on the conflict between individuals and society. He identified a set of what he believed to be basic

■ **Obscure and yet seemingly full of meaning,** *are dreams really trying to tell us something important about ourselves? Many psychoanalysts disagree with Freud about the importance of repressed sexuality, but nevertheless see dreams as revealing crucial information. Jung analyzed dreams in order to understand the aspirations that his patients could not articulate. Adler saw some dreams as rehearsals for dealing with anticipated difficult situations.*

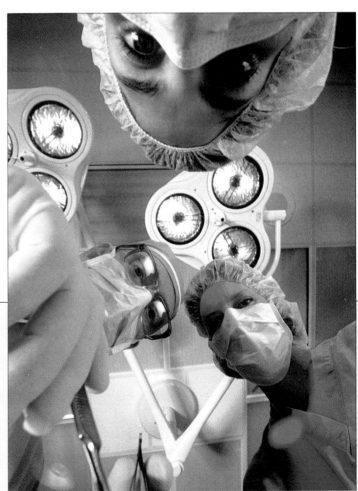

▲ **Sublimation** *is a mechanism for rechanneling unaccepted subconscious drives by turning them toward culturally admired activities. Sadistic aggression might be channeled as healing surgery. Freud believed that the arts and sciences are all subli- mations of sexuality and ag- gression. He thought that scien- tific curiosity, for example, is a sublimation of the desire to see one's parents copulating.*

human needs – such as the need to be creative, to be a unique individual, and the need to feel a sense of belonging. He interpreted mental disturbance as stemming from the difficulty of reconciling these needs with the demands and needs of society. The emphasis of all these later psychoanalysts, therefore, moved toward a more positive view than Freud's about the unsocialized id. They also saw more importance than Freud did in our overall environment.

Objections to psychoanalysis

There are many criticisms both of psychoanalysis and of its application in treating emotional problems. First, it is a theory based almost wholly on Freud's observation of his patients – mostly middle-class Viennese women – and so might not be more generally applicable. Second, the theory came out of Freud's own subjective interpretations and speculations, and it is difficult to test or to prove or disprove. For example, if there really is a correlation (something that has not in fact been established) between stinginess and neatness – the anal retentive personality – and early toilet training, this would not show that early toilet training *causes* this personality to develop. It is equally likely to be influenced by a mother's overconcern with cleanliness and tidiness. This would make her anxious to have her child toilet-trained as early as possible *and* make her train the child in every other aspect of neatness. Objections

FREUD'S ANALYSIS OF LEONARDO DA VINCI

■ Many critics have objected to the reconstructions that psychoanalysis makes of our pasts because, working backward, it is easy to explain things in ways which are totally erroneous. In a study of Leonardo da Vinci (1452-1519), the Italian Renaissance painter and scientist, Freud seems to have made mistakes that sustain some of this criticism.

Freud sought to understand two features of Leonardo's life – his artistic and his sexual inhibitions. There can be no doubt that Leonardo was highly sexually inhibited. He became virtually asexual for most of his life. Furthermore, his artistic creativity became strongly inhibited. Thus, although he started off painting more or less normally, he became slower and slower in completing his paintings and he eventually abandoned this work for research, until, at about the age of 50, he began painting again. It was in this period that the Mona Lisa was produced.

To attempt to understand Leonardo, Freud used all the biographical information that was available, especially about his early childhood, the crucial time for personality development in psychoanalytic theory. Freud made the following claims. Born illegitimate, and fatherless for the first five years, Leonardo was essentially seduced by his mother into a precocious sexual maturity which resulted in an intense infantile desire to find out about her sexual life. The instincts (important in his later life) to look and to know were aroused. He became, from the kisses of his mother, fixated on the erotic quality of the mouth. According to Freud all this childhood sexuality was repressed so powerfully that, throughout his life, Leonardo avoided all direct expression of sexuality. The desire to know and to see was sublimated into scientific research. His artistic work allowed sublimation of his sexual drives – for he painted laughing women (his mother) and beautiful boys – his mother fixation had made him essentially homosexual. (Without a man's conventional sexual interests to model his own on, the impressionable four-year-old had fixated on the beautiful boy that he wanted his mother – his only model for his own future interests – to desire.) When he became inhibited about paint-

Freud's theory emphasizes hidden causes that we cannot verify and gives little attention to what is actually known. The pitfalls he fell into when reconstructing the motives of historical figures are symptomatic of this failing.

to the psychoanalytic approach see too much emphasis on hypothetical hidden causes of mental conflict and not enough attention to what is actually on the surface and known – what the patient actually feels and needs, rather than what the psychoanalyst believes is in the subconscious.

The contributions of psychoanalysis

In spite of these criticisms, not many psychologists would deny that psychoanalysts have made an important and valuable contribution to the development of psychology.

Freud was the first to emphasize the importance of unconscious and unacknowledged influences on behavior. He also discovered the constraints of psychological repression and made the study of sexuality acceptable, highlighting its importance in problems of adjustment. In addition, his view that childhood development was of paramount importance in personality was an important contribution.

Present-day psychoanalysts see in their approach much that is of value but ignored by experimental psychologists. Psychoanalysts emphasize the importance of human sensitivity in psychotherapy – they consider it of vital importance to make patients feel better about themselves and learn to know and accept themselves fully.

In psychoanalytic and other forms of psychotherapy the aim is for the patient to achieve self-knowledge and self-acceptance. The essence of this approach is that it attempts to repair a split between an inner self and an outer self. This can be done only if you face up to your anxieties and conflicts.

Two thousand years ago, in ancient Greece, this was the ultimate wisdom of the famous oracle at Delphi. Written in gold letters above the entrance to her temple were the words "Know Thyself." This is the goal, too, of the Eastern mystic religions.

The strength of psychoanalysis is that the patient talks at length with a sympathetic listener. This enables you to be yourself without recourse to defense or posture. Both self-knowledge and self-acceptance can be achieved through this approach by the skills of psychotherapists in exposing and reconciling inner conflicts. **PK**

---

ing, it was because his inhibitions of sexuality gradually took over this aspect of his life too. His preoccupation with the mouth is reflected by the enigmatic expression in the Mona Lisa.

CRITICISMS

Freud makes much of a vulture fantasy that Leonardo had as a child and entertains the notion of a hidden vulture in one of the paintings. However, "vulture" was a mistranslation in a source that Freud worked from, and the bird Leonardo actually recalled from his childhood was a kite. This is not trivial since Freud considers that Leonardo was influenced by an ancient Egyptian tradition linking the vulture with motherhood.

Another error concerns an anatomical drawing of sexual intercourse between a man and a woman. In this picture the foot is wrongly drawn, an error that Freud accepts as psychological confusion, created by the heterosexuality of the subject, in the homosexual Leonardo. However, it has been shown that the foot was not drawn by Leonardo but added later by another artist.

◄ **Leonardo's Virgin and Child with Saint Anne** and a diagram of the vulture image, supposedly revealing a mother fixation.

► **Three versions of the sexual act**. RIGHT In Leonardo's original drawing there are no feet. CENTER An 1812 engraving by Francesco Bartolozzi incorrectly adds a right foot to the woman's left leg and a left foot to the man's right leg. FAR RIGHT The version that made Freud believe Leonardo was confused is actually an 1830 copy of Bartolozzi's engraving by Wehrt, a German lithographer, who has given the man's face a sour expression.

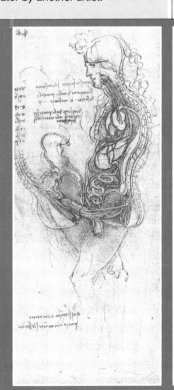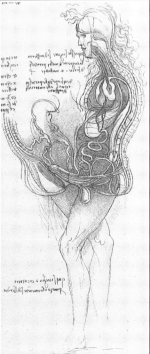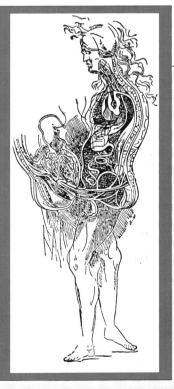

Personality Types

JUST AS chemistry has classified the elements, and physics has classified different kinds of energy and matter, so too psychology attempts to classify our personalities. Such classification is very difficult. Webster's Dictionary lists 17,953 different ways of describing what people are like and there is no one generally accepted method for organizing all these distinctions. Over the 3,000 or so years that people have been attempting to identify basic temperaments that underlie and explain personality differences, however, an increasing degree of insight has been achieved.

Are there really personality types?

The entire enterprise of classifying people as different personality types is only worthwhile if a person's behavior truly is consistent across different situations. There has always been controversy about this. Some argue that the situation rather than our personalities plays the largest part in how we behave. For example, a person who is meek and submissive at work can be domineering at home.

A major research undertaking to throw light on this question was carried out in the 1920s. In a monumental series of studies, over 10,000 schoolchildren were assessed for honesty, self-control and altruism. A total of 33 different tests were carried out. Ratings of reputation were also obtained from teachers and classmates.

In one test cheating was measured. Children were asked to score their own answers to a pencil-and-paper test. Some took this opportunity to improve their scores by changing incorrect answers. But unknown to the children, a duplicate of their original paper had been taken and so the researchers were able to compare answers before and after.

Another test of cheating assessed children's self-scoring on athletic tasks such as push-ups and long-jumps. Children were asked to record their own achievements, and then their claims were compared with what they actually did later when observed. By comparing results from different situations such as these the study concluded that "most children will deceive in certain situations and not in others."

However, now that researchers have had more experience of analyzing data, these findings have been reassessed, with correlations being based on more representative sampling of behavior than occurred in the original interpretations. It is now believed that the studies show that an individual child's honesty, self-control and altruism does not vary much from one situation to another.

Does personality last?

Does personality persist or does it vary as we age? The best way of investigating this is the so-called longitudinal method. In one study, personality ratings were obtained for 100 children interviewed in junior high school during the 1930s and then again 35 years later. The main conclusion was that the children had not changed much. Those who were rated "responsible," "impulsive" or "cheerful" as children tended to be rated in the same way as adults. In particular, children regarded as happy and relaxed tended to be the same in adulthood. There was, however, some evidence for a change for the better in children rated as unhappy and neurotic.

Another study was made of 763 English children in deprived areas who were rated by their teachers for extroversion and introversion when aged 10 years. Thirty years later an attempt was made to locate those who had acquired a criminal record or who had become psychiatric cases. Of those with a criminal record who were habitual offenders, 54 percent had been rated by their teachers as extroverts compared with only 3 percent as introverts. Of those who had received treatment for neurotic disorders, 44 percent

THE AIR STEWARDESS PERSONALITY

■ *Does our work make us behave in a certain way or do we bring to our work a personality that suits it? In a survey by the employment manager of an airline company, the 16 Personality Factor Questionnaire (see p91) was completed by 139 women who had been selected as promising candidates for training as stewardesses. They had not yet worked in this capacity. The diagram shows how they differed from other young American women.*

About 70 percent of young American women are more reserved than the average member of the airline group. Only 20

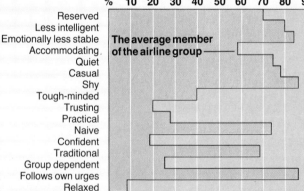

Air stewardesses and the 16 Personality Factor Test

	Reserved → Outgoing
	Less intelligent → More intelligent
	Emotionally less stable → Emotionally stable
The average member of the airline group	Accommodating → Assertive
	Quiet → Enthusiastic
	Casual → Persevering
	Shy → Uninhibited
	Tough-minded → Sensitive
	Trusting → Suspicious
	Practical → Impractical
	Naive → Sophisticated
	Confident → Apprehensive
	Traditional → Experimental
	Group dependent → Self-sufficient
	Follows own urges → Controlled
	Relaxed → Tense

percent are more intelligent. Even fewer are more emotionally stable, more uninhibited or more self-controlled. Only 10 percent are more relaxed and only about 20 percent more

trusting and confident. The work involves an element of danger or at least of dealing with stressful situations and awkward customers, while at the same time following strict

rules. Thus a high degree of mental health is needed.

In unusual or highly specialized occupations, large differences from the average personality are common.

Can we be sorted into distinct personality types? After long centuries of considering how to do this, we are still remarkably close to the ancient Greek list of temperaments: the irritable, melancholic, impulsive and phlegmatic.

had been rated as introverts compared with only 14 percent as extroverts. In general it seems that we are remarkably consistent, whatever the setting and whatever our age. It is "us" rather than the situation that we have to blame or praise for most of what we do.

Physiological theories of temperament

The ancient Greeks provide us with the earliest descriptions of basic temperamental types. The first great doctors, Hippocrates and Galen, decided that everyone belongs to one of four basic types, and Hippocrates argued that people developed according to these characteristic types because of excesses in particular body fluids or "humors." These humors were related to the four basic elements that the

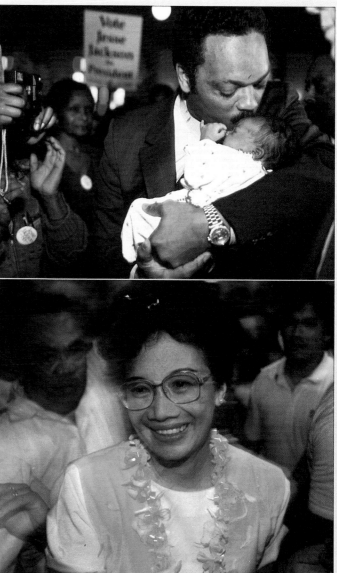

▲ **The situation helps to determine our behavior**, *but personality is a factor as well. As a part of their job, waiters strike servile poses* TOP LEFT *and air hostesses show a warm interest in children. The same people might behave very differently when they are not at work.*

However, to some extent we choose our work on the basis of what we think we are like, and also choose many of the other situations in which we find ourselves. Where others have a choice over matching us with a situation, they may judge our personalities in order to

decide – for example, when personnel officers try to judge whether we have the right temperament for the job, and voters assess the leadership qualities of political personalities. TOP RIGHT *An American politician brings personal warmth and extroversion to his*

chosen career. BOTTOM RIGHT *The widow of a Philippine leader has the presidency of her country thrust upon her by circumstances. She displays personal warmth but is perhaps less outgoing than a natural politician.*

Greeks recognized: fire, earth, air and water. Fire was supposed to be related to blood, and the *sanguine* type, whose blood was thought to be out of balance, had an optimistic, happy temperament. Earth was related to black bile, supposedly dominating the constitution of the *melancholic* type, who was depressed and anxious. Air was related to yellow bile, thought to abound in the *choleric* type – irritable and impulsive – and water to phlegm: the *phlegmatic* type was listless and not easily moved.

Apart from difficulty in accepting its view of what causes differences in personality, a problem with this picture is that people may not belong to only one of the four classifications. For example, someone might be unfortunate enough to be temperamentally both depressed and irritable. Another problem is that only extreme types are described. Most people tend toward the average. For example, the majority of us are neither optimistic nor pessimistic, but midway between the two. And the Greek fascination with the number 4 puts an artificial limit on the number of temperaments distinguished. Nevertheless, this classification remained popular for 2,000 years.

An outgrowth of Hippocrates' theory was the study of

CRIMINAL FACES?

■ *The Italian criminologist Cesare Lambroso (1835-1909) used physiognomy (the pseudo-science of facial features) to establish criminal types, including the three pictured* TOP. *Modern research has found hardly any evidence to support this approach. Before reading on, try to judge whether any of the photographs on the right shows the face of a criminal.*

RIGHT *This woman is not a criminal.* TOP RIGHT *Judith Ann Neelley awaits the death penalty in an Alabamba prison for women after killing a 13-year-old girl. Leonardo Vitale* BOTTOM RIGHT, *an accused Mafioso, was placed in an asylum for the criminally insane.*

▶ **Phrenology, the 19th-century study of heads**. *Franz Joseph Gall (1758-1828) and his followers believed that they had found a link between bumps on the skull and personality. The presence of an attribute such as kindness, or firmness of purpose, would be represented by a bump in a specific spot on the head and its absence by a depression. However, research has found no such relationships.*

The Greeks linked temperament to their theories of medicine. After these were abandoned, 19th- and 20th-century theories attempted unsuccess- fully to use external anatomical traits as a basis for personality distinctions.

other physical markers of temperament. People have always assumed that we can tell something about others merely by looking at them (see *Ch 4*). Indeed, such important questions as whether a stranger is a friend or foe, or whether an applicant should be chosen for a job, are often decided on such a basis.

The art of *physiognomy* (making inferences from a person's appearance) was particularly popular in the 19th

century. Standard drawings and, later, photographs were published showing the facial features of the typical criminal type, the artistic type and so on. More recent research, how- ever, has indicated that there is very little connection between personality and facial appearance. At least some of the attraction of physiognomy lies in the fact that facial fea- tures often bear a superficial resemblance to facial *expres- sions* (which do show something about the person behind the face – see *Ch 11*). For example, a thin-lipped person may look like someone with a repressed personality, because we often tighten our lips when suppressing anger.

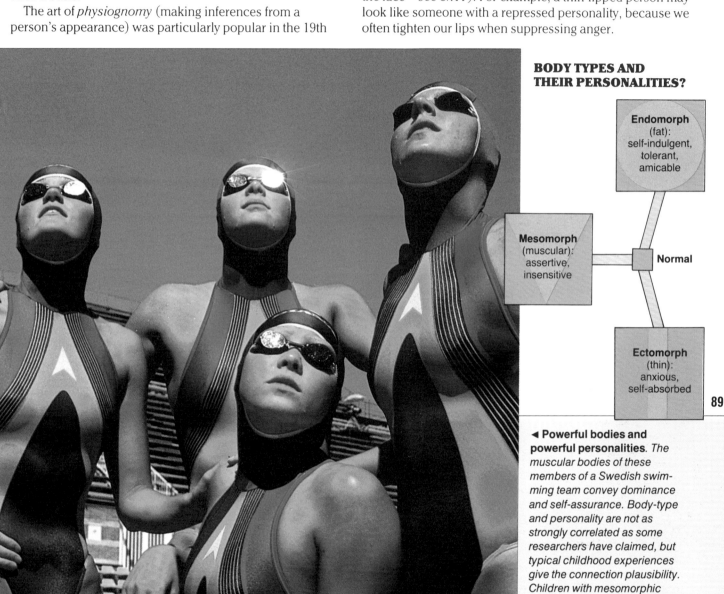

BODY TYPES AND THEIR PERSONALITIES?

Endomorph (fat): self-indulgent, tolerant, amicable

Mesomorph (muscular): assertive, insensitive

Normal

Ectomorph (thin): anxious, self-absorbed

89

◄ **Powerful bodies and powerful personalities.** *The muscular bodies of these members of a Swedish swim- ming team convey dominance and self-assurance. Body-type and personality are not as strongly correlated as some researchers have claimed, but typical childhood experiences give the connection plausibility. Children with mesomorphic body-types who can dominate childhood games and excel at sport are more likely to develop forceful personalities than deli- cately built ectomorphs, who may be bullied into an anxious introversion. In the endomorph, being overweight may lead on to a less active, less compet- itive personality.*

In the 1930s, in an effort to see whether *physique* is related to temperament, the American physician William Sheldon classified people in terms of three body types: endomorphy (fat), mesomorphy (muscular), and ectomorphy (thin). He then classified people in terms of temperament and claimed that he found a connection between the two. For example, endomorphs tend to be outgoing and sociable, mesomorphs assertive, and ectomorphs introverted. Some such connection had of course been recognized long before, for instance by Shakespeare in his play "Julius Caesar."

Let me have men around me that are fat;
Sleek headed men, and such as sleep o' nights.
Yond Cassius has a lean and hungry look;
He thinks too much: such men are dangerous.

However, the correlations that Sheldon reported from his research were excessively high, due no doubt to the fact that he rated his subjects' temperaments himself after studying their physique. Later work found only a 0.35 correlation between his temperamental types and his physical types – and not, as he found, a 0.8 correlation (a perfect correlation is 1.0).

Similar classifications have related physique to mental disorder. For example, it is documented that schizophrenia tends to be related to a thin physique, delinquency and psy-

■ **The "introversion/extroversion scale"** *finds a place for each of us, from the most quiet and retiring personality* LEFT *to the most outgoing* ABOVE. *Most of us are at neither extreme, but we are all in some degree either introverted or extroverted. You can test yourself on pages 112 and 115.*

90

FEMININE PERSONALITY, MASCULINE PERSONALITY OR BOTH?

■ *Psychologists once assumed that an essential of sound adjustment was for a man to have a distinctly masculine personality and for a woman to have a distinctly feminine one. In the 1970s, however, this view was strongly challenged by the investigation of a third type: the androgynous personality, combining the other two. The American researcher Sandra Bem defined masculinity and femininity on the basis of surveys of the traits people consider desirable for a man and for a woman. Masculine personality is conceived as assertive, independent and unemotional, while the feminine personality is seen as caring, understanding and cooperative. In surveys using the Bem Sex Role Inventory and similar questionnaires based on these principles, roughly a quarter of the people tested (including some women) are very masculine, a quarter (including some men) very feminine, and a quarter androgynous – combining both the masculine and the feminine ideals. The rest are neither particularly masculine nor feminine. Studies have found that androgynous men and women are more flexible in their behavior than sex-typed people and more creative: perhaps because creativity requires*

*Modern ideas about introversion and extro-
version have their roots in Jung's psychology.
Researchers have reinterpreted these two patterns as the poles of a personality dimension
that they can measure.*

chopathy to muscularity, and manic depression to fatness.
Here again, however, these associations represent only
slight tendencies.

Scientific theories of personality

More recent researchers have concentrated on personality types that can stand up much better to statistical
analysis.

Raymond Cattell reduced the thousands of common personality descriptions to 16 basic terms. On the basis of this
work he developed a questionnaire (the 16 Personality
Factor Questionnaire – or 16 PF) for personality assessment
(see p86). This has become the most widely-used measure
in the world. His method was to use what is called factor
analysis – a mathematical technique for identifying mea-

sures that belong together. For example, finding that warm
people also tend to be sociable, talkative and friendly,
Cattell arrived at a major dimension in which these traits are
grouped in the same category.

Hans Eysenck used similar research techniques, and
obtained results consistent with the Greek observation of
four basic types. But rather than forcing each individual into
one of the Greeks' four categories, Eysenck argues that it is
more logical to locate people on continuous dimensions.
He has interpreted the two most basic dimensions as those
of emotionality (also called neuroticism, instability or anxiety) and extroversion (with introversion being the opposite).
Extroverts are more outward looking, more cheerful, more
sociable, noisier and more energetic. Introverts are quieter
and more reserved. They prefer a few good friends to a lot of
outgoing acquaintances. They tend to be contemplative.
People who are low in emotionality are calmer and more
stable than those who are high on this scale: these tend to
be more excitable. A third dimension is "tough-mindedness" (see *Ch13*). High scorers can muster courage more
easily than low scorers. They find it easier to ignore their
own and other people's feelings.

The Eysenck Personality Questionnaire was developed to
measure these dimensions, and has become a standard
measure of personality in research studies.

The essential difference between the measures produced
by Cattell and Eysenck is that the types identified by Eysenck
are distinct from one another, while the traits identified by
Cattell are correlated. Eysenck argued for independent
dimensions because he was concerned with the theoretical
study of how different personalities develop, whereas Cattell

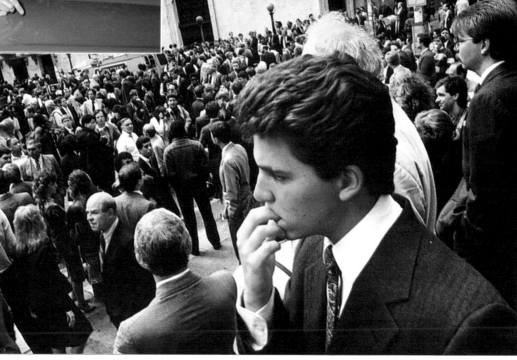

■ **Police need to be tough-
minded** *ABOVE. Financial
speculators RIGHT may find the
pressures easier to bear if they
are low on emotionality. Test
yourself on page 112.*

*both sensitivity and indepen-
dent self-assertion. Androgynous women have greater
self-esteem and are emotionally
better adjusted than feminine
women, apparently because
masculine independence and
assertiveness are highly useful personality traits.*

91

Like Hippocrates, Eysenck has suggested internal physiology and body chemistry as an explanation for temperamental differences. Two of Eysenck's dimensions can be combined to link personality "factors" with the four Greek humors.

favored correlated factors because he wanted to have many different ways of describing people for practical purposes such as testing for job suitability.

Your nervous system and your personality

Like Hippocrates, Eysenck has suggested a physical basis for individual differences. The theory that has emerged from intensive research is best described in terms of five levels:

1 At the most basic level there are inherited differences in those parts of the brain concerned with emotions, temperament, and personality.

2 These differences are a function of psycho-physiological differences – for example, in the brain's chemical and electrical activity.

3 These in turn lead to differences in conditionability and thresholds (such as sensitivity to pain).

4 Because of these physical differences, the characteristic personality differences in levels of extroversion and emotionality tend to develop.

5 This predisposition interacts with the environment (upbringing, school and social experiences, etc) to find expression in behavioral tendencies.

Eysenck suggests that greater activity or sensitivity in our nervous system would predispose us to develop a more emotional temperament. A simple test of this theory is to ask both stable and unstable people to plunge their arms and hands into ice-cold water for several minutes. Under stress such as this, measures of emotionality such as heart rate and blood pressure have been found to be higher in the unstable group, and their recovery time slower.

For extroversion, Eysenck suggests that underactivity or lack of sensitivity in the cerebral cortex (the outer coating of the cerebrum – the most highly evolved part of the brain) would lead us to seek out an exciting and stimulating life (see *Ch12*). It is found that extroverts tend to participate in dangerous sports, prefer highly spiced food and generally lead an active social life.

FOUR PERSONALITIES UNDER STRESS

■ Some people are more assertive than others: they express themselves more emphatically, especially by tone of voice, make more statements and ask fewer questions. They more freely make their needs and desires known. Not all assertive or unassertive people are alike, however. Some are extroverts, who show more facial expression, make more gestures with their hands and become more involved with people personally. The four panels below attempt to describe four personalities that result. They are based on studies of how each responds to a crisis or conflict.

■ **Unassertive introverts** tend to be cautious, analyzing their problems carefully in advance and organizing routines for coping with them. They get the facts right and live consistent, logical lives, according to principles. Cultivating fewer relationships than other unassertive people do, they behave less spontaneously. Making decisions is often difficult for them. In a crisis they tend to delay as they look for time to think, or collect more information. Their next step is to attempt to take charge with a well-thought-out plan. If this does not succeed they will go along with someone else's solution but may let slip recriminations if it fails. In dealing with them, be patient but persistent. As far as you can, back up your case with detailed, accurate information.

■ **Assertive extroverts** tend to be energetic, fun-loving and highly involved with other people. They react quickly to new situations, and may feel excited or worried about plans for the future while showing little interest in establishing routines. They express opinions forcibly. Under stress, they can become irritated and criticize other people's personal styles. They often go along with the ideas of a person they at first attack, but can be overpowering in their impulse to take charge if the ideas do not work quickly. If they cannot take charge, they may become withdrawn and gloomy. In dealing with them, avoid taking irritated comments personally. Try to suggest ideas for implementing their goals. Allow them to cast blame before discussing practical solutions.

■ **Unassertive extroverts** are unhurried, and more concerned with promoting relationships and avoiding conflict than they are with bringing about change. Amiable, supportive and outgoing in personal encounters, they are less likely than others to speak at a meeting, and more likely to try to make other people's ideas work. If they fail, they may criticize the others for expecting too much. If this approach does not help them, they may look elsewhere for reassurance that they are liked. If the situation demands it, they will take charge, but may feel anxious to justify their orders. In dealing with them, be reassuring. If they agree very quickly to your suggestions, beware of their becoming dissatisfied later about having given away too much too soon.

■ **Assertive introverts** are hard-driving, decisive, practical and efficient. They tend to put a higher value on being in control than they do on protecting their relationships, and they cultivate few close ones. They do not disclose as much about themselves as other assertive people do. They prefer either to work alone or be in charge. In a crisis they will tell others what to do, even when they have not thoroughly analyzed the situation. If this does not work they take the time to become better informed. Only when this fails to put them in charge are they likely to engage in personal attacks. They are the last of the four types to give in when they do not like someone else's plan. In dealing with them, stick to the facts. Persuade them by showing ways to achieve desired results.

92

Eysenck's model of how our temperament develops enables us to describe people at different levels. For example, on one level we can refer to someone as "accident-prone" or the "criminal type," and on another to the "extrovert" or to the "emotional type." Although such a classification makes sense at the theoretical level, critics point to the large number of individual exceptions. Indeed, Eysenck's stress on discovering general laws makes his approach more applicable to theoretical understanding than to particular individuals. **DKBN**

A SYNTHESIS OF 20TH-CENTURY AND MEDIEVAL IDEAS

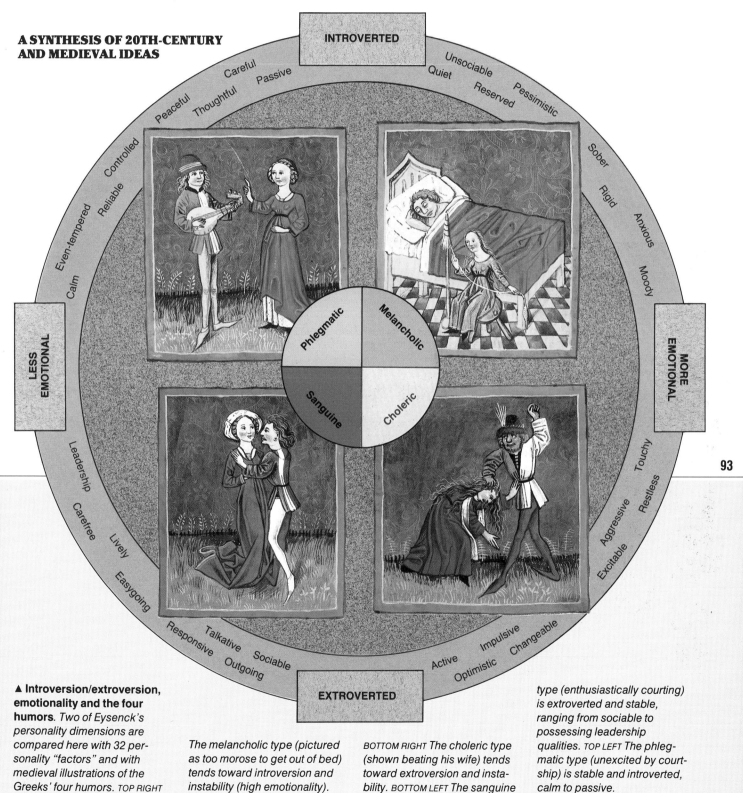

93

▲ **Introversion/extroversion, emotionality and the four humors**. *Two of Eysenck's personality dimensions are compared here with 32 personality "factors" and with medieval illustrations of the Greeks' four humors.* TOP RIGHT

The melancholic type (pictured as too morose to get out of bed) tends toward introversion and instability (high emotionality).

BOTTOM RIGHT *The choleric type (shown beating his wife) tends toward extroversion and instability.* BOTTOM LEFT *The sanguine type (enthusiastically courting) is extroverted and stable, ranging from sociable to possessing leadership qualities.* TOP LEFT *The phlegmatic type (unexcited by courtship) is stable and introverted, calm to passive.*

Expressing Your Personality

EATING a meal, waiting at the check-out counter in a super-market, giving advice to your children or just laughing out loud are all examples of behavior. And the way we behave in these different situations tells us and other people something about our personality.

Psychologists distinguish between *coping* behavior and *expressive* behavior. Coping behavior is the content of action – what you are actually doing. Expressive behavior is the *way* you do things. For instance, if you write a letter applying for a job, its content represents the coping behavior, the handwriting the expressive behavior.

The way you cope can show a lot about your personality (see *Ch 14*), but expressive behavior is very revealing too, because it is spontaneous. We are less conscious of the way we are walking than we are of why we are walking, less conscious of talking in a certain tone of voice and with a

certain rhythm than we are of what we are saying. Being less conscious of this aspect of behavior, we control it much less, and, although "self-monitors" and, especially, Machiavellians (see *Ch 5*) are skilled at managing how they present themselves, expressive behavior probably reveals more about us than most of us realize.

Sending facial messages

Most, but not all expressive behavior is the expression of emotions and attitudes through body language – nonverbal channels of communication. Each of the senses of a person you are with is an open channel for receiving expressive messages. Some of the most important are visual, and they are sent mainly by the face.

Scientists estimate that the human face can make about 250,000 different expressions. Cross-cultural research shows that people from regions that have never communicated have almost identical ways of expressing and interpreting six primary emotional expressions: happiness, sadness, surprise, fear, anger and disgust. There is cultural variation in the way people blend and recombine the facial elements that make up these primary emotions, so it can sometimes be difficult to interpret the emotions – and the personality – of a foreigner (see *Ch 20*). Much more of a complicating factor, however, is presented by facial *display rules* that vary from one culture to another, and even between the sexes. There are social conventions about how much emotion and what kinds of emotion it is appropriate to show in particular situations. For example, the Japanese try (usually very successfully) not to show negative emotions in public, often laughing and smiling to cover up. Many Mediterranean people *emphasize* their emotional display – for example, producing exaggerated crying during

▲ **Expressive faces** belong typically to extroverts, but even introverts can project a warm, self-confident personality with smiles and other facial gestures. Having an expressive face does not necessarily mean that a person is more emotional.

Those with immobile faces, especially men, who are usually more impassive than women, may have highly emotional personalities.

PERSONAL TASTE

■ *What we wear and the way we decorate a room reflect the purposes we have in mind. These may guide us in making such choices as wearing solemn colors for a funeral, for example, or painting the living room a relaxing cream, but the kitchen something brighter.*

We will also be influenced by a sense of the identity that we would like to express, wearing clothing that is typical of our sex, status, age group or sub-culture, decorating our walls with photographs and paintings of the family we belong to, mementos of places that are especially ours or posters about issues that involve us.

Personality, as well as identity, finds expression. The assertive person will display their identity more willingly. Extroverts may be drawn to the unconventional because it is more stimulating to seem different from the norm. They also prefer warmer, brighter, more arousing colors. Research has found ambitious people, particularly in conventional business professions, to prefer grays, dark blues or browns, both for their clothing and for the metallic finish on their cars. People who lack this kind of ambition usually choose brighter clothing and brighter colored cars without a metallic finish.

Our personalities are expressed not only by what we do but by the way we do it. Nonverbal signals like facial expressions, body language and tone of voice tell others more than we realize about the kind of people we are.

mourning, whereas northern Europeans expect each other to be more private. In most cultures, men are expected to be less vivacious than women and to hide fear more easily. This does not mean that men in general are less emotional than women. People whose emotions are hard to recognize

have been found to be more, not less, physiologically aroused than others: the effort of repressing emotional displays seems to increase the stress we are hiding.

With or without bearing all of these complications in mind, people form impressions of our individual personalities by the emotional reactions they see. People will judge mainly by your facial expression whether you are an anxious person, a warm one or a tough-minded one. Those who

Men who are only interested in the practical purpose of their clothing tend to be cautious people with low social motivation and a sense of dissatisfaction. Fashion-conscious men tend to be warm, helpful and slightly impulsive. Highly fashion-conscious women tend to be conventional in their social views. Women who are not interested in fashion and clothing design tend to be intelligent, confident and rather private.

Men with the most masculine personalities and women with the most feminine usually emphasize their masculinity or femininity by the way they dress and the way they decorate their surroundings. Perfumes and aftershaves are also used to express the femininity or masculinity that we sense in ourselves.

Even preference in food seems to express personality. One piece of research demonstrated that strong, self-confident and dominant women choose foods that are stronger tasting, sharper, saltier and more bitter than those selected by less positive women.

The warmth we convey to each other with smiles and other facial expressions relies on the use of cultivated gestures. Communicative people nod their heads, lift their brows and wrinkle their foreheads in ways that they know we will understand.

know of your cultural background, or know how to see through the more superficial sex differences, will probably understand you better than people who do not.

Conveying a warm personality

Facial expressions show much more than emotions. We also use them to convey attitudes – for example, interest, recognition, friendliness, disapproval, doubt. Culture and context have a very strong impact on this kind of expression

too: there are detailed, although usually unspoken, rules about how to show friendliness or disapproval, or about how much interest or amusement to display, to whom and in what circumstances. Among conventional facial gestures, for example, is the "eyebrow flash" – a quick lift of the eyebrows, usually accompanied by a smile. In most but not all cultures it would be unfriendly to omit this when signaling to someone that you have recognized them from across the room or down the street.

Much of the warmth that we convey to each other with smiles and other movements of the face is perfectly genuine, but not wholly spontaneous, because they are so often cultivated *gestures*. One of your standard smiles, for example, will make a pleasant social greeting when arriving for a dinner party. Another is the friendly but businesslike smile you use when sitting down at a negotiating table. A third will be a smile of attraction reserved for the opposite sex.

How warm the personality in your face seems will depend also on the way you nod your head, the movement of your eyebrows and the widening and narrowing of your eyes as you show other people how interested you are in their conversation. An immobile face will make you seem cold, distant and not willing to be involved. It is easier for an extrovert to display warmth – although an extreme extrovert may need to control the urge to wink and grin and wiggle the tongue more than other people can find it comfortable to watch. However, all of the conversational facial signals that we use *are* learned, and even if it takes more practice for some, anyone can use them.

An especially important feature of face-to-face communication is the amount of eye contact you exchange with your

---

GRAPHIC EXPRESSIONS

■ *When we write or draw we express our personalities almost without conscious control. Writing out musical notes, too, may express personality.* BELOW *Look at the ways three well-known composers – Bach, Beethoven and Mozart – wrote and try to identify them. If you are not already familiar with their personalities, think about the titles of some of their famous compositions: Bach's "The Well-Tempered Clavier," Beethoven's "Appassionata" and Mozart's "Magic Flute."*

Although our personal style of writing out words, sentences and notes is unique, however, the value of graphology (the

analysis of personality through handwriting) has not been demonstrated. Similarly, "projective" personality tests based on drawings have not been established as reliable (see Ch13).

Comparative measurements of the ways in which people's drawing and writing differ can be very accurate. But there is no scientific agreement about how to interpret these differences.

If you did not succeed in picking out Bach, the first of the three composers BELOW*, Mozart, second, and Beethoven, third, this reveals no greater inability in you than science itself suffers.*

PROJECTING A PERSONALITY

■ *Both what you do and how you do it tell others about the kind of person you are.* TOP RIGHT *Not merely the act of approaching a prospective partner, but an intense eye contact and an assertive, space-filling posture express self-confidence and masculinity. Removing her sunglasses helps the woman to lend warmth to the way she receives*

the approach. BOTTOM RIGHT *Some do not join the snake dance because they are too preoccupied with developing a relationship. Behind them, others give the impression that joining in is not their personal style. Among those dancing, posture and facial expression offer visual clues to varying degrees of extroversion.*

SEVEN WAYS OF EXPRESSING A WARM PERSONALITY

Spontaneous expressions of warm emotions	Facial gestures of interest and liking	Gesturing in illustrative, rhythmic and emphatic ways

partner. Extroverts and members of the warm-mannered "contact" cultures – for example, southern Europeans, Arabs, Latin Americans – exchange more eye contact, and so do women in general when interacting with other women. If you are out of your usual cultural surroundings, or if you are at one of the extremes of the introversion/extroversion scale, it may take a special effort to avoid using your eyes in a way that seems, on the one hand, distant or embarrassed, or, on the other hand, too intimate.

Sending messages with your body

In conversation we watch and react to one another's faces without paying as much attention to the rest of the body. You are unlikely to control your body as much as you do your face. This can be your downfall if you are telling a lie. Unless you are a very skilled Machiavellian, the embarrassment you feel about lying may show in the way your hand reaches up spontaneously to stroke your chin, touch your nose, pull your earlobe, or even cover your mouth. You may shuffle your feet or shift about in your chair. Normal gesturing is greatly reduced when we lie. We feel less free to illus-

| Exchanging eye contact | Standing close, leaning forward | Touching to show emotional support and acceptance | A warm and pleasant tone of voice |

DAYDREAMING

■ *Being lost in thought can create the impression of a dreamy, impractical personality. However, daydreaming is an activity to be encouraged. While in this highly relaxed state, we come to accept our failures, explore ways of dealing with difficult situations and, through reflection, learn more about ourselves.*

Research shows that children who daydream a lot are quieter than those who do so only a little. They are also much better at coping with boredom. The amount they fantasize seems to depend on their grow-

ing up in a secure, happy environment in which parents encourage them from an early age to develop their imaginative faculties – for instance, by reading to them at bedtime.

Children who do not daydream tend to be more violent than those who do, and there is evidence that adolescents who become aggressive or abuse drugs and alcohol lack a rich fantasy life.

Daydreaming continues right into old age but is most frequent during middle adolescence, after which it starts to diminish.

trate what we mean by tracing pictures in the air with our fingers or hands (showing people what we mean by "spiral," for example). We are less likely to emphasize the rhythm and the important points of what we are saying by unconsciously beating time in the way we usually do with our arms and hands. Children may even sit on their hands, unconsciously resisting the urge to put them over their mouth.

Our bodies also give us away when we put on an interested facial expression but forget to control a bored limpness in our limbs and a backward lean. Sometimes we try not to look interested, and we succeed in keeping a poker face but fail to check an urge to lean forward.

Any anxious mood tends to show up in the way we gesture. We tend to draw our limbs toward us, even hug ourselves. The hands tend to gesture toward the body and often touch it. Self-touching, especially on the head, has been found experimentally to improve memory in test conditions, seemingly because it calms us. Apparently it calms us as well when we are anxious in other situations, perhaps because the touch of someone familiar, even if only ourself, is reassuring and comforting. By contrast, when we gesture away from the body, in rhythmic, emphatic and illustrative ways, we convey and help to create in ourselves and others a relaxed and spontaneous mood and an impression of warmth. Increasing this type of gesture can be a technique for cultivating a more confident and warmer personality.

We also express warmth by how close we stand to one another. Finding the right distance is a matter of experiment – people will move away from you if you come too close; they will either move toward you or learn to accept that you are an emotionally distant person if you stand or sit too far away. In a context of self-assertion, a person who moves closer will convey a more effective personality than someone who steps back. A posture that increases the amount of

◄ **Drawing in upon herself,** Marilyn Monroe reveals a preoccupied and reflective side to her personality. She also shows an exaggerated femininity, holding herself in a way that takes up much less space than the poses that would be considered typically masculine.

► **Hands on hips** assert a determination to look ridiculous without feeling embarrassed. The folded-arms gesture of the man on the left suggests a desire to hide. Self-touching helps to calm and reassure us in stressful situations.

People who feel comfortable about touching tend to be more talkative, cheerful, socially confident and independent in their thinking. Women's voices tend to be assessed for sensitivity, enthusiasm and humor, men's for emotional power.

space you claim with your body – such as standing with hands on hips and elbows pointing out – will seem more assertive than standing with hands behind your back.

Studies have found that people who like to touch others and be touched are more talkative, cheerful, socially confident and independent in their thinking than those who do

not. They are nevertheless sensitive to social rules about where on the body it is appropriate to touch a stranger, a friend or a member of the family, and in what circumstances. People in contact cultures, and women who are interacting with women, stand and sit nearer to one another and frequently exchange touches to give reassurance or support or simply to emphasize conversational points.

Taking initiatives in touching gives an impression of personal dominance. For example, your boss will extend a

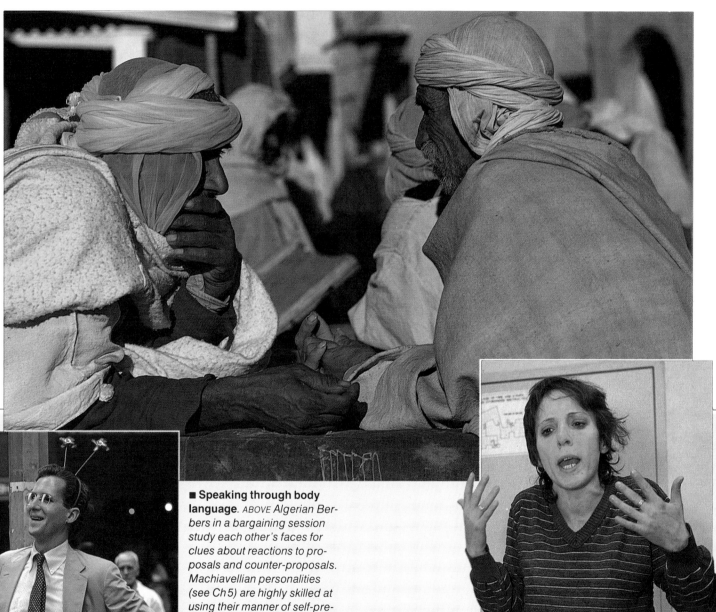

■ **Speaking through body language**. *ABOVE Algerian Berbers in a bargaining session study each other's faces for clues about reactions to proposals and counter-proposals. Machiavellian personalities (see Ch 5) are highly skilled at using their manner of self-presentation to win personal advantages. RIGHT An emphatic gesture expresses the vehemence of the speaker's opinion. The fact that she is gesturing toward herself suggests that she feels a frustrating lack of power to deal with a problem.*

In general, gesturing away from the body conveys a relaxed, confident and warm personality. Persistent gesturing toward yourself, self-touching and holding onto your hands or *arms, may convey an anxious personality and actually increase the level of anxiety in you and in the people you are with.*

hand in greeting before you do. Hitting and pushing express aggression. Slapping on the back in the right circumstances expresses friendliness. A handshake can express an energetic personality if firm, a passive one if limp.

Sending messages with your voice

It is not so much *what* you say, but how you say it that expresses your feelings. When the way a person speaks conflicts with what is being said, we tend to believe the tone of voice rather than the actual words. If, for instance, you call someone "honey" in a nasty voice, it is obvious you imply dislike. But if you say "I hate you" in a voice conveying fondness, perhaps accompanied by a warm smile, the other person knows you are expressing affection. Sarcastic humor offers probably the best example of the conflict that can

Men tend to enjoy sexual or aggressive humor and women intellectual or defensive varieties. Men and women show about the same amount of humorous talent, but women are often better at appreciating humor and men at creating it.

arise between words and tone of voice. We can define sarcasm as a message in which the information being transmitted vocally contradicts the information being transmitted verbally (the verbal content is usually positive, the vocal usually negative.) This is one of the reasons why some people do not easily understand sarcasm and may take the verbal content too literally.

The vocal aspects of speech other than words are called *paralanguage*. This includes loudness, speed of delivery, pitch, inflection, emphasis, breathiness, stretching or clipping of words, pauses, moaning, sighing, laughing, crying and so on.

EXPRESSING YOUR PERSONALITY WITH LAUGHTER

■ A particularly expressive aspect of nonverbal communication is laughter. It involves a massive physiological reaction. The contractions of the facial muscles are the most noticeable. But, in addition, there are many contractions of the diaphragm and abdominal muscles, so that the entire body shakes. As we reach full intensity, our blood vessels dilate and the production of tears increases until we may actually weep with laughter.

This physiological response is sometimes produced by physiological stimuli. The best example is tickling. Anyone who has played with young children knows how easy it is to make them laugh by tickling. But laughter requires more than a physiological stimulus. For instance, if you try tickling yourself, virtually nothing happens. And you can imagine what would happen if you tried to tickle a complete stranger in the street. For tickling to produce genuine laughter you need first a partner, and second a special relationship with them. Children laugh when tickled by their parents. But they will not laugh, and may even cry, when this is done by strangers. Similarly, if you are waiting for the bus in the morning and find one person laughing all alone, probably you and almost everyone

else waiting in line will carefully keep a distance.

Most laughter is a response to humor. Some people do not appreciate humor at all, and very rarely laugh. Others enjoy it more, and still others have a very highly developed sense of humor. They look for humorous stimuli by watching comedies or enjoying comic books and cartoons.

Different kinds of humor answer different needs. So one way of expressing your personality is to show a humor preference. There are five main kinds: aggressive, sexual, social, intellectual and defensive.

Aggressive humor is directed toward someone, transforming them into a laughable victim.

Sexual humor allows us to feel relaxed about a topic that makes people anxious.

Social humor can smooth relations between groups, reinforce group cohesiveness, or – as in political satire – try to influence our perceptions of social realities.

Intellectual humor allows us a momentary freedom from the tyranny of logical thinking by allowing us to play with words and concepts. Nonsense humor and puns are good examples.

Defensive humor can be black humor, making fun of frightening things such as

cancer, bad accidents and death. Another form of defensive humor is self-disparagement. Laughing at ourselves or at the macabre allows us to feel relaxed about situations that would be stressful if taken too

seriously. Furthermore, making fun of yourself may disarm those who might wish to attack you.

Research shows that men prefer aggressive and sexual humor, while women are more

By using techniques of voice analysis we can eliminate higher frequencies from recorded speech. Although words become unintelligible, the paralanguage remains. People listening to these recordings can easily tell if the message conveys liking or disliking. Some researchers have even proposed a formula to indicate the relative values of the verbal, voice and facial elements in judging a message.

They suggest that the face conveys 55 percent of the message and the voice 38 percent, leaving a mere 7 percent for the actual words. Although the formula is certainly not exact for every situation, many research findings clearly show that when there is a contradiction between the verbal and non-verbal message, most people will trust the nonverbal part rather than the verbal.

Paralanguage is one of the main vehicles we use to express personality. A deep tone is perceived as a sign of confidence and sophistication. Women tend to be assessed on the basis of tone of voice for their sensitivity, enthusiasm and sense of humor. Men tend to be assessed for their emotional power. Studies have correlated breathiness with lack of self-assertion. Soft voices with little resonance have been correlated with introversion. **AZ**

attracted to intellectual and defensive forms. Introverts choose mainly intellectual, social and defensive humor, whereas extroverts tend to like humor that is aggressive or sexual.

MAKING PEOPLE LAUGH

A humorous situation can happen by accident, but usually humor is created by people who have the special talent of making others laugh. They need a good memory for jokes or a creative imagination that allows them to link normally unconnected ideas in funny ways. They also need an assertive personality and enough individuality to make the unconventional connections that most humor consists of.

You can make a comparison between your skill at appreciating and your skill at creating humor by rating yourself from 1 ("very unlike me") to 5 ("very like me") on these statements.
1 I laugh easily.
2 I find many situations laughable.
3 I enjoy jokes more than do most of my friends.
4 When with my friends, I like to make them laugh.
5 My friends expect me to make them laugh.
6 If I could be a playwright I would write mostly comedies.
The first three statements measure humor appreciation, the rest humor creation. Research in the United States, France and Israel shows that there are no significant differences in how much sense of humor men and women have. However there is a difference in humor appreciation and creativity. As a group, men seem to be better at creativity while women are better at appreciation.

101

The Roots of Personality

BEING HUMAN, we naturally share much in common with other human beings. Yet at the same time we are all of us uniquely individual, with our own distinct personalities. Where do these personalities come from? Do we *learn* to be nervous or shy, assertive or aggressive? Or is that the way we are made from birth? Some people believe that personality is almost exclusively a product of environment – how we are brought up, how much we are punished or rewarded as children, and so on. An attraction of this view is its implication, that, in principle, at least, we can change if we do not like the way we are. However, much evidence points to the influence of heredity, as well. At the extreme, depressive psychoses and schizophrenia seem to have a strong hereditary element. We seem also to have our parents to thank or blame for tendencies toward anxiety, timidity, impetuosity, altruism, aggression and bad temper. We may even be, at least indirectly, the unwitting heirs to vocational interests and political attitudes. Heredity creates a temperamental framework within which our personalities can be *developed* and *managed*, but not chosen at will.

How different are we at birth?

Some of the tendencies that will make each of us unique as adults, such as differences in our ability to express and interpret emotional states, are already visible in very young babies with hardly any life experience.

Crying – the universal distress signal – comes naturally to all newborn infants, and facial expressions such as smiling and grimacing also appear in the early weeks of life. The need to form attachments with caregivers – people who look after us as babies – is also overwhelmingly inborn, as appears to be the infant's fear of separation from them. From the point of view of evolution, it is easy to accept that such common behavior patterns have assisted the growth and survival of the human species. But children vary considerably in the degree of their expression of emotion. Some are much more tolerant of strangers, of unpleasant tastes and even of being parted from their mothers. Others are almost predictable in their outbursts.

Already at seven or eight weeks, researchers have found, babies exhibit recognizable differences in intensity of reaction, activity levels, attention span, degrees of persistence and changes of mood.

Studies that have followed the same children from birth through their childhood years find that these differences persist despite emotional and social development and widening experience of the environment.

Beyond that, while many aspects of personality may seem to alter with age, there are still strong threads of continuity, particularly in characteristics that affect social interactions. Strained relations with others and neuroticism (being susceptible to such problems as anxiety, depression, phobias, compulsions and obsessions) have been traced back to high levels of emotionality in childhood. In turn, emotionality – how easily a child is upset – seems to be linked genetically to neuroticism in the natural mother. Similarly, children who score high on "sociability" – those who are not shy and mix easily, even with strangers – are much more

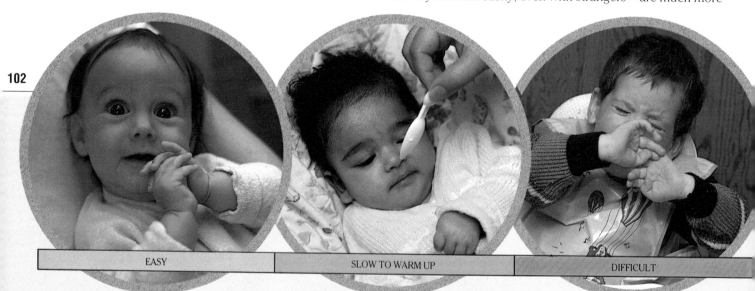

| EASY | SLOW TO WARM UP | DIFFICULT |

▲ **Frameworks for personality development**. *About 40 percent of infants have an "easy" temperament that encourages those around them to respond with pleasant and stimulating behavior. Happy moods and predictable feeding and sleep-* *ing patterns make them a pleasure to care for. They adapt quickly to new situations and will approach unfamiliar people and objects. About 15 percent of infants are "slow to warm up." They have fewer pleasant moods, a lower activity level,* *adapt more slowly and are at first withdrawn in new situations. Thus it is less stimulating for others to interact with them. About 10 percent of infants are "difficult." Their moods are unpleasant and they are withdrawn in new situations. They* *have irregular patterns of feeding and sleep and they have strong emotional reactions that can make their caregivers weary and tense. About 35 percent of infants are hard to classify.*

The environment that shaped and still influences your personality has itself been shaped in part by you. Since infancy, your own temperament has helped to determine how others will treat you and how you will choose friends and surroundings.

likely to become gregarious extroverts as adults. In fact, it has been suggested that sociability and its converse, fear of strangers, may be physiological in origin, and associated with the child's nervous system. Sociable children who develop into extroverts may have nervous systems that need higher levels of stimulation than those of introverts.

Children's temperaments

In one study of children's personalities, researchers followed 140 children up through to their teens, as well as many others for shorter periods. The children regularly saw trained observers, who set them standard psychological tests and recorded the results. Parents and, later, schoolteachers also provided information by reporting at regular intervals on their behavior.

Three distinct temperament profiles persisted over the period of the study. The "easy child" is very regular in its behavior patterns, approaches others easily, adapts quickly, has a low or mild intensity of reaction and is usually in a pleasant mood. The "difficult child" does not have regular patterns, withdraws from others, adapts slowly, has intense

WHAT KIND OF ENVIRONMENT AFFECTS US?

■ On average, different environments seem to account for about half of the difference between any two people's personalities.

What sorts of environmental influences matter? The family is an example of a "shared environment." But even close relatives or identical twins do not have exactly the same experiences.

Each of us has our own unshared, or "unique environment." This is partly imposed (eg the fact that you are the firstborn child in your family) and partly of our own making (eg the relationships that you develop with others).

If shared environment is important in shaping personality, then children raised by strict parents would share personality traits with other children who also have a strict upbringing. Likewise, children whose parents are more liberal should be noticeably different from strictly brought-up peers, and they should be similar in personality to other permissively brought-up children. In fact, however, the evidence suggests that this kind of environmental influence accounts for hardly any variation in personality traits.

Children who share an environment have not been found more similar in personality to one another than they are to those from very different backgrounds.

An example of a much more important childhood influence is the unique place that you occupy in your family's birth order.

Firstborns tend to be more conservative, reserved and achievement oriented – they seem to ally themselves more closely with their parents in order to overcome a sense of being displaced in the parents' affections by younger siblings.

A younger sibling may attempt to compete for parental and other attention by being more rebellious and more outgoing, and by making itself as unlike the older sibling as it can. It also seems, on the other hand, that younger siblings often model themselves on an older sibling. There is tendency, for example, for boys to show a more feminine style of personality, during childhood at least, if they have an older sister. Younger siblings in general receive less parental attention, especially in larger families.

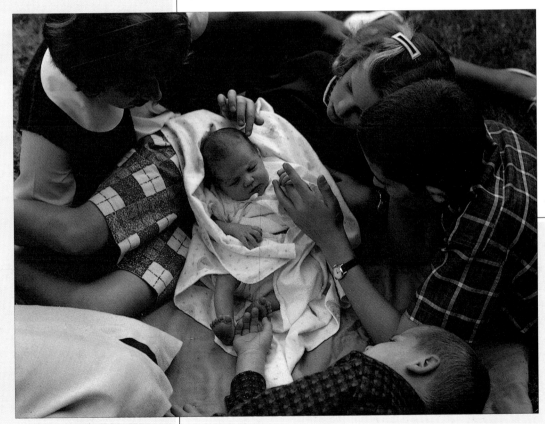

The circumstances of your adult life may also have an important effect. You are likely to adapt your behavior to particular social roles and strategies. This will color not only other people's impressions of what you are like as a person, but your own.

▲ **At the center of a new and unique environment**, an infant begins the long process of developing into a person. Inherited dispositions and the particular circumstances of her life will shape the experiences that make her. The environment that she shares with those around her – such as the fact that they all belong to the same family – will be of much less importance than factors that single her out – such as the fact that she is the youngest in a large family.

reactions and unpleasant moods. The "slow-to-warm-up child" has a low to moderate level of activity, is initially withdrawn in a new situation, adapts slowly, has a mild intensity of reaction and moods that are not so unpleasant as those of the difficult child.

If, as the evidence suggests, children are *inherently* different, then perhaps theories of parenting and education should take account of this. A difficult baby, whose intensity of reaction and responsiveness are high, might receive so much attention and stimulation from a talkative, playful parent that the child becomes overexcited, and then tired and irritable. It may be better just to lay the child down to sleep. What may be good for a child who is slow to warm up may be wholly inappropriate for the difficult child, and so

TWINS AND TRIPLETS REARED APART

■ Cases of identical twins or triplets who are separated during childhood and reared apart are fairly common. Often, however, these children are placed with relatives or family acquaintances, and so at least have contact with each other from time to time.

Much rarer are instances where genetically identical offspring are separated at birth, brought up well away from each other, and do not know of the other's existence until it comes to light much later on.

Only about one percent of all the cases studied are like this, and they do not provide a broad enough base for scientific comparison. The fact that both are adopted children may even account for some of the similarities between a pair of separated twins. Even so, the uncanny similarities unearthed offer fascinating hints of the role of heredity in determining personality.

ROBERT, EDDY AND DAVID

In 1980 American newspapers carried a report of triplets, none of whom had known of the other's existence. When Robert went to college, several students "recognized" him and called him Eddy. It turned out that Eddy had attended the same college the previous year, and not only looked like Robert but had the same birthday. After meeting, Robert and Eddy concluded that they were identical twins, and their story was taken up by the local press. David, on seeing their photographs in the newspaper, realized that he, Robert and Eddy must be triplets, and so he made contact. All of this came as a complete surprise to the adoptive parents, who had never been told about brothers.

Robert, Eddy and David not only look alike. They are all heavy smokers who use the same brand. They are extro-verts and gesticulate a lot when talking. They speak and laugh in a similar manner and all of them wiggle their tongues to accentuate a grin. They share similar tastes.

OSKAR AND JOCK

Identical twins Oskar Stohr and Jock Yufe were 47 years old before they met. They had been separated at birth and raised apart, Oskar by their grandmother as a German Catholic attending a Nazi school in occupied Czechoslovakia, Jock as a Jew by their father in Trinidad, Israel and the United States. Despite such distinctive upbringings, both have very similar profiles on objective personality tests. They both also wear wire-rimmed glasses and have a neatly trimmed mustache. Both like spicy food and sweet liquors. Both are absentminded, flush the toilet before use, store rubber bands on their wrists and have the peculiar habit of sneezing loudly in public in order to get a reaction.

THE "JIM TWINS"

The "Jim Twins," Jim Springer and Jim Lewis, were adopted as young children into separate families in Ohio. Despite differences in the environments in which they were raised, their personality profiles as measured by objective questionnaires are remarkably similar. At school, both liked mathematics and hated spelling. Before meeting at the age of 39, both worked as part-time deputy sheriffs after undergoing law-enforcement training. Both drove Chevrolets and repeatedly chose to holiday in St Petersburg, Florida. Both had dogs named "Toy." Both married and divorced women called Linda, had second marriages to women named Betty, and named their sons James Alan and James Allen.

Twin studies consistently find more similarities of personality between identical twins than they do between fraternal ones. Surprising parallels have been recorded in the tastes and the personality adjustment of identical twins reared apart.

on. Moreover, if some aspects of temperament remain stable through time, it may be possible to identify early on children who are more likely to experience personality disorders in later life and to take preventive measures.

The family connection

We inherit half our genes from each parent, and have on average half in common with our brothers and sisters. In looks and personality people are normally closer to their relatives than to outsiders, and more like their siblings than their cousins. But might not some of this be due to the shared family environment as well as to the shared genes? You might have developed as a very different person, for instance, if you had been kidnapped at birth and brought up by strangers away from your real family.

However, the results of adoption and fostering studies in many countries all point to heredity as a major influence on personality. Moreover, comparisons of a wide range of personality traits between twins have consistently shown much greater correlations between identical twins than between fraternal ones. Identical twins have all their genes in common, so that any differences between them can only be due to environmental influence. Such twins occur when the product of the fertilization of a single egg by a single sperm divides into two genetically identical individuals. Fraternal twins are the result of fertilization of two eggs by

two sperm and are related genetically like any other siblings except that they are born at the same time.

The patterns found show a tendency for identical twins reared apart to have more closely correlated personality traits than fraternal twins reared together. Correlations are measured from 0 (no correlation) to 1 (a perfect correlation). A review of 40 twin studies found a correlation of 0.7 for involvement in crime by identical twins, but only 0.3 for fraternal twins. The same correlations were found for alcoholism. The correlations for childhood behavioral problems were 0.9 and 0.4, for male homosexuality 1.0 and 0.1.

On the basis of twin studies, it has been estimated that on average, environment and heredity each accounts for about half of the variability in different people's behavior patterns. In one twin study, 69 percent of variance in sensation-seeking was attributed to heredity. In another, so was 60-70 percent of variance in extroversion.

Male and female

A vital part of our makeup is our sex. Are boys and girls, or men and women different psychologically as well as biologically? If so, this surely must affect the development of our personalities as we mature from children into adults. How far the differences in male and female behavior and, more controversially, in the social roles of men and women in general, depend on genes or cultural environment is a major aspect of the "nature" versus "nurture" debate, the debate about the extent to which heredity rather than environment makes us what we are.

105

◄ **A striking similarity in adjustment** *makes taste in home decoration a superficial part of this twin story. Roger Brooks* FAR LEFT *was raised in an orphanage under extremely unstable conditions, but grew up to be as socially adapted, balanced, good tempered and professionally successful as his brother Tony Milasi* LEFT *with whom he eventually co-hosted a television talk show called "Double Vision."*

▲ **Twin commitments**. *Drawn together because they share twinhood, these childless pairs are applying to adopt twins.*

The fact of being a twin is a special environmental influence that helps to shape interests and personalities. Studies of

twins reared apart, however, attempt to isolate just the fact that twins share their genes.

They cannot be explained simply in terms of our biology, but some personality traits that are regarded as typically masculine or as typically feminine probably reflect differences in the evolutionary pressures on men and women.

Traditional definitions of "feminine" include such epithets as "soft, tender, delicate." "Masculine" attracts descriptions like "spirited, strong, robust, vigorous." Attempts over the past two decades to undo these sex stereotypes do not appear to have succeeded. Many men and women, as well as boys and girls, are still expected to conform to sex-typical behavior patterns and often cheerfully perceive themselves as doing so. Thus men may deliberately try to be more assertive, competitive and status-seeking, while women tend to be more cooperative and caring.

How did these differences come about in the first place? If sex-typical behavior is largely cultural, a matter of learning and reinforcement, then it should be possible to change sex-role patterns by changing the learning environment. If however, they evolved along with the human species, and are in some way genetically encoded, then the possibilities of change would appear to be more limited.

Had evolution been easier, females could have done without males, producing offspring similar to themselves, and transmitting all of their genes to the next generation, instead of just half as in the case of sexual reproduction. In evolutionary terms, however, males are needed to distribute the genetic variations that arise through mutation. A population composed of identical clones of a single mother-

ancestor would have much less chance of surviving and reproducing through the millions of years of changing environments that our species and its forerunners have been able to adapt to. Because we are genetically diverse, we do not *all* die out when the habitat changes. Some happen to be preadapted to the new circumstances.

Males release enormous numbers of tiny, inexpensive sperm, which are really little more than mobile packages of genes. Females, on the other hand, produce small numbers of large, high-investment gametes called eggs. Egg cells simply await fertilization. Sperm frantically seek out the egg and compete to be the first to fertilize it.

Thus, because their gametes are precious, female mammals invest their reproductive efforts in pregnancy, giving birth and parental care. Male energies, however, are expended largely in competing with other males for females. In some species of mammals, males have violent territorial disputes over the right to acquire and protect whole female harems. Among the primates, and others with more complex modes of social organization, keenly contested dominance systems have evolved in which it is

■ **Risk takers**. *Personality testing finds large individual differences in how much risk we like to take, and heritability studies indicate that there is a significant genetic basis for these differences. Sensation seeking or caution can be encouraged by family or friends. Families that encourage risk-taking praise children when they overcome fears and achieve difficult or dangerous goals. Others try to teach prudence. But the underlying tendency toward or away from excitement is hard to alter.*

This makes sound evolutionary sense: clans and communities survive better when they have some members who will do daring things on their behalf, as well as others more certain to live and breed. **PK**

almost exclusively the "alpha" males who mate with the females. This pattern reinforces selection pressure for competitive, aggressive male behavior in future generations.

Perhaps, then, the sex-typical personality attributes that we associate with masculinity in human cultures have their roots in the evolutionary heritage of the male mammal. The genetic differences between men and women would seem to lend some support to this argument.

The genes that determine sex are carried on the sex chromosomes, designated X and Y. Individuals with two X chromosomes develop as females. Those with an XY constitution normally become males. A region of the Y chromosome engagingly called "Garden of Eden DNA" is responsible for the development of the testes. In its absence the same cells develop as ovaries. The testes not only eventually produce the spermatozoa, but also a group of hormones called the androgens. According to research findings, the androgens are almost certainly responsible for

HEREDITY IN THE AMISH COMMUNITY

Although our genes undoubtedly do affect our personalities, scientists know little about exactly which genes influence which aspects of behavior. So far most research has concentrated on the abnormal – in particular, mental illnesses such as manic depression. This is a severe personality disorder that affects about 1 percent of the population in the United States and Europe at some time in their lives. Relatives of known sufferers run, on average, a 10 percent risk of being affected, increasing to 24 percent for fraternal twins and 48 percent for identical twins.

By studying a closed community, researchers in the United States have managed to uncover a link between manic depression and a specific genetic defect. The Old Order Amish Community in south-

eastern Pennsylvania has remained relatively isolated and has genealogical records of its 12,000 inhabitants going back to the 30 immigrants who arrived there in the 18th century. Although the incidence of manic depression is no higher than normal in the Amish, it is possible to trace back its inheritance for generations.

Applying genetic techniques to blood samples taken from affected families, researchers have found a defective gene that is probably responsible for the disorder. The segment of DNA where this gene is located is indirectly connected with the production and control of dopamine, a vital brain chemical (see p110). The drugs that doctors prescribe for manic depressives are known to affect their levels of dopamine.

Only a small minority of the

carriers of the defective gene actually suffered any personality disorder, and even among identical twins the correlation is not high. These findings

support the view that personality, normal or abnormal, involves a complex interaction of our heredity and our environment. **GM RW**

◄ **Male and female**. Understanding how and why we are different involves understanding evolutionary pressures on the arrangement of the DNA (represented FAR LEFT in a computer-graphic display) from which our genes are made. We learn from family, friends and society how to have a masculine or a feminine personality, but male and female body chemistry (controlling, for example, levels of aggression and sensation-seeking) helps to determine what sex-role ideals humans are likely to adopt and live by.

what has been called "status-related aggressive behavior" in all mammals. Androgens are also present in female ovaries, but at much lower levels.

Very early on, before birth, the testes release a "burst" of androgens which causes cells in many parts of the body, including the emotional centers of the brain, to assemble androgen "receptors." After birth, the androgen in both males and females returns to very low levels. However, at puberty the testes in males release another burst, which activates the androgen receptors, including brain cells, causing a further masculinization of body and behavior.

Studies of adolescent boys who were prone to problem behavior, disobedience and fits of temper showed particularly high levels of the androgen androstenedione in their blood. Among teenage girls, too, those possessing relatively large amounts of this hormone (though much less than in boys) were more susceptible to defiant behavior and anger toward their parents. The problem of teenage delinquency may therefore be partly biological in origin.

It would be wrong, however, to try to reduce male aggressiveness and other sex-typical personality traits to evolutionary and biological fact. The same holds for the qualities we traditionally associate with women. In higher mammals, and in particular in humans, even behavior which has a strong biological component is by no means fixed, but is very flexible and under conscious control. Cultural influences, as well as experience and our own intelligence in handling situations, mediate. The roots of personality are deep and complex.

Brain and personality

The cerebral cortex is the outer covering, about 3mm deep, of the cerebrum (the "gray matter" of the brain). The cortex is made up of about 10 billion neurons (nerve cells).

Humans have by far the most highly developed cerebrum of any organism and it is in the cortex that our higher mental activities take place.

Researchers are a long way from an integrated and comprehensive understanding of how such structures of the brain, and how the body chemicals that affect them, influence personality. In particular, almost nothing is understood about how the brain changes when we *learn* a pattern of behavior. However, a foundation has been established from which to appreciate the biochemical and genetic component of personality.

Our genes determine the structure of our brain, its sensitivity to neurotransmitters (chemicals that affect the way nerve cells pass messages to each other), how efficiently hormones and other chemicals are produced in the body and how quickly they are destroyed after they have served their purposes. That an inherited variability between our brains

INTROVERTS AND EXTROVERTS

■ *The psychologist Hans Eysenck has developed a theory relating introversion and extroversion to the ease with which the cerebral cortex of our brain can be stimulated.*

Some people's cortex is easily stimulated because they are already in a high state of arousal. Others need stronger external stimuli to excite the cortex.

There is also a difference in the speed with which brain activity is inhibited after an external stimulus has had its effect. In some people arousal quickly subsides, in others this happens more slowly.

The link between these ideas and introversion and extro-

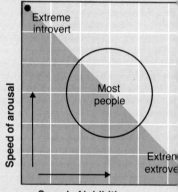

version is that extroverts are constantly seeking sources of external stimulation because their own level of cortical arousal is low. They are sociable, outgoing risk-takers who

THE HUMAN BRAIN

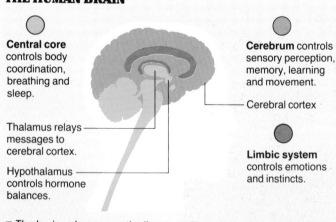

Central core controls body coordination, breathing and sleep.

Thalamus relays messages to cerebral cortex.

Hypothalamus controls hormone balances.

Cerebrum controls sensory perception, memory, learning and movement.

Cerebral cortex

Limbic system controls emotions and instincts.

■ *The brain, whose genetically determined variability underlies at least some of the differences between our personalities, is composed of three layers.*

1 The central core, made up of the thalamus, cerebellum and brain stem. These control involuntary actions like breathing, balance, coordination of body

movements and sleep. The hypothalamus, underlying the thalamus, has an important role together with the pituitary gland in regulating body chemicals and thus mood and behavior. It is associated with sexual response.

2 The mid-brain, or limbic system, including parts of the hypothalamus, controls emotion and instinctive behavior.

3 The cerebrum or gray matter. It has a left and a right hemi-

sphere and each hemisphere has a frontal and a hind lobe. The cerebrum is concerned with processing sensory data (sight, smell, touch, etc) with body movement and with the more complex aspects of behavior like memory, thought and language. The outer 3mm (0.1in) of the cerebrum — the cerebral cortex — is where most of this processing occurs.

We are each born with our own optimum level of stimulation for the cerebral cortex – the outer covering of the brain's "gray matter." People with introverted personalities seem to achieve their optimum more quickly and hold it longer.

contributes something to the differences in our personalities is at least suggested by the changes in personality that appear when the brain is physically damaged. It is also suggested by measured differences in body chemistry affecting neurotransmitters (see p110).

In 87 percent of cases where a person has suffered damage to the cerebral cortex, personality changes also occur. The cortex of the frontal lobes of the cerebrum seems to be particularly important. Damage to the frontal lobes tends to result in social irresponsibility.

The most famous case study of brain injury affecting the frontal lobes is that of Phineas P Gage, the foreman of an American railroad excavation crew, who was the victim of a premature explosion in 1848 that drove a 6kg (13lb) tamping iron through the left side of his face and up through his skull, destroying – at the very least – the left central part of the frontal lobe. Very shortly after the accident Gage was walking and spoke with "composure and equanimity of the hole in his head."

With the exception of the loss of sight in his eye, Gage recovered all of his faculties, all, that is, except his former personality. Gage's personality changed so much that his friends reported that they no longer "knew" him. Gage became fitful, irreverent, impatient and, on occasion, vacillated between obstinacy and capriciousness. His employers considered the change so marked that they could not return him to his former position. Gage, who was 25 years old at the time of the accident, died 12 years later.

In the past, mental patients with severe depression, anxiety, obsessions or neurotic fear were sometimes given "lobotomies" – fibers connecting the frontal lobes to the rest of the brain were surgically severed – in order to bring about a change to a more docile personality.

In the region of the temples, damage to the cortex can lead to impulsive behavior. Damage to the right hemisphere of the cerebrum tends to produce more changes in the way that people experience moods. However, damage to the left part of the thalamus (a region of the brain which underlies the cerebrum and receives incoming sensations) is more likely to affect mood than damage to the right part of the thalamus. Damage to some parts of the limbic system in the mid-brain can produce marked tameness, loss of fear and a loss of interest in other people. Damage to other areas of the limbic system, however, can lead to insomnia, restlessness and fidgetiness. **GM RW**

sleep less and have a higher sex drive than introverts. They also have higher pain thresholds. An extreme extrovert would also have rapid loss of arousal, and so need constant external stimulation.

Introverts have high arousal and/or not so rapid loss of arousal, as they need much lower stimulation from external sources.

In the diagram LEFT people who are introverted in some degree fall in the blue sector, extroverts in the red. Introverts in the top left quadrant are both more easily excited and slower to get over it. Extroverts in the bottom right both feel stimulated less easily and lose their sense of stimulation more quickly.

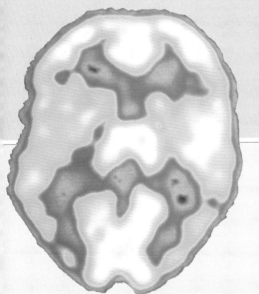

▲ **Patterns of brain activity** *in an introvert LEFT and an extrovert RIGHT as they both concentrate on the same task. They are watching a constantly changing video screen for a particular pattern of dots that the experimenter has asked them to look out for. These cross-sections of the brain are PET (Positron Emission Tomography) scans. To make the scans, a radioactive chemical similar to glucose (a sugar) is injected into the bloodstream. The radioactive chemical passes from the bloodstream into brain tissues and is used for energy like normal glucose. It concentrates most in sectors of the brain where the most energy is being used. Emitted radiation is measured and analyzed by a computer to give color-coded images. Red represents the highest amounts of energy used. Blue represents the lowest amounts. Here the introvert consumes less energy, particularly in the frontal areas of the brain (top of each scan), than the extrovert.*

NERVE CHEMICALS AND PERSONALITY

■ *When drugs such as amphetamines, alcohol and mescaline have their temporary effects on moods and behavior, they do this by affecting the level of activity of body chemicals known as "neurotransmitters." These are chemicals that excite neurons, the nerve cells that carry messages around the brain and nervous system.*

The levels and activity of neurotransmitters vary between individuals even without the fact that some people are under the influence of drugs and alcohol. Of central importance seems to be our individually inherited levels of an enzyme (a protein molecule that controls chemical reactions) known as monoamine oxidase (MAO). It has been directly linked with such traits of personality as extroversion, impulsivity and sensation seeking.

MAO is found in all body tissues, including the brain, and very high levels occur in the hypothalamus, an organ of the brain involved in regulation of behavior, especially sexual behavior. The easiest way to measure MAO is in blood samples. There are consistent differences between individuals in the amount of MAO in their blood cells. It is assumed that these differences also apply to MAO levels in the brain.

LEVELS OF MAO

High sensation seekers, people who are higher in sociability, ego strength and leisure-time activity levels are low in MAO. Low sensation seekers tend to have high MAO levels. Animal studies agree – research on a colony of monkeys found low MAO levels in those males that were more dominant, more playful, aggressive and more sexual while high MAO monkeys tended to be solitary, inactive and passive. Low MAO levels have been found in chronic human schizophrenics, alcoholics and drug users.

BRAIN CHEMICALS AND DRUGS THAT AFFECT THEM

■ *It has been estimated that there may be up to 200 different neurotransmitters (chemicals that have a role in transmitting messages between different parts of our brain).*

Each chemical has an effect only on specific parts of the brain that recognize them – they fit with chemical receptors in the membranes of cells, rather like a key into a lock, and only brain cells with the right lock respond.

Many of the drugs that affect our emotions, behavior and therefore (temporarily) our personality have their effects because they either increase or decrease the effectiveness of particular neurotransmitters. For example, morphine has a very similar chemical structure to the body's own natural painkillers and fits the same receptors that they do. Only a few neurotransmitters have been identified. Here are some of the better known ones and the drugs that affect them.

Neuro-transmitter	Role	Drug	Effect on neuro-transmitter	Effect on experience and behavior
Noradrenaline	Increases arousal and brain activity; controls moods	Barbiturates Alcohol	Decrease	Sedatives
		Amphetamine Cocaine	Increase	Stimulants (can cause a schizophrenic-like state)
		Mescaline Cannabis	Increase	Psychedelic
Dopamine	Arousal	Chlorpromazine	Decrease	Antipsychotic: used to treat schizophrenia
Acetylcholine	Muscle contraction	Atropine – (from deadly nightshade)	Decrease	Slows mental processes; relaxes involuntary muscles
		Muscarine (from *Amanita muscaria* – "magic mushroom")	Increase	Psychedelic; can cause convulsions and death
Serotonin	Dampens arousal; involved in sleep; anti-depressant	LSD	Decrease	Produces schizophrenic-like state: hallucinations, personality changes
Endorphins	Suppress arousal; decrease anxiety and tension; natural painkillers	Morphine Heroin	Increase	Calm central nervous system; decrease anxiety; promote euphoria and self-confidence

What is the link between MAO and personality? Its function is to regulate the activity of several neurotransmitters. They are carefully controlled by balancing their production and destruction, and MAO is involved in the destructive part of this biochemical balancing act. MAO levels are found to increase as we grow older (and become less sensation seeking) and to be, on average, higher in women than in men.

The full chemical consequences of low or high MAO levels are extremely complex. However, the effect on levels of two neurotransmitters in particular has been shown to be important. These are dopamine and serotonin.

DOPAMINE

Dopamine is closely related to and can be converted into noradrenaline, which helps to stimulate the nervous system, muscles and respiratory system when we are roused to action. Dopamine seems to increase our ability to respond to weak

▶ **Sensation seekers** *tend to have low levels of MAO (monoamine oxidase), an enzyme that influences the rate at which the body breaks down key nerve chemicals. Low levels of MAO mean that dopamine and noradrenaline, which help to keep us roused for action, are more readily available.*

110

> *Our preferences and our desires are influenced by a complex system of nerve chemicals controlling the levels of arousal that stimuli produce in us. Variations in brain chemistry help to create the variations between our personalities.*

MONOAMINE OXIDASE AND PERSONALITY

■ *Several personality differences have been correlated with above-average and below-average levels of MAO (monoamine oxidase) in blood samples.*

HIGH MAO

*Low sensation seeking.
More likely to seek solitude.
Less likely to take risks or to seek variety in sexual and drug experiences.*

LOW MAO

*High sensation seeking.
Seek social activities.
More likely to drive fast, take risks, smoke cigarettes and take drugs.
Eight times more likely to commit suicide.
More antisocial behavior.*

stimuli, especially those involving a reward.

Rats lacking dopamine will respond normally to strong stimuli like tasty food or the stress of being nearly drowned but are sluggish in responding to less dramatic stimulation – for example they will fail to build a nest to warm themselves in cold conditions.

Dopamine is also thought to be involved in the expression of aggressive and sexual behavior. So if MAO is low, and dopamine therefore high, we might expect increased sexual and aggressive behavior and greater likelihood of responding to weak stimuli.

However, we should beware of simplistic interpretations, because MAO is not the only factor controlling dopamine or any of the other neurotransmitters, nor is dopamine the only influence on the behavior traits mentioned.

SEROTONIN

Serotonin inhibits brain activity. Low levels can lead to fearful and hypervigilant behavior in animals, and serotonin is thought to have a role in reducing our level of activity under conditions of long-term stress. It also plays a crucial role in sleep. Depletion can lead to total insomnia. Serotonin levels have been found to be reduced in brain tissue from depressed people who have committed suicide. So it seems to have a role, too, as a natural anti-depressant.

SEX DIFFERENCES

Assessment of individuals for sensation seeking shows consistent sex differences. This suggests that the sex hormones produced by the male testes and the female ovaries may somehow affect this aspect of personality. The male sex hormone testosterone is linked

to aggressiveness and research now suggests that testosterone levels are also related to sensation seeking and impulsiveness. Moreover, there also seems to be a link with MAO. It has been found that this enzyme is inhibited by testosterone (giving the effect: low MAO, high sensation seeking) and is also affected by the female sex hormone, estrogen. Estrogen, levels of which vary markedly during the menstrual cycle, can also lower MAO levels and this could explain some of the mood changes associated with different phases of the menstrual cycle.

Precisely how MAO affects the fine balance of neurotransmitter levels is not yet understood but its role in destroying excess levels of dopamine (which increases brain activity) and serotonin (which decreases brain activity) are probably crucial.

Assessing Your Personality

ASSESSMENT of personality is attempted by career counselors, marriage counselors, clinical psychologists, educationalists and job interviewers, and a great deal of research time and effort has been put into creating useful personality tests. The two principal kinds that are used are projective tests, which need to be interpreted subjectively by an expert, like the Rorschach inkblot tests – see p114 – and personality questionnaires or "inventories," which, once developed by an expert, can be scored objectively by anyone. The latter are the most common method, and probably the most accurate. They are also the only tests that can be used in self-assessment. However, to consider deeper or very particular aspects of your personality you may need to rely on the insights of friends or on unproven techniques.

Are personality tests reliable?

In psychological measurement all tests should be *reliable* and *valid*. A reliable test is one that gives the same score when you are retested, or if a different scorer uses it. A valid test is one that can be shown to measure what it claims to measure. Of all types of personality test, personality questionnaires are the most reliable and valid and this is why they are widely used.

However, there are some obvious problems with inventories. One concerns the variability in our feelings and behavior. Most people are sometimes cheerful and lively and other times not at all. In addition, although we may appear lively and cheerful in social situations, underneath we may feel nervous and awkward. Outward behavior can be a cover for inner anxiety – so which is the real personality to be measured? The answer is, of course, that both are and good tests take account of both.

Another major problem in personality assessment is whether or not we are always willing to answer questions truthfully – and, even if we are, do we always know what the truthful answer is? There are many instances where someone may be untruthful or inaccurate – if they are applying for a job, for example, or if they believe they are in some way abnormal and want to cover the fact, or simply if they want to appear to be "better" than they really are.

One way of solving this problem is to ask people who know the tested person well to answer questions about their personality and behavior. A more subtle approach is to include within the inventory questions designed specifically to test truthfulness or bias. One set of questions, for example, is designed to measure the tendency some people have

---

A PERSONALITY QUESTIONNAIRE

■ *In this personality test there are three scales. Answer yes or no to each item as honestly as you can with your first reaction. There are no right or wrong answers. When you have finished, turn the page.*

SCALE 1

1 Do you enjoy talking?
2 Are you often bored at parties?
3 Are you sociable?
4 Are you rather a quiet person?
5 Do you like to work fast?
6 Do you like a nice, quiet, peaceful setting?
7 Are you thought of as witty and amusing?
8 Do you like jobs that need a lot of concentration?
9 Do you like really energetic. pastimes?
10 Are you really a shy person?

SCALE 2

1 Are you rather moody?
2 Can you take criticism easily?
3 Do you find it hard to sleep well?
4 Are you calm and easy-going?

5 Do you often feel wracked with guilt?
6 Can you easily put fears for the future out of your mind?
7 Do you sometimes just worry about everything?
8 Are you usually cheerful?
9 Are you really rather easily annoyed?
10 Do you take everything in your stride?

SCALE 3

1 Do you enjoy gambling for high stakes?
2 Are you a careful driver?
3 To win a game do you sometimes bend the rules?
4 Are you frightened by the idea of deep pot-holing?
5 Would you enjoy watching a bullfight?
6 Do you think that puppies and kittens are sweet?
7 Do you think insurance schemes are just a waste of money?
8 Do you think hurtful practical jokes are bad?
9 Do you enjoy really fast driving?
10 Do you think there should be stronger laws against drugs?

Personality questionnaires provide reliable and valid information about our personalities, but they are based on broad distinctions. Less well-proven techniques attempt to achieve a more individual and probing assessment.

toward acquiescence – to prefer to answer "yes" or "true" rather than giving negative answers. This tendency can bias an entire personality inventory and can be detected only by including a suitable "acquiescence test."

Also included might be a scale designed to detect people who are anxious to appear good – people who answer "false" to such statements as "I sometimes feel angry." Other scales detect those with a tendency either to exaggerate or to be defensive.

Some tests, like those illustrated on these pages, derived from Eysenck's Personality Questionnaire, measure such individual personality traits as extroversion, emotionality and tough-mindedness. Cattell's Sixteen Personality Factor Test breaks up these factors into sixteen scales that include anxiety, guilt proneness, self-control, conscientiousness, suspiciousness and aloofness. The widely used Minnesota

Multiphasic Personality Inventory (the MMPI) is made up of several hundred questions and aims to assess a range of more clinical traits such as feelings of persecution and mania. An individual's scores are compared with the responses made in the past by other subjects and a detailed personality profile is obtained.

Only objective assessment involving detailed personality inventories such as the ones described, and often also including someone else's assessment and the skills of an expert tester, can be really reliable. You can try the tests here. They are given to illustrate how personality inventories work as well as to provide some insights into your own personality. A variation on the personality inventory which you can try is the *Q-sort*, designed to reveal aspects of your self-image, and your level of self-esteem (see p116).

The self-knowledge that comes from questionnaires can often tell you more about yourself than you could have known without this kind of assessment. You may, for example, discover that in spite of what other people want you to be, you are in fact a sensation-seeking extrovert who is rather rigid and highly self-controlled. This can be useful in contemplating jobs or in understanding why you get on with some people and not others.

■ **Personality self-assessment** *is something we engage in almost daily, when we decide what to say about ourselves in conversations with someone close* LEFT, *when we see how we behave in important situations* TOP *or when we ask whether we are the kind of person to wear the clothes or drive the car that we see in a window. Assessment techniques developed by experts can complement this process, but not all can claim to be more scientific.*

113

Projective tests are designed to bring out our inner feelings and conflicts as we describe what we see in an ambiguous or vague shape or say how we would complete a story. The results are very difficult to interpret objectively.

Plumbing the depths of your personality

"Projective" tests are designed to uncover the deeper layers of our personality, those aspects which are usually hidden from us – motives, desires and conflicts. Although there is a huge variety of projective tests, certain features are distinctive.

Generally they consist of ambiguous pictures which you are asked to describe. Because the picture is ambiguous, it is assumed that your description reflects something about you rather than something about the picture. This is why the tests are called projective – the person tested is supposed to have projected their own inner feelings and conflicts into the description; so the more vague the test picture the better.

Another important aspect of projective tests is that there is a certain freedom of response. Your description of the stimulus is your own, in your own words and style. This is quite different from a personality inventory where subjects are compelled to choose between set items.

The best-known projective personality test is the Rorschach Test invented by the Swiss psychiatrist Hermann Rorschach (1884-1922). This consists of ten symmetrical inkblots. Any resemblance in the inkblot to anything is quite fortuitous. Descriptions must, therefore, be projections. Certainly the response "this is an inkblot" would be regarded as highly defensive.

The Thematic Apperception Test (TAT) was developed by the Harvard psychologist, Henry Murray. This test consists of pictures of people in various settings. Here the ambiguity lies in the people's expressions and in the precise nature of what is going on.

TAT has spawned many relatives because it has been found so useful. There is a Children's Apperception Test (CAT) where all the figures are children or parents. There is

an animal version of the CAT, where animals replace humans, in the hope that children will identify more easily with the animals, if the picture is at all threatening. Projection is thought to take place when the subject identifies with one of the figures in the picture. In a typical picture used in the TAT, a boy sits before a table where there is a violin. If you were to describe the boy as hating his lessons you would be scored low on need to achieve. If he is described as fantasizing about his concert successes all over the world, your score would be high. In the CAT, a bed can be faintly discerned with lumps in it. If the child talks about his parents fighting or making love, an Oedipal conflict will be scored. If he said it is like his own bed, this would be a neutral response.

The Blacky Test uses pictures of dogs in family situations

■ **Inkblot tests.** *ABOVE The woman in red is telling a psychologist what she sees in an inkblot similar to these RIGHT. The psychologist will take the woman's interpretations of the blot as projections of personality. She may score her high in strength of ego if the woman sees a figure moving boldly (eg a flying hawk). Seeing a house cat may be scored as indicating passivity and dependence. If the figure is seen in only a small part of the blot, easily marked off from the rest, this might indicate a need to be exact and accurate.*

▲ **Projecting personality into drawings,** *a depressed male mental patient makes even the sun look bleak, while a well-adjusted young woman has a boy wave a flag. Her house BOTTOM is cheerful and inviting. The house of a psychotic mental patient TOP looks unhomelike. In spite of an intriguing potential, however, experts have failed to develop reliable personality tests based on drawings.*

with Blacky as the hero. This test taps Freudian variables – for example, the castration complex card of this test shows Blacky about to have his tail cut off. In France a similar test has appeared which substitutes a pig for a dog.

An entirely different kind of projective test is sentence completion. For example, "Every morning when I get up, I feel..." The House-Tree-Person Test requires you to draw a house, a tree and a person. Each drawing is then interpreted. For example, a big house is taken to show a strong sense of the self you present to the outer world.

The accuracy of projective tests

Projective tests are often contrasted with personality inventories not only because of their freedom of response, but also because they are open to a much more personal and idiosyncratic form of interpretation than questionnaires. Users defend them by pointing out the projective tests can tap the personal, private conflicts and experiences that no others share, and take account of the person's uniqueness.

Like Freudian theory, however, projective tests have been severely criticized by experimental psychologists on a number of counts. First there is poor agreement between different scorers and between the same scorer on different occasions. This is known as low inter-scorer reliability. It is difficult to see, therefore, how scores could be valid – that is, measure what they claim to measure. There is, indeed, almost no sound experimental evidence that supports their validity. Furthermore, the scores can be shown to be affected by such things as the sex of the tester, his or her race, and what people taking it believe the test to be about. **PK**

SCORING YOUR PERSONALITY QUESTIONNAIRE

■ *The personality scales on page 112 are all scored out of 10. If you have answered yes to an odd-numbered item, score 1, and score 0 if you answered no. If you answered no to an even-numbered item score 1 and 0 if you answered yes.*

Remember that in personality questionnaires, unlike tests of ability, such as intelligence tests, it is neither better nor worse in any way to obtain a high or low score.

SCALE 1
This measures extroversion and introversion. The extrovert is outward looking, cheerful, sociable, noisy, energetic. The introvert is the opposite of this; quiet, rather reserved, preferring a few good friends to a lot of cheerful companions, a contemplative person. If you scored 8 or more on scale 1, you are a clear extrovert. If you scored 3 or less you are equally clearly an introvert. All other scores are about average.

SCALE 2
This measures emotionality. The low scorer is stable, calm and easygoing, phlegmatic and unflappable. The high scorer reacts with strong emotions to whatever happens – cheerful one moment, depressed the next, anxious sometimes, then cheerful. A score of 8 or more means that you are a person of strong emotional feelings. A score of 3 or less means that you are truly calm and stable, a useful trait for jobs that may be stressful. All other scores put you around the average.

Look at your scale 1 and scale 2 scores together to see which of the four traditional temperamental types on page 93 offers an approximate description of your personality.

SCALE 3
This is the tough-mindedness scale. Most people tend to be rather low on this dimension. The high scorer is a person who likes risks, is daring and is not strongly affected by the feelings of others or by worrying about what might happen. On this scale a score of 8 or more would be relatively rare and indicates a person who would be well suited to high risk occupations where courage and the ability to ignore feelings is important. Men tend to score higher than women on this scale. Most people, of both sexes, score between 0 and 5.

115

HOW ASSERTIVE ARE YOU?

■ *For a rough measure of your assertiveness, chose a completion for each of the following statements.*

1 *In conversations and discussions, I mostly*
   a *ask questions.*
   b *make statements.*
2 *When I disagree with other people's opinions, I usually*
   a *try to change the subject.*
   b *tell them.*
3 *In meetings you should always try to*
   a *understand everyone's ideas.*
   b *make sure everyone understands you.*

4 *When explaining ideas, I*
   a *give lots of detail.*
   b *try to be brief and simple.*
5 *I am usually*
   a *careful and deliberate.*
   b *quick.*
6 *I usually show emphasis by*
   a *a facial expression.*
   b *my tone of voice.*
7 *When making a point I*
   a *lean back.*
   b *lean forward.*
8 *I like other people to*
   a *give me details.*
   b *give a concise picture.*
9 *In a standing conversation I hold my hands*
   a *loose or behind my back.*
   b *on my hips.*

10 *I prefer to*
   a *do a good job*
   b *stick to the schedule.*

For each **a**-*answer count -1, for each* **b**-*answer 1.*

A very negative score indicates that you may need to assert yourself more.

A very high score suggests that you may be overpowering others and could benefit from being a better listener and more patient.

Your assertiveness score and your score on scale 1, page 112, show which of the personality profiles on page 92 is approximately yours.

THE REAL AND THE IDEAL SELF

■ *"I wish I were more like Ruth; she really is such a loving and caring person." "Isn't he incredible! If I had half his energy, I'd be a millionaire by now." You have probably said or thought something like this more than once; we all have, and probably meant it as no more than a compliment or comment on somebody's better fortune. However, remarks of this kind have another significance: they say something about our own shortcomings, and the ideals we hold but cannot match.*

ROOM FOR IMPROVEMENT

Within the first few years of life, we develop an awareness of an "actual self" that we conceive ourselves to be, and an "ideal self" that we would like to be. There is always room for improvement in everyone, but if the gap between the two is overly wide, low self-esteem, guilt and a sense of failure can become considerable, and unnecessary, burdens. This is especially true if deeply ingrained moral or religious values are involved. If we are unable to live

MEASURING THE GAP BETWEEN YOUR REAL AND IDEAL SELVES

■ *Psychologists often measure self-image by means of the "Q-sort." A typical Q-sort comprises 100 self-referring statements, individually printed on pieces of card. The person sorting them categorizes them into nine groups, representing nine levels of similarity – from "completely unlike me" to "completely like me." The statements can include such things as "I get upset easily," "I am a likable sort of person," "I can concentrate well" and so on. The content can be easily changed to fit whichever particular aspect of the self-image is under scrutiny. It may, therefore, be used to ask people to rate themselves on anything from appearance to intelligence, from occupational suc-*

cess to standards of morality.
The cards can be sorted in many different ways, but to get some idea of the discrepancy between what people conceive of as their actual and ideal selves, they must sort the cards twice – first, on the basis of "How I am at present," then "How I would like to be."

There is, however, a limit on how many cards can be put into each of the categories, so that the statistical "normal distribution" required by this technique can be created. Therefore, if people are given 100 descriptive statements to be sorted into nine categories, they will be required to spread their responses.

Forcing the choices into a distribution pattern means that

it is easier to correlate the scores of different people, but this is also an effective way of making people discriminate more between the qualities they have or esteem most and least. Without such a rule, "How I would like to be" sortings might attract top scores on every socially desirable attribute presented, without necessarily giving much idea of the sorter's own ideal self.

SELF TESTING

A simplified alternative to the Q-sort can easily be created (SEE BELOW). Such an exercise naturally lacks the precision of a Q-sort or other professionally administered personality-analysis techniques. Nevertheless, it may help you to make a first

	Very like me	Like me	About half and half	Unlike me	Very unlike me
Adaptable	✕			✓	
Generous		✕		✓	
Successful		✕	✓		
etc					

▲ **Self-test Q-sort**. *To get a rough measure of the gap between your real self and your ideal self, make a list of about 25 positive and negative traits that you consider important. Rule and label five vertical columns and beside each trait check the column that is appropriate when "me" refers to you as you think you actually are. Then put a cross in the column that would be appropriate when "me" refers to the person you would like to be.*

◄ **Ideal self becomes real**. *Heather Bannerman of Edinburgh, Scotland, proved that her ideal weight of 57kg (125lb), although 54kg (118lb) distant from her real weight, was not unrealistically distant.*

Measuring the distance between your image of the person you are and your image of the person you wish you were can help you to assess your self-esteem. A large gap suggests unrealistic ideals. A small one is healthy.

◀ **Unattainable ideals** *undermine our self-esteem. Adolescence especially is a time of low self-esteem and fascination with cult figures whose successes cannot be emulated but whose own well-known sense of being incomplete makes them objects of identification.*

incompatible with our self-ideal. In this way, acts of appalling cruelty, dishonesty, and depravity have been performed by people whose consciences and self-esteem appear quite unaffected. Terrorists, for example, tend to consider their brutality and inhumanity as justifiable retribution against their persecutors and necessary steps toward attaining their ideal of peace, justice and mutual understanding.

Such extreme examples may seem relatively rare, but the process is common enough. A more everyday example is the parent whose aggression toward a child is at variance with a self-ideal as a good-natured, caring person. If you can persuade yourself to believe that the child is wicked or in need of correction for his or her own good, you may then be able to regard quite unjustifiable behavior as legitimate and even commendable. It is a strategy which, in a limited sense, can work well, but all such distortions of experience and denials of real motives are, ultimately, self-destructive.

Even if we are unaware of our self-deceptions and unintentional hypocrisy, others tend to sense them and become unable or unwilling to provide us with the closeness and esteem we need so much. Unless we can distinguish between our actual and ideal selves, and be prepared to acknowledge or somehow reduce the gap between them, personal growth, mutually supportive relationships, self-confidence and self-esteem are always at risk.

approximation of the gap between your actual and ideal selves. At the least, it will provide food for thought and should suggest one or two lines of action.

First, you may discover that some of the guilt or sense of failure you may feel is due to having adopted or accepted quite unrealistically high standards or aspirations. If you are neither a saint nor a genius, and do not expect to be either, a readjustment of your ideal self may lead to a great reduction in self-critical feelings or behavior.

Second, as long as there is no insuperable obstacle preventing your success, acknowledging and assessing the gap between your actual and ideal selves can provide the necessary guideline and spur to practical self-improvement. Rich may be the prize of understanding what kind of people we really are, but it is not enough. If we are to grow and become "self-actualized" people, we must also get to know the person we aspire to be. **BWPW**

up to high standards and expectations of ourselves, we may be overwhelmed by a sense of failure and worthlessness. Even highly successful, saint-like people can have this happen if their own standards and criteria of success are higher still.

NARROWING THE GAP

However, forces within the self are usually hard at work trying to narrow an otherwise intolerable gap and so protect self-esteem. One psychological strategy is to distort our perception of the behavior that is

Becoming Well Adjusted

SUCCESSFUL personality development means constantly adjusting to changing physical, mental and social capacities. When you were an infant and child you adapted to increasing demands from your parents and environment, to competition from brothers and sisters, to the fact that you were a boy or a girl. Adolescence required adjustment to new sexual feelings and potencies and brought a crisis of identity as you tried to become less emotionally dependent on your parents. You are still developing as you make occupational, marital, parental and sexual adjustments, weather a mid-life crisis, or get used to retirement.

Being "well adjusted" involves more than passively fitting in. It means coping effectively, even assertively, with the problems in your life. Becoming well adjusted in a new stage of development may depend on the opportunity to observe and learn from people who are good models of the particular social, work or relationship skills that matter. Success may be influenced by the level of emotional support you receive from others. It can also be affected by unpredictable changes. Events like marital breakdown, the death of someone close, job loss, even the excitement of winning a lottery, can greatly add to the normal stresses in your life and make them harder to manage.

How you adjust also depends on personality itself. Possibly from the beginning, temperamental differences affect responses to change and stress. In addition, a part of personal growth that crucially affects each new crisis in your life is the style you develop for coping with change and disruption. Each of us needs a style that suits our own temperament and personal circumstances.

The influence of temperament

Our earliest personality differences persist and influence not only our behavior but the responses of people in the environment that we are trying to adjust to. For example, the 40 percent of children classed as "temperamentally easy" (see *Ch 12*), have many fewer confrontations with their mothers and they are more likely to receive parental praise than the 10 percent classed as "difficult." Their mothers are less likely to be irritable, their teachers more likely to be approving. A difficult offspring puts a strain on parents, whose irritability then interferes with their ability to soothe the child, who becomes even more sensitive and less adaptable.

Circumstances greatly affect the degree to which a given temperament is adaptive. When raised in a rather bleak children's home or in famine conditions, children with difficult temperaments have a better survival rate than others. Presumably, they receive more food and attention at the expense of less demanding peers and possibly develop fewer psychological problems.

European and American parents have been observed to be far more bothered by babies waking up in the middle of the night than parents in Puerto Rico or Kenya. Middle-class parents show higher expectations than working-class parents that children should sleep and feed in regular patterns, adapt readily to new people and situations and feed and dress themselves. The difficult children of middle-class Westerners, therefore, seem to be at a greater risk of becoming poorly adjusted.

However, the child's temperament, rather than the parent's

ADJUSTING TO YOUR NATURE AND YOUR ENVIRONMENT

■ *LEFT A difficult environment for a difficult child. Difficult children of middle-class Western parents may find it slightly harder to adjust. Working-class and third-world parents have lower expectations and are more tolerant of children who adapt slowly and have irregular feeding and sleeping patterns. It is harder for a child to win comfort from parents who feel stressed by its behavior. Unfavorable starts and unfavorable temperaments can be compensated for as children develop adjustment skills.*

Adjusting to crises and new situations is part of the lifelong process of personality development that we all undergo. The personality that we develop is itself an important factor in how well we adjust to life's problems.

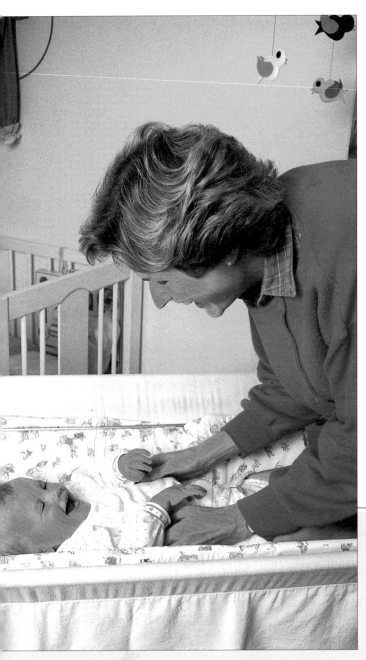

attitudes, may on balance be the most important component in the complex question of how well adjusted it becomes. Psychologists have traditionally blamed children's psychological problems on their environment in general and on the mother's behavior in particular – but the concept of the difficult child is now recognized as more than the invention of tired and disgruntled parents.

The environment we are born into and the pattern of emotional responses with which we are born are a matter of luck. However, as we develop we learn how to modify both. We learn by trial and error what kind of environment suits us, and we seek it out in our career decisions, our choice of friends and marriage partners and in everything we do to create a personal lifestyle.

Even those with the extremes of temperament may make very successful adjustments. The most highly introverted person in the community may in the end find contentment tending a remote lighthouse. The most tough-minded should probably not try to settle down to a quiet life but seek suitable risks and challenges. People who have very intense emotional reactions will seek soothing companionship and calm occupations.

It is not always possible to find the niche that you can adjust to easily, however, and even when you do, events are unlikely to leave you in perfect harmony with your environment for long. You have to adjust anyway. To some extent you can change the environment you fall into. You can ask

■ *ABOVE An easy child in an easy environment. In favorable circumstances, a temperamentally easy child is likely to experience few adjustment problems. Its cheerful personality and predictable pattern of behavior encourage parents to respond positively.*

■ *RIGHT A difficult environment for easy children. Passive or uncomplaining children may find it harder than difficult children to adjust when raised in bleak conditions. Difficult children demand and receive more attention. Here children work at making sacks in an orphanage in South Vietnam.*

your employer, for example, to clarify your duties. (One survey revealed that a major source of stress for about half of the employees in the United States is that too much of the time they do not know what they are supposed to do.) To some extent you can change your behavior – many temperamentally shy people, for example, can learn how to be more assertive, in relatively small but useful ways. To some extent you can learn to bear more easily the things that, for the moment, at least, you can do nothing about. Two traits of

personality help with all three of these adjustments – an *internal* "locus of control" and an *external* and *specific* "style of attribution."

Do you take an internal or external view?

Your "locus of control" (see *Ch 3*) is the way you see control over your life. You have an internal locus if you think of yourself as being in control, an external locus if you see impersonal events and the choices of other people as more

FINDING YOUR VOCATION

■ *TOP A life of religious seclusion requires a temperament that makes it possible and satisfying to be devoted to ideals of self-sacrifice and contemplation, and to have the discipline to resist very ordinary desires. Religious orders are quick to discourage candidates who seem suited to freer and more stimulating surroundings. Novices are required to fulfill long apprenticeships before committing themselves fully.*

■ *LEFT Drawn to stressful and competitive work, a trader at the Chicago Mercantile Exchange shouts to make himself heard. In the phrase of Hans Selye, father of the study of stress, each of us has our own amount of "adjustment energy" and an optimum level of stress that we must attain to fee sufficiently stimulated. Stress works against us only when we cannot control it – when we cannot match it to our personal needs.*

We learn by trial and error what surroundings we can readily fit into, and our choices of career and lifestyle favor them. However, we may need to adapt to unsuitable environments, modify them, or simply bear with them.

important. An internal locus helps people to cope successfully with stresses and changes of all kinds. The more you *see* your life under your own control, the more likely you are to *try* to control it and to consider setbacks as temporary and not too distressing. People with an external locus may at times feel optimistic, but they are optimistic about their luck rather than their personal effectiveness.

Often people have a sense of control in one part of their life but not in another. For example, your successes in a particular realm – academic achievement, football, being a parent – might make it seem second nature to you to set and achieve targets (getting an A, making the team, getting the children to bed on time). In other areas, however, you may see yourself as "not the kind of person" who takes charge of their destiny. You hope to fall into an interesting job, but do not consider that you could find one through your own job-finding abilities. You wish your marriage partner would become more interesting again, but you do not take steps yourself to revitalize your marriage.

We can all take lessons from ourselves in how to develop the more effective self-image that would make us more adaptive people. The fact that you can learn skills and pursue purposes in one area of your life is evidence that you have the potential to be more effective in others.

In contrast to locus of control, it is an advantage for your "attributional style" to be *external*. Attributional style is our habitual way of explaining who or what is to blame when things happen to us. For example, when their relationships break up, one woman may say: "He couldn't keep up with me. He was envious of my success," while another may say "He got bored with me; I couldn't keep him interested." The first explanation is external. It is much less likely to lead to depression then the second, internal, attribution and likely to lead to more successful coping.

Do you take a specific or a global view?

Another aspect of attributional style is whether it is *specific* or *global*. A person failing an examination may either say "I'm not much good at writing under pressure, I'll do better next time" or "I can't do anything right; I'm no good." The first is a specific attribution – in other words the cause is seen as temporary – while the second is global – things will never change. The specific way of interpreting the failure is the more optimistic and positive one. It is likely to be more successful – more productive of useful adaptation – than the second.

People who explain unwelcome events in internal, unchanging, global terms have a predisposition toward depression. Those who give themselves external, specific explanations that leave the door open to change are not only

WORK, LIFESTYLE AND PERSONALITY

■ *People with different personalities enjoy different work and lifestyles. The highly extroverted person, outward-looking and sociable, is not likely to find job satisfaction in a solitary occupation where relationships with other people are not of prime importance. A very introverted person, likely to be quiet, reflective and rather reserved, might find it extremely difficult to adjust to the police community relations work seen RIGHT in New York's notorious Ninth Precinct.*

Personality is important not only at work but in sexual and marital relationships as well. Marital satisfaction is greatest when the wife shows as many typically feminine traits as her husband shows masculine ones – in other words a very masculine man is more likely to have a successful marriage relationship with a very feminine woman, while a man who is not strongly sex-typed is more likely to have a happy marriage with a woman who is not strongly sex-typed. As regards traits without a sex bias, however, the more similar a couple are the better.

Sexual attitudes are also related to personality traits. For example, high scorers on extroversion and tough-mind-edness scales (see Ch 13) tend to be sexually adventurous and unrepressed while more anxious individuals are likely to be inhibited and feel guilt more readily. Some leisure activities seem particularly suited to the extrovert and sensation seeker, like wind-surfing, hang-gliding and parachuting. Our personality is an important determinant of what we enjoy or dislike in many important aspects of our lives. **PK**

likely to avoid depression but to be more successful in many areas of their lives. For example, in one study, 100 insurance salesmen were assessed for their habitual types of attribution. The ones with positive styles sold 25 percent more insurance than the others. Students with positive attributional styles do better academically. What causes such characteristic styles of explanation? No one really knows. A child may imitate the parents' explanatory styles or the attitude of its teachers. It may be that a child who is always blamed for things may develop an internal style. It is also possible that the explanations that occur early to a child for events such as the separation of parents may set a pattern for the interpretation of future losses and difficulties.

The way in which we cope with events has been shown to play an important role not just in psychological adjustment but also in our physical health. There is now a great deal of evidence to suggest that stressful life events, particularly bereavements and professional and economic pressures, can trigger or aggravate physical illness (see *Ch 23*). A person who interprets these unwelcome events in terms of

THE RESILIENT PERSONALITY

■ *Some people have a resilient personality that makes them face challenges and adjust to them rather than running away from them. They have a strong sense of self, both in terms of feeling good about themselves and in having a sense of personal power (termed an internal locus of control – see main text).*

Such hardiness is characterized by a willingness to confront problems, to reshape situations by flexible approach and imaginativeness, and also by active coping. It is associated with a resistance to physical illness as well as to depression, despite stressful events.

Researchers have examined resilient children who survive or even thrive under hardship that

would devastate others. Children brought up under extremely severe conditions (eg with mentally disturbed parents or in war zones or areas of civil disturbance such as Northern Ireland) have been studied. The ones who cope well with hardship and traumas believe they can exercise control over their lives, despite the bleakness of their circumstances. They find they have an opportunity for choice and decision where others would see no opportunities for personal action. For example, one girl who had been abandoned by her parents and had no food in the house except some stale bread cheerfully cut three slices and prepared herself a "bread sandwich."

◄ **Confronting bleak circumstances.** *TOP Boys and girls attend a funeral after a fatal incident in Northern Ireland. BOTTOM Scavenging cheerfully* *for the necessities of life in a Philippine rubbish dump. Children who believe they can exercise control cope well with hardship.*

Resilient personalities have a strong sense of self. They feel good about themselves and feel they can face challenges and adjust to any problem. They find opportunities for choice and decision where others do not.

internal, global and unchanging causes, blaming themselves or circumstances that cannot change, may be more likely, because of their pessimistic style, to suffer from stress-related health problems. Depressive explanatory style is a health risk, probably on the scale of smoking, drinking and lack of physical exercise.

Failure to adjust

Some of us are particularly – and most of us are fairly – well adjusted. Only a minority – about 15 percent at any one time – are maladjusted to the point of suffering from a mental disorder. Such disorders are usually temporary – and are therefore not themselves aspects of personality – and most are associated with specific situations to which sufferers have not adjusted. However, some traits of personality are associated with a higher risk of disorder.

Neuroses are the commonest and mildest forms of mental disorder, but they are nevertheless quite serious. Neurotic

people may behave in markedly abnormal ways; they may be so afraid of heights as to avoid going upstairs in a two-story building; they may check 15 or 20 times that their front door is locked before going to bed at night. However, neurotic individuals retain sufficient insight to realize that their thoughts, behavior and feelings are not appropriate to the circumstances.

Most neurotic people have emotional problems. About half of them are troubled by excessively high levels of anxiety; this may concern specific objects such as spiders, airplanes or snakes and will usually, but not invariably, lead them to avoid coming into contact with their feared object.

People with anxieties about social situations, such as meeting strangers or eating out, are more likely to have personality traits that include feelings of inadequacy and low self-esteem. Others will experience anxiety that is independent of specific situations; their anxiety suddenly overwhelms them and is of such intensity that they may fear that they are going to die. Such attacks of panic are so debilitating that they make an individual feel vulnerable in any situation where they feel trapped and unable to have access

THE RESILIENCE OF ELEANOR ROOSEVELT

■ *A famous example of a resilient personality was Eleanor Roosevelt (1884-1962).*

Her mother, who could not bear to be touched by her, frequently ridiculed her in front of guests. Her father was an alcoholic. Eleanor was raised by her grandmother, a cold and strict woman.

Nevertheless she became one of the most popular and admired American figures of the century.

Famous as a humanitarian, she was committed to political and social issues, particularly those involving women and minority groups.

When she became engaged to Franklin Delano Roosevelt, 30 years before be became President of the United States, she was active in community service work in New York and introduced him to the squalid living conditions of the underprivileged. She was a mother of

six and a delegate to the United Nations, where she co-authored the Universal Declaration of Human Rights. One of her many books is entitled "On My Own."

ABOVE *She gives voice to some very definite opinions of her own as she and President Roosevelt attend a public function in 1936.*

to a secure base of safe environment. It is not surprising then that some people who experience such attacks – agoraphobics – prefer to stay at home and avoid crowded places.

People suffering from *obsessive-compulsive neurosis* may complain of unwanted thoughts which erupt repeatedly into their minds. They can experience almost irresistible urges to do something unacceptable or aggressive (eg shout rude words or push a passer-by under a lorry) although they rarely succumb. They may perform repetitive ritualistic actions in an attempt to exercise control. Typical compulsions would be washing their hands many dozens of times each day in order to avoid infection, or checking perhaps 20 times that the gas taps are off.

People who are more likely to develop obsessive neuroses include those with a very limited ability to express warm and tender emotions. Perfectionists who show an unusually great interest in detail, an excessive devotion to work and productivity and find it very difficult to make decisions are susceptible. So are people who insist on controlling others.

Other neurotics suffer more from *depression* than anxiety. Sometimes their melancholy mood is linked to an external event such as a job loss or the break-up of a relationship; their sadness is, however, disproportionate to the event. Neurotic depressives can generally cheer themselves up for a while.

The difference between a neurotic depressive and a depressed person who does not suffer from a psychological

▲ **Situations that we cannot control**, such as growing older, can be the most stressful. They point to the need to include in our mix of coping abilities the art of acceptance. The actress Joan Crawford, shown here, was noted for taking charge of matters that affected her. She demanded perfection from her children and was made director of the international corporation that her late husband had headed. This distinction came to her not as his widow, but because of her own hard-driving promotional work. She reported profound distress, however, including losing her fundamental sense of control, at the prospect of aging.

ASSERTIVE ADJUSTMENT

■ *"Adjustment" has a passive ring, as though it means simply fitting in with the world as you find it. In reality, many of the most well-adjusted people have very assertive personalities. Even nonassertive adjustments involve taking action, and even when adjustment means learning to live with a situation that you cannot change, assertive people may do this better.*

When you find that you and your environment do not fit with each other satisfactorily, you can try to change the environment. For example, you paint your house a color that you like better or you ask your neighbor to stop having noisy parties.

Especially when these attempts involve asking others

> **YOUR NEIGHBOR'S PARTIES ARE NOISY. DO YOU...**

COMPLAIN?   JOIN IN?   MOVE?

to adjust to your needs, they would be called self-assertive. There are also nonassertive ways of changing your environment. If the neighbors are having a party, you might close the windows and put in ear plugs, or you could go out.

In many cases, it is useful or necessary to adapt to a situation by a change in your own behavior. For example, people have been forming a poor impression of you, and so you self-assertively decide to dress better. A particularly self-assertive strategy would be inviting yourself to your neighbor's noisy party and joining in. A nonassertive behavioral change is where you simply comply with others' wishes.

Sometimes, there is nothing you can do. Your noisy neighbor is the chief of police and his noisy guests include the mayor. The parties are not enjoyable when you join in and you cannot afford to move

house. Assertive coping in situations like this involves reminding yourself that no situation is permanent and keeping alert to the ever-present possibility that an opportunity will arise to act constructively, for example by helping to vote both of them out of office at election time.

People who cope assertively are often pleasant and likable. They may be as likely to see and do something about other people's needs as about their own. Those with aggressive personalities often do not cope as well. Some people have an intense, hard-driving personality identified as "type A" by researchers into heart disease (see Ch 23). In particular, type A men who have a sense of time urgency and an easily provoked hostility suffer extremely intense levels of stress when they have to bear with unwelcome situations. In some cases, an insistence on controlling others can contribute to compulsive neurosis (see main text). Making reasonable demands on others, however, is adaptive and healthy.

People who adapt their own behavior willingly in their relations with other people have cooperative, less demanding personalities. They are often very likable. Those who put up with difficult situations easily will find patience a useful trait of character. It is important, however, to combine cooperativeness and patience with assertiveness if you are to maintain self-esteem. Entirely cooperative and patient people will eventually be seen by themselves and others as inconsequential, as tools of other people's purposes.

Successful adjustment combines being cooperative and patient with being assertive when you have reasonable demands to make. It means accepting the losses and limitations that change brings, while exploiting new possibilities.

disorder is thus a matter of degree. In addition to their melancholic mood, however, those with neurotic depression as opposed to everyday blues may suffer from disturbance of sleep, loss of appetite, loss of sexual drive and lack of energy.

In some mental disorders, the *psychoses*, affecting no more than 2 percent of people, failure of adjustment is very severe. There is such a degree of impairment that sufferers are unaware that anything is wrong and yet are unable to meet many of the demands of everyday life. One of the commonest of the psychoses is *schizophrenia*. The thinking and

behavior of sufferers will be grossly disordered; they may feel that they are being controlled by alien forces or may be certain that their most intimate thoughts are known to other people. Often such people report hearing voices that keep up a running commentary on their actions or discuss them in the third person. No specific personality type is associated with schizophrenia.

Another common psychosis, *manic-depressive psychosis*, is characterized by mood swings from depression so profound that sufferers may believe themselves to be totally evil to a state of excitement and elation when they feel so full of energy as to need no sleep and to be capable of starting an apparently unlimited number of new projects resulting, in fact, in costly failures. **AH PF**

PURSUING THE POSSIBILITIES

■ *LEFT Changing the environment is an important aspect of adjusting to circumstances. Here a wheelchair-bound garden enthusiast has had flower and herb beds built to a level where he can reach them.*

■ *ABOVE Enjoying old age. Each stage of our lives offers its own distinctive limitations and possibilities. A good adjustment is one that accepts the limitations and pursues the possibilities.*

Personal Growth

MOST OF US know of innumerable ways in which we could be better people, yet we find it difficult to know where or how to begin. If asked, we could probably pour out a catalog of wished-for changes such as wanting to be more assured, decisive, popular, independent, kind and/or creative. Often, we are especially aware that there is room for improvement in our capacities as friends, lovers or parents. There are in fact many ways to begin, but all of them have in common becoming very involved with other people. "Growth workshops" such as assertiveness training groups and encounter groups, and even friends, can help you to achieve a better understanding of yourself – and help you change aspects of your personality that may be hampering your development.

Learning to be more assertive

Among group therapies, and filling an increasingly widely felt need, is assertiveness training. Its purpose is to help people stand up for themselves, to say no inoffensively when they feel someone is taking advantage of them, to pursue their own goals in a less inhibited way, and to communicate needs and feelings better.

Official programs to rehabilitate aggressive offenders or aggressive mental patients sometimes include assertiveness training, in order to teach them how to have a more con-

structive impact on others. Most of the programs available commercially, however, or in community or continuing education centers, are attended by people who believe they are too mild. Participants discuss, act out and analyze the circumstances and reasons for this. Then they act out situations again, using social skills modeled by their instructor – such as looking people more directly in the eye, and smiling and speaking confidently when making a request. They discuss problems ranging from being unable to respond appropriately to rudeness and poor service at a restaurant to being the one who always gives in to other people's wishes.

Apart from the damage it may do to self-respect, being too submissive often leads to an accumulation of repressed hostility, and the resulting eruptions of anger can cause guilt and embarrassment. Unless relieved in some way, resentment at always being put upon and the self-rejection that may follow explosions of anger can stunt social and emotional growth.

Assertiveness training may help you to be more effective in impersonal situations. It may also improve your relationships, which work best where the principle of give-and-take

▲ **Becoming more assertive** *is a personal-growth aim for many. Clenching your fist to resist domination is only one part of self-assertiveness. It also includes knowing how to express positive feelings without embarrassment.*

▶ **Good relationships and self-acceptance** *are both an aim of and a means to personal growth. Other people teach us more about ourselves when they are close to us.*

Personality enhancement may mean becoming more assertive, more sensitive or more in control of your own actions. People who are very close to you can help, and so can group workshops. Personal growth requires involvement with others.

applies fairly and there is clear communication. Assertiveness training may help achieve this balance not only by teaching you to assert your self-interest better, but by teaching what some instructors call "positive assertiveness" – the knack of saying what you like about other people, paying them compliments (and accepting theirs without embarrassment) and involving yourself with them without seeming overly ingratiating, intrusive or domineering.

Learning to be more sensitive

Two common forms of group therapy probe deeper, attempting to make us more aware of ourselves and more sensitive to other people.

T-groups are used mainly for improving the communication and negotiating skills of managers. Sitting in a circle, small groups discuss organizational or personal problems. Participants are encouraged to act not only as sympathetic critics of one another's ideas, but to give feedback on any-

thing about each other that might seem appropriate, including attitudes, manner and mannerisms. Members find that they are able to communicate and exchange personal feelings to a degree that would never occur elsewhere. They become more sensitive to other people's way of seeing things and learn why others react to them as they do.

T-groups can be a valuable self-improvement technique for anyone. However, their broader development has been eclipsed by *encounter groups*. These groups of about 6 to 16 people meet for an hour or so every week for months or even years, or the encounter may be an intensive one over a period of a few days or even a single day. How long the group will exist may be set in advance or this may be left open-ended. It will tend to be highly informal, people often sitting on the floor to avoid conference or business-meeting styles of discussion. All encounter groups are nondirective. No one person chooses the content of the discussion.

Beyond being there and getting things under way, an encounter group leader has little function. At first, when participants are getting used to the group and there is a certain amount of confusion, some will become impatient or angry about this. The leader may clarify what is said or done, and provide encouragement as necessary, but will offer no interpretations, structure or purpose beyond explaining the general objective – that everyone taking part will help every-

127

▲ **Talking about yourself** in a growth workshop or group-therapy session means overcoming inhibitions. The reaction of listeners is usually to support and help a speaker. To encour- age free discussion, growth workshops are often kept very small, with participants sitting comfortably in a circle.

one else to achieve a realistic and honest self-image. This they will attempt to do by discussing one another's difficulties, how well or badly they seem to be managing them and how they feel about one another.

In the early stages, polite conversation may be the keynote, or tentative statements from members as to what they are looking for and why they have come. As they get to know each other better, they will probe more deeply into motives, attitudes and ways of relating to the group and other people. Questions and disclosures become increasingly personal,

and advice and criticism are exchanged more freely, as are opinions about one another's personality and character.

Sometimes, an encounter group may opt to help individuals act out their problems – to see how they handle, for example, rows with their partners, children or employers. The central character outlines a typical scenario and plays his or her own part, with members of the group taking other roles. Afterward, everyone analyzes how appropriately the central character behaved. Alternatively, members can use others in the group as stand-ins for significant people in

GETTING CONTROL

■ *Everyone has some problem that they wish they could control better. The most obvious examples are in areas where we think we really should be exerting more willpower, and somehow we cannot – we feel unable to control our weight, our smoking or our tendency to give in when other people become demanding.*

In other words, in some parts of our lives we have an "external locus of control" (see Chs 3, 14). People who are externals in matters of weight, for example, are liable to see their actual or anticipated failure as the consequence of factors beyond them: hormone or metabolic variations between

slim and fat people, or the impossibility of refusing what is pressed on them by friends, family or advertisers. Eating may be seen as a response to stress, or it may begin to seem that there are no really effective diets available.

People who have an internal locus of control in these matters, however, might adjust their weight in spite of having the same metabolism as an external, in spite of having food urged upon them, in spite of feeling stress and without adopting any other dietary strategy than eating less.

The helplessness that we have about some aspects of our lives is a learned one. We have

heard how difficult it is to do a certain kind of thing, and when we have tried we have failed. The important thing for anyone setting out to undo this learning is to avoid failure and to reward their successes. This means being realistic and clear as to what constitutes success. The ultimate goal may be losing a certain number of pounds, or being more assertive, but completing the prescribed daily exercise or achieving a weekly target of reasonable refusals to unwelcome demands is a safer measure of success.

Small steps are preferable, and may be rewarded through a contract with yourself. Small food treats or other extrava-

gances could serve as rewards while giving up some favorite food or TV program could be a punishment. However, punishments should be used with care and not allowed to increase the counter-productive tension and anxiety usually associated with fighting ingrained habits. Above all, be prepared for failure so that setbacks and small lapses do not seem catastrophic.

Hypnotherapy can also help. You can be given the suggestion that you will feel relaxed about meeting new people or resisting the temptation to smoke or whatever else makes you anxious. It may take several sessions, but this works well if there is also a conscious determination to change. Even by developing a routine of getting into a relaxed mood and imagining yourself doing with ease the things you find difficult, it is possible to make them easier.

▲ **Members of a "chocoholics" society,** *meeting for a weekend of chocolate as the main ingredient in every meal.*

The first element of any successful attempt to become more resistant to self-indulgent habits is to genuinely want to

change them. The second is to unlearn the belief that you are helpless to stop them.

Encounter-group members sometimes have direct confrontations, but mainly they help one another to solve problems and to develop a new and more realistic self-image. Most report that afterward they are more spontaneous and self-accepting.

their lives, and express their feelings to them. Emotions may even be expressed more physically by, for example, someone screaming at and punching a pillow that represents someone who generates anger and frustration. There is both a release of emotion and a shared insight.

Confronting others and yourself

Once powerful emotions begin to be expressed, direct confrontations between encounter-group members may occur. The defenses behind which you hide your true self will probably be revealed. Weaknesses in your personality and in how you relate to others will almost inevitably be exposed, and it can be distressing when others begin to say why they do not like you and why they have little sympathy for your self-created difficulties or even contempt for the way you deal with them. Once we see them for what they are, however, we can choose whether or not to discard any

of these aspects of self and open ourselves to change. Therefore, the purpose of mutual criticism is not as destructive as it may appear – it clears the way for rebuilding.

In fact, much of what happens in an encounter group is supportive and caring, with members helping one another solve problems and revealing the positive and admirable sides of one another's personalities. In the end, every member will have to come to terms with what they believe to be the good and the not-so-good aspects of themselves, and synthesize a new and realistic self-image from all they have learned about themselves and their effects on others.

Some people drop out, hurt or disillusioned, and occasionally, someone will have a serious breakdown. Whether a breakdown was already coming and they joined the group as a last resort, or whether it was precipitated by the stress of encounter-group participation is usually hard to judge. Those who have negative experiences are, in any case, a very small minority. So too are those whose lives are changed in any very obvious way. When this does happen, it is usually a matter of people deciding to change jobs – generally moving away from materialistic and authoritarian concerns to more democratic and humanistic ones. More often,

◄ **Personal growth for managers.** *At this training camp, Japanese managers perfect their social skills BOTTOM, and practice wholehearted group involvement TOP. Subjects also include giving orders, building self-confidence and expressing opinions unself-consciously. Night hikes and calisthenics at 5.00am promote physical self-discipline.*

▲ **Tactile sensitivity.** *In this variation of the encounter group method, members try to increase their self-awareness and consciousness of others through touch. Touch therapy breaks down personal defenses and inhibitions and encourages self-expression. Interpersonal communication is enhanced as members become more sensitive to the attitudes and reactions of those around them.*

changes tend to be subtle and subjective, and assessing the effect of being in an encounter group depends a good deal upon what ex-members have to say. A minority report that there has been no improvement in their personalities. Far more say they have benefited from the experience – mainly by becoming more sensitive and sympathetic toward others, behaving less artificially in their relationships and being more open and spontaneous in the things they do. They also place a high value on their greater self-knowledge which, in many cases, has allowed them to shed useless feelings of guilt and inferiority and accept themselves.

Friends and personal growth

Relationships are both an important goal of personal growth and a *means* to personal growth. They are a goal of our lifelong development – throughout childhood, and long into adulthood, most people's relationship skills improve – because we need some combinations of friends, an intimate partner and/or close family ties for social stimulation, emotional support and help. For example, the people who are closest to you probably do more than any mere acquaintance to support your self-esteem – they share opinions, interests and often a sense of family or community identity with you, and they like the fact that you are like them. The help that very close friends and intimate partners give, however, also includes constructive criticism and sometimes quite blunt personal assessments. A relationship is an open-ended and often quite intimate encounter, and so it is invaluable as an aid to knowledge about, and development of, your inner self.

For some, having this aid to personal growth may be rather more complicated than enrolling for assertiveness training or joining an encounter group. You have to estab-

No one likes to be proved wrong, but if someone close to you really thinks it necessary to get you to see or do things in a new way, it may be to your advantage to postpone saying no until you have given each other a fair hearing.

lish or improve your relationships first. The skills needed to make and keep friends, however, are not hard to learn for those who know how to see things from other people's points of view.

Friendships usually begin with acquaintanceships. Consequently, it would be wrong to minimize such practical problems as having to stay at home with dependent relatives, being naturally shy and timid, having transport problems in the evening, not being physically attractive and not having a particularly interesting job to talk about. All these affect the ease with which initial contacts are made and kept up. However, commitment and practice have more to do with making friends than luck.

Impression management (see *Ch 5*) is an important (even if often unconscious) part of everyone's technique for making friends. Opportunities for friendship can be created by making yourself attractive and pleasing to others. First impressions are particularly important (see *Ch 4*). If the first few pages of a book or the first ten minutes of a television program are dull, readers and viewers will turn to something more interesting, and the same thing happens with personal appearance and conversational style.

One way of finding out about your own conversational style is by listening to see how often you use the words "I" and "my" in conversation. It can be surprising to discover just how frequently these occur, not only as opening gambits but also as interjections when other people are talking. Whatever the subject, there are always plenty of people waiting for an opening to talk about themselves or about someone or something closer to their own interests. Those

HANDLING DISAGREEMENTS

■ We make the most of close relationships when we use the trust established within them to help us lower defenses and accept friendly criticism of at least some aspects of the self we usually try to keep hidden. There are, of course, dangers in this kind of communication. Once criticisms are expressed strongly as personally important views, discussion easily tips over into a quarrel that will never have a real winner.

No one likes to be proved wrong, but if your friend or marriage partner really thinks it necessary to get you to see or do things in a new way, there are techniques for coping with

this. Instead of letting them stress the differences between you, ask them to remind you about how much they agree with you on everything that is

not disputed. Then, having reinforced this basis for trust, it is important to postpone an entrenched "no" about the rest. Consider the arguments and

the evidence together. It is remarkable how often we flatly contradict one another and plunge into heated arguments when, had we asked more questions, a full-scale clash of personalities could easily have been avoided.

Be ready to admit freely where you seem to be wrong or misinformed while never being smug or triumphant when the other is.

Attentive listening and a warm, open attitude will not only help prevent bluster and a descent into personal conflict, they should also ensure that, whatever the final outcome, the relationship is not damaged.

who can and do listen attentively, ask questions and show a genuine interest in the person to whom they are talking, are more than halfway to becoming highly regarded and valued companions. Of course, this is not the same as cultivating total self-effacement. It is a matter of balance and, in the first instance, of learning to control your own sense of self-importance and desire to impress. As a relationship develops, you will of course talk about yourself – in more and more personal detail. But this process of self-disclosure will proceed by turn-taking stages (see p55).

Modest listeners and gentle persuaders are always preferred to those who are cocksure and overbearing. And those who take the trouble to study other's tastes, wishes and sensitivities are liked best of all. Even the smallest sign of caring is important. Anyone concerned with improving their social skills should make sure that they can remember not only people's names but whatever else they have learned about them: their home and family, anniversaries, job problems and interests. We are much more likely to be drawn to someone who communicates happiness and warmth than to a person who seems aloof and gloomy. It may take a lot of effort to replace a habitually distant or cold expression with a smile or to create a convincing show of interest in others, but these may be important first steps. **BWPW**

131

■ **Relationships and personal growth**. *TOP LEFT* and *TOP RIGHT Picking that one special person out of the vast crowd of humanity and then hanging on to them is a central challenge of everyone's life. An indispens-* *able aim of personal growth is to become more skilled at forming relationships and at making the personal adjustments that help them to last. RIGHT Friendships, as well as closer intimacy, matter to our well-being. They are made possible chiefly by taking a genuine interest in others and in the things that matter to them.*

2

YOUR EMOTIONAL WELL-BEING

PART TWO

The World of Your Emotions

LIFE without emotions would be unimaginable. No love, no jealousy, no hate – no driving passions to destroy us or to lift us to heights of ecstasy. Emotions are a part of us. Yet the words "emotion" and "emotional" are often used in a negative sense, as the opposite of reason, as something we might be better off without. Could we really dispense with our emotions? Indeed, why did we acquire them?

Emotions are universal

Since the time of Charles Darwin (1809-82) scientists have considered that emotions are by no means confined to the human race, but extend far down the animal kingdom. Primates, dogs, cats, birds, even rats and mice express emotions in various ways – through sounds, postures, movements, facial expressions, and even odors and color changes. Whether fish have emotions, or worms or insects, is still unclear.

Our emotions are recognizably similar to those displayed by animals, and, in fact, we attribute them to our own pets. Dogs have been reported to show signs of "depression" when their owners died or went away, leaving their food and becoming listless.

Others have been known to growl and bark in seeming jealousy when they saw their owners embracing. A cat in a confrontation with a dog bares its teeth, arches its back and erects the hair on its body to make itself look bigger and more threatening. In much the same way, two men who get into an argument after having too much to drink, square up to each other as they get more heated, sticking out their chests and even doubling up their fists.

Emotions also cut across time and across cultures to convey the same messages in virtually any context. When a team of scientists from the United States visited a remote tribe in New Guinea and showed them photographs of American students with facial expressions displaying happiness, anger, fear, sadness, disgust and surprise, the tribespeople easily identified four of these. Fear and surprise were difficult for them to distinguish.

These and other findings support the view that similar emotions are fundamental to all human groups. For instance, children born blind, deaf and brain-damaged display the same emotional reactions as normal children. They smile when they are given things, laugh when they are tickled, spontaneously embrace other people on occasions and cry when they are hurt or left in unfamiliar surroundings.

Why some emotions are innate

The evidence of research suggests that some emotional behavior is innate. Babies and young children have instinctive emotional reactions and these help a mother and child

EMOTION IN CHIMPANZEES

■ *Perhaps the greatest justification for the enduring belief of humans in their basic kinship with animals is seen in the chimpanzee. An angry chimp will sulk and display fits of temper, just like a human. Young chimps will hold their breath, pound their heads on the floor, and pull at their hair when they are prevented from having something they want. When finally offered food or a toy, the chimps will sometimes refuse the object they wanted in the first place. In laboratory research chimpanzees have expressed signs of terror on being shown a plastic model of a chimpanzee's head. Chimpanzees and gorillas in the wild may give help to youngsters in trouble even though it means going into dangerous areas. This seems to be a form of altruism.*

Chimpanzees who have been raised like children display human emotions. In 1930, Harry Raven, a curator at the American Museum of Natural History, bought a baby chimp from hunters in Africa who had just killed its mother. He took the chimp, named Meshie Mungkut by some African children, and raised it with his family. Meshie developed human patterns of behavior – she rode a tricycle, looked after the baby and had perfect table manners. Raven was forced to sell her to a zoo when she became sexually mature. When he visited her a year later she rushed into his arms and clung to him.

Being emotional is part of being human, but do we really need emotions? The goals that made them useful for evolutionary survival – deterring aggressors, attracting mates, forming social bonds – are still as pressing as ever.

135

▲ **Emotions around the world**. TOP LEFT *Exhilarated by victory, a German tennis star jumps for joy. His clenched-fist gesture expresses triumph.* TOP RIGHT *Being photographed has put a Urueu-wau-wau Indian boy of Brazil into a mood of hilarity and a cashew fruit has become ir-* resistibly funny. In the massive physiological reaction involved in laughter, a simple joke may even reduce us to tears. BOTTOM RIGHT *Exuberant crowd partici-pation is a feature of this tradi-* tional event in Siena, Italy, where parishes compete in a horse race around the main square. Emotions are amplified by being shared. The linked arms and hands of these sup- porters express their unity of feeling. BOTTOM LEFT *Tears roll down the cheeks of an English-woman as she watches her husband depart for a long and dangerous absence at sea. Emotions like joy and sorrow are basic to human experience and recognizable worldwide.*

to communicate with each other. No baby is taught to laugh or cry, nor do adults need any previous experience to understand these signals immediately. The cry of the infant, typically associated with separation, is almost universal among mammals, prompting the mother to remedy the situation. Also common to mammals is play, in which young males are generally more aggressive than young females. Mothers prescribed artificial hormones while pregnant, however, have produced female infants who are more aggressive in play. Emotional behavior is not entirely learned but reflects nervous system development, affected by body chemistry. This is normally under the control of the genes we inherit from our parents.

Looked at in terms of evolution, the newborn mammal is most vulnerable to the environment and to predators and relies on body signals and other communication displays to increase its chances of survival. The infant must attract the mother's attention and support and the mother must reciprocate immediately. There is no time for either to become conditioned to their situation. Emotions are a vital part of this communication system and so need to be present in the infant from birth.

How are emotions useful?

Emotions are universal because they are useful. When Darwin described the behavior of an angry cat confronted by a dog, he recognized its aggressive posturing as an aid to survival. Those cats who adopted it were more likely to deter an attack and live to produce offspring. Other species too – birds, toads and frogs, and some reptiles, as well as humans – may try to puff themselves up to look bigger so as to frighten off a potential aggressor. When animals are in critical situations – for example, under threat, or seeking prey or a mate – their emotional displays convey information to potential adversaries or partners about what the ani-

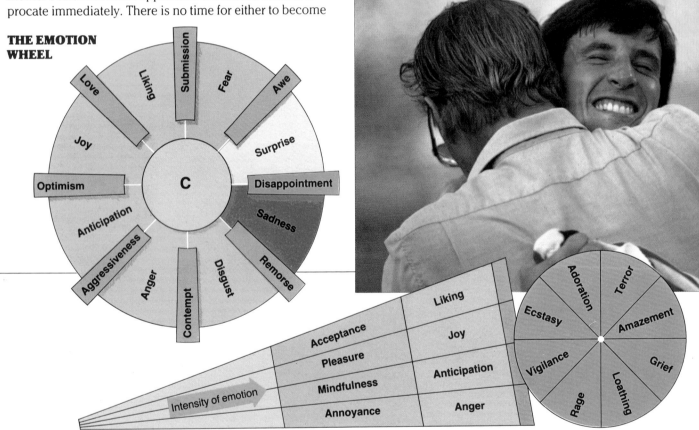

THE EMOTION WHEEL

■ The emotion-wheel diagram TOP shows the relations between eight primary and eight secondary emotions of medium intensity.

The primary emotions that appear next to each other, like the primary colors in a color spectrum, are not sharply distinguished but blend into one another: blue and yellow blend into green, and fear and surprise blend into awe, anger and disgust into contempt.

Another aspect of the analogy between color and emotion is that in both cases an infinite variety of blends is possible. The diagram is not intended to show the full range of emotions.

Some emotions are opposed, and rather than blending they conflict. In the wheel, a C for "conflict" stands between pairs such as joy and sadness, disgust and liking, because they cannot both be expressed at the same time, and experiencing both at once would result in emotional deadlock.

The emotion wheel is a cross-section of the three-dimensional emotion model BOTTOM. This model shows the various intensities of emotions, based on questionnaires in which college students rated the intensity of emotion words on a scale of 1-11. High-intensity emotions BOTTOM RIGHT are rage, ecstasy, amazement, terror, grief and loathing. Low intensity emotions are acceptance, pleasure, mindfulness and annoyance.

We use emotional behavior to communicate our needs and intentions to others and prompt them to give way to our demands or give us sympathy and help. Positive emotions attract other people to us and strengthen existing relationships.

mal might do next. In this way, the animal retains some control over the situation.

The same applies to other, more complex emotional expressions in humans. Most of us have at some time experienced the hurt of being rejected after a relationship with someone we had grown fond of. A common reaction of a rejected lover is one of sadness, or even to break down and cry. The tears convey the sense of loss and a threat to well-being.

Sadness evokes sympathy and consolation in other people and may even induce the loved one to return. Such emotional behavior communicates the injured party's needs to others and urges them to provide for these needs. So even

"negative" emotions may be useful in helping us to achieve our goals and stabilize a situation that is getting out of control. Even more so, "positive" emotions – such as expressions of happiness or joy – attract other people to us, providing friendships and social support.

Emotions can also act as "amplifiers," without which we may be oblivious to the dangers of a situation. An underwater swimmer who is running out of air will be acutely aware of the situation and will be driven by fear to fight hard to reach the surface in order to breathe again. By contrast, some World War II pilots who lost their oxygen supply while flying at high altitudes did not realize what was happening – the effect on the brain cells is gradual, and so there was nothing to warn them of the danger, no emotional trigger – and they blacked out and crashed.

Emotions are complex

The complexities of life, of our relations with the world about us and with other people, are reflected in the complexity of our emotions and in the language we use to describe them. We commonly speak of having "mixed feelings" toward someone, or – more extremely – of having a "love-hate" relationship. From early on we experience ambiguities of feeling. A child's parents are the source of rewards,

■ **Emotional bonding.** *ABOVE LEFT An athlete receives joyful congratulations from his father during the Olympic Games. ABOVE Grieving relatives after a disaster at sea. Hugging at moments of high emotion reinforces ties. Animals, too, instinctively seek physical con-* *tact when under stress. Chimpanzees threatened by an aggressor move together and hug one another before attacking.*

▲ **Signaling distress**. *Just as a baby cries to secure its mother's attention, emotional displays in later life – looking distressed, crying or running away – promote our survival by communicating our needs and prompting others to give help and consolation. Though we often keep them private, emotions are designed to be ex-* *pressed. We use sounds and postures signaling anger or fear to warn off aggressors or alert each other to possible danger.*

137

The death of a relative can provoke anger, guilt and a sense of helplessness as well as grief. Resolving such mixed and confusing feelings is an important part of coming to understand and accept yourself.

pleasures and good things, but at the same time they set limits, enforce discipline and curb unacceptable forms of behavior. The child loves them for their compassion and care, but may feel resentment and frustration when it cannot have its own way. Humans are not unique in having mixed emotions. The facial expressions of dogs in aggressive mood usually betray some signs of fear.

Over the centuries, philosophers and psychologists have considered that certain emotions, such as fear, anger, joy and sadness, are more basic emotions, from which most of the others derive. Eight emotions are represented as basic in the diagrams on page 136. Some researchers recognize more. Basic emotions occur at various intensities. We distinguish between feelings of annoyance (mild anger) and rage (strong anger). Fear ranges from apprehension to panic, sadness from feeling blue to feeling grief-stricken.

In reality, emotional feelings are more complex than this, having many components. For this reason it is often difficult for us to put our feelings into words even when we try to be candid about them. For instance, people generally experience intense mixed feelings after the death of a spouse or parent. Sometimes a person's grief is combined with anger, out of a feeling of having been abandoned by the deceased. Sometimes the feeling of the person left behind is one of sadness mixed with pleasurable anticipation because of the opportunities that will be opened up for pursuing new

goals. Sometimes feelings of guilt or helplessness are also present.

Most of us have so many emotions churning around inside us that it would be impossible to analyze them all. Sometimes people express their emotions unconsciously by indirect means. Frown lines on someone's face are often signs of persistent anger or frustration, and yet that person may be unaware of these feelings. Other people walk around with a downturned expression as if they had a permanently unpleasant taste in their mouth. The implied feeling of disgust may not be conscious. Dentists occasionally find that people who grind their teeth a great deal do not realize that they experience any anger.

If you ask someone about their emotional state you are likely to receive an incomplete answer. This is partly because of convention – we do not bare our feelings so readily – but also because that person does not really know the answer. As we become better acquainted with people, we learn to recognize their emotional states without having to ask. In other words, we become familiar with their personality.

Personality traits are recognizable mixes of emotions that characterize how an individual reacts in certain types of situation. Hence, we might say someone who habitually thinks of the future with sadness has a "gloomy" personality, if they generally look to the future with optimism, we say they have a "bright" personality . When someone seems to be dominated by extreme personality traits, we begin to refer to them in clinical terms. A person who seems ab-

THE LANGUAGE OF EMOTIONS

■ *Surveys carried out to explore the language of emotions have shown that we employ a wide range of vocabulary to describe our emotional states. A sample of people who were asked to describe the feelings that they associate with depression produced between them an extensive list of expressions.*

Interestingly, in describing what is apparently a state of mind, there are references to physical symptoms such as feeling "tired" or "sleepy" – and even impulses to action (for example, wanting to "withdraw") and biological changes such as having "no appetite."

One respondent directed the ill feeling outward onto the world: "Everything seems useless, absurd, meaningless." Many other emotions are also multifaceted. No one description by itself can express what is felt.

- *"I feel empty, drained, hollow, understimulated, undercharged, heavy, sluggish."*
- *"I feel let down, tired."*
- *"It's an effort to do anything."*
- *"I have no desire, no motivation, no interest."*
- *"I feel sorry for myself."*
- *"I lose all confidence in myself and doubt myself."*
- *"I feel vulnerable."*

- *"I feel insignificant."*
- *"I want to withdraw."*
- *"Everything seems absurd."*
- *"I feel as if I'm out of touch, can't reach others."*
- *"My body wants to contract."*
- *"I have no appetite."*
- *"I can't smile or laugh."*
- *"My chest feels heavy."*
- *"There is a lump in my throat."*
- *"It's as if I'm suffocating."*

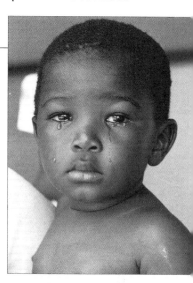

EXPRESSIONS THAT ARE DIFFICULT TO INTERPRET

■ *Faces often reflect mixed feelings.* RIGHT *His attention caught by the camera, a child is beginning to forget an unhappy incident. He shows both passing sadness and newfound curiosity.* FAR RIGHT *Expressions that seem out of place can be difficult to interpret. Exhaustion prevents a winning Formula One racing driver from enjoying his victory. Hands appearing from below keep him on his feet as a mixture of happiness, relief and confusion shows in his face during the cup presentation. Getting to know someone's* personality may help in divining their feelings, but complex emotional reactions often resist analysis. Sometimes, it may be very difficult to describe your own emotional state (see Ch18).

EMOTIONS AND THE BRAIN

■ The parts of the brain known collectively as the limbic system are thought to be the most important for the emotions. They developed early in evolution and control our arousal response to danger ("fight or flight" – see Ch 21) – our own limbic system functions basically like a reptile's. We have a more varied emotional life than other, less advanced animals, however, because our highly developed cerebral cortex – the thinking part of the brain – interacts with the limbic system and attempts to control it.

Emotional control is influenced by other structures within the brain including the brain stem, and also by a number of biochemical systems. The nerve chemical serotonin, for example, influences mood, and dopamine helps to rouse us and keep us alert (see Ch 12).

Stimulating the brain electrically helps pinpoint the mechanisms that control emotion. Doctors use electrical brain stimulation in diagnosis and epilepsy, Parkinson's disease and treating pain. Patients report a wide variety of feelings: anxiety, anger, disgust, pleasure, sadness, surprise.

There is no single brain center for a particular emotion. Instead, a group of structures integrate the various fragments of behavior (such as clenching your fist, narrowing your eyes, raising your voice) that define each emotion. The same emotion can in fact be produced by the electrical stimulation of different brain areas.

Aggressiveness can be inhibited by stimulating part of the limbic system. During stimulation, normally aggressive animals can be touched or petted.

normally gloomy all the time might be described as a "depressive," or someone who seems to have uncontrollable energy and is always on the go as "manic."

Do emotions have a future?

Strong emotions are as common today as they ever were. People still experience the joys of achievement, possession, marriage, love and children, and the sorrows of parting, illness and death. The survival of emotions in modern society is ensured because they reflect the reality of dangers, losses, pleasures, pains and challenges.

In addition, emotions persist because of the genetic basis evidenced by the similar facial expressions of emotion in diverse cultures, by consistent patterns of emotional development and by studies of twins. These suggest that our temperaments are inherited (see *Ch 12*). It is well-known that animals can be bred for specific temperamental qualities. Research has also shown that there are well-established neural pathways in the brain that are associated with the emotions.

If the controlling forces for our emotions are in our genes, emotional changes in whole populations can only occur slowly and over a number of generations. It would take an almost unimaginable change in living patterns and environment to rearrange the gene pools that determine the emotional tendencies of future generations. **RP**

Emotional Development

AS ADULTS, even though we have learned not to give too much of ourselves away, we experience an extraordinarily rich range of emotions.

Yet all this complexity begins with a baby whose first emotional reaction is to cry; indeed, other than a gurgling contentment at mealtimes, this appears to be our only emotional reaction for the first few weeks of our lives.

The way something so primitive becomes so intricate and complex is the major part of our emotional development. We develop emotionally, however, for the whole span of our lives.

Early smiling and early crying

If you pick up and play with a young baby, your reward will often be a smile. This happens at such an early age that it is probably a built-in reaction. A baby seems to be programmed to smile at the sight of a human face, and this reaction first occurs at about eight weeks of age. However, it is equally clear that the way we smile can be changed by our experiences. A quick look around shows us that some people smile much more than others, and all in their own distinctive styles. Children vary too. If they are brought up in an environment where they are not much encouraged to

STAGES OF EMOTIONAL DEVELOPMENT

■ *Even from birth infants show consistent patterns of expression that can be recognized as emotions. More than 100 patterns have been identified, including facial expressions such as closed-mouth smiles, pouts and grimaces, as well as noises ranging from laughs and squeals to soft wails. The "social" smile, produced in response to attention by the mother or other caregiver, begins at 6-8 weeks and develops over the first year of life.*

Only a limited number of stimuli will provoke a change in the facial expression of a very young child. For example, a high-pitched sound more readily prompts a smile than a low-pitched one and humanlike sounds are preferred to pure tones.

A baby's earliest smiles are produced by a single muscle, but as the pattern of interaction between the child and the mother, and between the child and the environment, becomes established, so the smiles become more complex. Changes in the baby's facial expressions combined with movements of the head or body communicate its needs and desires to the mother. The positive emotions of pleasure and joy develop into love by about the age of three.

Negative emotions develop in parallel and also increase in complexity – from distress, anger and fear through disgust, envy and jealousy. Distress caused by separation from the *mother begins at three or four months, becoming more acute over the next couple of years. At about six months, the presence of strangers causes distress. This tendency reaches a peak at eight months, but then gradually declines.*

These early developmental patterns are remarkably consistent for normal children and for children who are born blind or deaf, as well as among children from diverse cultural backgrounds. Identical twins are closer in their emotional behavior than other siblings.

Research has suggested that three types of attachment influence the development of the emotions. The earliest of these involves trust and a bond of dependency between the mother and infant (see p142). Next, as the infant matures, the mother encourages separation and greater reliance on play with other children – the "peer affectional system" – through which the child begins to acquire the basic social skills that will be needed in adulthood. Finally, relationships with the opposite sex become important – the "heterosexual affectional system" – and the individual learns about dominance behavior, courting and social and sexual behavior.

In the course of development, more and more events serve as emotional stimuli – criticisms, presents, teachers' comments, money and so on. At the same time, the emotions become increasingly complex and serve deeper purposes. **RP**

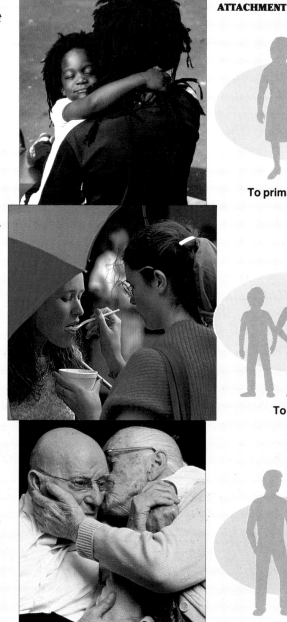

THREE KINDS OF ATTACHMENT

To primary caregiver

To friends

To intimate partner

A lifelong process, our emotional development transforms our infantile reactions into the adult's intricate system of communication. Its early course can profoundly affect our ability to interreact and form relationships.

smile, as used to be the case in institutional homes, then they simply stop smiling. In fact, in extreme cases, this type of upbringing can lead to emotional apathy and a withdrawal from social contact.

Like smiling, crying also seems to be built-in. Yet it too can be changed by our experiences. There are two quite distinct types of crying in young children. The first – and the one that often occurs at the moment of birth – is reflexive, an automatic reaction to pain or extreme discomfort, the most common cause being hunger. Later, young children learn a different kind of crying – crying to get attention or to be given something. If you listen carefully to a baby, you will hear distinct cries of pain and of frustration.

Becoming attached to a caregiver

It may still be uncertain how much our emotions depend on our genes and how much on the environment, but at least it is clear that most of them exist in primitive form by about the age of two, and that they depend very much on the attachments that develop between us and our parents – particularly our mothers, as it is usually the mother who spends most time with the developing child. Two lines of research have pointed to the importance of this attachment. The first and best known is on the social and emotional development of rhesus monkeys, which involved rearing young monkeys with surrogate "mothers." Some of the "mothers" were made of wire and some of wire covered with cloth. The monkeys with cloth mothers developed normally but those with wire-only mothers became emotionally disturbed. This seems to show that the basis for the formation of the first emotional attachment in life comes from having a warm and physically comforting mother.

We have to bear in mind that a child's emotions may develop in a very different way from those of young animals. Certainly, our emotions are far more varied and complex, as the second important line of research has shown. This was conducted among normal families, in institutions and even in the more artificial surroundings of the laboratory. It showed that some children who were permanently separated from their mothers soon after birth, without adequate

PATTERNS OF ATTACHMENT

■ *Psychologists have observed that children's attachment to their mothers follow three typical patterns when they are put into strange surroundings.*

Children aged about one year to 18 months who are secure are calm and easy when their mothers are there. They play well and are friendly to strangers. If the mother leaves they become upset and quickly go to her for comfort when she returns. About two-thirds of children are like this.

Mildly insecure children (about one-quarter) appear detached from their mothers, not noticing whether or not they are in the room. They are as easily comforted by strangers as by their mother.

Very insecure children (about one-tenth) are very anxious in strange situations, stay close by their mothers and become most upset if their mothers go away. When she returns they seem to experience a mixture of fear and anger.

■ **Secure attachment** *to parents. LEFT Responsive mothering promotes a stable emotional bond – observable at about 8 months – that will contribute to a child's later stability, self-* *reliance and confidence in relationships. ABOVE An infant may show attachment later to a father who is not the primary caregiver, but the basis for this can be established early.*

Children who have working mothers are often more emotionally stable than those whose mothers stay at home. Provided the substitute care is good, they are more independent and sociable, and may perform better at school.

replacements, quickly developed serious emotional disturbances. Also, by as early as six months, attachments become so strong that any breaking of them can lead to quite severe emotional damage. Adoption should occur in the first rather than second six months of life.

The early pattern of attachment is very important to a child's later emotional development. Consequently, insensitive or unresponsive mothering – or perhaps an inborn difficulty for the baby in forming a happy relationship with its mother – can lead to insecure attachment. The child may become socially withdrawn and less able to form new relationships. Such children also become frustrated and angry, and typically do not persist at solving problems.

Fathers too are vitally important at this stage. In the traditional family, the father generally provides more fun and excitement than the mother, although it is the mother who is turned to for comfort. Also, of course, other children of the same age provide examples of qualities such as generosity, which are important to a child's emotional development. Indeed, as with experimental monkeys, companions of the same age can in some circumstances make up for a lack of adult attention. What is critical to children's emotional development is that there should be some person to whom they can become attached in the first months of life.

How important are social influences?

It is, of course, very difficult to work out what someone else is feeling. With a child or baby this is especially difficult. Yet in spite of this, there does seem to be clear evidence that emotions develop in a surprisingly regular way. Development begins with attachment and the social smile, which sets the scene for a link between the infant and familiar people and places. After this, the way the emotions unfold depends on what happens in the child's thinking processes and motivations.

Research has now shown that infants from the age of three to six months learn to imitate their mother's facial expressions – they are especially responsive to body language at this age.

This means that most of the subtle emotional expressions we know so well begin in a simple, primitive form in the first few months of our children's lives. It also means that parents have a profound and probably long-lasting effect on their children's developing emotions. Parents can make or mar their children's future social and emotional lives by

▲ **Attachments to peers** *gradually begin to supplement attachments to caregivers. Small children such as these in a Soviet day nursery, however, are still many years away from being able to rely on each other, rather than on parents and teachers, for dependable emotional support.*

WORKING MOTHERS

■ *What are the emotional effects on a child of having a working mother? The answer depends to some extent on what happens to the child instead of being with its mother. So long as the substitute care offers good emotional support, children seem to benefit from having a working mother. Young girls in particular become more independent and better socially adjusted and even do better academically. Placed in the same situation, boys are also more independent and better adjusted socially than they would otherwise have been, but they do not share the same academic advantages. This depends, however, on social class. Sons of working-class working mothers do seem to gain academically.*

It might be thought that the daily separations of the mother and her young child would upset the emotional links between them, which could be unfortunate for the emotional development of both, not just the child's. However, although children who stay with a daycare teacher may form bonds with that teacher, they still prefer their mothers, especially when they are upset.

Socially, children who attend daycare centers gain over those who do not. They tend to be more self-sufficient, more cooperative, more socially at ease, although they are also less polite and more aggressive than those who do not. Of course, this is only so if the daycare center is stimulating. If the center is dull, depressing and lacking in stimulation, the child will suffer emotionally.

their expressions, body language and general responsiveness and affection.

It is easy to see the specific emotions gradually appear in the first two years of a child's life: excitement, pleasure, distress, wariness, fear, anger and, after these, the more complex emotions such as envy and jealousy. Certainly, after the age of about two, emotions become more involved and more intricately bound up with a wider and wider range of social events. Increasingly, it is how the child sees and thinks about the world that makes the difference. It is therefore very important that, as children grow older and begin to find out how well they can cope with things, their parents devise situations that encourage them to test themselves against their social world, so that they can safely experience emotions such as frustration and anger, interest, excitement and pleasure.

What do animals teach us about ourselves?

If you talk to people with pets, particularly dogs, you will find that they "know" that some animals are born more emotional than others – and they are right in this. Dog breeders actually select emotional traits. We also know that some animals are born with specific inbuilt fears. For example, birds brought up in nests fear natural predators such as hawks. It is almost impossible not to imagine that fears are similarly built into us – perhaps at least a fear of the unknown, or more specifically a fear of the dark.

One of the most interesting ideas to spring from the study of animal emotions is that of *critical periods*. This is the notion that there are periods of time in the lives of young animals when they are especially sensitive to social events. These are times when, for instance, if they are removed from familiar places or familiar animals of their own kind, they become very emotionally distressed . There are also times

that are ideal for forming emotional bonds or experiencing things that will make them into more or less emotional creatures as adults. Photographs of the rather eccentric-looking Nobel Prize-winner and student of animal behavior Konrad Lorenz show him walking around followed by a group of goslings. This came about through that critical period very early in a goose's life when it is programmed to follow the first moving object it sees. This is usually its mother but in this case it was Lorenz, who was out to prove a point and became stuck with what are called "imprinted" ducks. It

PLAYING AT EMOTIONS

■ *Playing at emotions helps children to develop them. Acting out roles in which play characters are angry, determined, brave, caring and concerned, frightened, sad or joyful is a way of exploring and understanding the range of feelings involved in human interaction. Early play at giving each other emotional support and loyalty prepares the way for the mature friendships that will follow in later years.*

After the age of two, emotions become intimately bound up with a wide range of social activities. Playing at these activities helps a child to deal with increasingly complex feelings by providing safe ways of practicing emotional expression.

may be that human infants imprint in some similar way.

Another strand of work on emotional development in animals is based on experiments with young rats. The rats were given the essentials of life, and then provided with one extra experience each day, for example, being picked up and stroked for a few minutes. It did not seem to matter what extra experiences the young animals were given – any attention, even an occasional mild electric shock, made them into less timid, less fearful, generally less emotional adults. If humans are at all like animals, the lesson is clear: any attention that can be given to a child will make it calmer as an adult.

Emotions beyond childhood

Emotional development does not end at the age of two, of course, but goes on increasing in richness, though as we get older we are discouraged from showing our feelings. What is becoming increasingly clear to psychologists is that those of us who had childhoods in which the emphasis was on hiding our feelings are especially careful to conceal them as adults, and experience much more anxiety than people who have been brought up to be more expressive. This again suggests how important very early experiences are for our emotional lives. Our ability to control our social relations tends to improve with age, so adult emotion is probably more conscious, variable and dependent on who we are with and what we are doing than emotion in children. However, although adults hide most of their feelings, this does not mean that they are not experiencing them. Elderly people in particular report that they find others disapprove of them expressing emotion, and there is evidence to support their claim. It is somehow disturbing to see an older person without full control over emotional expression, but we only feel like this because of the way in which we have been brought up ourselves. It depends on what our culture expects us to believe.

It is very likely that, although our emotional expressions become more and more inhibited with increasing years, our actual feelings change very little. There is no reason why the 70-year-old should not be as helpless with love or anger or sorrow as the 17-year-old. **KTS**

PLAY IS A SERIOUS MATTER

■ Children work hard at play, treating it as a serious business. Why? What are they getting out of it? One thing seems to be that children use their play as a way of learning how to deal with the world, and in particular with things that would otherwise be emotionally overwhelming. For example, if a young boy is slightly frightened by his father, then it might just help to walk up and down wearing his father's slippers or banging something with his hammer. It is almost as if the child is thinking: if I am like him and he is like me, he won't hurt me because I wouldn't hurt myself.

Play and emotion are probably related in a number of ways. For example, when children become emotional about something, they are likely to start playing, although not of course if their emotion is so extreme as to make it impossible. If the children are experiencing the emotions of interest and enjoyment, their play is likely to be even better than before. On the other hand, if children's play is blocked or thwarted in some way, they are likely to become angry or anxious. Children who are frustrated with a broken toy or by another child who takes something they are playing with seem instantly to regress to the emotions they used to experience when they were younger.

Another of the interesting links between play and emotion comes from a mixture of fear and excitement. This raises the interest of a child considerably. It is very similar with adults. Many of the things we do in our leisure time involve the seeking out of a kind of "safe danger" – most outdoor sports are like this and even competition itself has an element of this about it. Of course, if fear becomes too much, play will stop. Play seems, then, to be important to us all, whatever age we might be, as it helps us cope with and even enhance our emotional lives.

▲ **Adult play.** *Like the child who is well balanced, the well-balanced adult finds an outlet in play for imagination and emotional impulses. Playing at exercising control over a railway empire can be practice for taking a controlling view of your real-life destiny.*

DEVELOPMENTAL TURNING POINTS

■ There are some emotional crises that everyone faces, simply by growing up and growing old. They are almost always crises for others as well – for the parents of the growing child, for the love object of the adolescent or young adult who is experiencing a crisis of intimacy, or for the children and marriage partner of the developing adult. The American psychoanalyst Eric Erikson sees eight major turning points in life's journey.

TRUST VERSUS MISTRUST

The first crisis occurs during the first year of life when the baby develops a balance between trust and mistrust as a result of an interplay between its own temperament and its environment.

A healthy baby with parents who are consistent in meeting its demands is likely to develop a basically trusting nature. On the other hand there is the "difficult" baby with gastrointestinal distress and harried parents who may in addition be tense about their work. They may have been unable to find a reliable person to care for the child and, although they usually respond immediately to its cries they often let it cry itself to sleep. This baby is likely to find the world confusing and unpredictable and may become an anxious and untrusting adult.

There are of course many babies with upset tummies and reliable parents, just as there are those with regular digestive systems and parents who provide the most irregular care. As in all crises, there are many nuances that determine the outcome.

BECOMING INDEPENDENT

The two-year-old battles with life's second crisis – autonomy versus shame and doubt, where attempts to become an individual can be either nurtured or stifled by parents. At three years old children reach the third turning point, where they start to develop their initiative but can also be made to feel guilty about their attempts at independence.

During this time (until about six years old) the child is struggling with concepts of "me," "mine," "I can do," "I'm good," "I'm bad." At the same time the parent is wondering why Lisa must get into everything, why Jimmy says "No" to every suggestion. Should Johnny be allowed to play with his food? Why does he so often have a tantrum at the market? Why does Jane insist on taking her filthy blanket to school? The mind of the preschool child may seem an enigma.

These are normal crises in most families but they can result in stress for parent and child when the parent cannot tolerate the child's desire to explore and feel competent. It can be equally stressful if the parent sets no limits, and the child is out of control. The child then senses the lack of boundaries and feels anxious about the power he or she may have in the world.

OUTSIDE INFLUENCES

On entering school the child is curious and eager to learn. This fourth stage is an important turning point for the child and the family. Until then most of the child's influences are likely to have come from within the family, especially from the parents. Now, as the child ventures into a new world, he or she comes under the additional influence of teachers and peers.

It has been suggested that a child from a family that is different from the family of his or her peers may be ostracized. "Being different," however, may also help the child gain certain strengths of character if the family is supportive and close knit.

On entering school, the child becomes less dependent on the family as the sole source of emotional security. At this point he or she can develop a sense of competence or inferiority. Most of us can remember a time in school when, having let our minds wander, we were asked a question and were overwhelmed by a feeling of stupidity when we were unable to answer it. A minor incident like this can produce a major emotional response. However, despite the child's anguish over how competent he or she might be, this is often a settled period in the family's life.

ROLE CONFUSION

By contrast, the fifth turning point, adolescence, can be a highly unsettled time for the whole family. Erikson described this crisis, which occurs between the ages of 12 and 18, as one of self-identity and role confusion. Many adolescents are painfully self-conscious, feeling that everyone in the world is looking at them. They consider the smallest blemish "hideous," one hair out of place "gross." Adolescence is also a turning point physically. At no other time is growth so rapid. Sexual maturation occurs, and new sexual feelings are experienced: hot flushes, butterflies in the stomach, unexpected erections, sweaty palms, erotic dreams.

The future, an unknown, can be frightening. No longer a child and preparing for life as an adult, the adolescent wonders who he or she is and "who will I become?" This can lead to role confusion as the adolescent may not be able to piece together from the many possible roles a coherent sense of self. Later in life, as part of the seventh turning point – adjustment to adult life – the "midlife crisis" reflects this earlier storm and stress of adolescence.

The parent's mid-life crisis often occurs at the same time as the adolescent crisis of the child, and can be exacerbated by the adolescent being at the zenith of physical agility and in-

▲ **Both ends of the lifespan.** We develop emotionally from birth to death. Old age brings

EARLY SCH
YEARS

PRE-SCHOOL YEARS

TODDLER YEARS

THE FIRS
YEAR

Eight major turning points mark our emotional development. They require us to cope with new and challenging demands on our self-confidence, our understanding of others and our appreciation of our own abilities to adjust and adapt.

dulging an intellectual bent for sarcasm. Family relationships may be strained and this is a turning point in terms of renegotiating roles of parent and child. For the parent, the crisis is one of productivity and despair, often bringing thoughts of lost dreams – "What have I accomplished?" "Who am I?" "Is that all there is?" The crisis is in truth very similar for both parent and adolescent child. Suicide rates are highest for males between 40 and 45 or in late adolescence.

INTIMACY VERSUS ISOLATION

In between these two turning points, the young adult evolves from the adolescent stage into a crisis of intimacy versus isolation. This is the period when you can begin to establish intimate relationships with other people. However, you may be rejected or the relationship may fail: worrying about the negative possibilities can cause withdrawal from social contact. Nevertheless this is generally the period of partnership formation.

ADJUSTING TO ADULTHOOD

Parenthood, even more than marriage, ushers in life's seventh crisis – adult life with all its attendant responsibilities. Few events bring more novel demands into the lives of young adults. The birth of the first child is actually a critical period in the evolution of the family and in particular for the working woman. For her the consequences of choosing to have a child are often curtailment of activities. She will have less free time and her income and energy will be reduced.

Life is filled with irony. After what may often be great emotional turmoil, a couple makes the decision to have a child or children. Then, some 16-20 years later, they suffer the loss of their children and are faced with the "empty nest." This can be a time of much anxiety and the "mid-life crisis" referred to earlier. It often coincides with the menopause, a time when many women begin to feel they have lost their attractiveness and, without children to care for, their reason for being. However, there is research to suggest that the departure of children from the nest may not be a significant crisis. Rather, it is children who do not leave home "on time" and who do not make normal progress who are more likely to cause their parents stress.

REAPING THE HARVEST

The eighth and final life crisis occurs in old age when the individual looks back on his or her life either with a sense of self-fulfillment and satisfaction or with despair. At this juncture people may feel that they are gaining the benefits of hard work or well-managed relationships. They may take pleasure in the thought that they have made or done something that will live on, or that they have grandchildren who represent new life and survival of the family identity. But they must also come to terms with death. If earlier crises have not been resolved successfully old people may be overwhelmed by a sense of despair, feeling bitter about their lives and unable to face death. **HWR**

ADOLESCENCE

YOUNG ADULTHOOD

MIDDLE YEARS

OLD AGE

practical and emotional challenges and new relationships. Grandparents can play an important role in the lives of their grandchildren whom they see as guarantors of continuity.

LIVING WITH AN INTERNAL PARENT

■ *When we are stressed, anxious or afraid, our instinctive response is to reach for comfort from other people, like a child who is frightened by a nightmare and automatically runs to its parents.*

This response is good both for children and for adults. Studies of abused children or children involved in natural disasters have found that those who seek comfort from adults suffer less pain and adjust more successfully. Adults who express their troubles to a confidant seem to be at less risk of illness than those who bottle up their emotions (see Ch 23).

However, when children turn to parents, they do not always receive the most effective support, nor the best example of how to deal with stress. Many people do not completely grow out of nonadaptive strategies that they learn in this way. They internalize a parental voice that tells them for the rest of their lives how to respond to emotion. Some psychological therapists make this internal parent a focus of their attempts to help people to understand themselves. Here are the main types of internal parent that they identify. Your own might combine features of more than one of these.

THE CRITICAL PARENT

A child internalizes this type of parent by growing up in a very strict environment with rigid rules about when to accept emotion and what emotions to accept. For example, the real parent criticizes the child for feeling afraid. Later the adult's internalized critical parent suppresses fear and it may become anger.

Parents whose emotional control is poor – for example alcoholics or schizophrenics – also tend to produce in their children a critical internal parent. The child vows not to be like the parent and develops independently an internal voice

■ **Nurturing parents** *allow children to express their emotions and to seek help when necessary. It is of advantage to adopt this as your own internal parenting style.*

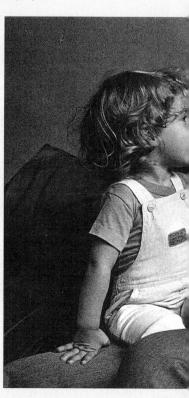

The CRITICAL INTERNAL PARENT tells us to control our emotions → We turn fears and anxieties into anger and depression

The GIVING INTERNAL PARENT tells us to help others and suppress our own needs → We feel but hide resentment about the demands others make

The DISCONTENTED INTERNAL PARENT tells us that life is unsatisfactory → Situations that should fill us with anticipation make us gloomy

The DISAPPOINTED INTERNAL PARENT tells us that we are unsatisfactory → We feel that we and others are unworthy

The NURTURING INTERNAL PARENT tells us that we deserve love and comfort → We express our emotions freely, receive social support and solve problems

> *In a sense, we all have within us an "internal parent" who tells us how to respond to emotional stress. This internal voice tends to reflect the example that our real parents set when reacting to our emotional needs and to their own.*

that controls all emotions. With a critical internal parent, you tend to demand constant high performance and perfection of yourself. This may make drugs and alcohol tempting as they allow some relief and pleasure. The favorite emotion of someone with this internal parent is anger. The anger often turns inward to depression.

THE GIVING PARENT

People with this internal parent are usually unaware of the fact that the only time they feel connected to others is when they are giving. They choose a partner and friends who will take and take but offer little in return.

Excessive giving leads to exhaustion, resentment and depression. The giving internal parent allows you neither to ask for care nor to get angry at others.

Unlike people with the critical internal parent, who refuse to allow themselves medical help, those who internalize the giving parent will seek help if physical

symptoms begin to threaten their capacity for giving.

THE DISCONTENTED PARENT

In some families the parents are successful, healthy, have a supportive partner and a good job – they have everything but happiness. They are complainers and usually were raised by one or more parents who were chronic worriers. They teach their children to be so negative that no excitement or anticipation can be experienced and the need to face choices or decisions leads only to depression and anxiety.

THE DISAPPOINTED PARENT

This kind of parent may be extremely successful but feels disappointed with their child, from whom they demand constant perfection. Also in this category are parents who see themselves as failures and are disappointed with themselves and with everyone else. The child in either case has a built-in sense of disappointment and feels discouraged and ineffec-

tual whenever facing danger or opportunity for success.

As adults people with disappointed internal parents may even make poor vocational and romantic choices almost as though they are trying to insure that they will live a life of disappointment. They have what psychiatrists call a "self-defeating personality." Drug addicts and their partners often have the disappointed internal parent. Rather than seeing her life as full of possibilities, a woman with this internal parent will become upset, irritated and annoyed about her situation when faced with the choice whether to be a career woman or a homemaker.

SEX DIFFERENCES

In most Western cultures the critical parent is predominantly male and the giving parent predominantly female. This helps to explain some of the differences in the emotional problems of the sexes. Men traditionally have more problems with anger and violence, perhaps partly as a result of the critical parent. When afraid, men often feel they are not permitted to admit it or ask for help – they are expected to suppress their fears and worries. Anger and aggression may result. This chronic anger contributes to men's higher incidence of heart disease, suicide and child or wife abuse.

The critical parent insists on the domination and control of self and of others. Women seem to be more willing to risk the loss of control that is part of loving and needing someone. Feeling a lack of control, the male critical parent takes refuge in overwork, anger and criticism.

The giving parent dreads selfishness and anger. If your role in life is to give, to provide emotional support and be understanding and compassionate, anger and self-centered behavior are unacceptable.

Women with this internal parent often belong to the older generation. They devote their lives to taking care of their husband, children and friends. Uncomfortable about asking for care, they may turn to food for comfort and become overweight. The depression that results is caused by resentment turned inward and by a repressed fear of asking for love. The giving parent demands that giving to partner and children should not diminish even if the woman has a career. Recent generations of women are more likely to develop the critical internal parent. The greater number of options open to them means more pressure to do everything perfectly.

THE NURTURING PARENT

Many children are lucky enough to have parents who allow them to feel their emotions without guilt and to seek comfort when they need it. Instead of suppressing pain and turning it into anger or depression, the loving and positive internal parent that the child takes with them into adult life will allow pain to be felt as sadness and fear, and allow the adult to follow the best and most natural way of responding to a crisis: asking friends for comfort, letting sadness and anger out, and allowing rest and constructive distractions. People who do not pride themselves on being stoic, on being independent and on keeping their problems to themselves, but who instead ask others for support and advice, have a milder experience of distress and resolve their difficulties more successfully.

It is not, however, essential that you should have had a 100 percent nurturing parent in your childhood in order to develop a nurturing internal parent. People are resilient, and for thousands of years, while loving and staying loyal to their parents, they have sought new and better ways of thinking and of living. **RM**

Understanding Your Feelings

WE TEND to think that knowing how someone else feels is never quite the same as knowing how we feel ourselves. When *you* experience an emotion, it may seem, you are the only person who can have any real knowledge of what is happening to you – others can know in a sense, you might feel inclined to say, but only at second hand, and they will always have to accept on trust that what you say about your feelings is true and the behavior you use to display them is genuine.

Against this view, however, stands the fact that people often have difficulty interpreting their own emotions. Sometimes, others know better what we are feeling than we do ourselves. They are able to interpret our feelings by helping us to assess what we really think about the situation we are in and helping us to realize that we feel the same impulses that almost anyone else would who thinks in the same way. They might help us to see that we are afraid, for example, by bringing home to us (however little we may wish to admit it) that we know we are in a dangerous situation and want to get out of it. They help us to understand whether we are in love by talking to us about what we expect in a romantic partner, what we see in the person we are involved with, and what we feel motivated to do for that person. Emotions, then, are not simple things that we experience alone, but complex elements of the life we share.

The raw materials of emotion

Experts researching emotions see in them three closely related strands. First, emotions of any intensity involve physical arousal. Second, emotions involve judgments and beliefs. Third, they involve behavior.

Some researchers take the view that *all* emotion involves physiological arousal: if there is emotion, it should be possible to measure in the laboratory some increase in heart rate, breathing, sweating and muscle tension. Does this mean that interpreting an emotion always involves interpreting a physical feeling? This seems particularly disputable. No one can feel joyful, excited or stressful emotions (see *Ch 21*) such as anger or anxiety, without a quickening of the pulse, but we do experience a range of calm and tranquil feelings at the opposite end of the scale.

When the body does become aroused, however, we easily give the arousal an emotional interpretation. Examples of this have been demonstrated in experiments. People who are injected with the hormone adrenaline have an increased heart rate, quicker breathing and muscle tremors. It makes them feel very jumpy and twitchy. Volunteers who are given adrenaline injections can be induced to interpret their aroused mood very differently, depending on the circumstances. Left in a waiting room with a stranger who (as part of the experiment) begins to act euphorically (making paper

A quickened pulse, sharper breathing and a sense of alertness may accompany an upsurge in our emotions, but these physiological changes do not tell us which emotion in particular we are feeling. It is what we think that matters most.

airplanes, playing basketball with the wastepaper basket, etc) they tend to become euphoric. Waiting with someone who behaves angrily (complaining, tearing up a question-naire, storming out of the room), they tend to become angry. These effects are not seen in people who have been injected with a harmless salt solution rather than with adrenaline. An effect *is* seen in people whose bodily arousal comes from hard physical exercise. When they are provoked, they react more aggressively than people who have not exercised.

The surprising thing, however, is that the patterns of bodily involvement in emotion are not at all clear. Although anger, fear and happiness seem very different to us, each of them lifts the body into much the same state, readying it for

whatever action may be appropriate. Even with very sophis-ticated measurements, experts have not managed to find consistent patterns of arousal for specific emotions.

The impact of beliefs

In real life, the interplay between arousal and our percep-tions of the world around us is complex. Perception is usu-ally a key factor in our becoming aroused, not just in our finding an explanation for the arousal. Judging a situation to be dangerous, outrageous or delightful both arouses our emotions and gives a name to what we feel: fear, anger or joy. In fact, it is very difficult to perceive anything in the world about us without interpreting it – without trying to judge what it is and whether it is likely to be good, bad, dan-gerous, safe, interesting or unimportant. Of particular im-portance are *attributions* – judgments of who or what has caused the situation that we encounter. Your personal style of attribution (for example, whether you always blame yourself when things go wrong) can have a profound impact on your emotional life (see *Ch 26*).

Perceptual judgment seems even to affect how much *sensation* we feel. Dogs experimentally reared in isolation, without the opportunity to learn such basics as the avoid-ance of fire, will sniff curiously at a lighted match, placing the nose dangerously close. Normal dogs recoil with yelps of pain.

From the point of view of distinguishing one emotion from another, the key question seems to be what you feel like doing with your aroused body: do you feel like running away in fear, fighting angrily, or working or playing enthu-siastically at the activity to hand? Our expressions of strong emotions definitely signal more than the mere fact that we are aroused. They show what we think about the object we have found arousing: for example, we see it as threatening

151

◄ **Different reactions to the same situation** *show in the faces of two friends as they ride the big dipper. The girl on the right feels an enjoyable exhila-ration, but her companion is beginning to interpret her own state of excitement as fear. People of the same age and cultural background often have different emotional responses to a situation, because temper-amental factors and past expe-rience lead to differences in the way we assess what is happening.*

◄ **Moments of uncertainty** *TOP LEFT usually leave us equally unsure of what to do, of what we should think, and of how we feel. Judgment, emotion and action intimately reflect each other.*

◄ **A high state of arousal** *BOTTOM LEFT demands an expla-nation, and this preacher com-municates both arousal and explanation to his audience. Few of them will doubt that they are moved because of the message, and the message will consequently have a greater impact on their lives than if it had been delivered in a more sober style.*

Beliefs and judgments give our emotions specific flavors. This helps to explain why our feelings can change so quickly, without any corresponding changes in our physiological state, and why repressed feelings have a way of flooding back.

and dangerous (fear), threatening but possible to oppose (anger), or nonthreatening and very welcome (pleasure) (see *Ch 20*).

Interpreting our emotion may be mainly a question of getting clear in our own minds the significance we have attached to the object of emotion. This may very often be unproblematical, but in cases of self-deception or of very involved and potentially inconsistent thinking, it can be difficult to understand what our own feelings are.

Internal organs are neither sensitive enough nor fast enough to be the seat of our complex, fast-changing emotions. Judgments, however, can be virtually instantaneous, and so can account for the speed with which some emotional experiences plunge us into gloom or lift the spirits with great urgency. It is also the subtle differences between judgments and beliefs that produce the subtle differences between emotions.

They also help to account for individual differences in our emotional responses. Two people in the same situation, who have equally sensitive nervous systems, may nevertheless feel very different emotions (and different intensities of emotion) because they have had different experiences in the past, have different expectations, different systems of belief and different needs.

The persistence of beliefs and judgments helps to explain why repressed emotions have a way of flooding back. You may perceive that you have been offended in a way that matters but force yourself to stay calm and show friendly behavior to a rude neighbor. If you do not have convincing reasons for revising the judgment that you have been badly

treated, however, its frustrated emotional expression may build up to the point where a completely inappropriate person becomes the victim of your anger.

Emotions in relationships

Some of the most difficult emotions to fathom are the feelings we have for other people. This is because relationships involve such a complex meshing of the past and present thoughts and behavior of those involved. Also (and depending on how significant the relationship is) it is because our interests are so greatly affected. We do not easily admit that we feel jealous because this may imply that we are more dependent than our pride can accept.

A particular problem for many is the question "Am I really in love?" It can be a confusing one when television and romantic novels so often present an image of love as a state of arousal. This is to overlook many other dimensions of the feeling. You can love someone without feeling intensely about them every moment. What matters most is how you perceive your relationship and the motivations that this perception inspires in you.

We often hide from ourselves the resentment we feel about a partner in a relationship, and we do not face up to it until it explodes in a full-blown crisis. This kind of internal emotional conflict can usually be traced back to a conflict of beliefs. In the excitement of romance people can make themselves blind to anything in their partner that might be

◀ **Solitary reflection on how you feel** *about your relationship is seldom as illuminating as talking to your partner or a friend. You may find it possible to reassess your own expectations in constructive ways when you try to articulate them.*

▶ **Conflicting feelings** *lie behind most of our overindulgences. Knowing that you are breaking a diet or jeopardizing your health creates a sense of inward dissatisfaction. Solutions may include blinding yourself to your inconsistencies or bringing your aims and your actions into line.*

considered a fault. Yet gradually, as the excitement wears off, they begin to notice things that do not match many of the beliefs they in fact have about what it should be like to share a life with another person. In some degree the disappointed partner does not voice these concerns because they can be very difficult to articulate, especially for people who come from a family that does not easily express needs. Also the disappointed partner does not want to create conflict in the relationship. In addition, he or she may find it hard to believe that they are dissatisfied even in small ways with the behavior of someone they love – the common view is that loving someone means considering them ideal. As

the disappointment builds and they find it more and more dissonant (see box) to behave in a committed way toward someone who does not fulfill their needs, they may suddenly announce to themselves that they are no longer in love.

It is much better to investigate the issues at an earlier stage – especially in the relationship formation stage – but even during a crisis in a relationship it is worth asking a friend or your partner to help you to spell out the conflicting thoughts behind your conflicting emotions. Your partner will find it easier to make you feel fulfilled when your needs are known, and your expectations themselves may benefit from constructive reconsideration. **KTS**

HOW WE DEAL WITH INCONSISTENCY

■ *You may have particular difficulty interpreting your own feelings when you fail to maintain a harmony between your beliefs and your actions. Psychologists give the name "cognitive dissonance" to the anxiety we feel on perceiving such inconsistencies. There are three ways of*

reducing this kind of conflict. First, you could abandon either your actions or your beliefs to bring them into line. The obvious solution in the case of someone who smokes and believes that smoking is harmful would be to stop smoking. Alternatively, you could stop

reading about the harmful effects of smoking.

Second, you could try to swamp your beliefs with counterarguments. For instance, you might say to yourself: "My father smoked like a chimney and lived to the age of 95."

Finally, you might play down

the importance of the whole issue, so that although the dissonance is still there, it does not seem to matter so much: "We've all got to go sometime, and it might as well be through doing something enjoyable."

Dissonance is a matter of degree and is at its strongest when there are few good reasons for acting in the way that you do. This was shown in an experiment in which each volunteer was persuaded to spend an hour engaged in a very boring task, then to tell the next volunteer that it had been very interesting. The pay for this was either $1 or $20. All the volunteers did as requested, and later they were asked how much they had actually enjoyed the task. Interestingly, those who had been paid $1 said that they had enjoyed the task much more than those who had been paid $20.

According to the theory of cognitive dissonance, those who were paid $20 felt they had a reason for lying as requested. However, those that were paid only $1 had no real excuse for going along with the experimenter and lying, but they had done so. This made them uncomfortable and produced the motivation to change their attitudes, memories and thoughts in order to bring them all into line. It was as if they were thinking, "I must have enjoyed it more than I seemed to at the time, because I'm not the sort of person who would lie for $1."

153

How Moods Come and Go

EMOTIONS are feelings, often lasting for just moments. Think of the rapid succession of them that you experience as you watch the news on television: perhaps anticipation, then alarm, then curiosity on hearing what the main stories will be; then pleasure, then anger, then mirth on learning the full details of each.

Feelings that last, or that keep recurring, match our *moods*. A mood is a temporary disposition to have a certain kind of feeling. For example, you may be in an angry mood when you are watching the news. You will still feel many emotions, but your anticipation, curiosity, pleasure and mirth will be considerably dampened, and your reaction to things that give you negative feelings will be stronger than it is when your mood is better. When your mood is angry, you may also react with quite different emotions than you usually do – feeling disgust about a particular news item instead of the amusement you would feel on another occasion. You may fail to be moved by something that would otherwise make you glad.

It is clearly an advantage to be in the right mood for the occasion. If you have to fight, it is better to be in an angry mood (so long as it is not a blindly angry mood) than a frightened one, and, most of the time, we would prefer to be in a good enough mood to enjoy the advantages that we have, to notice the good as well as the bad in people, and to notice the opportunities that surround us to live more effectively. What, then, affects our moods, and how is it possible to manage them?

The way people behave and what they seem to think of us – especially what *we* think of ourselves – are major determinants of our moods, and our personalities can influence the moods to which we are prone (see *Ch 26*). However, impersonal determinants of moods also affect us – aspects of our physical surroundings (such as the weather),

◄ **Environment and mood.** *TOP LEFT An absent friend may be the main reason for feeling down on a rainy day, but the weather too makes its contribution. BOTTOM LEFT A release from work pressures and a stimulating change of routine help to explain the sense of well-being that we have on vacation. The locations we choose for our holidays also matter. Negative ions in sea breezes, and warm, sunny weather all enhance mood, though excessive heat can cause irritability and even aggression.*

► **Creating an ambience.** *For a festive event, a festive mood; crowded streets, decorative lighting, bright costumes and energetic dancing set the tone of the April fair in Seville, Spain. Dressing up and being with friends who are enjoying themselves are stimulating in their own right, but noise, bright lights and intense colors can greatly enhance the effect.*

Our constantly changing feelings reflect moods that may persist for hours – or even days. To what extent are they affected by our surroundings, the weather or the season, stimulants, depressants and our own body chemistry?

mood-altering substances, our own body chemistry. We cannot always control the way we feel, but awareness of these factors may help us to avoid unwelcome swings of mood.

The impact of the environment

Outside temperature, wind speed, barometric pressure, humidity, rain, fog, thunderstorms and even clouds have all been blamed for making us feel the way we do. Phases of the moon, sunspots and the effect of high altitudes have also received attention. The effect of seasonal changes in the number of daylight hours may be another factor in determining how we feel (see box).

The scientific evidence for a link between most environmental factors and mood is not strong. Researchers have tried to correlate changes in specific, easily measured events that reflect mood – suicide rates, hospital admissions for psychiatric disorders, and crime (especially homicides) – with environmental phenomena, but they have failed to establish a clear relationship.

However, a link has been demonstrated between mood and two particular aspects of the environment. The first is between the feeling of well-being and the type of electrical charge in the atmosphere. Generally speaking, the presence of negative charges – in the form of negative ions – has a favorable effect on mood. The absence of negative ions and a prevalence of positive ones have both been linked to headaches, irritability, increases in blood pressure and low or depressed mood.

The most common example of a change in ion pattern that affects mood occurs with winds of the type called the "Fohn" in Switzerland, the "Sharav" in the Middle East, the "Sirocco" arising over the Sahara and affecting the Mediterranean coast of Europe, the "Mistral" sweeping down the Rhone valley in France, and the "Chinook" occurring on the eastern side of the Rocky Mountains in North America. These warm, dry and persistently strong winds follow a weather front in which the electrical charges include an excess of positive ions. Indicators of low mood have been found to increase as these winds begin to blow.

How negative ions affect the body to improve mood is not known, but a commercial industry has now developed to supply negative ionizers for homes and offices, where appliances, equipment and smoking may affect the quality of the

air. An open window may have just as much effect. Waterfalls are an especially good natural source of negative ions.

High altitude is a second area where research has been able to show a clear relationship between mood and environment. Its effects include both physical and emotional symptoms, such as insomnia, listlessness, mental and physical fatigue, poor memory, inability to concentrate or make clear judgments and sometimes irritability or even an exaggerated sense of well-being. Unlike the situation with positive ions, studies have shown that high altitude has a direct effect on the body: the lack of oxygen in the air interferes with the ability of the body cells to carry out essential chemical processes. When moving to a much higher altitude than the one your body is adjusted to, you may need a short period of readjustment.

Less scientific but nevertheless important research suggests that other environmental factors have an effect on mood. We are more likely to report feeling happy and satisfied with life as a whole when there is sunshine, moderate warmth and low humidity. For example, market research companies have found it easier to conduct surveys of the general public on sunny days than on gloomy ones. Also, people tend to give higher tips in restaurants when the weather is bright.

Living in a sunny climate, however, does not seem to make us happier than living in a cold and wet one. It seems that we adapt to the prevailing climate and soon become bored if it is always the same. Changes of season, and, especially, an *improvement* in the weather, are welcomed.

Our surroundings can also be important for our mood. Nature can give a sense of peace and tranquillity, and can deepen our feelings of contentment. People seem happiest when they are surrounded by wild, natural countryside. Water scenes can create this feeling, and their appeal has been linked to our evolutionary past. Also important is depth of view: people like to look across an expanse of countryside or water.

Mood-altering substances

The most dramatic temporary effects on mood come from drugs, whether prescribed, legal (for example alcohol) or illicit. An enormous number of substances can alter mood in different ways, but generally they fall into two classes: stimulants ("uppers") and depressants ("downers"). Both types are sometimes prescribed by doctors to relieve stress and anxiety.

The most popular recreational drug is alcohol, a depressant. The widespread belief that it is a stimulant results from the effects it has when taken in low dosages: relaxation and a lessening of inhibitions. However, its depressive physical effects can be profound as the dose increases: the loss of the usual controls on behavior by a slowing down of brain activity can cause aggressive outbursts, and very high doses result in stupor, coma and, finally, death. Drugs such as

► **Social drinking** can be enjoyable and harmless. In small quantities, alcohol slows the nervous system just enough to produce a happy, relaxed mood, promoting sociability. In excessive drinking, the depressant effect of alcohol may release aggression and cause loss of control and judgment. Because alcohol and its chemical derivatives remain in the bloodstream for several hours, mood swings, irritability and loss of concentration may continue long after an initial euphoria. Alcoholics try to stabilize their mood with more alcohol.

Alcohol depresses the nervous system. Nicotine and caffeine stimulate it and rouse the body in general – they can make us more sensitive to irritating stimuli. Drinking more than six cups of coffee a day may increase tension.

nicotine and caffeine increase the body's level of arousal so that stimuli that might otherwise be only mildly annoying are much more likely to become major sources of provocation; a ticking clock is a good example. If you drink more than six cups of coffee a day you risk feeling anxious and tense.

A major problem with trying to analyze the link between drugs and mood is that the effects of chemicals are hard to predict. The reason for this is that moods are the result of a complex interplay between various physical events, both inside and outside the body, and the judgments (see *Ch 18*) we make about them.

Moods and body chemistry

Hormones are chemical messengers, secreted by organs of the body, that are carried in the body fluids to specific tissues that they can affect – tissues whose cell membranes have the right chemical receptors. *Neurotransmitters* are more local, released by nerve cells and received by neighboring nerve cells. Hormones control body formation and growth as well as day-to-day physical functions. Neurotransmitters and certain hormones have a profound effect on our moods.

The impact of hormones on mood is complex and, to a degree, unpredictable. Cortisol, for example, a hormone produced by the adrenal glands, affects nervous tissue, and it can cause depression in some people, occasionally to the point where they may seriously contemplate suicide. Other people – or even the same people at different times – may experience quite the opposite reaction: cortisol may make them feel happy, or at least protect them from feeling ill at ease about something that would otherwise cause them concern. In fact, the latter is the most common reaction when cortisol and similar hormones are given for medical reasons.

It is difficult to study the effects of hormones because, when they are given in unnatural doses as tablets or injections, they may not cause the same reaction as when they are secreted by the body in small, regular pulses. Nevertheless, we can learn something about their effects on mood by observing how people react when they are used as medication, and by observing mood changes in women throughout their menstrual cycle.

Most women will testify to changes in their moods during the month or so between one period and another. These coincide with alterations in the levels of the major female sex hormones, estrogen and progesterone. Both increase at midcycle and then begin to drop to a low point at about the time bleeding begins. This coincidence in itself suggests, though it does not prove, a relationship between hormones and mood.

157

◄ **Making a tense mood worse** *during a break at the Paris Stock Exchange. The relaxing effect of smoking a cigarette is short-lived and deceptive. It relaxes only the anxiety you feel about being without something on which you depend. Overall, tension is greater because the nicotine in tobacco increases physical arousal and contributes to eventual tiredness. Breaking the habit may increase irritability and tension at first, but it allows steadier nerves and greater alertness in the long run.*

Scientific support for this has come from studies of women suffering from premenstrual syndrome (see box), who were given the hormone progesterone during the last few days of their cycle and whose symptoms were dramatically relieved. Other information has emerged from studies of women who reported feeling irritable, quick-tempered or anxious after taking some of the early oral contraceptive pills that contained high levels of the hormone estrogen.

By some estimates, over 200 neurotransmitters may be involved in the day-to-day working of the nervous system.

LIGHT AND DARK

■ *Many people complain of feeling tired and depressed during the winter months. They tend to oversleep, move sluggishly and eat more, especially foods rich in carbohydrates. These low spirits usually begin to lessen with the onset of spring, and energy and the desire to be active returns during the summer months.*

Winter depression, or "seasonal affective disorder" (SAD), involves the hormone melatonin, secreted from the pineal gland in the brain. The gland does not manufacture melatonin in light, and so usually very little is secreted during the day. At night, levels of the hormone peak. In people who suffer from winter depression, the peak times for melatonin secretion change with the season. Exposure to a bright light, equal in power to about ten 100-watt bulbs or more, for up to an hour at both ends of the day, may help to relieve depression by extending the day length.

■ **Working by day and by night.** *ABOVE A bright, sunny office makes a pleasant, tranquil workplace. LEFT Night shifts can affect our moods adversely by allowing production of the hormone melatonin to extend into the daytime as we sleep with curtains drawn. Most artificial nighttime lighting is too weak to halt melatonin production, which normally peaks at 2 or 3am. Adjustment to altered rhythms varies between individuals but may take up to six days. Changing shifts each week allows you little time to adapt. Resulting fatigue and sleeping problems can cause irritability and depression. Changing shifts every three weeks, instead, reduces adjustment difficulties. Disrupted patterns of melatonin release also help to explain jetlag.*

Some people who suffer from depression in winter are able to improve their mood by sitting under a strong light at the beginning and the end of the day: an artificially lengthened day seems to make hormone production more regular.

Only a few have been identified, and the most important of these are dopamine, noradrenaline, serotonin and the endorphins. Noradrenaline and dopamine are closely related and both are involved in arousal – most stimulants have their effect on us by inducing increased secretions of one or the other of these two neurotransmitters, or by imitating their chemical behavior. Depressants such as barbiturates and alcohol induce a decrease.

Serotonin dampens arousal and acts as a natural antidepressant. Evidence suggests that about half of obese people are deficient in serotonin production. The carbohydrate foods that they like to eat in such quantity help to stimulate serotonin production, however, and this is why eating helps to put them in a good mood.

The neurotransmitters known as endorphins are natural painkillers. They suppress arousal and anxiety. Drugs such as morphine and heroin appear to fit the same receptors in cell membranes as endorphins do, and so to substitute for them. **SMH**

PREMENSTRUAL SYNDROME

■ The changes in a woman's feelings, moods and behavior that we now call "premenstrual syndrome" (PMS) have been known at least since the time of the ancient Greeks.

Although it is difficult to be sure exactly how many women suffer from PMS, community surveys indicate that about 80-90 percent notice some premenstrual change and, of these, perhaps 30 percent must make a significant effort to cope with it. About 5 percent of women suffer enough to require some sort of treatment, while 1 percent are severely disabled by its effects.

The most common emotional symptoms of PMS include tenseness and irritability or a depressed or low mood. These are almost inevitably associated with, among other symptoms, breast tenderness, a feeling of bloatedness, headaches and sometimes a craving for sweet or salty foods. Research in 1987 found an increase in impulsiveness during the premenstrual phase in a small sample of women.

Symptoms can start 7-10 days before bleeding, and are not usually relieved until the period commences (see graph RIGHT). This timing is important in deciding whether tension is part of the menstrual cycle or due to another medical problem.

The causes of PMS are not known. One theory suggests that the changes in the levels of the hormones estrogen and progesterone during a

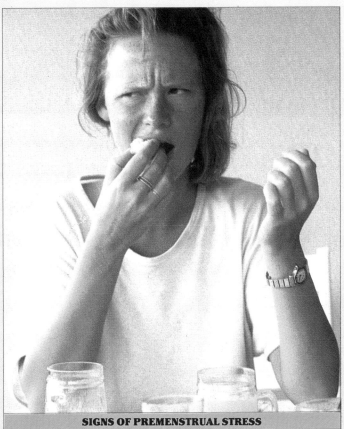

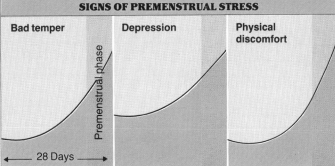

SIGNS OF PREMENSTRUAL STRESS

Bad temper | Depression | Physical discomfort

Premenstrual phase

← 28 Days →

woman's cycle may play a role, but studies carried out on large groups of women have not been able to confirm this. Researchers have also looked into the possibility that low

levels of endorphins, the body's natural painkillers, may be a factor, but, again, studies have not produced reliable results. Others have examined diet and water retention as possible

causes, but without finding any consistent pattern.

Some experts believe that the symptoms of PMS may be maintained or worsened by a stressful environment or other psychological factors such as poor coping skills. For example, negative feelings and ideas can become closely linked with any cyclic or regular event that is accompanied by unpleasantness; these associations can then lead to unpleasant moods – and an increase in pain and discomfort – when the event (in this case, the next bout of premenstrual symptoms) is expected.

There are a number of treatments available for PMS, but whether they are successful is an individual matter. Doctors can prescribe progesterone to alter the balance of the female sex hormones. This treatment suppresses the menstrual cycle so that no periods occur. Some women have been greatly helped by nonprescription remedies, such as evening primrose oil or vitamin B6. (Caution is required even though these substances are available over the counter, as overdoses can be toxic: women have suffered nerve damage by taking too much vitamin B6.) Others have found a combination of exercise and diet helpful, particularly if there is a reduction in sugar intake. However, successful self-management of PMS also involves learning how to cope with and minimize stress, and the best results seem to occur in a supportive environment.

Expressing Your Feelings

FEELINGS may seem very private – known for certain only to you. Ultimately, however, they are inseparable from an outward expression. Feeling angry means feeling like making an angry face, like clenching your fist, like speaking harsh words and perhaps striking a blow. You may hide joy or sadness, but only with effort, and the effort will be one of controlling your urge to behave outwardly in a way that others can recognize as emotional.

Much of the time, it is beneficial *not* to restrain the emotional impulse to express yourself. We have an emotional life chiefly because it makes us send out messages that need to be communicated.

The emotions in our faces

One way of expressing an emotion is to tell someone what you feel. When your feelings are especially subtle or complex this will probably be an important step in making it clear even to yourself what they are (see *Ch18*). However, with basic emotions, it is of relatively little importance whether you use words at all and what words you use. Saying privately to yourself "I feel angry" has much less to do with feeling angry than the urge to hit someone does, and, similarly, when you say "I feel angry" it is difficult for others to see this as an expression of anger unless your facial expression, tone of voice and other nonverbal signals agree. Some researchers estimate that the literal meaning of your words accounts for only 7 percent of the influence that your overall behavior has on people trying to interpret your emotions (see *Ch11*).

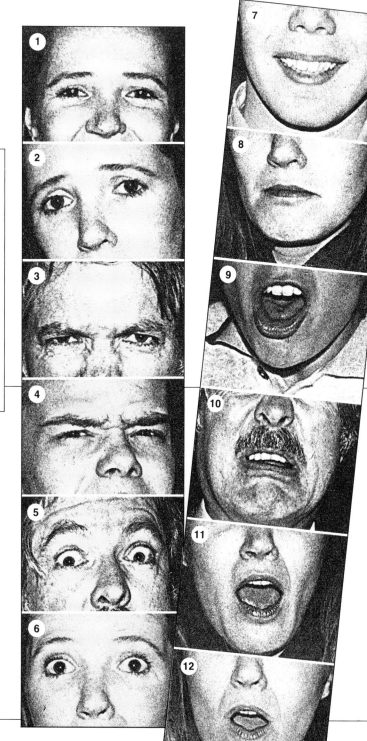

DO EXPRESSIONS CREATE MOODS?

■ *Facial expressions may do more than signal to others how we feel – they may actually influence our own moods. There are nerves directly connecting the muscles of the face to the brain's mood-controlling hypothalamus. Also, contraction of the muscles involved in smiling is known to have an effect on blood flow and temperature within the brain.*

The "facial feedback" theory of emotions dates back to the 19th century, when the Ameri-can philosopher and psychologist William James observed that by composing his facial features, he felt better able to bear the grief he was suffering over the loss of his parents.

Smiles, like yawns, are infectious. Smiling at someone usually prompts them to smile back, even if they are not much in a mood to smile. The physical action of smiling back, however, may itself have the power to alter their mood for the better.

USING THE FACE TO EXPRESS EMOTIONS

■ *We use our intuitive knowledge of spontaneous emotional expressions to send less spontaneous messages when we choose. Frames (1) and (7) show the eyes and the mouth of happiness. In (13) a young woman uses them in a natural but posed expression of pleasure, reinforced by posture – with a friendly forward lean. Frames (2) and (8) are the eyes and mouth of sadness. In (16) a young man poses the mock sorrow that he displays when he wants to warn friends they are being too sarcastic. Frames (3) and (9) show angry eyes and mouth, frame (17) mock anger, while (4), (10) and (14) show disgust: a wrinkled nose is essential. In (5), the eyes of fear have raised lower lids, unlike the eyes of surprise in (6), but in (11) and (12) the mouth of fear and the mouth of surprise are similar. In (15) an attempt to convey anger produces a blend that looks much more like fear. In (18) a young man poses the blend of happiness and surprise he would use to greet guests arriving for a party. Social rules and concern for relationships require us to show pleasure when greeting.*

Your tone of voice and your facial expressions communicate emotions much more convincingly and effectively than words do. Heightened aware-ness of how we tell each other what we feel can improve the quality of relationships.

They estimate that facial expression, by contrast, carries on average 55 percent of your message. The face with its almost infinite variety of expressions is a wonderful trans-mitter of emotion. The more of other people's faces we can see, the better we can interpret what they are feeling.

There is convincing evidence that we are born with our most basic facial expressions of emotion. The evidence for

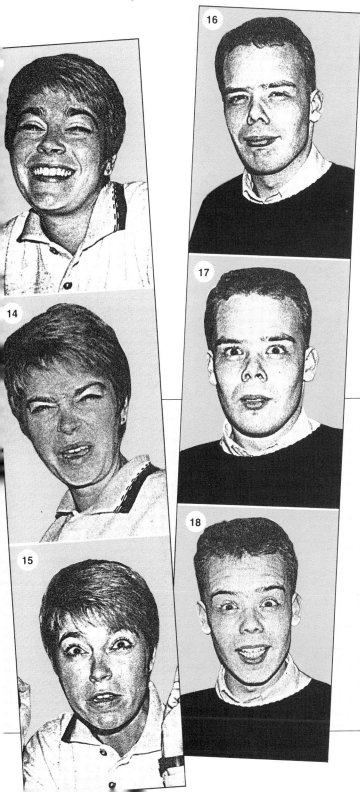

this comes from the observation that facial expressions are very similar across all cultures, and also from studies of people who are blind from birth. At first, their range of facial expressions is the same as that of the sighted. Only later, as other people's facial repertoire increases with experience, do the blind appear slightly less expressive.

Different authorities recognize as few as six and as many as ten basic emotions whose facial expressions are recog-nized in very similar ways across many different cultures. Each basic emotion has a range of intensity, such as that shown diagramatically for eight basic emotions in *Ch16*, and this spectrum of intensity appears in facial expressions. Thus, for example, our looks of attention range from interest to excitement, happy expressions range from enjoyment to joy, surprised faces include startled ones, distressed faces include anguished ones, angry faces can be enraged and the face of fear anything from frightened to terror-stricken.

Our expression of emotion is even more versatile than this, for basic facial expressions are made up in turn of

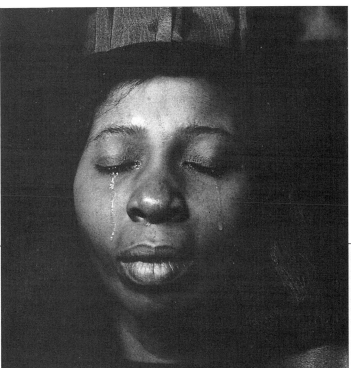

▲ **Letting tears flow** *helps to discharge tension. Analysis of genuinely emotional tears reveals minute quantities of stress-related chemicals not found in the tears we shed over peeled onions. This may help to explain why there is no sense of release when onions make us cry: the relief we feel through genuinely emotional weeping might be the result of a reduced concentration of certain stress chemicals in our blood. Exces-sive control over your emotions may in any event make you inwardly tense, and keep levels of stress chemicals high. This may increase your susceptibil-ity to disease (see p172).*

161

basic elements that can combine in an almost infinite variety of ways. Happy eyes have wrinkles around them, sad eyes have raised brows and lowered upper lids; angry eyes have a penetrating stare with tense lids (sometimes the brows are lowered and drawn together); the eyes of fear have raised lower lids, and the brows are drawn together; surprised eyes are open wide, with raised brows. Any of these eyes can combine with the mouth that usually goes with them (smiling for happiness, downturned for sadness, either pressed together or pushed forward aggressively for anger, open in surprise and fear) – or they can combine with another to make a blend requiring more observant interpretation. You might see sadness in the downturned mouth and at the same time anger in the penetrating eyes of someone you have disappointed. A common blend is anger and disgust: in disgusted anger, the wrinkled nose of disgust combines with angry eyes and mouth instead of with the curled upper lip, raised lower lids and lowered brows of *mere* disgust.

Emotion in your voice and body

It is not surprising that when we try to read another person's feelings we concentrate on their face. However, the quality of their voice also carries an important part of the message – 38 percent of it, if attempts to quantify so precisely can be taken seriously. It is not just the look of pleasure in another's face that tells us they are glad to see us but the warmth and enthusiasm in their voice. We judge people's confidence by how steady and resonant their voices are. Talking on the telephone, we can see the other person's sad face vividly in our minds when we hear their sad tone.

We can also read something about another's emotions from their body. In terms of actually identifying an emotion, we are likely to attempt this only when no other means are available. For example, speaking to a large crowd whose faces are too distant to see clearly, you may judge whether they are interested in what you are saying by whether their posture is alert and forward-leaning or bored and limp. You might judge by gestures and postures whether your neighbors down the street are having a tensely aggressive or relaxed and friendly conversation.

■ **Body language** is mainly facial, but gestures and posture usually amplify messages sent by the face and voice. LEFT Indians mourning the death of a national leader show their grief in a hand-on-heart gesture that signals deep sorrow. The woman intensifies this with a backward lean. Her companion shows distress mainly through his facial expression but in addition feels a need to touch someone. ABOVE The contemptuous feelings of this spectator toward a soapbox orator in Hyde Park, London, are expressed in his lazily casual stance. His facial expression may be difficult for the speaker to interpret from a distance, but crossed legs, an oblique lean and an open-hand gesture convey the listener's confidence in his own superiority. Less obvious aspects of our body language often reveal emotions we would prefer to keep hidden: tapping feet express impatience or nervousness; clenched fists, tension or anger.

*Body language amplifies the emotions that you
express in your face and voice. Moving closer to
someone or touching them intensifies intimacy or
anger. Posture can tell you whether others feel
bored or interested by what you have to say.*

Usually, however, our bodies and our gestures amplify
feelings whose primary expression is in the face and voice.
Social conventions about the distance we keep from others,
depending on whether we know them well or only slightly,
make changes in our posture or behavior emotionally
significant. Any increase in how close we stand or sit and
how often we touch means an increase in the level of
emotion – perhaps more intimacy, perhaps more aggression. The face and voice are also amplifiers: raising your
voice and looking straight into your antagonist's eyes are
ways of raising the tension between you; increased smiling
and increased eye contact similarly heighten a sense of
intimate arousal.

You can verify these effects on arousal for yourself. Stare
continuously into a person's eyes during a conversation.
Not only will you find it difficult, but you will also see the
other person become very uncomfortable. Then try taking a
surreptitious half step toward them. You will cross the boun-
dary of what they find comfortable, and they will take a half

step back, probably quite unconsciously. With care, at a
party, for example, you can slowly move someone backward right around the room.

Emotional signaling

The reason why emotions are so very similar everywhere,
despite the differences between cultures, is probably because our feelings are so very primitive. They have served a
useful adaptive function throughout the history of humanity.
For example, anger mobilizes energy and builds defenses
for the good of the species. Similarly, fear prompts escape
from danger, and the emotional bonds of love and friendship make it possible for us to pursue joint survival in highly
adaptable social groups.

If emotions are so basic it is not surprising that their
expression is universal. Any other system would cause too
much confusion so that survival might be threatened. If you
could not tell roughly what another person's facial expression meant, you could fall into danger or miss a great opportunity. This even works across species. The difference
between a ferocious and a friendly dog is fairly obvious to
humans. At a very basic level, it is important for emotion to

163

DISPLAYING EMPATHY

■ *Emotional expressions and
their recognition make up a very
basic type of communication. It
is through this that we come to
understand what emotions
mean, not just for ourselves, but
for other people. It is as near as
we can get to feeling things as
others do.*

*This sharing of feelings
depends on empathy – an emotional reaction springing from
the sight of someone else experiencing an emotion. Empathy is
not the same as sympathy.
Sympathy is feeling sorry for
another person's plight. It does
not embrace any emotion other
than a form of sorrow or sadness; it is not, as is empathy, a
matching of your emotions to
those of the other person.*

▶ **Sharing her anguish,** *two
women support a bereaved
friend. The face of the woman
on the left reflects empathy for
the victim in her distress. Empathy also causes the woman on
the right to show resentment at
the photographer's intrusion.*

be expressed obviously and clearly – it helps in survival. Cries of alarm, for example, do this rapidly, widely and effectively.

Ethologists, who study animal behavior in its natural setting, believe that emotional expression has evolved through what they call ritualization. This is what happens when an action is changed to give it a communicative value which it

did not have before. For example, bared teeth in an animal often indicate an angry threat; originally they were, without much doubt, a preparation for attack.

Within the animal world, emotional expression serves a number of different kinds of function. *Group togetherness* is seen in the emotional signals involved in attraction and interaction, particularly courtship, dominance and submis-

WHEN MORE INFORMATION MATTERS

■ *Incomplete information may leave us guessing about another person's feelings. We interpret emotional displays first by changes in facial expression and other body language. We may check the context to make sure that our interpretation makes sense, but basic emotions are usually clear from their expression alone. However, to understand complex responses we need more information.*

ABOVE A wide-eyed, openmouthed stare unmistakably expresses surprise. Is there also a sense of alarm? What is there to be alarmed about at this school reunion? RIGHT Is this woman extending a cheerful greeting to someone outside the picture or making a gesture in response to something the boy is saying? Is the man reacting to the woman, to the boy or to someone beyond?

Recognizing what others feel is often easier if you understand the context. Normally we assess facial expressions and other body language first and then check whether our impressions make sense in the actual situation.

sion. *Signals about the rest of the world*, particularly in the form of warnings, may be given by sound, by sight (the flashing white tail of the rabbit) or even chemically in fish. There are hundreds of *signals of threat*, from some birdsong to gorillas beating their chests. Two further kinds of animal emotional expression concern communication between rather than within species. They indicate either a readiness for attack (eg cats' hissing and back-arching), or a readiness for contact (eg purring). It is interesting that we are so easily able to communicate our basic emotions to our domestic pets such as cats and dogs, and they to us.

Emotions in context

Despite cross-cultural, even cross-species, similarities in emotional expression, how and when an emotion is expressed is still of great significance. Psychologists once believed that context was the most important factor, and that if we could not see the context then we could not recognize the emotion. This is now known not to be so; it is possible to recognize an emotion from its expression alone. However, a knowledge of the context, particularly what led up to the emotion, does help in its interpretation.

Think of the difference between a smile between two friends and a smile between two enemies. Then, too, imagine your reaction to someone laughing at a funeral, or looking guilty when winning a competition. Such discrepancies between emotion and context make us seek an explanation.

Normally there are two stages in such a search. We judge the expression and then use the context to check our judgment. Sometimes we find an explanation. "She looks angry.

▲ **Repressing emotions and expressing them**. *TOP Inscrutable outward expressions often convey a desire not to display what is felt within. Averted eyes* and immobile features resist interpretation. When others keep their feelings hidden, we are prompted to seek an explanation by examining the context. *ABOVE A frustrating situation provokes different intensities of a shared emotional reaction. To recognize anger and exasperation in these* faces, representing many nationalities and cultures, there is little need to understand that they are at an airline check-in counter during flight delays.

What's happened? Who said something? Ah yes, there's her mother. She's obviously upset her again." Sometimes we have to check back on our first assumptions. "She looks angry. Who's said something? That's odd; there's no one around. Perhaps I was wrong. Does she really look angry?"

Controlling your emotions

When we try to deceive other people about our feelings we attempt to do so by controlling our voices and our body language, especially our facial expressions. Since the hands and arms are the next best senders of information after the face and voice, we usually try to control them as well, but often we do not do this as attentively. The feet and legs are the least effective at sending information, and, when we are trying to deceive, we often forget to control them.

We frequently comment on facial expression – "You're smiling a lot today, what's happened?" or "What's that frown for?" We very rarely comment on a person's feet or legs. It seems inappropriate to say, "Why do you keep jogging your

feet up and down?" or "Why do you keep squeezing your legs together like that?" However, when someone is in an emotional state and attempts to control it, the emotion leaks out in nonverbal behavior of which they may be completely unaware. Not many of us pay much attention to what our hands and feet are doing. So, if you want to check if someone is in a more emotional state than their words would have you believe, check the feet and legs first and then look for telltale signs in the hands.

If you are really observant you will also be able to see people giving themselves away with their facial expressions. We make what are called micromomentary (that is, very fast and fleeting) facial expressions. It is as though the mask slips now and again, and just for an instant the anger or the anxiety or even the secret pleasure shows through until self-control is re-established.

Social rules require us all at some times to control the way we express emotions. The rules vary greatly from one culture to another. For example, the Japanese are much less

▲ **Coordinated enthusiasm** *is the crowd response at a baseball game in Tokyo. Crowd-behavior experts have timed to hundredths of a second the* synchrony of groups of several thousand English football fans flicking supporter scarves during chants. The feeling of anonymity that comes with crowd membership allows people to release emotion more easily than they can in small groups. However, this can also lead to uncontrolled mob aggression, or the uncritical acceptance of ideas, when crowd manipulators take charge.

In one form of therapy, participants attempt to explore their emotions by paying close attention to what they feel when they adopt aggressive or meek postures and facial expressions, or think themselves into happy or angry moods.

likely than Westerners to show amusement in public, but they find many of the same sort of things amusing, and in private their laughter will be just as uninhibited.

Too strict a control over your emotions can be harmful. In extreme cases, if emotions such as anxiety or fear persist for a long time and are repressed, this can have marked effects on the body, and lead to physical illness (see *Ch 23*). Asthma, stomach ulcers, skin disorders and heart disease can have an emotional element.

Lack of emotional expression can seriously undermine relationships. If you allow yourself to feel too inhibited about expressing affection, or convince yourself that your displays will be artificial and inadequate, you may be depriving your partner of a basic need.

You may seriously limit your own potential to form successful and satisfying relationships if you always suppress the expression of your own needs. A sound relationship is one that is fulfilling to both parties and a partner cannot satisfy longings without knowing about them. In working relationships, too, it is when you speak up that those who are associated with you will have their best opportunity to spare you the emotional conflicts that work often creates.

Emotion therapy

It is possible to use the control of emotional expression in very positive ways. Therapists have developed techniques of emotional control that you could apply to yourself.

If you are having a problem with a particular emotion, it is sometimes possible to generate another emotion which then obstructs it. The most obvious way of doing this is to learn to relax at will. You cannot, for instance, be at the same time both anxious and relaxed, or angry and relaxed. Another possibility is to play a self-assertive role: it is difficult to be self-assertive and anxious at the same time.

One of the main ways of gaining control over our own emotions is to learn as much about them as possible. You should try to explore exactly what is going on when your body is in a state of emotional arousal and to pay close attention to the signals it gives you. One way of doing this is to assume various bodily postures or facial expressions, and to hold them and think about the feelings they generate. Or you could think yourself into being happy or angry, sad or fearful, then explore the feelings and try to relax to inhibit or thwart them.

Playing such emotional roles by using one emotion to inhibit another, and fully exploring facial expression and bodily posture, can be a step in the direction of developing a more flexible and more effective personality. **KTS**

STAGED EMOTIONS

■ *Two of the most important and yet most primitive ways in which emotion is both communicated and released are through music and drama.*

Music is sometimes used in therapy to relieve anxiety. Some farmers even play music to their cows to increase their milk yields. Most people make some use of music either to fit in with and so amplify their moods and emotional states, or to change them.

Drama has great emotional impact. Many plays explore the emotional lives of their characters and invite the audience to empathize with them.

Stage theorists place a great deal of emphasis on the production and manipulation of emotion through physical and postural control on the part of the actors.

This is only a formalized version of our emotional communication in everyday life, in which we all play roles and use our bodies to manipulate the emotions of those around us.

▲ **Feelings run high** *in the audience at a Punch and Judy show. The rawest of human emotions have been portrayed by the puppet Punch in millions of performances worldwide since his first appearances in 17th-century Italy.*

167

Anxiety and Stress

WHEN WE face a challenge – whether it be physical attack by an assailant, trying to remember someone's name or the need to adjust to an upsetting change in our pattern of life – we all feel anxious. It is part of our natural response to stress. How much anxiety you feel partly reflects the seriousness of the challenge you face. It also reflects your style of coping, which can make the difference between a level of anxiety that helps you to perform effectively and one that overwhelms you.

Three stages in your response to stress

Long before humans evolved, animals developed a "fight or flight" response: a capacity for sudden alarm in the face of danger – for example, from a predator; or a challenge – for example, an opportunity to capture prey. This is a survival mechanism in which a surge of hormones and nerve chemicals rouse an animal to a fully alert state and make its body ready for action. The nervous system becomes highly stimulated, heart rate increases, muscles tense and breathing quickens. "Fight or flight" is the *alarm* stage, the first of three stages in an animal's response to stress.

In the next stage – *resistance* – body chemistry adjusts (in particular, there is a steady flow of adrenaline) in order to keep the body at a more easily maintained level of arousal during the time needed to fight or to get away.

If the challenge can be neither met nor escaped and it continues for a long time, the animal will eventually enter a third stage – *exhaustion* – when the resources for arousal and resistance are used up. It happens, for example, when wolves take turns chasing a single deer.

Humans respond to threats and challenges in the same way, and this is a central feature of emotional life. The involuntary physical reactions of the alarm stage may be triggered even when you merely imagine something that you

ANXIOUS TO RESPOND EFFECTIVELY

■ *Anxiety is the emotion most commonly felt when people are under stress. After the initial feeling of alarm FAR RIGHT that grips us when we recognize a threat or a challenge, we try to deal with the situation. There is a period of uncertainty when we do not know what the outcome of our efforts will be, and at this time we all feel some degree of anxiety. This may be mingled with an enjoyable excitement, as in the case of the tense security officers TOP anxious not to miss any detail of the illegal drugs deal that they have* *staked out. Emotions appear less intense in the little girl BOTTOM finding her way through a maze, but she feels uncertain too, and touching her tongue gives her comfort. All of us also have experiences, from time to time, of excessive anxiety – anxiety that interferes with our ability to act effectively. A small minority of people suffer from a "generalized anxiety syndrome": they feel at least mildly anxious most of the time, often without finding a specific reason for it, and under stress they may become overwrought.*

We are under stress whenever we are faced with a challenge, and we feel anxious as we try to escape or to overcome the challenge. Only when we feel helpless does the anxiety become severe enough to interfere with our ability to act effectively.

THE FIGHT OR FLIGHT RESPONSE

■ Next time you become anxious, you may notice the following changes:

Rapid pulse
Increased perspiration
Tightened stomach
Tense muscles
Pounding heart
Shortness of breath
Gritting of teeth
Clenching of the jaw
Inability to concentrate
Extreme restlessness
Heightened emotions

These are all part of the "fight or flight" response. Helpful to our evolutionary ancestors, struggling to survive in the wild, they sometimes benefit us today. For example, they may help athletes achieve peak performances or executives meet near impossible deadlines. In these cases, energy is expended in a constructive way.

However, in modern society, the fight or flight response is often self-defeating. Waiting in traffic jams, looking for misplaced papers, obsessively mulling over insoluble problems, can cause more anxiety and physical strain than a challenge that we act upon.

A feeling of stress mobilizes the body's resources for immediate action. The rate, strength and regularity of the heart beat increase. The spleen contracts. Sugars are released into the bloodstream for energy, and the blood supply is redirected from the skin and the internal organs to the muscles and the brain. The blood's tendency to clot increases, to reduce loss of blood if fighting or fleeing causes injury. Breathing deepens as the bronchial tubes dilate. The pupils of the eyes dilate to enhance vision. Complex changes in the balance of hormones have an impact on the immune system (see p172). If this energy is not released through action, it can work against us.

are afraid of, such as snakes. You are all the more prone to arousal when you think about an upcoming situation, as when you are told that you might have to give a speech tomorrow. In the alarm stage, feelings range from anticipation, excitement, even joy (when the challenge is a welcome one), through resentment and anger (when the challenge is unwelcome) to anxiety, fear or panic (when you are not confident of meeting the challenge).

The resistance phase is when you work to meet or evade the challenge – preparing and giving the speech, or persuading event organizers not to call on you. Some degree of anxiety – a feeling of uncertainty about the outcome – goes with our resistance to any genuine challenge. It is the most characteristic emotion of stress. Sometimes it is a pleasurable, mild anxiety, sometimes a strong but stimulating one. With body chemistry working in favor of heightened alertness and activity, you may be surprised at the exceptional energy that you find in yourself, at how easily you are able to cope with a difficult situation.

Sometimes, however, we feel a helpless, uncontrolled and very destructive anxiety. When we feel truly helpless in the face of a threat we feel neither an angry urge to fight, nor a frightened urge to flee. Instead our anxiety expresses itself as withdrawal into depression (see *Ch 28*). This can still be a stress response, accompanied by physiological arousal even if not by aroused behavior. This is why depression can be so tiring.

With or without a period of helpless depression, people often fall into a state of exhaustion as they try to overcome or endure impossible situations (see *Chs 23, 24*). However, this third stage of the stress response is not the inevitable outcome of a long-term problem. By effectively managing stress it is possible to put up with a lifetime of situations that are never fully resolved.

Life crises and daily annoyances

The current level of stress in your life is the sum of two factors: first, the number and seriousness of any life crises (see *Ch 22*) to which you are currently adjusting; second, the level of annoyance that you face in your daily life. Life crises include any event that causes a major upset or major excitement, such as getting married, losing a partner or being passed over for promotion. Daily annoyances are irritating – frustrating or distressing events such as you might experience when looking after small children, getting to and from work or working in a busy and noisy office.

The most concrete attempts to measure overall stress are based on life crises. However, there is no straightforward relationship between how stressed you feel and the number and magnitude of present crises. One reason for this is that some people who feel highly stressed are bothered mainly by daily annoyances. They do not face major changes in their lives, calling for personal adjustment, but ever-present irritations and difficulties. Many may be very small by themselves, but they add up to a high level of stress.

The two sources of stress can amplify each other. When you are having difficulty adjusting to a crisis, daily annoyances can seem much harder to cope with. Small frustra-

EXAMINATION NERVES

■ Everyone meets situations in which anxiety robs them of the performance that they are trying to achieve: for some, these include thinking of the answers during an examination.

As with any other kind of performance (see the graph on p185), we think more efficiently and more productively when we are under some emotional pressure. As pressure increases, we become more and more alert problem-solvers. Performance and judgment are likely to be impaired, however, when you cross your individual stress threshold and become upset or angry.

If the task is very complex, requiring conscious attention, being emotionally aroused may quickly hamper your performance. However, there are many tasks that we can perform automatically while thinking about something else. The "automatic processing" within the brain that makes this possible is handled by the cerebellum, a part of the brain that is less influenced by emotional arousal than the cerebral cortex, which processes our conscious mental activity.

This means that practicing a skill is worthwhile even if you are likely to become anxious when you need to perform. It is possible to feel very anxious in an examination and still perform well, if the questions have been accurately anticipated and the answers thoroughly learned. The confidence won by sound preparation may even help to relax you.

▲ **Daily annoyances,** *such as the inconveniences of traveling to work in large and crowded cities, are a constant background source of stress. They shrink our capacity to cope with the extra stress we must bear* when we experience crises in our personal lives or extra pressures at work.

Coping style can make the difference between a level of anxiety that aids your performance and one that overwhelms you. Good coping means not only problem-solving but knowing how to calm yourself and seek help and reassurance.

tions also drain some of the energy that you have for adjusting to major crises. It is important to be prepared to read the signs of too much stress (see *Ch 23*) and to make allowances when the pressures in your life are becoming too great.

At least as significant in making life crises an unreliable measure of stress is the fact that we all have different coping abilities and different levels of support from friends and relatives when we face a crisis. The amount of stress that you feel might be quite different from the amount felt by someone else who is in a very similar situation, but copes less well and receives less support.

Controlling anxiety

In novel, unpredictable and dangerous situations, the adrenal glands release the hormone cortisol, but as we see opportunities to control the situation, or persuade ourselves that it will pass, cortisol levels fall, and so does anxiety. This

is called "problem-focused coping." The way in which you perceive the problem is a key factor in keeping arousal to a manageable level when you are under stress: it pays to think positively.

"Emotion-focused" coping also has a calming effect. This is where you relax your anxiety simply by saying to yourself "Relax...," or by making a joke, by seeking the comfort of a friend or even by comforting yourself with self-touches (especially to the face and other parts of the head) or self-hugs. A survey of middle-aged men and women found that they used both emotion-focused and problem-focused coping in almost all of the challenges that faced them.

Coping style has a strong impact on the amount of stress that your life can sustain. It may even have the effect that, the more crises you struggle with, the more adept you become at adapting to changes and upsets – so that you feel less stressed by each.

The "hardy" personality is identified as suffering the lowest stress from life crises. People with this personality have a sense of commitment and involvement in life and an expectation that they will find ways of controlling or at least influencing events that affect them.

After a succession of life crises, some people become chronically depressed. This is less likely to occur when the person attributes the occurrence of crises to temporary factors that they can change. ("I was passed over for promotion because I didn't try as hard as I could have.") It is more likely to occur if the person attributes the crisis to unalterable factors (see *Ch 14*). **AER**

DETECTING A LIAR'S ANXIETY

■ The principle underlying a polygraph test (lie detector) is that, if lying causes anxiety, then heart beat, pulse rate and other variables will be affected if you dishonestly answer questions.

Lie detectors are not foolproof, and it can be difficult to tell whether they are accurate or not. If you are innocent but emotionally excited simply by being asked the questions, your bodily responses might make it appear that you are lying. If you are a practiced liar you could be relaxed enough to fool the machine, even giving a pretended emotional reaction to a neutral question.

Increasingly more sophisticated techniques, however, also exist. For example, emo-

tional reactions are sought to clues that only the guilty person would recognize as critical stimuli: this is known as "guilty knowledge." **KTS**

▶ **Detecting lies on Wall Street?** *By a disputed means, an investigator attempts to shed light on an insider-dealing scandal in New York's closely knit financial community.*

THE IMMUNE SYSTEM UNDER STRESS

■ Most of us do not become ill every time we are exposed to viruses such as colds and influenza, and many people believe that being under a strain is one of the factors that make the difference when they do catch something. In schools, for example, colds and sniffles seem to take over toward the end of term. Studies have shown that stress hampers the ability of the immune system to cope with disease.

ONGOING STRESS

Studies of people suffering from depression, anxiety, severe loneliness or a high level of recent life crises find a weaker immune response than that of randomly selected groups. Even ordinary work stress can have an effect: medical students taking their final examinations had lower immune-cell activity in their blood than they did one month earlier.

Coping abilities make an important contribution to immunity. Comparisons have been made between groups rated by psychologists as "hardy" (with good coping skills) and groups rated unhardy, both burdened with about the same high number of life crises and the same level of daily pressure.

Hardy people have a stronger immune response, although even theirs weakens somewhat when they are under a strain.

Reducing stress can increase the effectiveness of the immune system. One study tested 45 elderly people. Each was randomly assigned to one of three groups: a relaxation training group (see Ch 25), a group given increased social contacts, and one given no treatment.

Over a one-month period, those who had received relaxation training showed signifi-

POSITIVE THINKING AND ILLNESS

■ The powerful effect of our emotions on intellectual and physical fitness has always been a major tonic used by physicians in the treatment of the sick. When medical treatment was unsophisticated and medicine consisted mainly of herbs and lotions, physicians often had little more to offer their patients than emotional support and encouragement. Sometimes this was achieved solely through the patient's belief in the treatment. Research has consistently found that most of us will show a "placebo effect" – improvement in our condition when we think we have received medical treatment, even though the "medicine" is a placebo (a substance incapable of affecting us). With the development of effective medi-

cines, the powerful interaction between emotions, thought and physical well-being seemed less important. However, physicians often continued to choose not to tell their patients how ill they were, fearing that the knowledge might send them into decline, and few would have argued with the idea that trust in the treatment you are receiving and belief that you will continue to live play a vital part

in the process of recovery. Recently, psychologists and physicians have revived their interest in this aspect of treatment. Some people believe that when you suffer from a serious illness your state of mind may be the most important factor helping you to recover. One woman who had leukemia and was expected to die imagined the cells in her body as happy faces while she was receiving

chemotherapy treatment. She also reflected on all the things she still wanted to do in her life. Another who underwent radiotherapy for colon cancer visualized the radiation as bubbles eating up the bad cancer cells, like the toilet cleansers destroying germs in television commercials. Both women survived their illnesses and believe that their mental exercises played a part in recovery. **RLS**

▶ **Training for victory.** Stricken by cancer in 1980, jockey Bob Champion could not give up his dream of riding the winning horse in Britain's prestigious Grand National. Thanks partly to chemotherapy and partly to his faith in life, he is still alive. During his treatment, he personally supervised the recovery of his mount, Aldaniti, from a broken leg. They rode to victory in the Grand National in 1981.

The hormones and body chemicals produced in stress can disrupt the effectiveness of the cells that work together to fight disease. Learning how to relax is one way of reducing acute stress and strengthening the immune system.

cantly enhanced immunity. No significant changes were found in the other two groups.

Distressed people are more susceptible to infectious disease, and they recover more slowly and suffer more complications. Loss of immunity due to stress is likely to be more important in older people, whose immune systems are already weakened.

BODY CHEMISTRY

The hormones and body chemicals released when we feel strong emotions (see p168) are what hamper our immunity. The immune system is a system of many different kinds of cells that communicate with each other by chemical messages that are capable of being disrupted when other chemical activity is high.

The body produces immune cells in the bone marrow. About half of them travel to the thymus gland, located just under the breastbone, where they mature. Three kinds of "T" cells (for thymus) work together. "Helper" T cells enhance the germ-fighting activity of other immune cells. "Killer" T cells attack and destroy virus-infected or potentially cancerous cells. (The immune system is important in fending off not only the germ-caused illnesses, such as influenza, but is also crucial in eliminating renegade cells that might produce cancers.) "Suppressor" T cells turn the helper cells off when they are not needed. (This stops them from attacking healthy tissue.)

A second component of the immune system, the "B" cells (for bone marrow), mature in the marrow. By chemical means they recognize foreign cells, and chemically stimulated by helper cells, they manufacture the germ-fighting molecules known as "antibodies." These are tailor-made to be effective against specific invading germs. Antibodies traveling in the blood attach to the germs they are designed to disable.

A third category of immune cells are the "natural killer" cells that attack any diseased cells that they encounter and send out chemical alarm signals to the T and B cells.

Most of the time, stress-induced disruptions of this system are not great enough to heighten significantly our risk of cancer or serious infection, although coming down with a cold may be a genuine sign of too much stress. When people feel helpless in the face of great and long-lasting distress, however, low immunity can be life-threatening. **AER**

▲ **Coming down with influenza**. *Usually our immune system destroys the viruses that constantly invade our bodies. Occasionally a virus to which we are not immune spreads through the community, but not everyone becomes ill. One of the factors that promotes resistance in those who are spared is the ability to cope well with pressures, thus keeping down the levels of stress chemicals that may interfere with immune cells developing new defenses.*

CRISIS EVENTS

■ In one study, bereaved men and women had a weaker immune response two months after the death of their partner than they had when their partner was dying. The test was made by taking blood samples and measuring the level of immune-cell activity. Another study of bereaved women evaluated them for grief symptoms such as mood swings, suicidal thoughts, insomnia and weight loss. Those showing the most severe symptoms also showed the biggest decrease in immunity. The researchers then evaluated women whose partners were healthy: they all had a healthier immune system. Recently experiencing a high number of any of the other typical life crises (such as losing your job or moving house) also tends to go with weaker immunity.

Facing Life's Crises

WHAT does the word "crisis" mean to you? To most people it is associated with disruption and strain. But professionals do not define "crisis" in negative terms. A crisis is inherently neither good nor bad. It is simply a turning point – an emotionally significant event that changes your life. Whether the change is for the better or worse will depend partly on the nature of the event and its timing. Equally important is the way you adapt to or cope with what is happening.

Life is punctuated by developmental crises, which are natural *stages* of everyone's life, from forming our first attachment to a caregiver to adjusting to old age (see p146). There are also crisis *events*, such as falling in love, winning a fortune in a lottery or being bereaved. Some crisis events are environmental, depending on the whims of nature, such as hurricanes and floods.

Personal crises

Research has verified that losing someone who matters to you – through their death, through divorce or through separation from them – is the most upsetting event that most people expect to experience. The death of anyone close to us brings us up short, reminding us of our own mortality. Not only are we vulnerable at this time to thoughts of our own death but childhood fears of loss and abandonment are also rekindled. The death of a partner is one of life's most devastating experiences: a new widow, for example, usually takes a minimum of two years to adapt to her position. This greatest of life's crises involves powerful feelings of grief. Understanding the usual stages of grief can help you cope with your own feelings during bereavement or help you to give effective emotional support to a bereaved friend or relative. Counselors refer to the importance of "working through" the grief process. A person who adapts too quickly to a loss may later suffer long-term despair or depression, or find that they are unable to love again (see Ch29).

Grief is not, of course, caused only by death. Separation and divorce, major crises in the life of an adult, also involve initial grieving. It is normal to feel angry, hurt or rejected. But adults have mature defenses which can help them save their self-esteem and reconstruct their lives. After the initial loss, the crisis may mean a positive change, bringing growth, an awareness of potential and new challenges.

The children involved in a divorce, however, are more vulnerable to its lasting effects, often feeling bereft and abandoned. Many feel guilty, believing that they are in some way responsible for what has happened. In fact, the two most frequent causes of grief for children are divorce of parents and death of a pet.

Women, especially, often bear a heavy financial burden after a divorce and, like their children, find that their stan-

▲ **Separation is a major crisis**. *Companionship is usually an essential ingredient of happiness, and ending a close relationship can be painful. Almost inevitably, separation means changes – sometimes considerable – in our domestic and social patterns, and these make emotional demands on us. But separation can also have positive results, teaching us more about our own needs and abilities. A temporary separation provides an opportunity to review the relationship and reassess strategies for developing its potential.*

A crisis is a turning point, in itself neither good nor bad. The outcome can be influenced by your habitual approach to challenges and by your social support network. Seen as a pivotal point in your life, a crisis can bring positive change.

dard of living changes drastically. The stress of adjusting to a new, often poorer neighborhood, and of the combined task of earning the family's living and giving adequate supervision to children adds considerably to the emotional burden of separation. Where divorce happens later in life, the "displaced homemaker" finds herself, after 20-30 years of marriage, with no marketable skills. Many of these women have no adequate savings and face grave economic

crises. Today more women protect themselves with pre-nuptial agreements, which specifically detail appropriate financial arrangements in the event of a divorce.

Not all individual crises are associated with grief. Taking out a mortgage or becoming pregnant also involve major adjustments in your life.

Crisis events

Studies of life events have resulted in the following list, starting with those that have the greatest impact and ending with those with the least. Some are very positive events,

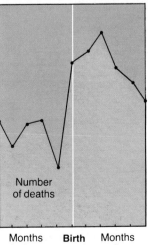

■ **Reacting to disaster**. *In the immediate aftermath of a public tragedy people tend instinctively to keep together for mutual support. Individual reactions vary from fear to stunned immobility. Covering the face with the hands is a typical response: even if there is no longer anything distressing to see we try to shut out the mental picture and deny the reality of what has happened.*

▶ **Death is the ultimate crisis**. *Yet research indicates that to some extent even death is under our control. The will to live is evident in the fact that among people who are old and frail the number of deaths is highest in the period shortly after their birthdays. It seems that some people can keep themselves alive for an important occasion.*

Number of deaths

Months before | **Birth month** | Months after

such as marriage or the arrival of a new baby, but they are emotional crises because of the adjustment challenges with which they confront us.

1 Death of partner
2 Divorce from partner
3 Separation from partner
4 Jail term
5 Death of close family member
6 Personal injury or illness
7 Marriage
8 Dismissal from work
9 Marital reconciliation
10 Retirement
11 Change in health of family member
12 Pregnancy
13 Sex difficulties
14 Gain of new family member
15 Business readjustment
16 Change in financial state
17 Death of close friend
18 Change to different type of work
19 Change in number of arguments with partner
20 Taking out a large loan (eg mortgage)
21 Foreclosure of mortgage or loan
22 Change in responsibilities at work
23 Son or daughter leaving home
24 Trouble with in-laws
25 Outstanding personal achievement
26 Partner begins or stops work
27 Change in living conditions

GETTING AWAY FROM IT ALL

■ *Research shows that vacations, however happy, are an emotional strain for many individuals and families. Some vacations go wrong, of course: airport delays, unsatisfactory hotels and polluted beaches are just some of the typical complaints. But even if you experience none of these hardships and return invigorated, your break from routine will have made both physical and emotional demands on you. Vacations can be hard work – more so, perhaps, than you consciously recognize. The initial planning and organization, the need to adapt to a lifestyle different from your usual one and the compulsion that many of us feel to "make the most of every minute": all this may be fun but it is also potentially stressful.*

Expectations tend to be high and this can lead to disappointment, even when no major setback occurs. The expectations of individual members of the family or group may differ: it requires compromise and care to harmonize these differing hopes.

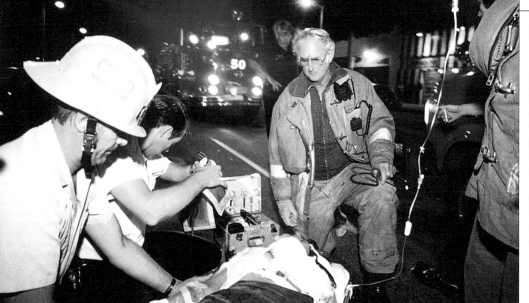

DISRUPTED LIVES

■ *Accidents happen quickly, LEFT but the crises they create for victims may last for years, through disruption of earnings and lifestyle. The impact of sudden unemployment TOP can be comparable. Work not only brings financial rewards: it bolsters these Japanese shipbuilders' sense of identity and competence, and it is an important source of friendships. Loss of a job damages more than earnings: it can erode self-respect and impair relationships. But this can also be a positive turning point. In reorganizing a disrupted life people often find rewarding new directions in which to develop.*

Research has identified a long list of common personal events that bring major changes in our lives, requiring us to make extensive adjustments. These "life events" include not only distressing changes but ones generally regarded as welcome.

28 Revision of personal habits
29 Trouble with boss
30 Change in work hours or conditions
31 Change in residence
32 Change in recreation
33 Change in church activities

This list is seen from the perspective of an adult. But many of the same life events are critical for children and young adults. For a child, changes at work are replaced by changes at school. Going to school for the first time is a major event in any child's life – as it is for the child's parents as well. Leaving school is also a turning point and changing schools may require considerable, and potentially stressful adjustments.

Why me?

Events often occur over which we have little if any control, and which are not among the burdens (such as bereavement) that we accept as part of anyone's life. The great depression of the 1930s is an example of a crisis of this sort. In a study of people who grew up during this period it was found that although families suffered great economic hardship – significantly altering the nature of family relationships and family life around the world – there were nevertheless some positive outcomes. For instance, economic conditions often meant that the father, until then the typical breadwinner, was out of work. In these circum-

stances the children and wives pitched in to make ends meet. As a result, some households became more egalitarian. But this period in history left deep emotional scars on many people.

Drastic economic changes are not the only such turning points in life. Natural disasters, such as floods or hurricanes, may also have long-lasting effects.

Victimization, too, can be seen as an uncontrolled, undeserved crisis. Since murder, burglary and rape are not common experiences, most of us take an attitude of "infantile omnipotence" toward them: the belief that "it could never happen to me." This is a common defense mechanism. After a tragedy, then, and particularly after a crime has been committed, a typical response is "Why me?" Surprise is inevitable. We are off guard. We cannot be continually vigilant, nor can we function well if we feel perpetually vulnerable. What happens in sensational crimes exposes a central human fear – vulnerability and loss of control.

An important factor that affects our reaction to a crisis is the extent to which the event is predictable and can be prepared for. Even though we cannot control the weather, with appropriate warning we can prepare ourselves for serious occurrences such as floods and hurricanes. Random events, however, are truly frightening, making people bewildered, confused and angry. When there is a rash of housebreakings in nearby neighborhoods or an unapprehended child rapist is active in the area, we feel anxious, no matter how carefully we improve household security or supervise our children.

▲ **Positive life events** *are also crises. A newly married couple faces important tasks in adjust-* *ing their own relationship and their relationships with other people. The marriage may also* *mean other very significant changes, such as moving to a new house or changing jobs –* *both of which make great, potentially stressful, demands on us.*

Handling a crisis

A crisis is nothing more or less than a change and change is essential to the intricate pattern of a rich and rewarding life. But change, whether for the better or worse, can be difficult to handle.

If you have nurtured relationships with friends and family you will find crises easier to resolve successfully. Research suggests that in times of crisis those who have social support suffer far less from stress than those who are left to cope alone. This is particularly true if you have lost someone close to you: people you know and trust can help with everyday arrangements so that you do not have to jump straight back into daily responsibilities.

How you handle a crisis may also depend on the extent to which you feel in control. People who feel they have or should have complete control – which is impossible – may feel guilty and depressed when they come up against uncontrollable events. But it can be helpful to cultivate the belief that you can control many aspects of your life. The old adage "Give me the strength to change that which can be changed, and accept that which cannot, and the wisdom to know the difference" is crucial to the successful outcome of a crisis.

Giving a devastating event human dimensions can make you feel less helpless. Here is how the American psychologist and philosopher, William James, described his experience of a traumatic event, an earthquake:

First I personified the earthquake as a permanent individual entity. It came, moreover, directly to me. It stole in behind my back, and once inside the room had me all to itself, and could manifest itself convincingly. Animus and intent were never more present in any human action, nor did any human activity ever more definitely point back to a living agent as its source and origin. All whom I consulted on the point agreed as to this feature in their experience; "it expressed intention," "it was vicious," "it was bent on destruction," "it wanted to show its power," or what-not . . . the perception of it as a living agent was irresistible. It had an overpowering dramatic convincingness.

Earthquakes are particularly devastating because of their erratic nature. William James encapsulated the event by personalizing it. He was trying to understand his reaction and check this against the reaction of others. Making meaning out of a catastrophe is one way of handling fear.

Support groups

Someone who is going through a serious crisis may find it particularly helpful to talk to people who have undergone similar experiences. It may be enough to talk to one fellow-victim: a woman who has had a miscarriage, for example, may find it comforting to talk to even a stranger who has been through this crisis and knows how it can affect her life. It can be more emotionally supportive knowing that someone empathizes, does not just sympathize, with you.

Sometimes it can be helpful to discuss the condition or event with a group of people who are in the same position. There are now support groups for all major (as well as many uncommon) misfortunes and afflictions – such as bereavement, children's disabilities and AIDS. Often, after a major disaster, the survivors and the families of those who died find great comfort in organizing a formal group where, together, they can discuss the practical problems arising from the tragedy and work through their grief. **HWR**

◄ **Shocked disbelief is a common reaction to disaster**. *A major catastrophe – such as an earthquake or an airplane crash – is rare, and we wonder why we, in particular, seem to have been singled out. We feel a sense of outrage and of unreality: "This can't be happening to me!" Survivors and bereaved relatives often form associations – meeting regularly to discuss the event, their feelings and practical problems such as compensation. This empathetic mutual support is often more important than the sympathy of other friends and relatives.*

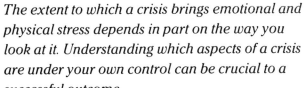

The extent to which a crisis brings emotional and physical stress depends in part on the way you look at it. Understanding which aspects of a crisis are under your own control can be crucial to a successful outcome.

Nancy Tilton   Todd Tilton

179

HANDLING THEIR CRISES

■ *TOP* Discovering that you are infertile is an emotional crisis: personal and cultural expectations are disappointed. Many couples feel angry and may deeply envy others who have children. Depression is very common. However, about half the cases of infertility, like this couple in front of television cameras, celebrating the birth of their test-tube twins, are treatable. Those less fortunate can expect to experience many of the symptoms of grief (see

Ch 29) and will need to come to terms with their loss. LEFT *Preparation can lessen the stressful effects of a crisis. Knowing exactly what will happen and how we can expect to feel gives us some sense of control over events. It is particularly important to explain impending crises to children. Here a six-year-old girl learns about the heart surgery she will shortly undergo.*

Signs of Stress

SOME stress is good for us. To enjoy life we need to feel stimulated – problems, challenges and excitement keep away boredom and depression. If there is too little pressure to get things done, we fall into a state of inertia from which it is difficult to rouse ourselves – the common saying "If you want something done, ask a busy person to do it" reflects the low levels of performance that we expect from people who are underchallenged.

High levels of stress, when they are properly managed, can bring dramatic advantages. Up to a point, performance improves with increasing pressure. A sense of high achievement and high self-esteem may help us to cope successfully with higher and higher levels of stress and with intermittent periods of very intense demand. When we reach the optimum, we feel a marked zest for living and enjoy being fully stretched.

However, everyone has a stress threshold, a point where more pressure becomes counterproductive. Pushing past this point leads to a dramatic fall in productivity and con-

tentment, and in the long run health problems can develop. These adverse effects of stress are all too evident when they occur, but usually the early signs go unnoticed, because they seem minor and because we are distracted by pressures. However, learning to read the signs is an essential part of successful stress management.

Acute and chronic effects of stress

The remarkably consistent physical reactions referred to in *Ch21* as "the fight or flight response" – for example, rapid pulse, tensed muscles, pounding heart, shortness of breath and heightened emotions – are the *acute* (short-term) effects of stress. This is the adaptive response that rouses our bodies and minds to meet danger or a challenge. Everyone experiences it from time to time.

The acute effects of stress can sometimes be mistaken for a heart attack and, in extreme cases, people may be rushed to the emergency room, but examination shows that they are really suffering from a panic attack. In this case, mis-

BOREDOM AND STRESS AT WORK

■ *The most reliable way to tell how much stress a person experiences in their work is to ask them.*

Early research centered on the work itself, but psychologists now agree that the individual's own ideas about a job provide the most reliable information. However, some generalizations about different kinds of job stress can be made.

Those who are understimulated at work, because of inadequate challenge or lack of opportunity to use their skills, seem to suffer more psychological problems, such as job dissatisfaction, low self-esteem and depression, but they have fewer work-related effects on their physical health.

In contrast, people who are overloaded appear to run a higher risk of cardiovascular disease.

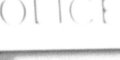

▲ **Arriving at work in the morning,** *do you feel that you are looking forward to the stimulation and the challenge of your job, or do you feel caught up in a situation you cannot control? Stress is involved in both reactions. It is unhealthy only in the latter.*

▶ **Moments of high stress** *can be part of any job. They do not harm us, so long as we rest between them. Work that constantly overloads a person with ongoing stress, however, especially when they do not wind down successfully in the evening or at the weekend, can be a serious risk to health.*

Successful stress management includes learning how to read the early-warning signs when the pressures in your life are becoming too great. Changes in behavior, as well as many physical and psychological clues, should be noted.

reading the acute signs of stress leads to more stress.

Panic attacks are uncommon. When we are under stress, we tend to concentrate on the circumstances that we are dealing with. We are not very conscious of our internal physical reactions to the situation, and being unaware of ourselves in this way probably helps us to get on with problem-solving.

Even when acute effects are very pronounced, they are not dangerous to a healthy person. So long as the problem is resolved and we rest afterwards, there is no need to be especially aware of them.

However, many sources of stress are ongoing or follow one upon the other. When one problem is solved, another takes its place.

Sometimes several problems confront us at once, and the decision about where to begin is daunting in itself. Although no one problem amounts to very much, the sheer volume of challenge overwhelms us.

When there is no relief from pressure, *chronic* (long-term) effects of stress appear. These effects are not consistent – two people may respond to the same amount of ongoing stress in strikingly different ways. Chronic effects *should* be made objects of self-awareness. Even though they are sometimes difficult to interpret, they are signals that you should adjust your lifestyle or your work habits before worse problems emerge.

Stress and heart disease

When we say that someone is "sick with worry" or "dying of a broken heart," do we literally mean that worry and heartache can harm you physically? For most of its history as a scientifically disciplined field (from about the mid-1700s), medicine would have dismissed such notions. There was no scientifically understood chain of causes and effects that could link emotions to physical health. Today,

181

▲ **Rural boredom.** *People who find life in the country stressfully understimulating are sometimes baffled by the longing that city dwellers have for quiet surroundings. The bright lights, crowded streets and constant noise of urban life provide a tonic for some, a constantly annoying background for others.*

Time urgency, hostility and competitiveness are the most important characteristics of the Type A personality – the person most at risk of allowing frustrations and delays to be so stressful that they become a cause of heart disease.

however, an understanding of stress hormones (see *Ch 21*) has provided the link between mental state and physical health.

This link was recognized at an early date in the case of hypertension, or chronic high blood pressure. During the Second World War, British physicians found characteristic symptoms in 27 percent of 695 men who had been involved in desert warfare for one year. Even with the danger behind them, these soldiers continued to show raised blood pressure, rapid pulses, pale faces and enlarged pupils.

In normal health, peaks of high blood pressure occur several times a day as normal stress reactions gear us up to face challenges or respond to stimulating events. In victims

of hypertension, blood pressure stays at the peak levels. A consequence is that blood vessels are weakened and eventually may burst. When this happens in a major artery of the brain, the result is a stroke, causing debilitating or fatal damage. Rapid circulation of blood in prolonged high blood pressure can also result in weakened kidneys and a weakened heart. Both may eventually fail.

Strokes and heart disease may also result from hardening and narrowing of the arteries. Fatty deposits (plaque) on arterial walls, which may in part result from excess blood

---

TYPE A OR TYPE B – ARE YOU A STRESS-PRONE PERSON?

■ *As early as 1910, the great British physician, Sir William Osler, noted that "it is not the dedicated, neurotic person who is prone to heart disease, but the robust, the vigorous in mind and body, the keen and ambitious man. . . whose engine is always at full speed ahead." Much later, heart specialists proposed a description of the "Type A personality" who is prone to stress-related heart disease: this kind of person displays an intense, hard-driving competitiveness, a persistent sense of time urgency and is easily roused to hostility. By contrast, the Type B person is relaxed and easy going. Studies of initially healthy individuals seem to support the claim that a Type A personality is a risk factor for heart disease, but studies of those already at heightened risk due to a previous heart attack or due to other traditional risk factors (such as high blood pressure), have failed to confirm its importance. Recently, attempts have been made to refine the concept of the Type A personality to specify clearly its harmful elements. Attention has focused on anger and hostility, which have been found especially to predict future heart disease.*

To test whether you have a Type A personality, complete the following questionnaire. Take your time answering the questions. Answer yes or no in each case. It is important to give as frank an answer as possible. Feel free to ask someone who knows you well how you should answer. Some of the items, such as the way you talk, may not be apparent to you, but would be to others.

 1 *Are you unhappy in your work?*
 2 *Do you bring work home from your job?*
 3 *Does your work include frequent deadlines that are difficult to meet?*

 4 *Do you think about your work in the evening and on weekends?*
 5 *Do you find it hard to fit into the day everything you have to do or want to do?*
 6 *Do you lack the time to prepare for contingencies – to think ahead about what you will do when a plan does not work as expected?*
 7 *Do you find yourself hurrying and writing unclearly as you fill in checks or other routine papers?*
 8 *Do you dislike taking the time to do jobs in the home?*
 9 *Do you hurry when you are reading?*
10 *Do you feel guilty about resting if there is work to do?*
11 *Do you eat quickly?*
12 *Do you often feel impatient?*
13 *Do you find it almost unbearable to have to wait in line or to travel behind a slow vehicle?*
14 *Do you find it irritating to watch people do things less quickly than you can?*
15 *Do you clench your jaw or grind your teeth?*
16 *Do you often try to do two things at once, eg listening to someone while thinking about something else?*
17 *Do you tend to evaluate performance in terms of numbers?*
18 *Do you gesture emphatically in conversation, eg clenching your fist, bringing it down on the table or pounding it into the palm of your other hand?*
19 *Do you have a tendency to finish the sentences of others for them?*
20 *Do you frequently interrupt in conversation, and hurry others to finish what they are saying?*
21 *Do you accentuate key words even when there is no need for emphasis?*
22 *Do you speak more rapidly at the end of sentences?*
23 *Do you find yourself repeatedly bringing conversations around to yourself or subjects that interest you directly?*
24 *Do you pretend to listen to others while remaining preoccupied with your own thoughts?*

Every yes answer scores 1 point. A person who scores 16 points or more may be significantly more at risk of a heart attack than average.

fats mobilized for energy during stress, harden these walls and create narrow passages. During stress our blood clots more easily than normally (presumably as an adaptation against losing too much blood during violent action). Blood clots can catch at narrow points in hardened arteries in the brain and stop the flow of blood, causing a stroke in the form of oxygen starvation.

In the heart condition known as *angina pectoris*, coronary arteries feeding the heart are narrowed by fatty deposits. They may fail sufficiently to expand the supply of oxygen to the heart during stress. Chest pains result. A form of heart attack, a *coronary thrombosis*, occurs when a blood clot lodges in one of the coronary arteries, blocking completely the oxygen that it supplies.

Heart disease, then, can be a sign of stress. Your doctor is likely to take a heart attack or a hardening of the coronary arteries as a reason for asking questions about your lifestyle and suggesting ways of avoiding pressures and excitement, and of coping more effectively with those that cannot be avoided. However, this is a late date for stress management. It is desirable to be aware of the problem before your health is damaged.

Medical check ups can help by watching for high levels of stress hormones in blood and urine samples. Another danger sign is high levels of glucose sugar in the blood – blood sugars are a stage in mobilizing blood fats. Your doctor will also be concerned if you have constantly high blood pressure or a constantly high pulse rate. You can keep a check on your own pulse rate, and can notice for yourself such chronic effects (experienced by some but not others) as an enduring dryness in the mouth, excessive sweating, dilation of the pupils, difficult breathing, hot and cold spells, recurrent numbness and tingling in parts of the limbs.

UNDER PRESSURE

■ *ABOVE Time is money for businessmen in Buenos Aires hurrying to their appointments. RIGHT Problems accumulate over the telephone for company directors planning a publicity campaign. Some stress is essential to a productive work routine – for example, the stimulus of fighting to meet deadlines and getting to meetings on time. Managing these pressures effectively includes knowing when to take a needed rest.*

One very common and reliable physiological warning of too much stress usually goes unheeded. When we are faced with a problem, muscles tighten in preparation for action. In conditions of ongoing stress, unrelieved muscle tension in the neck often leads to a headache. At this point we may try to remedy the situation by taking painkillers. But this approach does nothing to change the source of the stress and so prevent a recurrence of the problem. Nor does it really remedy the cause of the pain – muscle tension. It is much better to be aware of the headache as an early sign of stress. Other signs of too much muscle tension include lower-back pain and even facial twitches. With practice in self-awareness, it is not too difficult to notice muscle tension even in advance of the headache and to take coping measures, such as voluntary relaxation (see *Ch 25*).

Other physical signs of stress

Among illnesses brought on by stress, those of the heart and circulatory system are the most significant. Men going through the stressful six months following the death of a wife, for example, are more likely to die during this period than men who have not been bereaved, and although the likelihood of all fatal illnesses increases, heart disease is an especially common cause of death.

Even heart disease, however, is not a sure sign of stress. The effects of chronic stress vary widely from one individual to another. Stress is never the sole or the only possible explanation when things go wrong – many other factors, such as lack of exercise, being overweight, poor diet, family history and toxins in the working environment, for example, can contribute to heart disease. It is all the more true that coming down with a cold or having an attack of asthma is an imprecise indicator. Nevertheless, one strategy to consider if you develop such symptoms as an ulcer or a skin rash or have an upsurge of a complaint that is common to you is to take a new approach to life's pressures. There are numerous health problems whose causes are thought frequently to include stress.

During stress, blood flows away from the abdominal region to feed the limbs and the nervous and respiratory sys-

▲ **Eating on the run**. *Taking too many fast-food meals is a behavioral effect of excess stress. It is also a contributing factor to some stress-related health conditions. The physical effects of stress chemistry on the digestive system are compounded by a poor diet, and indigestion, heartburn, bowel problems or peptic ulcers may result.*

▶ **A stressful environment** *compounds the stressful effects of time urgency. Transport problems in big cities – traffic jams, crowded subways and unavailable taxis – add to the pressures of keeping a tight schedule. In such frustrating circumstances our fight-or-flight mechanism keeps us aroused even though action is blocked.*

Under emotional strain people often neglect their health. They may miss preventive checks and even ignore symptoms. Feeling too tired or too short of time, they may stop taking exercise and risk becoming overweight.

tems instead. Indigestion and heartburn can result from accumulations of digestive acid in a now inactive stomach. Poor eating habits (especially too much fat) also make a contribution. In those who are prone, peptic ulcers can develop through excess digestive acid burning holes in the lining of the stomach or the duodenum (the upper part of the small intestine where it joins the stomach).

In some people, prolonged stress can involve bouts of diarrhea or constipation or both, with pain in the lower abdomen – in a condition know as "irritable bowel syndrome," to which low dietary fiber contributes. A more severe condition is "ulcerative colitis" – the bowel becomes ulcerated and must be treated with anti-inflammatory drugs.

The immune system may fail to function effectively during prolonged periods of severe anxiety or depression, as stress hormones inhibit the responsiveness of white blood cells to bacteria, viruses and cancer cells (see p172). Resistance to

minor colds and influenza as well as major infections and cancers may be reduced.

In some cases, asthma (constriction of the bronchia, the tubes that let air in and out of the lungs) and a tendency to overbreathing (taking in too much oxygen and blowing off too much carbon dioxide) are badly aggravated by emotional excitement.

Migraine headaches can be triggered by stress. These headaches are not due to muscle tension but to spasms and relaxations of the blood vessels supplying the brain. In many sufferers, they occur especially when emotional arousal increases the flow of blood.

Under too much pressure, some people break out in hives or develop unexplained itches, often in the anogenital region. Acne, eczema and psoriasis may be aggravated. Rare cases of alopecia (sudden baldness, with hair falling out in handfuls, and even loss of eyebrow and body hairs) have been linked to stress.

Emotional tension can contribute to impotence in men and painful intercourse in women. A reduced sex drive can

▲ **Showing the strain**. *TOP LEFT Former US President Richard Nixon at the height of his career. TOP RIGHT Under extreme stress during the Watergate scandal. BOTTOM LEFT His signature as he takes office in 1969. CENTER Clarity begins to fade and BOTTOM RIGHT a scrawl appears just before he resigns in 1974.*

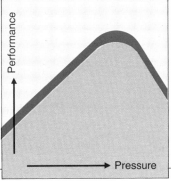

◄ **Recognizing your pressure threshold** *helps you to use stress to your advantage. Performance improves in proportion to rising pressure – up to a point – a different point for each person. Then more pressure becomes counter-productive: increasing it causes a steep slide in the quality and quantity of useful activity. This deterioration may be more apparent to others than to the person who is affected. Sensitivity to the signs, however, can alert you to a need to take breaks, establish priorities and reassess goals. A clear absence of them can reassure you that new challenges may be worth attempting.*

become a pattern during periods of chronic stress, as can irregular menstruation and aggravated premenstrual stress in women. Tension may reduce the chances of conception even when intercourse is complete.

Other health reasons for avoiding too much stress include the fact that it makes us more accident-prone. Under emotional strain, people also often neglect their health. They may fail to keep up preventive checks or neglect important symptoms, such as breast lumps. When people are under heavy stress, they often reduce the amount of exercise they have. They feel too tired to go to the swimming pool or arrange a tennis match, or doing this seems like an unwarranted detour from solving pressing problems.

Stress and work performance

Besides helping you to avoid health problems, of course, it is worth noticing early signs of stress because they can tell you that your performance is on the point of suffering, and that keeping up the pressure will have the opposite effect from the one you are pursuing – quickly and effectively reaching your goals.

It is as well to heed the warning if you are often physically very tired at the end of the day and wake up in the morning feeling unrefreshed and unwilling to move until galvanized by the thought of the work there is to do. This is a sign that your productivity has peaked and is probably slipping under the weight of fatigue. If there is still much more work to do

KEEPING A STRESS DIARY

■ *People sometimes worry that, trying to be aware of their own reactions, they will become pre-occupied with stress. However, this usually does not happen unless they feel helpless about their problems. Combined with an understanding of how to control stress levels (see Ch 25), self-awareness is a life skill.*

It requires practice, for the brain is like a filter that keeps information about our own selves out of consciousness. It processes a massive amount of information and focuses our attention selectively, mainly on external objects and events. Voluntarily turning your attention to how you feel, however, can provide useful information. Is this a day or a time of day when you should feel relaxed and refreshed? Instead, do the muscles in your limbs feel tight? Do you feel tired? Is your pulse racing?

One of the most effective ways to discover your own stress level is by keeping a diary. The patterns that emerge usually suggest strategies for coping better.

The diary should contain a note of the stress level, rated from 1 to 10 on your own subjective assessment of how much more stressed you feel than when totally relaxed. There should be information about the circumstances, activities or people involved, and any other details you think may be useful. You may find that certain situations or people raise your stress level. You may find that you are under greater stress at particular times of the year – for example, if you are a school teacher, you will not be surprised to find greater signs of stress toward the end of each school term, after several weeks' build-up of pressure.

You may find that you are under greater stress at a particular time of day. This is normal. Some people show peak performance in the morning, while others do better in the early evening. One reason why people may handle stress better during different parts of the day may be diet. Skipping lunch or drinking a great deal of tea, coffee or other drinks containing caffeine may reduce your ability to concentrate or may increase a tendency to overreact when challenged.

Regular high levels of stress may not pose problems so long as regular periods of relaxation (see Ch 25) are also a part of your day. Relaxation relieves the high state of arousal associated with stress, and it restores your capacity to meet pressures. It is therefore important to continue your diary into the evening and weekend hours. You may find that stress spills over from the working day into the evening, a particularly important pattern to take note of, for this is where the problems associated with chronic, unrelieved stress begin.

SIGNS OF STRESS CHECKLIST

■ *Are you under too much stress? Here is a checklist of common physical, psychological and behavioral signs of chronic stress. Indicate the degree to which you have ex-* *perienced each of them over the past four weeks, choosing a number from the following scale: 0 = never, 1 = occasionally, 2 = frequently, 3 = constantly or almost constantly.*

None of these symptoms is a guaranteed measure of excess stress, but if several affect you frequently or constantly, and other causes are difficult to identify, you should read Ch 25.

PHYSICAL SIGNS
Tension headaches or migraine headaches.
Difficulty in falling or staying asleep.
Fatigue.
Overeating.
Loss of appetite.
Constipation or diarrhea.
Lower-back pain.
Allergy problems.
Hives.
Skin rashes.
Indigestion.
Aching neck and shoulders.
Twitches.
Ulcers.

PSYCHOLOGICAL SIGNS
Nervousness.
Anxiety.
Irritability.
Depression.
Anger.
Feeling withdrawn.
Feeling that you do not want to do the things you have to .
Feeling emotionally drained.
Suffering from nightmares.
Finding difficulty in remembering.
Losing your sense of humor.

BEHAVIORAL SIGNS
Reduced quality of work performance.
Lower productivity at work.
Mistrust or hostility toward associates.
Missing appointments or deadlines.
Absenteeism or shirking responsibilities.
Minor accidents, increased errors.
Indecisiveness.
Problems with sexual performance.
Using drugs.
Excessive use of alcohol or tobacco.

Your reactions to stress may be stressful to your family and friends. Unable to control the source of stress, they must suffer your irritability, loss of humor and lack of time. It may be clear to them and not to you that you need to rest.

before the crisis is over, you will probably do it quicker and better if you take a few days off.

Other warning signs are difficulty in sleeping, indecisiveness, forgetfulness and mental blocks and difficulty in pronouncing words toward the end of the day. You may find yourself prone to nervous laughter, even to trembling, and to impulsive behavior.

There may be jobs you used to do in a few hours, but now they seem to go on forever. It becomes increasingly difficult to recover your concentration after interruptions. Normal levels of stimulation – the presence of other people, ringing telephones – combine with excess pressure and your own reduced vigor to leave you feeling disorganized and distracted. But you may begin to be productive again when alone – for example, in the late afternoon when everyone else has left the office.

A positive strategy is to lower the level of stimulation when you are trying to get things done. Even if you pride yourself on your ability (normally) to concentrate, create uninterrupted quiet times. Take breaks in order to relax. Decide on an order of priorities and stick to it. A less constructive way of coping is to give yourself over to distractions, getting nothing done except reacting to other people's initiatives. The high priority items do not get done, and the work backlog keeps growing. So does the pressure.

Some people try to cope with feeling swamped at work by devoting weekends or evenings to catching up. But this can create further stress by taking away the time for necessary

relaxation, and the situation may worsen if family and friends begin to feel resentful about losing your time and attention, or about the bad temper with which you drive at household tasks compressed into a smaller and smaller time slot.

Stress and relationships

Reactions to stress can have serious consequences for both personal and workplace relationships. Tension caused by stress can make you lose your sense of humor – though you might not know it until someone tells you – or you might find yourself overreacting to small irritations, blowing up suddenly at people or becoming impatient with them. Approaching an encounter with a friend or colleague in a state of irritation is likely to lessen your ability to express your point of view, listen effectively and take in new information. You may easily feel opposed or not understood. (Under excess stress many people become hypersensitive to criticism.) As a result the meeting can become frustrating for both parties. Both of you will leave it with a sense of ill will that may be revived when you next meet.

Remember that your reactions to chronic stress are stressful to your family – all the more so because they have no control over the situation that is driving you. *They* must wait helplessly for the crisis to pass, while you at least have some sense of bringing about this solution. Their failure to feel a sense of progress may infuriate you – it may seem disloyal and undermining, because you rely on that sense of progress to keep going. But the chances are that it is only too obvious to them that your progress would probably be better if you took proper rests. **AER**

► **When the pace of competition becomes a strain,** *we tend to carry the strain into our relationships. One sign of this is losing your sense of humor. Another is overreacting to small irritations. Under excess stress many people become hypersensitive to criticism. They may feel opposed or not understood by family or colleagues. Tension caused by the personal conflicts that may result can make it all the more difficult to deal with the original problems.*

Emotional Breakdown

EMOTIONAL breakdowns occur when people experience an excess of "nerves," anxiety or stress. They occur not only because of the demands that are made on the victims, but because of the way they cope with these demands. If they cope badly, stress and internal conflict can build up alarmingly. Reducing this internal conflict involves becoming aware of its source and adopting new coping strategies: developing new interests, rebuilding self-confidence and, most importantly, learning to communicate again with other people.

Stress and strain

"I found I couldn't concentrate on anything, and I couldn't sit still. I was tired and exhausted, but even so, waves of panic would sweep over me. Eventually, I started crying all the time and people knew something was wrong."

"My husband came home looking for me. I heard his voice but I couldn't move. I was too frightened by the bedroom, even by the furniture. Finally he found me crouched up against the corner of the room. I just stared at him..."

These descriptions of the experience of emotional breakdown are very different, but the main feature of both is a feeling of being so completely overwhelmed by stress that it is impossible to continue with everyday life. The right amount of stress can be a positive influence, challenging and motivating us so that we perform better (see *Ch 23*). Too little stress, or the absence of outside demands, can lead to

feelings of dissatisfaction and boredom. In fact, it has been found that in times of war and other extreme circumstances when people are exposed to unusually great stress, the incidence of breakdowns actually decreases.

Stress by itself does not cause breakdowns. It is merely a force or group of forces acting on the individual. Difficulties arise only when people are not able to deal with stress as it

BURNOUT

■ *"Burnout" is having an emotional breakdown through job stress. It happens when a person identifies too closely with an idealized role and has unreasonably high self-expectations. Victims are frequently members of the caring professions – nurses, teachers, social workers, therapists. The typical victim is excessively dedicated. They work long hours, usually for little pay, and tend to invest a lot of extra time and energy in their job.*

They ignore material discomforts and identify fully with what they feel are the more spiritual rewards of the job. They may also be loners who may feel indispensable and unable to delegate responsibility.

There are also organizational pressures involved in burnout. The victim may come into conflict with red tape or inadequate resources which work against the desire to help clients. Quite often, for example, the junior nurse has to face the combined conflicts of not being able to care for patients in the way he or she expects because of resource cuts, together with a high level of responsibility in her job but low social status in society at large.

Sufferers go from active coping to a loss of purpose and a cynical attitude toward work and life. They may go through a phase of distorting their achievements to lessen guilt. Sullen, irritable, and angry at their job and others, they denigrate everything, finally making errors and becoming exhausted. The remedy for burn-

out involves intensive social support systems, restricting priorities, setting shorter, more realistic goals in their work and using collective support systems to change the organizational structure of their profession.

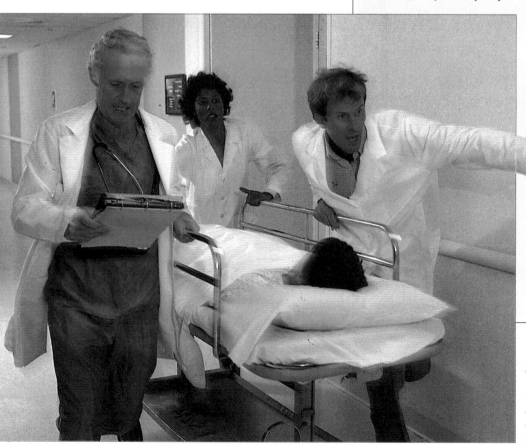

◄ **Under an intense daily pressure**, *emergency-ward medical staff rush a patient to the operating theater. Internal conflicts between high personal standards of care and the obstacles to fulfilling them can lead to "burnout."*

If we cope badly with stress, internal conflicts can build up alarmingly, and lead to an emotional breakdown. This can be devastating, but the experience may also be a turning point from which to rebuild in new directions.

occurs and allow it to build up. When this happens, they try to function under an excessive load, and *strain* develops – an excess of stress that works against us.

A favorite analogy of our mechanistic age is to think of ourselves as "human machines." Like other machines, we work better if kept in good order and in daily use. However, we can only take so much stressful wear and tear: any more and we are heading for mechanical failure, or emotional breakdown.

Once strain develops the analogy ends, because, unlike machines, humans supply their own internal strain. It occurs when the things in life that we identify with and strive toward pull us in opposite directions at the same time – as if we are on a broken raft in the middle of the ocean, desperately trying to keep the pieces together so that we can stay afloat. This conflict produces increasing feelings of tension and restlessness until, eventually, we are unable to make decisions or sometimes even to move. We have, in fact, reached breaking point.

Why do we feel internal conflicts?

People often perform more than one role in their lives – union official/teacher, fire fighter/lay preacher – and for most, having multiple roles broadens and enriches their lives. However, when these roles are by nature incompatible, and yet the person fully identifies with them, conflict is created that can lead to an emotional breakdown.

There are many women, for example, who have successfully combined a full-time business career with the role of mother. But a woman who believes that a good mother is always available for her children, and a good businesswoman spends all her time at the office, will be in conflict if she tries to adopt both roles.

TIPPING THE BALANCE

■ *People who are teetering on the edge of a breakdown often show certain definite signs. They are increasingly withdrawn from reality, perhaps becoming progressively preoccupied and secretive. Their behavior may become bizarre and apparently irrational, and they will have less and less honest communication with others. Sometimes people feel irritable, tired and tense, and they may complain of sleeplessness, physical discomfort and anxiety.*

If a person has reached the breaking point, almost anything can push them over the edge. Most can identify some small event that was the "straw that broke the camel's back." For one, upsetting a jar of jam was the crucial factor. The jam went everywhere, she was unable to get it back inside – so she gave up there and then. For another, a harsh word from an employer was the final straw.

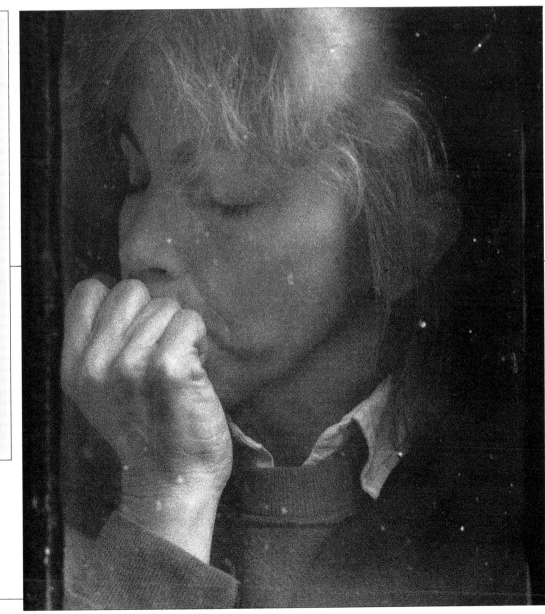

▶ **"I started crying all the time**.*" When there is no relief from the strain of internal conflict, stress can become so great that the tiniest extra challenge can become overwhelming.*

Alternatively, if she feels that the quality, rather than the quantity, of the time spent on each role is the important factor, conflict is less likely to arise. Many people combine seemingly impossible roles successfully, and they do this by working out a way of life that makes no conflicting demands on their identity.

Another kind of conflict occurs when the reactions and rewards we wish to receive from others do not match those we actually get. We may feel that we do everything in our power to be loved but are still rejected, or we may work hard to impress the boss but continue to be ignored. Often this is because the means we have used to get what we want have been inappropriate.

For instance, some of us may complain that, despite all we have done, we have failed to receive an important promotion, but on examination we may find that we acted in a self-defeating and desperate manner, or that we have been somehow offensive in our approach.

Sometimes conflicts occur because our goals are actually unattainable. They may be completely unrealistic – perhaps we want to be loved by everyone all the time – or it may be that those we expect to reward us (emotionally or materially) are unable or unwilling to do so. The latter often happens to people who have suffered the loss of a relationship due to bereavement or breakup: they may be unable to stop behaving in ways that used to provide them with rewards from their loved ones but no longer do. This then leads to a conflict of behavior and expectation and, frequently, breakdown.

Conflicts in self-expectation occur when people decide that they must simultaneously achieve two basically incompatible goals. This could be a student who expects to go out every night instead of studying but still wants to get a good degree. Very often these individuals are unaware that what they are trying to achieve is impossible. They may be genuinely ignorant of the incompatibility of their strategies or,

MANAGING CONFLICTS

■ *LEFT Anxiety about role conflicts – for example, concern that maternal responsibilities may hamper your effectiveness and flexibility as an executive – is only one of the internal conflicts that can lead to emotional strain. Conflict can also occur between the love or recognition that you believe you deserve and what you actually receive. Conflicts of expectation result too when we set unattainable or highly conflicting goals for ourselves. ABOVE Getting it off their* chests. *Nurses protesting over their pay and working conditions make an uninhibited spectacle of themselves in the streets of London. When problems about your job begin to upset you, it is important to take action of some kind. Communicating with your employer is often a useful first step before looking for another job. The problems may be open to solution, and you will at least get practice in making your views known.*

Most people who have breakdowns feel stranded – unable to discuss their anxieties with others. Surprisingly, people who constantly complain to their friends about their lot in life are not the ones who break down emotionally.

more likely, they cannot decide which goal to identify with and concentrate on. They are unable to meet their own expectations and an overwhelming conflict builds up.

Coping with emotional conflict

We all have times when life makes conflicting demands on us, but in most cases we cope with this by modifying our behavior and our own demands. Usually we can see beyond the conflict because we are not tied to our initial expectations. For example, if we have been looking forward to a vacation and, just at the last moment, one of our children falls ill, we can cope with the disappointment by knowing that we can go another time and, besides, the well-being of those we love is of far greater importance than the anticipated pleasures of any holiday.

However, it is essential to know that an emotional conflict exists if we are to deal with it successfully. Unfortunately, we may not always be sure of our underlying feelings, and since life is often unpredictable, we can be caught unawares by some external event, such as loss of a job or sudden illness in the family. A man with low self-esteem, for example, who defines himself in terms of the job he feels society expects him to do, might not understand why he feels depressed and less masculine when he suddenly loses that job. Without knowing that his real problem is a lack of self-esteem, he would not be able to deal successfully with the conflict.

One common yet contradictory method of coping with conflict is to avoid committing ourselves to any particular course of action, including any that could possibly relieve us of our conflicts. Instead of trying to steer a clear way through our problems, we construct reasons to remain in turmoil, usually out of a fear of the unknown. Someone may claim to want a love relationship desperately but fear the demands they believe such a relationship would bring. Although they may go through the motions of trying to meet prospective partners, their manner and actions are so self-defeating that they will never form a relationship with anyone. The strain caused by this conflict – wanting a partner but preventing themselves from finding one – may cause them to retreat further until they are completely unable to go out and face the world. It would have been far better if, before reaching this low point, they had examined their behavior and taken steps to change it so that their chances of forming a relationship were increased. However, many people find changing the status quo very frightening and refuse to do anything to alter their circumstances, even when their current situation is causing them great pain.

The importance of communication

A breakdown is as much about an inability or a lack of opportunity to communicate problems to others as it is about not coping with them. Most people who experience breakdowns feel stranded and unable to discuss their anxieties with others. Very often they have false expectations about themselves and about how others see them, and this can prevent them from communicating their feelings. This is particularly true of those in positions of authority or those with jobs that involve listening to and helping others.

Surprisingly, people who constantly complain to their friends about their lot in life are not the most likely to have

◀ **Making a joke of it.** *One of the most important advantages of friendships is that they allow us safely to make fun of the causes of strain in our lives. Employees at a company picnic may release tension by ridiculing the company procedures that frustrate them daily. Wives joke to each other about their husbands' lack of attention; husbands joke to each other about wives' lack of understanding. With tensions eased, it is often possible to return to work and to other relationships in a more constructive frame of mind.*

breakdowns. They have found, no matter how inadequate and annoying for their listeners, a means of sharing their problems that will make it easier for them to cope. On the contrary, those most at risk are usually quiet, seemingly controlled individuals, whose expectations of themselves do not allow displays of emotion, and whose calm demeanors hide long-standing depression and a detachment from the rewards of social activity and support.

Recovering from breakdown

Of those who suffer emotional breakdown, the majority make a good recovery. In fact, many people emerge with a new perspective on life that allows creative possibilities

People who have had a breakdown may feel at the mercy of events or even of their own thoughts. It is important for them to develop confidence, to be able to feel in control when they address the problems that face them.

they never had before. Recovery usually depends on five factors. First, and most important, is the ability to view old conflict-producing habits in a new light. *Cognitive therapy* helps people to challenge their expectations of themselves, and to view reality and other people as less threatening than before (see p247). They become more flexible and learn how to discuss and clarify their personal and social expectations, eliminating any conflicting ones.

Another way to develop a more flexible approach is to participate in a broader range of activities. Research has shown that people prone to breakdowns tend to identify themselves totally with the way they perform. It is therefore very hard for them to stand back from a failure and say, "Well, that happened and it hurt, but there are other things I am more successful at." Exploring new areas of activity will help overcome this tendency to feel that one failure is evidence of a total lack of worth.

A third important factor is learning to feel in control. Those who have had a breakdown may feel at the mercy of events or even of their own thoughts. It is important to develop confidence in order to cope with stressful events. A confident person will be able to address a problem head-on instead of fearfully withdrawing from it and allowing imagination and false expectation to take over.

If your employer gives you a work assignment, but you are not exactly clear about what to do, you may lack the confidence to ask for more information. You might feel that you

▲ **Taking up a new interest** *during recovery can boost self-esteem and lighten a dull routine. A range of activities means a wide scope for success: if you know there are things you are good at, you are less likely to be overwhelmed by failures in other aspects of life. A hobby* *you can do alone increases your self-reliance. Joining an evening class or discussion group means meeting new people who may reinforce the social support system crucial to a well-balanced emotional life.*

Build close friendships with people you find supportive

Minimize fatigue and strain by improving your physical fitness

Discover new activities that offer opportunities for success

BEATING EMOTIONAL BREAKDOWN

Develop a more flexible approach by re-evaluating your expectations

Cultivate a more confident approach to potentially stressful events

THE POSITIVE ASPECTS OF BREAKDOWN

■ *For most people, having a breakdown is the most devastating experience of their lives, but it can have some positive consequences.*

Having let go of the all-absorbing conflicts that eventually led to breakdown, victims may for the first time in many years find an opportunity to reappraise their whole system of values, changing their identities and giving their lives a new direction.

Many artists and political and religious figures have found their purpose in life as a result of a breakdown.

Ongoing reappraisal, however, is to be preferred. It helps us to avoid identifying with fixed and unrealistic expectations.

"I FEEL IN CONTROL OF MY LIFE AGAIN"

■ *A man who made a very successful recovery tells his story in these words: "My breakdown happened a year ago, though looking back, it had been brewing for much longer. My job as a school principal was demanding. I would spend weekends stewing about problems I had with my teachers, who did not seem to respect me and disliked the reforms in teaching methods I was expected to introduce. I wanted my family to support and reassure me but they resented my preoccupation with work and my constant irritability.*

Suddenly everything started to fall apart.

I was unable to make decisions or concentrate. With the prospect of failure looming, my life lost its direction – the future was a blank. One afternoon a secretary found me sitting dazed in my office, unable to move or even speak.

Sessions with a psychologist helped me see that I hadn't really wanted to run a school. My new job allows me more time for my family and for new interests. It uses the talents I really have and I feel in control of my life again."

are somehow supposed to know what is required and so you go away in confusion.

This conflict becomes increasingly upsetting. If you were a confident person, you would immediately ask for more information, avoiding conflict right from the start. You might even go up in your employer's estimation because of the interest you have shown.

The importance of the fourth factor – an intimate social group – should not be underestimated in preventing or overcoming breakdown. A group of close and trusted friends with whom you can share ideas and let off steam helps to diminish feelings of isolation and the sense of having to cope all alone.

However, not every group is beneficial: if everyone in it has similar problems and shares the same perspective, a "pressure-cooker" atmosphere can develop, and this increases tension instead of reducing it.

A final factor, important to all areas of mental and physical well-being, is physical fitness. Those who are fit seem to cope better with the early effects of strain. Perhaps this counteracts the extremes of fatigue that can add to the psychological difficulties of overcoming conflicts. Fitness also raises mood, putting us in a better frame of mind and enabling us to be more flexible when we encounter stressful events.

To prevent breakdown it may help to remember three "F"s: Fitness, Flexibility (in thought as well as activity) and Friendship. There is also a fourth "F": Fun. Having fun and, in particular, being able to laugh at yourself, are important ways of putting conflicts in perspective. **KPO**

193

◄ **Creating their own entertainment,** *two spectators are unconcerned that rain has stopped play. Making the best of a bad situation does not come naturally to everyone, but is a habit worth cultivating if you are recovering from a breakdown. It is part of learning how to accept unexpected problems and disappointments without distress. Allowing yourself to have fun occasionally and forget everyday concerns helps keep problems in perspective.*

Learning to Relax

LIKE EVERYONE else, you probably have a set of stress "triggers" that work to your disadvantage – particular situations that alarm you or make you impatient when it would be much more useful, and perhaps even better for your health, to stay calm.

For some people, stress is triggered when they notice that the line of traffic in which they are waiting has stopped moving, or, when they are at home, they hear a siren and remember that a member of the family is out of the house. Does your heart stop beating when your supervisor approaches you to ask about progress?

Arriving at work tired and angry because of the traffic, spending an evening worrying about something that has only a minute chance of having happened, finding yourself unable coherently to pass on essential information to a superior – these are all to be avoided. But how is it possible to feel more relaxed in such situations?

Drawbacks of tranquilizers and alcohol

People face stress-triggering situations better when they are in a relaxed state to begin with, and that is why many who are going through a period of high stress resort to tranquilizers such as valium. These provide a very convenient and often reliable method of staying calm. However, there are a number of drawbacks to using alcohol as an aid to coping with stress.

Repeated research shows that people who have one or two drinks a day live longer, on average, than teetotalers. In particular, they are less likely to die of heart disease. One explanation that has been put forward, is that having a drink when you get home helps you to unwind and so have a more relaxing respite from your work. Too much of this good thing is, of course, bad for you: people who take more than two drinks a day tend to die younger than teetotalers.

However, people who are neither teetotalers nor regular drinkers do best. Those who have less than the one drink a day, and as little as one in a month, live the longest.

It is worth remembering as well that the chemical by-products of alcohol stay in the blood for many hours after your drink has given you that nice relaxed feeling. Since these are the chemicals that give you a hangover when you drink too much, it is possible that they contribute, even when you only take one or two drinks, to all of the other causes of tiredness and irritability next day that eventually make you look forward so much to getting home and having a drink. When you are going through a period of especially great pressure at work, you may find it surprising how much more energy you have if you cut down on your already moderate intake of alcohol.

Both tranquilizers and alcohol, when it is taken at inappropriate times, can produce too much relaxation and lead to drowsiness when you need to be alert. Also, the calming effects of these drugs can weaken over time as your body develops a tolerance for them. You will feel a need to increase your dose. Addiction is a serious danger: dependency may develop with long-term use of valium as

► **Experiments in the kitchen** are part of the relaxation in this couple's lifestyle. Though it often seems impossible to summon energy after a demanding day, active recreation with friends or your family is more restorative than television viewing. Thirty minutes daily of gentle exercise that makes your heart beat faster can also help: it leaves you feeling refreshed, and even people who are only moderately fit find stress much easier to bear.

To manage stress effectively, it is essential to cultivate the habit of relaxation. Regular rest and relaxation help to keep tension low. Routine muscular relaxation exercises also help, and they can be used strategically when pressures mount.

well as with overuse of alcohol. In some circumstances tranquilizers may be necessary in the short term to bring anxiety down to levels that allow us to learn how to cope without drugs. However, whenever possible, chemicals should give way to improved lifestyle and improved coping methods. You might beat all the longevity averages by learning how to relax without taking a drink.

If you automatically reach for a cigarette when you experience a stress trigger, you are pursuing a particularly self-defeating relaxation strategy. Nicotine, the most important drug in tobacco smoke, is a stimulant: smoking makes you less relaxed (see *Ch 19*).

A more relaxing lifestyle

Very often, when people are under stress, they complain that they do not have enough energy to do anything in their leisure time. As a result, they vegetate each evening in front of a television set. Rather than doing less and less, the antidote to this lack of energy is often to do more, because a lack of challenge and fulfillment in leisure time contributes to fatigue. Exercise, in particular, discharges tension, and

195

■ **Relaxing situations** *help us to put tensions aside, but it is useful too to learn relaxation techniques such as those mentioned on page 196. Your muscles may be more tense than you realize, even when you sit reading. In a workplace experiment, one group of workers learned a relaxation method and practiced it twice a day. A second group sat quietly twice a day. After eight weeks, the relaxation group had a lower number of health complaints and fewer days of illness. They had higher scores on work performance tests and showed higher job satisfaction.*

A MUSCLE-RELAXATION EXERCISE

■ The following instructions are for "progressive muscle relaxation." This relaxation technique consists of first tensing then letting go each of the main muscle groups in your body and learning to associate the word "Relax" with the feeling of letting go.

You should spend about 15 minutes per day practicing. Gradually, you will reach deeper levels of relaxation, and reach them more quickly. Eventually it should become possible to feel fully relaxed even in a crisis, simply by saying the word "Relax" to yourself or by taking one or two deep breaths. This will give you a strategic tool for keeping in control when your personal stress triggers might otherwise work against you.

BREATHING

1 Sit or lie comfortably with your eyes closed.
2 Breathe deeply. Hold your breath for a moment and then let it out slowly. You will feel yourself becoming more relaxed. Repeat this step two more times.
3 Breathe more naturally and allow yourself to think only of your breath going easily in and out as you feel more and more relaxed.

TENSING

In each of the next ten steps (4-13) tense the particular muscles mentioned for 5-10 seconds, let them go and let your mind dwell for about 30 seconds on how relaxed they are. The tensing will help you to recognize muscle tension more quickly later and know when you need to relax. The contrast between muscle tension and what you feel afterward will enhance the relaxation.

7 Put your chin on your chest to make your neck tense, then let your neck go limp.
6 Tense and then relax your shoulders.
5 Move your hands up to your shoulders to make your arms tense, then let your arms go limp.
4 Clench your fists tightly, then let your hands go limp.

START TENSING HERE

8 Close your eyes tightly, then relax and feel the relaxation in your upper face.
9 Clench your jaw, then relax it and feel the relaxation in your lower face.
10 Tense and relax your stomach and chest.
11 Tense and relax your thighs and buttocks.
12 Tense and relax your calves and legs.
13 Tense your feet, curl your toes, and then let them relax.

RELAXING

14 Allow a few moments of rest with calm and regular breathing. Allow yourself to feel comforted by your sense of relaxation. Let the relaxation spread deeper and deeper.
15 Go slowly through the muscles of your body again without tensing them. Allow a wave of relaxation to pass through each part of your body. If you can feel tension anywhere, let it flow away.
16 Think of the relaxation everywhere in your body.
17 Think of the easy flow of your breathing, in and out.
18 Spend about a minute thinking of the word "Relax" each time you breathe out and thinking of how relaxed you feel.
19 Count slowly from 1 to 10, feeling progressively more refreshed and awake. Open your eyes. You will feel refreshed, awake and relaxed.

LEARNING RELAXATION THROUGH BIOFEEDBACK

■ "Biofeedback" means recording a person's physiological responses and simultaneously feeding this information back to them. It is used for training people to control their responses. For example, in the treatment of tension headaches by biofeedback, electrodes are placed on the forehead, neck or jaw. The signal from the electrodes is amplified and converted to a sound or a light display that the patient can read. The patient can experiment by voluntarily tensing the muscles of the face and neck and noting the difference in signals. When instructed to reduce the level of tension, people are usually able to change in the desired direction, even without knowing how to accomplish the change, and the feedback reinforces this ability. Using relaxing imagery or other techniques, they will find that the tone will change to indicate more and more relaxation, and their goal will be to discover how much more relaxed they can allow those muscles to become.

The most common use for biofeedback is in relaxation training, but research indicates that it is rarely more effective than methods which do not involve technology. When it is used, it is combined with unaided home relaxation practice, such as the progressive muscle relaxation technique, and studies have found that the home practice is the most effective part of the treatment. The time and expense involved in attending biofeedback sessions or buying biofeedback equipment may well be unnecessary.

▲ **Headaches** are often caused by muscle tension. Muscles begin to hurt when kept tense for long periods of time. Long-term muscle contraction during stress has been found in people prone to headaches and jaw pain. Taking a painkiller is less effective than avoiding the onset of pain altogether through relaxation.

From a scientific point of view, relaxation means a lengthening of the fibers in the muscles. It is not simply a matter of sitting quietly or sleeping, for at such times it is quite possible for your muscles to be contracted by tension and remain unrelaxed.

this is energy-giving, not energy-consuming. Research has found that people who are physically unfit are more physiologically aroused by stressful events and feel them more keenly: they are more alarmed, or more angry. Regular aerobic exercise, however, has been shown to reduce the intensity of their reactions. Aerobic exercise is any activity, such as jogging or swimming, kept up for 25-30 minutes, that significantly increases your intake of oxygen. You can tell that you are exercising enough by taking your pulse: subtract your age from 220 and aim for a pulse rate that is 60 to 75 percent of this figure. When you are unfit, you will easily reach this target in gentle exercise with short rests. Gradually you will find yourself wanting to exercise harder because your heart can perform so much better.

If the demands that you face do not leave you any leisure, it is time to review your goals in life and reassess the realism of the way you pursue them. No one can be effective without rest and recreation each day and without taking a day or two off each week to relax with family and friends.

Letting your muscles relax

From a scientific point of view, relaxation means a lengthening of the fibers in the muscles attached to your skeleton. It is not simply a matter of sitting quietly or sleeping, for at times like that it is quite possible for muscles to remain contracted by tension.

Muscle relaxation can be the welcome result of listening to a favorite, calming piece of music, having a neck massage or hearing a good joke. To these means it is useful to add conscious techniques of relaxation that can be used anywhere and at any time. This is a skill that makes it possible for you to turn down your inward level of tension at will, even as you sit at your desk or stand at the front of a classroom, as the day's pressures mount.

Whichever of the many relaxation techniques you use, you will need to do four things:

1 Focus your attention on a word or sound that you have learned to associate with relaxation.
2 Disregard any competing thoughts or any worries about how well you are doing.

197

■ **Calm in mind and body**. *ABOVE By increasing the strength and mobility of muscles, the ancient Indian art of yoga helps to ease tension. Meditation, the mental aspect of yoga, also helps. It too can produce a highly relaxing effect on the muscles. The kind of meditation relevant here involves assuming a relaxed posture and repeating a set word or "mantra," letting its sound fill your mind. Widely used in India is the mantra "om," meaning* "one" *in the sense of the unity of all being. RIGHT In prayer, people achieve the benefits of relaxation through putting from their minds their daily concerns and allowing themselves to feel a passive dependence on a deity.*

3 Keep yourself in as comfortable a position as possible, so that your muscles have little work to do.

4 Keep environmental stimuli to a minimum – for example, by closing your eyes.

It is helpful to be able to do this, and thereby achieve relaxation, without depending on props, such as candlelight. The times when you will most need to relax are probably not going to offer a relaxing ambience. Many techniques have been developed to help people learn to relax in this way.

REDUCING "TYPE A" BEHAVIOR

■ *Learn to relax and you may live longer. In a four-year project in San Francisco, stress-prone men who had already had a heart attack had a lower heart-attack recurrence rate after learning relaxation techniques.*

The project involved 850 heart-attack victims. More than 95 percent of them were found to have Type A personalities (see p182) in an interview: the interviewer was able easily to provoke frustration, anger, and time-urgency.

One group received standard medical counseling. Another group (of 592) received standard counseling plus advice about Type A behavior.

The medical counseling was given by heart specialists. It consisted of advice and information about diet, exercise, drugs and treatment.

The additional Type A behav-

ior counseling included training in progressive muscle relaxation, advice about rethinking beliefs that lead to hostility and time-urgency, and advice about restructuring some stressful aspects of life. Specific Type A behavior drills were also included. For example, if participants found themselves hurrying to make a light, they would be required to backtrack for one block in order to remind themselves of how self-defeating such hurrying is in the long run.

Those participating in this program of behavioral change showed significantly less Type A behavior over the four years. In each year of the project, only 2.96 percent, on average, suffered a further heart attack. A far less dramatic decline in Type A behavior and recurrence occurred in the medical counseling program.

"Progressive muscular relaxation" is the name for the technique outlined in the box on p196. "Autogenic training," developed in Germany, has six exercises to be practiced several times a day. First, imagine that your limbs feel very heavy. Say to yourself: "my feet are becoming heavier, my legs are becoming heavier," and so on. Second, imagine that your limbs feel pleasantly warm. Say "my feet are becoming warmer," and so on. Third, tell yourself that your heart is beating more calmly and more slowly. Fourth, tell yourself that your breathing is becoming slower and deeper. Fifth, tell yourself that the upper part of your abdomen feels pleasantly warmer. Sixth, tell yourself that your forehead feels pleasantly cooler.

With the completion of each step it is useful to take a slightly longer breath and suggest to yourself that you have reached a deeper level of relaxation, with a more complete unwinding of muscular tension. It is important simply to *let* the relaxation occur. Avoid trying to force yourself to relax.

Overcoming stress triggers

Not only can relaxation techniques keep you in a relaxed mood, but they can be used directly to keep you calm when stress triggers are released. When you have practiced enough to build a strong association between your tech-

Relaxation techniques can be used to keep cool in stressful situations. You can make yourself calm in preparation for predictable crises. By imagining them, you can practice feeling calm in ones that happen without warning.

nique and genuine muscle relaxation, you will find it possible to transfer the association to a less elaborate form of your ritual – one that you can use strategically at a time of stress, perhaps simply by taking a calming breath and saying to yourself "relax."

Your relaxation technique can also be used to make you less sensitive to your personal stress triggers. First, make a list of what these triggers are. Notice which things set your heart pounding, make you sigh in exasperation, or make you think of lighting a cigarette or making coffee. Look especially for the triggers that produce reactions that are out of proportion or make matters worse.

In the case of triggers that occur at predictable times, you can use your relaxation technique to make yourself especially calm in preparation for the stress. This should be combined with positive-thinking. Often when we face stress, we make our emotional reaction worse by thinking of stress inducing interpretations: "I know this can't work," "This is always an impossible time of the day." This can impair your ability to deal with the problem. It is more helpful to say "I know I'm finding this hard now, but every day I'm going to get better and better at it" or "I know that it seems hopeless, but that's because I'm so emotional at the moment; as I learn to do this more calmly, I know I'll be able to work out a better way."

When you cannot predict when a certain stress trigger will next occur (for example, when an interoffice memo will arrive from your supervisor), you should practice the relaxation routine while imagining the event. Put yourself into a state of deep relaxation and then imagine the memo arriving while you continue to relax. Practice this a few times and be prepared to act it out in real life when the memo does arrive. Rehearse and have ready something positive and encouraging to say to yourself.

By associating relaxation with a stress trigger, both in your imagination and in real situations, you may eventually extinguish the conditioned emotional reaction that you began with and replace it with a calm, relaxed response. You will be better placed to act and think in a more appropriate way. **AER**

PUTTING A BRAKE ON TRAFFIC NERVES

■ *Driving makes us tense. It is dangerous combining high speed and close proximity to other fast-moving vehicles. Also, although in other aspects of life we can to some extent control who we interact with, this is not the case while driving, and when another driver is inconsiderate we feel helpless. Hurling abuse, using the horn or taking revenge by subjecting them to the same discourtesy, are unlikely to be effective and are likely to leave you more worked up.*

Certain conditions have to be satisfied if expressing anger is to make you feel better:

1. *You direct the anger at the person responsible.*
2. *You express the right amount of anger. Too little will leave you with a feeling of self-effacement. Too much may cause guilt.*

3. *The person does not retaliate, but acknowledges and accepts your point of view. These conditions will seldom be met when you are driving. As a result, giving vent to anger further drives up your stress level. What then is the alternative, since aggravation is bound to occur?*

One important strategy is to keep your background tension low enough that irritating events on the road do not lead to outright anger. Use of relaxation techniques, possibly at each traffic light, may be helpful. Rather than regarding each stop as an obstacle, you might think of it as part of a routine that gives you opportunities to relax, or review plans for the day. It also helps to develop the habit of checking bodily tension while driving, in order to release tension that may have developed in the shoulders or neck.

When aggravating situations occur, be prepared for them. It is naive and unrealistic to expect that everyone is going to drive appropriately. Assume in advance there are going to be problems and use them as opportunities to practice not being triggered.

Experiment with ways of letting go of the anger so that it does not build up uncontrollably. When someone cuts you off, think of alternatives to the habitual and inflammatory explanation that they are inconsiderate or that it is deliberate.

Perhaps they are lost, unused to the traffic conditions or are just having a bad day. See which response makes you feel better in the long run.

◄ **Watching fish** *has been found to reduce the watcher's blood pressure measurably. So have relaxation exercises. Keeping pets reduces stress in heart-attack victims. In one survey 28 percent of nonpet-owners and only 6 percent of pet-owners died in the year following a heart attack.*

▶ **A lifetime of traffic tension** *shows in the face of an Italian taxi driver. The frustration of losing time and opportunities makes traffic delays stressful for everyone. Practicing relaxation techniques behind the wheel is a constructive form of relief.*

Positive Thinking

THE BRAIN is the organ of both thought and emotion, which are indivisibly intertwined. Your mood can influence the way you look at the world: what you notice, what you remember and the things you say. Similarly, your thoughts and attitudes affect your moods. Although body chemistry (see *Ch19*) is a more immediate determinant of mood, this in turn seems to be affected by our judgments about the world we find ourselves in, and especially our judgments about ourselves. Taking a positive view of the world and of yourself is easier when your mood is good, and it is easier to be in a good mood when you take a positive view, especially if this motivates you to behave in self-reinforcing ways.

Reacting positively to other people

Encounters with other people have a major impact on our moods. For example, it has a lasting positive effect when people show an interest in what you have said, find you sexually attractive, or tell you that you have done something well. This seems to imply that our moods are at the mercy of others. However, the effects that others have on us are not due solely to their behavior but also to the expectations that we ourselves bring into the process. Researchers have identified three stages that each of us controls to some extent when meeting others, and these help to determine the way we feel in social situations.

If, for example, you are going to a party, in *stage 1* you have a specific idea about what it will be like for you, and this expectation is likely to come true. If you think, "No one is going to talk to me," there is an excellent chance of exactly that happening. This becomes a self-fulfilling prophecy, because the unsociable mood that it produces in you hampers you from taking conversational initiatives, and it may cause you to use facial expressions and other body language that make you seem unattractive. This is far less likely to happen if you go to the party with an open mind and a friendly approach.

In *stage 2*, you consciously or unconsciously evaluate what is happening in an encounter. You might approach a group at the party with the intention of starting a conversation, and they ignore you, perhaps by walking or turning away. You can evaluate this situation in a number of ways. You could be negative and think, "They probably don't like me," or you may ask the self-doubting question, "How have I offended them?" However, you could be more open-minded and think, "They might not have seen me," an evaluation that would not reflect badly on you. Whether you are negative, neutral or positive in your outlook directly influences the quality of your mood.

In *stage 3*, you come to a conclusion about why something has happened – in this example, why you were ignored. There are three ways of answering the question, depending on your personal *style of attribution* (see *Ch14*). First, you may consider whether it is something about you that is at fault (an *internal* cause): "Am I unattractive in some way?" You may instead regard the cause as *external*: "They don't seem to like anyone today." Second, you might

---

MOOD OR PERSONALITY?

■ We all experience a wide range of emotions throughout the day, but we are not prone to exactly the same responses in the same situations. Partly, this is because we are not all in the same mood, but also, at a deeper level, we have different personalities: some of us are inclined to be gloomy and others to be cheerful (see Ch10).

The fact that personality is one of the determinants of mood, however, is not a reason for thinking that our moods are beyond control. Personality is only partly determined by such heritable factors as our body chemistry – learning and experience also have a considerable effect. To see whether personality is a factor in any of your own moods complete this questionnaire.

For each of the 30 emotions listed, first rate yourself on your present intensity of feeling. Score 1 if you do not feel the

HOW INTENSELY AND HOW FREQUENTLY DO YOU FEEL...

■ Rate intensity first, then go through the list again for frequency.

	7	Cozy	19 Happy
	8	Desperate	20 Scared
	9	Inspired	21 Glad
	10	Desolate	22 Dejected
	11	Benevolent	23 Sympathetic
	12	Cruel	24 Quarrelsome
1 Cheerful	13	Joyful	25 Still
2 Afraid	14	Panicky	26 Tense
3 Willing	15	Protected	27 Interested
4 Bad	16	Lonely	28 Rejected
5 Friendly	17	Even-tempered	29 Understanding
6 Angry	18	Resentful	30 Violent

emotion at all, 5 if you are feeling it very intensely.

SCORING

The questionnaire measures the degree to which you are relaxed, happy and calm. To calculate the degree to which your present mood is relaxed, add up your self-ratings for emotions 1, 7, 13, 19 and 25, and subtract the sum of your self-ratings for emotions 2, 8, 14, 20 and 26.

For happiness add up your self-ratings for emotions 3, 9, 15, 21 and 27. Subtract the sum of your self-ratings for emotions 4, 10, 16, 22 and 28.

For calmness add up your self-ratings for emotions 5, 11, 17, 23 and 29. Subtract the sum of your self-ratings for emotions 6, 12, 18, 24 and 30.

It is possible for scores to range from -25 to +25, depending on whether you are feeling very much in that mood or not at all. Most people score within the range of 10-15 points either side of zero.

When you have assessed your present mood, complete the questionnaire again, but this time rate yourself on how frequently you feel each of the 30 emotions. Score 1 if you never, 5 if you very often feel it. Calculate relaxed, happiness and calmness measures in exactly the same way. This time they tell you whether you are temperamentally relaxed or tense, happy or gloomy, and calm or irritable. Comparing your mood scores with your temperament scores can help you judge whether your present mood is, in fact influenced more by your personality or by your situation.

Your own expectations and attitudes influence your feelings as much as other people do. Making a habit of positive thinking and planning for mood-enhancing activity are ways to manage your emotions, to make them work for you.

regard the cause as *stable* or *unstable* – in other words, is it a permanent thing: "They don't like me because I'm foreign," or something temporary: "They're just reacting to the way I'm dressed." Third, you might regard the cause as *general* or *specific*: "They've never liked me," or "They are annoyed because I'm late." Believing in external, imper-

manent and specific causes will leave you feeling better.

The kind of image we have of ourselves will largely determine the way we feel, as well as our ideas about why things happen. Those with a negative self-image will tend to make negative interpretations of social encounters, which will lead to negative moods. Those with a positive self-image, however, are more likely to interpret events in a way that allows them to continue to feel good about themselves.

Of course, moods can also be catching. We have all

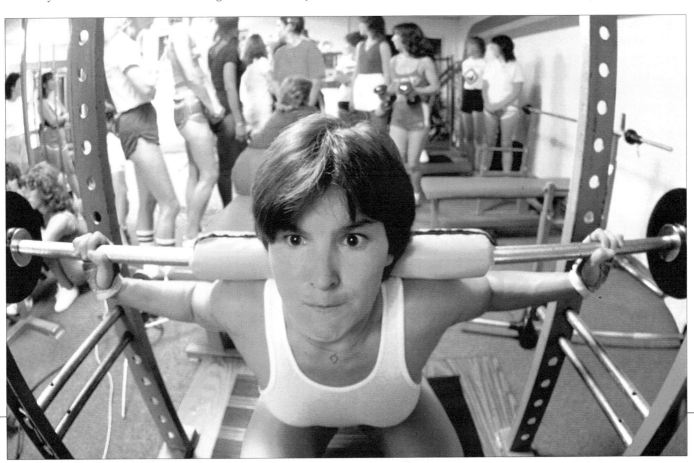

POSITIVE MOODS

■ *ABOVE A mood of determination holds a bodybuilder to her task. Believing that you can succeed is an essential ingredient of the will to succeed. RIGHT Getting full enjoyment from social situations may involve cultivating positive expectations and a friendly approach. LEFT Seeing the funny side of things and helping others to do the same helps this man to release tension and tolerate the tedium and the strain of heavy labor.*

known people who make us happy or depressed simply by the way they act when we are with them. In experiments, volunteers whose emotions were roused with an injection of the hormone adrenaline became happy if a companion seemed happy, angry if the companion seemed angry (see *Ch18*). Clearly your own mood is one of the factors influencing that of the people who might, if their mood is right, find you interesting or sexually attractive. Simply behaving as though you were in a good mood can help others to help you to feel good. **SMH**

Memories and moods

Our emotions and moods can affect the way we remember things, and what we remember affects our mood.

In memory studies, people are sometimes put into a depressed or a very cheerful mood – for example, by means of hypnosis. In one experiment, people are hypnotized and asked to become very happy or sad by trying to remember a scene in which they have been deliriously happy or grievously sad. Then they are given a learning task – for example,

a list of 16 words to remember later. Next, their mood is reversed (from happy to sad or sad to happy) and they learn another set of words. The idea is to try to recreate a real-life sequence in which a variety of moods and memories are experienced. Dramatic "state-dependent" effects are observed: when volunteers are in a sad state, they recall more of the words that they learned while sad than they do of the words that they learned while happy; similarly, when they are in a happy state they recall more of the words they learned while happy.

This principle of state-dependent memory can be usefully applied when you are trying to control your mood. When it becomes difficult to get out of a sad mood, it is worth noting that research with depressed people who constantly feel despair, despondency and melancholy shows that they tend to recall only the unpleasant episodes in their lives. Even more disheartening, their mood makes them interpret present events as depressing, reinforcing their sadness and storing up yet more sad memories. The development of this circle – from depression to perceiving and remembering

The point is that…

…you haven listened to a word

202

■ **Giving vent to a hostile view**. *Effective mood management does not mean always keeping an even temper. Anger may sometimes signal a loss of control but it can equally signal a determination to oppose what you do not accept and make your influence felt. LEFT Demonstrator and counterdemonstrator confront each other with passion. A jabbing finger helps the man to communicate how much the point he is making* *matters to him. RIGHT He leans forward, using his posture to make it clear that he is not simply mentioning but asserting what he says. Anger galvanizes us for action in a fight or an argument. However, it may also concentrate attention in ways that interfere with communication. When angry, we do not listen effectively. Anger is catching – thus angry words may fail to win us a sympathetic ear.*

Moods can affect the way you remember things, and what you remember affects your mood: you make a sad time worse by remembering only sad times. You can break this cycle by trying actively to recall happy experiences.

negative incidents in life, to deeper depression, and so on, may be the reason behind chronic despondency.

This relationship between emotions and thought has led some psychologists to develop therapeutic techniques that interrupt the cycle. Placing a mildly depressed person in a more cheerful environment may be enough. This might be achieved by a change of job, taking a long cruise, or spending time with friends who think positively. For more intractable cases, therapy may need to focus on personal history, with particular emphasis and reinforcement on remembering and noticing the more pleasurable aspects of life.

Sadness and happiness are not the only moods that are affected by memory. If you are trying to put yourself into a confident mood, you will succeed much better if you make a point of calling up memories of the times when you have acted confidently. Reminding yourself of all the times when you have felt frightened and nervous will reinforce the mood you are trying to avoid. **RLS**

Getting into a good mood

The events that trigger bad moods are often beyond our control. Nevertheless, there are practical ways of taking charge of our moods. Some of them are remarkably simple,

but lasting effects may require thoughtful and persistent re-organization of your everyday routines. In 1910, the French pharmacist Emil Coué pioneered a self-help therapy that aimed to increase good health and a feeling of well-being. His followers repeated to themselves the simple statement: "Every day, in every way, I am getting better and better." More than five decades later, students were asked by the American psychologist Emmett C Velten Junior to read 50 statements, first silently and then aloud. The statements were selected to have the same effect that Coué aimed at,

203

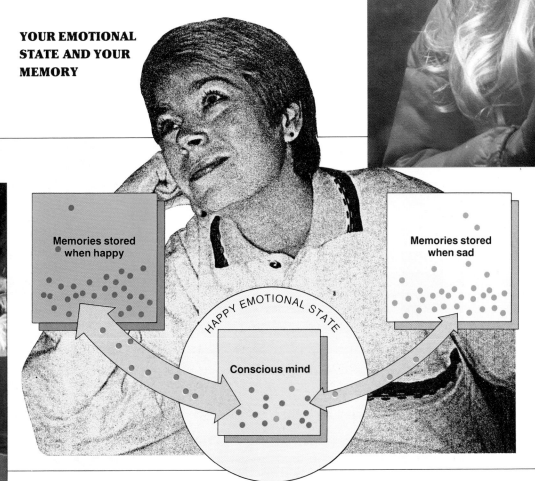

YOUR EMOTIONAL STATE AND YOUR MEMORY

Memories stored when happy

HAPPY EMOTIONAL STATE

Conscious mind

Memories stored when sad

■ **Mood and memories**. *How you feel in the present influences what you remember about the past. Laboratory experiments have shown that, during low moods, memory channels to sad experiences are more open. Channels to happy experiences in the past tend to open best when you are in a good mood: places, sounds, smells, all trigger pleasant memories. When you are happy, an upsetting event in the past ABOVE will come to mind less easily than an entertaining time spent with friends FAR LEFT.*

for example, Velten's students read the phrases "I feel great" and "Things are looking up." The main finding of this experiment was that the mood of some of the students was immediately enhanced, although for only 10-15 minutes. A similar effect was produced each time the procedure was repeated. Since then, the Velten technique has been further refined. The 50 statements have been reduced to 12, so allowing more time to concentrate on each one. People are also encouraged to imagine themselves as being in the mood suggested, and sessions are arranged at the time of a rewarding activity such as a break at work.

Velten's and Coue's technique is an example of auto-suggestion – giving yourself a suggestion such as a hypnotist might give you. If you became adept at self-hypnosis, would the heightened suggestibility that you achieve in the hypnotic state help to make the Velten technique more effective? In fact, when people under hypnosis receive the suggestion that they are happy, they report feelings of self-confidence and self-esteem, they feel socially competent, they are more charitable in their descriptions of social events, and they tell more cheerful stories and make more positive free associations: when asked to say the first thing that comes into their minds, they tend to say something cheerful. However, attempts to extend this positive state beyond the hypnotic trance by giving a long-term post-hypnotic suggestion have not been very successful.

Planning for mood enhancement

The most successful attempts at controlling mood for longer periods have been achieved by therapists who teach their clients to make systematic attempts to enhance mood by restructuring daily activities. Participants keep diaries of

204

▲ **Music enhances mood** at any age: mothers frequently quiet their children with a song. Musical expression covers the full range of emotions and different styles are more or less congenial depending on your mood. Rousing tones and a fast pace jar with a depressed mood, though slow, mournful music may make matters worse. Music's strong powers of association are part of its effect. Deliberately selecting music that puts you in mind of favorite past events can help to relieve present tensions and dissatisfactions.

Recording your reactions to events in a diary allows you to pinpoint activities that put you in a good mood. Dining out, being with friends and dressing up in smart clothes are generally found to be mood-enhancing.

their reactions to different events so that a plan can be formulated to pursue in particular the activities that work for them. Typically positive activities include sitting in the sun, eating tasty meals, taking pleasure in doing work well, and being with happy people. With suitable planning, mood can be enhanced for a whole day. Other activities that usually enhance mood include dining out, dressing up in clean clothes, winning a competition and achieving something at work. Some, such as telling jokes and giving good news or presents, can work for both giver and receiver. Since all these have a short-lived effect, the trick is to make a habit of them, to obtain frequent boosts of mood enhancement.

Moods of intense happiness, known as "peak experi-

ences," may be caused by almost anything that you especially value. The birth of a much wanted child would be a good example. Peak experiences are more common for self-actualizers (see *Ch1*). They have solved so many of the basic problems in their lives that they have more attention available for the wonders that anyone could appreciate if they could take notice. In an American study, a questionnaire designed to measure self-actualization was given to a group of 500 randomly selected adults and to 222 people who had applied for permits to make use of the wilderness areas of the state of Illinois. The researchers predicted that this second group would have higher self-actualization scores, because they were attracted to the esthetically pleasing and physically challenging environment that could provide opportunities for the peak experiences. The prediction proved correct. **DKBN**

◄ **Aerobics in the sun** *keeps these Frenchwomen looking and feeling good. Making the effort to exercise is difficult if you are not in the mood, but overcoming initial reluctance may help you to establish a habit that reinforces self-esteem and encourages posi-*

tive attitudes. Physiological evidence has been found of the directly beneficial effects exercise can have on mood (see p247). Looking your best also provides long-term mood enhancement by increasing self-confidence.

▲ **Enjoyment of natural splendors** *has been found in surveys to be easier for more highly "self-actualized" people – those who believe that they have met their basic requirements for nourishment, health, safety, love, belonging and self-esteem. With basic concerns*

out of mind, they find it possible to actualize some of their most distinctively human potentials, including the capacity for profound appreciation of the environment.

Dealing with Fear

FEAR is a basic human emotion that occurs in the face of real or imagined danger. It prepares us to take action in a crisis, and it is adaptive because it makes us feel like avoiding or running from the things that can harm us. But sometimes we attempt to overcome fear – for example, when we judge it better to stand up to a threat than to evade it. We may especially want to overcome fear when it is irrational – when it does not warn us of any real danger at all but unproductively interferes with our lives.

Rational fears

We tend to think of fear as meaning just one thing, but it actually consists of physical, mental and behavioral components. Physical changes include increased heart rate, trembling, sweating, dry mouth, pallor, faintness. The mental aspect is your *feeling* of fear, when you identify something as an object of fear: for example, you realize you are afraid that you will look awkward when you stand up to give a speech, or you are dismayed at facing the accusations of your employer over a mistake you have made. Recognizing the object of your emotion as an object of fear is just one part of a complex process of identifying the emotion that you feel. (On another occasion you might interpret similar physical reactions as anger – see *Ch 18*.) Fear behavior includes the outward display of your reactions: for example, avoiding or running away from the object of fear.

One way of dealing with this emotion is to suppress fear behavior – confronting the object of fear, instead of avoiding it. This can be very adaptive. Unfriendly dogs are less likely to attack if you look assertive and confident, more likely if you look frightened. People form a more positive impression of you if you seem in control of your fears. You also

form a more positive impression of yourself. Studies of first-time parachutists find that those who show bravado during the days approaching their jump find it easier to go through with the jump – no matter how transparent their self-deceptive claims not to be afraid may seem to others.

In many circumstances, however, it can be very helpful to express what you feel. Letting others know what your fears

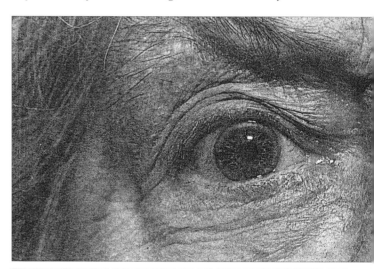

PREPARING FOR OCCUPATIONAL DANGER

■ *Anticipating real danger to physical well-being can make us prepare for crises and avoid harm. In occupations that require an ability to master fear, effective training and effective equipment build confidence.* LEFT *A policewoman must look assertive, confident and in control if she is to perform her job well.* ABOVE *Painting the Golden Gate Bridge in San Francisco requires concentration. A securely attached safety belt helps.*

To be gripped by fear may be a normal and even a lifesaving experience, and apprehensive foresight can protect us from real danger. Irrational fears (or phobias), however, can unproductively interfere with our lives.

are makes it possible for them to reassure you that your fears are not unreasonable, and to help you find ways of dealing with them. Both of these forms of social support help to ease the level of arousal, and this may improve your

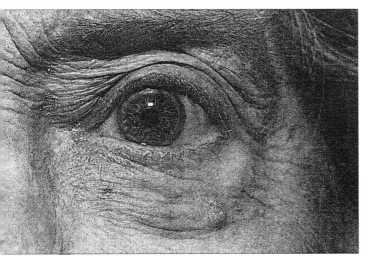

performance in dealing with the object of fear, as well as with all of the other problems of life that need attention. It is especially useful to seek social support by expressing fears when they concern long-term situations that you can do little about – for example, someone you love is in a war zone, and talking about it helps you to bear the anxiety. Social custom makes it more acceptable for women to seek help for almost any kind of problem than for men to do this, and this may help to explain why women are more expressive of fear.

Irrational fears

Although fear is a normal and universal experience, people sometimes develop the nonadaptive fears known as *phobias*. These can seriously affect their lives. The word "phobia" is derived from the Greek *phobos*, meaning "terror"; it is also the name of a Greek god who, it was believed, could instill terror and panic in enemies. It has been estimated that nearly 8 percent of all adults have a serious enough phobia of one sort or another to justify seeking treatment. Uncounted numbers have mild phobias that may be no more than a source of annoyance or occasional embarrassment. In large-scale American studies, women have reported more phobias than men do.

If you are afraid to walk up to a wild tiger, there is nothing irrational about your fear. If, however, you are terribly frightened of pigeons, and refuse to go anywhere near them, your reaction would be considered phobic. Psychiatrists and clinical psychologists consider phobias to be neurotic disorders, and refer to them as "phobic neuroses" or "phobic anxiety." Despite these labels, a phobia is not a serious mental disorder. Many people have ones that do not affect their lives drastically, and those of children are usually only transient, disappearing as they grow older.

207

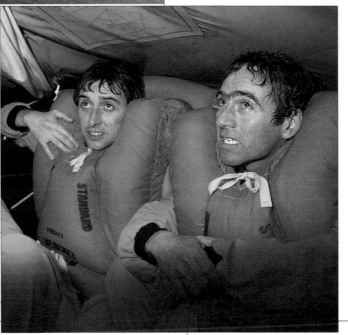

■ **Ready for the worst**. *Practicing the correct use of their lifeboats and other life-preserving equipment helps these offshore oilfield workers to avoid panic and follow established rescue procedures in the event of an accident. Planning in advance what you should do when your home or place of work catches fire can add to your sense of security and your presence of mind in an emergency.*

People can develop phobias about a wide range of things: situations, animals, objects. However, some are more common than others.

The fear of going out (especially alone), of traveling and of being alone is known as *agoraphobia*, a word that comes from the Greek *agora*, meaning "assembly place" or "market place." This is by far the most common phobia, accounting for over half of all cases in which people seek treatment. Unlike other phobias, the symptoms of which only occur when triggered off by a particular kind of situation or object, agoraphobia tends to be characterized by generalized anxiety, which may be present most of the time. It usually begins between the end of adolescence and about the age of 35 and the severity may fluctuate. Severe agoraphobia is quite disabling: the agoraphobic may become completely housebound because going out would lead to great anxiety, feelings of unreality ("not being there," "not me") and panic attacks. This can, of course, make treatment difficult, since to get to a doctor or clinic, the agoraphobic has to go out. Many chronic agoraphobics develop lifestyles to suit their problem: other people do their shopping, someone always accompanies them if they do have to go out and – in a few cases – they ensure that someone is *always* with them.

Social phobia is the fear of social situations and activities, such as meeting people, speaking before a gathering and eating and drinking in public. It is a severe form of the social anxiety that we all sometimes feel. About 10 percent of people who seek medical help for phobias suffer from this, and, like agoraphobia, it tends to begin after adolescence, although rarely lasts beyond the late twenties. The social phobic becomes extremely anxious in company, and may blush, sweat or stammer. In some cases, the person is unable to look directly at anyone, and will totally avoid eye contact. If this phobia is prolonged, it can lead to serious consequences since the person is unable to cope in an adequate way with public encounters, work with others or face an interview.

Everyone worries from time to time about becoming ill, but those suffering from an *illness phobia* – between 10 and 20 percent of all phobics – do worry about it continually. In this way, it is similar to hypochondria, but while the latter involves an overconcern about health in general, illness phobia focuses on a particular disease, usually one that is being widely publicized at the time – cancer, venereal disease, heart disease, AIDS. Anything associated with it, such as television programs, books or signboards, can cause the person to become extremely anxious.

Animal phobias – fear of specific animals or insects, commonly spiders, bees and wasps, cats, dogs, horses, snakes, rats and mice – tend to originate in childhood, and constitute less than 5 percent of all phobias seen by psychiatrists and psychologists. This small number is undoubtedly only the tip of the iceberg, however, since most animal phobics do not feel the need for help. Except for their phobias, there is nothing wrong with them, and, as long as the feared animals can be avoided (which is not difficult in many cases), they can lead normal lives.

◀ **Animal phobias** represent a small percentage of all phobias treated by experts, but it is likely that many more people than those who seek help suffer. Unlike the woman shown here, most manage to avoid the feared animal, and so they do not feel a need for treatment. The most common animal phobias are fears of snakes, spiders and small, furry animals such as mice.

▶ **The most commonly treated phobia** is agoraphobia (fear of crowds and open spaces). Severe agoraphobia may force a person to become completely housebound, since going out alone may lead to distress. Lifestyle is seriously limited: it may be difficult to arrange always to have someone with you when you have to go out or to find someone to do errands for you.

Nearly 8 percent of adult Americans report some form of phobia, in many cases triggered by fear of a particular kind of situation, object or animal. Women report more phobias than men, and they are more willing to seek help.

There are a great many other specific phobias – fear of thunderstorms, crowds, enclosed spaces, darkness, fire, flying, dental treatment, funerals and coffins, heights and so on. These simple phobias may begin at any age, and like animal phobias, they have no generalized effect on a person's life, even though, as far as the feared object or situation is concerned, the phobia may be severe.

Mysophobia is, however, a special case. People with this fear of germs and dirt often develop an obsession – that is, they begin to fear not only the germs and dirt but also the consequences of contamination, and the thought of this intrudes unwelcomingly into their consciousness. In turn, this leads, in many cases, to compulsive handwashing and cleaning rituals. However, the phobic nature of some of these people is very clear: their irrational fear can be focused on a very specific substance (eg dog dirt), or it can be wide and unspecific (eg "any form of dirt," "all germs"). They can go to great lengths to avoid coming into contact with these things, in some cases feeling that only their own bedrooms are safe, and confining themselves to them. In less severe cases, they may continue to carry out most of their daily activities, but carefully avoid obvious sources of contamination (eg shaking hands, using public toilets), and engage in elaborate decontamination rituals if avoidance fails. The late American industrialist and millionaire Howard Hughes is a well-known example of someone with a severe germ phobia: at various stages of his life, his activities were drastically curtailed as a result.

Here are some of the most common phobias and, in parenthesis, their objects: *acrophobia* (heights), *aerophobia* (flying), *ailurophobia* (cats), *aquaphobia* (water), *brontophobia* (thunder), *claustrophobia* (enclosed spaces), *cynophobia* (dogs), *erotophobia* (making love), *haphephobia* (being touched), *hematophobia* (blood), *nyctophobia* (the dark), *ochlophobia* (crowds), *ophidophobia* (snakes), *phobophobia* (fear itself), *pyrophobia* (fire), *xenophobia* (foreigners), *zoophobia* (specific animal or animals in general).

How phobias begin

There are different views about what causes phobias. The *psychodynamic theory*, expounded mainly by Freud and his followers, considers phobias to be manifestations of deeper fears or conflicts, usually going back to early childhood.

Among suggested causes of irrational fears are: subconscious conflicts; exaggerated promptings of instinct; reactions learned from early traumatic experiences; accepting culturally transmitted beliefs; and imitating other people.

The problem is seen as lying in a person's own desires and feelings, which for some reason the conscious mind cannot accept. This leads to a displaced fear about an innocuous object, which is actually a cover for the true fear or conflict. Thus when people complain of, for example, a fear of spiders, this is supposed to be a symbolic substitute for something deep in their subconscious mind. Although, this is an interesting theory, it is quite difficult to test, and certainly the experience of most clinicians and researchers who deal with phobics does not give it any credence.

The other major explanation of the origin of phobias is the *learning*, or *behavioral*, theory. According to this, phobias are learned reactions: objects and situations associated with painful or traumatic experiences become the focus of phobias simply because they are associated with these types of experiences. Unlike the psychodynamic theory, this one can be tested experimentally, and indeed there is evidence that phobias can be acquired in just the same way. For example, in a famous early (and somewhat cruel) experiment, the American psychologist John B Watson was able to "create" a phobia in an 11-month-old boy. When the boy was first shown a white rat, he reached for it with no sign of fear; however, every time he touched it, Watson made a loud sound that frightened him. The boy quickly developed a fear of rats.

However, not every case fits this model. The onset of many people's phobias is not marked by a painful or frightening experience, and it is also known that people can acquire phobias through "modeling": observing and copying other people's fears, especially those of family members. In addition, culturally transmitted beliefs and views can contribute to the development of this disorder – for example, many people are afraid of snakes even though they have never been near one. Thus, phobias are acquired not only through direct experience but through indirect experience as well.

There are further factors to consider. For example, not everything is equally likely to become the object of a phobia – in fact, the range is fairly narrow. This selectivity suggests that there may be a biological predetermination in the sort of things to which people develop phobias.

Finally, there is the question of instinctive, or innate, fears – the natural fears that occur in humans as well as in

▲ **Enjoying a dangerous hobby**. *A preference for leisure activities like skydiving, mountaineering and ski jumping is counted by psychologists as a mark of a risk-taking temperament. This personality trait has been linked to the complex system of nerve chemicals within our bodies controlling our response to arousing situations (see Ch12). Combined with a resistance to feeling concerned about the feelings of others, and about the consequences of actions, risk-taking is the basis for the "tough-minded" personality type (see Ch13).*

■ **Glory and profit**. *Some people, such as this stunt pilot* LEFT, *rolling his open-cockpit airplane over in mid-flight, deliberately accept danger, both for personal fulfillment, through enjoyment of an exciting lifestyle, and for financial reward.* RIGHT *Stunt men allow themselves to be set alight, thrown off roofs, involved in car crashes. People with a risk-taking temperament are drawn to many of the situations that phobics specifically avoid.*

animals. For instance, young children are quite rightly afraid of the dark, of strangers, heights and so on; some fears develop at particular ages; and some disappear as a person grows older. This has led some writers to suggest that the important question is not how and why phobias are acquired, but why some people do not lose their innate fears in the course of time, as others do.

How phobias can be overcome

Some phobias simply go away, but unfortunately, this does not happen in the majority of cases. If a phobia assumes disabling proportions, it is advisable to seek help, rather than wait in the hope that it will spontaneously disappear; most psychiatrists and clinical psychologists undertake treatment of phobias, as do a few family doctors. There are two main forms of therapy: psychodynamic and behavioral.

In *psychodynamic therapy*, the best known form of which is psychoanalysis, an attempt is made to explore the patient's subconscious mind to unearth – and help resolve – an underlying conflict or other factor assumed to have caused the phobia. However, the results of this type of therapy for phobias are not very impressive, and it is also an extremely time-consuming exercise as a course of therapy may take up to three years.

Behavioral therapy is a relatively recent development. When used to treat phobias, it aims to train the person to face the feared object or situation with no anxiety or discomfort. The strategy used to achieve this is "exposure": phobics are exposed to the objects they fear, thus countering their usual response of avoiding them. The actual details of the exposure procedure can vary – it may be done in small, gradual steps, when it is called "systematic desensitization," or it may be prolonged and

intense, when it is called "flooding." Sometimes people are taught relaxation techniques so that they can deal with the anxiety that can occur during exposure. And the exposure itself may be carried out in the imagination, when the phobic is asked to conjure up the feared object in his or her mind, or it may be done in real life, with the feared object actually present. Many therapists now use a combination of the two, and they almost invariably couple this with

THE BIRTH OF A PHOBIA?

■ *The root cause of a phobia, according to many experts, is a painful or traumatic experience in childhood. An early fright may repeat itself as a "learned reaction" when similar situa-* *tions arise. It is possible, too, that some people feel instinctive fears more powerfully than others do, or fail to overcome them in the same way as they grow older.*

◄ **Treating a phobia**. *Although some phobias disappear naturally, others require professional assistance. This treatment for fear of flying attempts to train the sufferer to feel more relaxed in the air. In a series of gradual steps, including sitting in a stationary aircraft while practicing relaxation techniques inspired by Yoga – such as breathing deeply by inhaling and exhaling with the abdomen, head back and hands outstretched – the trainee learns to feel confident and self-controlled during air travel.*

To overcome irrational fears you must confront them one by one. This can be achieved in small steps with the help of a friend or a relative. In more serious cases, help should be sought from a professionally qualified therapist.

"modeling," when they demonstrate how to react without experiencing fear.

Needless to say, the actual behavioral treatment of any individual is always tailored to his or her particular problem. It may also contain elements other than exposure and modeling – for example, social phobics may also be given training in basic social skills. These are crucial aids to confidence in social interactions. The results of behavioral therapy for phobias are impressive, and it is the treatment of choice for these problems.

What about drugs? While it is true that many doctors still prescribe tranquilizers, and these may help to reduce anxiety temporarily, they do not have any specific effect on phobias, they can be habit-forming, and, in general, they are not considered to be suitable treatment for such illnesses.

Coping with a phobia

How can we help ourselves, or someone close to us, in the event of a disabling phobia? As far as possible, the feared object or situation should not be avoided. The main principle is exposure – confronting the fear instead of running away from it – and this can be done in gradual steps. If the phobia is a mild one it can be helpful for a trusted friend or family member to handle, in the presence of the phobic and in as comfortable and nonfearful a way as possible, the focus of the phobia. The affected person can then begin to participate in this activity. If the phobia is severe, however, the best course is to seek professional help: proper therapy can be very effective. **WPdS**

THE CASE OF AN ARACHNOPHOBE

■ Janet, a 25-year-old woman, asked for help with an arachnophobia (spider phobia). Although she had always been somewhat afraid of spiders – she remembered running away from them as a child – the problem had become acute about a year before when, during a visit to the zoo, she saw some very large bird-eating spiders. Since then, just the thought of spiders made her very anxious, and even very small spiders frightened her.

She found she could not go into a room if she thought a spider was there; unfortunately, since she lived in the country, she often came across them. During the day, when her husband was away at work, she confined herself to her bedroom and kitchen, and avoided the other parts of the house and the garden. She wanted to move to a less rural area, but realized that this would not actually solve anything. Her husband was very supportive, but felt

she needed professional help. They went together to their family doctor, who referred Janet to a clinical psychologist.

The treatment was fairly straightforward, and consisted of a program of desensitization in both imaginary and real-life situations. After Janet gave the psychologist details of her problem, they assembled a list of fear situations involving spiders, starting with the least

fear-arousing ("seeing a picture of a spider in a book") and ending with the most ("a large, hairy spider on my hand"). In between, there were many intermediate items – eg "holding in my hand a tightly closed glass jar with a very small spider in it," "picking up a dead spider and throwing it out of the window."

Janet was taught relaxation techniques, and the desensiti-

zation only began when she was able to perform these well. During each session she was asked to sit comfortably in an armchair and relax, keeping her eyes closed. The psychologist then asked her to imagine the various items on the list, starting with the least fear arousing. When she was able to imagine that item with little or no anxiety, they proceeded to the next – two or three items were covered in this way. After a few sessions, Janet was exposed to real spiders, in a similar step-by-step fashion. She was also given homework, which she did with her husband's help. For example, she had to catch a little spider from her garden and put it into a bottle, and keep it on her window sill.

Janet made very good progress. In the end, she felt she was no longer afraid of spiders, and was able to go about her house and garden quite freely. And she no longer wanted to move.

A STEP-BY-STEP PHOBIA TREATMENT

 1 Write down a list of fear-arousing situations

2 Learn relaxation techniques

3 Practice relaxation as you imagine each item on the list

4 Practice relaxation as you gradually expose yourself to the actual situations

 5 Seek professional help if the phobia persists

Overcoming Depression

MOST of us know what it is like to feel depressed. At any one time between 5 and 9 percent of women and 2 to 3 percent of men will be suffering from depression that is bad enough to need treatment and many more will be feeling generally low and helpless, their energy drained and their work and relationships impaired.

Depression is a range of *feelings* and a tendency to *behave* in a certain way. In some cases it may also be a *biological* state of the brain.

"What's the point of anything?"

When we are depressed our feelings are negative. Depression saps our mental and emotional energy – we feel empty, sluggish and understimulated. We feel we have lost contact with other people and we want to withdraw into ourselves. Depression can make us feel physically as well as emotion-ally distressed: there may be an inner ache, a sinking feeling in the chest. We will probably feel that we cannot cope and that we are, in some way, to blame for our unhappiness.

People who are depressed typically stop mixing with other people. This has two negative effects. The first is that they deprive themselves of many of the emotional rewards of social contact simply because they see fewer people. The second is that they seek to obtain their customary level of emotional reward from fewer people. Those few often begin to resent this increased dependence and they themselves may withdraw. This reinforces the depressed person's feeling of being abandoned. He or she will tend to cry more, to become forgetful, to be indecisive and to lack concentration. Even the smallest task seems to need a huge amount of effort.

Is depression more than extreme sadness?

Everyone has experienced sadness. In times of bereavement or other misfortune we may find that we cannot sleep or sleep too much, that we lose our appetite or eat too

▲ **Depressing work saps moti-vation**. *Doing a boring task does not necessarily put you into a state of depression. But if there is a big gap between your expectations of the nature and rewards of a job and the reality* *of your working life, the buildup of frustration can be stressful. Research has found that stress more often results from a tedi-ous and repetitive job than from a job that requires high-level decisions.*

■ **Sadness and depression**. *Feeling sad about the death of a great leader, like these Yugo-slavs* TOP, *is different from be-ing depressed* RIGHT. *The mourners know why they are sad. Depression, though it may result from a tragic experience, permeates the sufferer's life. Often it takes the form of list-lessness – an inability to per-form everyday tasks. A severely depressed person may even be afraid to get out of bed to con-front the world, yet receives no comfort from this passivity.*

Depression is a common affliction – we all know what it is to feel helpless and hopeless. Whether a crisis leads to chronic depression, and how we cope with this, is affected by the way we normally perceive and deal with problems.

much. Similarly, if we lose our job it is natural for us to feel anger and sadness: these are normal reactions to certain severe life events. Short-term depression of this kind is common. But in due course the symptoms of a bereaved person will usually pass (though telling them that may not be helpful) and the anger of someone who has lost their job may be a spur to making positive changes. We *know* why we feel so miserable and this sort of depression usually lifts with time, with our own efforts and with the support of family or friends.

Long-term depression has similar symptoms but is more embedded and irrational. It is like a form of propaganda – telling us lies about ourselves, other people, the world and the future. The sufferer becomes entrapped by their unrealistic, negative perceptions. They believe that they are useless and unloved and that the future looks hopeless. This sense of hopelessness is what leads some chronic depres-

LEARNING TO BE HELPLESS

■ *A sense of helplessness is characteristic of depression. You may well feel unable to cope even with problems that are well within your capabilities. Most of us experience major stress from time to time but not all of us become chronically depressed and helpless. Why have some learned to react in this way, and can they unlearn the habit?*

Researchers now believe that our thinking style, even when we are not depressed, influences how vulnerable we may be. Two aspects of habitual thinking style are important: our "self-focus" – how much we focus on ourselves when things start to go wrong, and our "attributional style" – how we know events are caused.

SELF-FOCUS

Read the statements below and choose which of the alternative ways of completing them suits you best.
1 *When something makes me sad*
   a *I try to divert my attention to other things.*
   b *I lose all desire to do anything.*
2 *When several things go wrong on the same day*
   a *I can still do things as if nothing had happened.*
   b *I really don't know what to do with myself.*
3 *When a new appliance falls on the floor by accident*
   a *I concentrate fully on what should be done.*
   b *I can't stop thinking about how this could have happened.*
4 *When I am in pain*
   a *I am able to concentrate on other things.*
   b *I can hardly think about anything else.*

If you look at each pair of alternatives, you will see that the one marked (a) indicates that you concentrate your attention outside yourself when you are under stress – that is, you show "action orientation." The (b) alternative indicates that you concentrate on yourself following stress – that is, you show "state orientation." Whether you are state or action oriented can affect how vulnerable you may be to depression, but it depends also on your attributional style. In other words, though dwelling on things when they are going wrong can be a positive way of sorting matters out, it may have the opposite effect if you are the kind of person who usually interprets negative events in an internal, stable and global way (see Chs 14, 26).

215

sives to commit suicide. Modern psychotherapists work to help seriously depressed people question their negative feelings. In cases of mild depression, it can be helpful to take a similar approach. The next time you feel really low, catch yourself as you think "There's nothing to look forward to anymore," "Even my favorite hobbies just make me feel worse." Try turning those negative statements into questions. Ask yourself: "Is there really nothing to look forward to?" "Can't I think of anything that would make me feel a little better?"

Relearning anticipation

The feeling that we can no longer get pleasure from being with favorite friends or from doing favorite activities is the most common symptom of depression. How much we enjoy anything is regulated by two different systems in the brain. The first regulates how much we *anticipate* – look forward to company, work, food or a hobby. The second controls how much we enjoy the activity as we do it – a *consum-*

matory reward. When we are depressed the anticipatory reward mechanism often fails although the consummatory reward mechanism may remain active. As a result, while we may enjoy a dinner party once we are actually there, we do not learn to look forward to the next one. If we are to overcome depression, we must recover our ability to energize ourselves for the next activity.

One way of relearning anticipation is to choose three activities as targets for the coming week. It is important that they should be ordinary events – for example, asking a friend for coffee, baking your own bread, digging the garden. The objective is to re-establish your pleasure in day-to-day existence. Write down each activity and then, underneath each one, note down three things you will enjoy about doing it. Start each sentence, "I will enjoy..." to force yourself to think of the positive rewards. It is as if the anticipatory mechanism in our brain has become weak through disuse and must be coaxed back to health. A target activity might read as follows:

▲ **The depressing view from a high-rise apartment.** *Our external as well as our immediate surroundings profoundly affect our mood. Here the bleak outlook is exacerbated by the social isolation of living in a high-rise. The tall buildings that used to be a feature of urban planning are now regarded as potentially detrimental to emotional well-being, especially for women who are at home with young children all day. Our personality type affects our ability to adapt to adverse conditions. A resilient person (see* Ch 14) *believes that they can to a large extent control their lives. If housing is scarce and unemployment high we may not be able to move to more congenial accommodation. But we may be able to change our immediate surroundings and our social behavior and this, in turn, can affect our reaction to desolate conditions.*

MANIC DEPRESSION

■ *A small number of people experience depressions that alternate with mood swings in the opposite direction. If that opposite swing is very extreme, they may be experiencing mania. During their periods of high mood, manic depressives will be more active at work, at home, socially or sexually. They will be more talkative than usual and their thoughts will race. They will have an inflated self-esteem and a few may believe they are a great world figure.*

Manic depressives will typically lose their powers of judgment and self-control, perhaps spending too much money, making foolish business decisions or drinking recklessly without being aware of the potentially very serious consequences.

Researchers do not know how or why the brain switches into mania but many now believe that the cause is more likely to be genetic than with other kinds of depression.

Looking forward to a meeting or activity can be almost as enjoyable as the event itself, but depression dulls anticipation. An important stage in overcoming depression is to learn once more how to look ahead with optimism.

Digging the garden: I will enjoy the fresh smell of the newly turned earth. I will enjoy being out in the fresh air. I will enjoy choosing some bulbs to put in for next spring. When you have made your list, decide which day is best for your activity. In the days beforehand, spend a little time once or twice each day visualizing yourself doing the activity and try to feel the enjoyment of the things you listed.

This technique may be very difficult for some people. If you cannot make it work, ask yourself why. Perhaps the target is too big? Digging the whole garden at once is unrealistic – choose a task that can be achieved. Perhaps you are not good at knowing when to stop for a rest? Dig a small plot, then stop while you have the energy to appreciate your achievement. The rest of the garden can wait until later. Perhaps you have chosen an activity that depends on someone else? If you are unsure whether they will be able to help, your target may be at risk. You should take care to choose an activity you can accomplish yourself. Perhaps you simply feel you do not have the energy, a common feeling in de-

pression. Turn that negative feeling into a question: "How much energy do I have for this task just now?" One way to find out is to start the task. Frequently the energy to continue comes once we have overcome the initial hurdle.

Reawakening past pleasures

Another common effect of depression is that our usual likes and dislikes are reversed. Close friends may seem unbearable: we may find we prefer to be with people we know far less well. Favorite activities now irritate us.

Michael was 53 and had been depressed for nine months. He used to enjoy doing things with his hands, especially woodwork. He enjoyed gardening moderately but he did not particularly enjoy working on his car. However, since becoming depressed, he found that working on the car was all that he felt energetic enough to do. He had no enthusiasm for gardening and the very thought of his workbench made him feel worse. His likes and dislikes were turned upside down by his depression.

To help yourself recover past pleasures, make a list of all the activities you enjoyed before you started feeling low: for example, walking, gardening, meeting friends, sewing,

DEFEATING DEPRESSION: SOME SUGGESTIONS

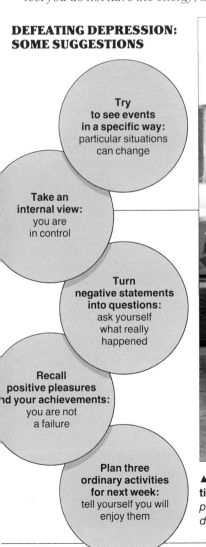

Try to see events in a specific way: particular situations can change

Take an internal view: you are in control

Turn negative statements into questions: ask yourself what really happened

Recall positive pleasures and your achievements: you are not a failure

Plan three ordinary activities for next week: tell yourself you will enjoy them

▲ **The excitement of anticipation** *is one of our most common pleasures. Someone who is depressed, however, tends to hold in view only the task ahead and not the satisfactions. But by learning again to anticipate and cope with minor activities, they can recover their ability to tackle major tasks with enthusiasm and vigor.*

going to the park, etc. Arrange them according to how much pleasure they used to give, with the most pleasurable at the top and the least pleasurable at the bottom. Start with an activity at the bottom of the hierarchy, one of those that only gave a small amount of pleasure. Try doing it for just a few minutes each day. Setting your own timescale, gradually move up your list. Never force the pace. If you feel uncomfortable at any stage, move one step back down the hierarchy and try again soon. In time, you may regain the enjoyment of your favorite activities.

LEARNING TO BE REALISTIC

■ When you are depressed you think in terms of extremes and this lowers your mood even more: "Nobody wants to see me," "I am a burden to everyone." Because one friend cannot meet you, you feel as though none of your friends care for you any more – an absolute conclusion that was based on very insufficient evidence.

How can you stop yourself doing this? The next time you feel low, try to remember what went through your mind just as you felt your mood slump. Perhaps your partner said, "I am just going out." What was the thought in your mind just before your mood changed? Was it "My partner doesn't care about me," or "Nobody wants me to go out with them?" Sadly, some of us may indeed have real problems in our relationships that need to be tackled. However it is still worth asking if the negative reaction is the most appropriate one. If your partner goes out, does that really mean he or she does not care about you? Is there no other evidence of their love? It will help if you ask yourself, "Would I interpret this particular event in a more positive way if I were not feeling depressed right now?" So, for example, if you failed an exam and were thinking, "I've always

been a failure, I'll never pass an exam," ask yourself if there is another, more positive interpretation. Ask yourself how you would see things if you were not (understandably) upset just now, or how you will see things in a few months' time when the crisis has passed.

The chemistry of depression

Research suggests that there is a link between some forms of depressive illness and depletion of neurotransmitters in certain brain areas. (Neurotransmitters are chemicals exchanged by nerve cells as an essential part of their functioning – see *Ch19*.) This is often called endogenous depression, to indicate that it arises from inside the individual.

Endogenous depression is usually contrasted with reactive depression where a person reacts to the stress of a critical life event (see *Ch22*) such as illness, unemployment or bereavement by suffering a depressive breakdown, but this distinction does not seem to be clear-cut.

Observation shows that there do seem to be differences between the two kinds of depression. Someone who is suffering from reactive depression following a crisis such as bereavement will usually feel better, if only briefly, if a friend says a kind word to them. In contrast, someone suffering from endogenous depression will be unable to experience even fleeting pleasure when something pleasurable happens. Endogenous depressives are also more likely to suffer

Our usual likes and dislikes may be turned upside down in times of depression. It can be helpful to make a list of favorite activities and then work gradually through them, from the least to the most emotionally challenging.

weight loss and early morning wakening, where they wake at 4.00 or 5.00 in the morning and cannot get back to sleep. They are also more likely to suffer a regular variation in mood during the day, being more intensely depressed in the morning.

However, despite these differences in symptoms, research has found similarities between the two kinds of depression. Endogenous depressives, too, have usually experienced severe life events in the few months before their illness. Perhaps the truth will turn out to be that we all have certain biological programs in the brain. Some of us tend to react to stress in one particular way: we may be sleepless at night rather than in the morning, we gain rather than lose weight, we feel irritated and hostile rather than miserable. We can sometimes detect these tendencies in a mild form when we are under slight stress. The next time social or work pressures make you feel mildly stressed, try to observe your reactions. When we experience major

stress, we may be predisposed to develop either endogenous or reactive depression. Researchers have already discovered indications that it is our experience as individuals that influences which type of depression we may develop. If we have lost a close family member through death, then depression experienced in later life is more likely to be of the endogenous variety. If we have lost someone through separation or divorce, then any later depression is more likely to be reactive. These are general trends and will not be true of everyone. **JMGW**

◄ **An unrealistically negative interpretation of events** *is characteristic of depression. Even positive gestures of affection or concern may be misunderstood. A depressed person cannot react with their former warmth and spontaneity, and a negative style of thinking may become habitual unless consciously resisted.*

■ **Enjoying small pleasures** – *an outing with the family or a moment of shared fun with your partner. People who are depressed often find that their normal rewards and incentives have been thrown into reverse. Disconcertingly, they now seem to prefer the activities they only moderately enjoyed before they were depressed and find themselves shunning old friends in favor of people they were less*

close to. Experts refer to this condition as "motivation reversal." Surprisingly, a way of overcoming this is not necessarily to force yourself, initially, to resume your favorite activities or to see your closest friends. Rather, you should start with the things that used to give you only small amounts of pleasure. By gradually working up your list of past pleasures – from the least to the most enjoy-

able – it may be possible to re-establish your former hierarchy of preferences.

219

Coping With Grief

SHOCK, horror, disbelief, despair, resentment, anger, misery and relief are some of the natural reactions you can expect to feel when someone who is important to you dies. The extent and duration of grief can vary greatly, depending on how close you were to the person who has died and on the circumstances of their death. Following the death of a child, for example, or of an adult who has undergone a long and painful or disabling illness, grief is likely to be intense. In contrast, the death of an elderly person at the end of a long and happy, healthy life is likely to be less severe for younger, nondependent relatives, though it will, of course, be devastating for their partner.

Grief has been analyzed in different ways but many researchers agree that we experience grief in four main stages. The first stage is a time of shock and disbelief, fol-lowed by the second when we feel the acute pain of loss. The third is characterized by anger and guilt, while reinte-gration is the fourth and final stage. It is important to re-member that there may not be clear divisions between one stage and the next and that no two people have exactly the same experience of bereavement. However, understanding the typical progression of grief can help us understand the intense and sometimes conflicting emotions that we experi-ence when we mourn. It can also help us support people we care about when they are bereaved.

It can't be true!

When someone close to us dies, our immediate reaction will be one of shock and disbelief. This stage is quite short, lasting from the time of death until after the funeral. The

FUNERALS HELP US TO FACE REALITY

■ Accepting the death of some-one we love is part of recover-ing from the trauma of loss. The need to deal with practical arrangements helps this pro-cess. The funeral and the cere-monies accompanying it have considerable therapeutic value. We seem to have a deep need to mark major events in our lives with rituals that express the reli-gious, social and psychological aspects of our own culture. A funeral gives those who mourn a way of making an important statement about their love of the deceased and the pain of bereavement. When someone has been lost at sea or a murder victim's body has never been found, the bereaved families can experience great difficulty in working through their grief. They often feel very strongly that they have unfinished busi-ness that cannot be completed until they have buried the body.

After the funeral ceremony relatives and friends may often gather to share a meal and to reminisce. This custom can be very supportive to the bereav-ed. It can also provide a stimu-lus for strengthening or renew-ing family relationships and even friendships.

In some cultures, such as Australian aboriginals, the funeral rites and ceremonies can last for two weeks. During this time, mourners are encour-aged to express their feelings.

■ **The expression of grief** is affected by social customs. LEFT Black is the chief color for a funeral in Ireland, red in Ghana CENTER, and white in Thailand RIGHT. Funerals give the community the opportunity to honor both the dead person and the bereaved, and they give the bereaved an opportuni-ty to find an outlet in ritual for their emotion.

Grief is a complex emotion with which few of us are practiced at coping. Understanding the stages by which it usually develops can help both the bereaved and the friends and relatives who would like to give them their support.

shock will often be experienced as physical sensations. The bereaved person will probably feel weak, shaky, cold and breathless. They may feel as if they are choking and their head and heart seem to pound. These physical symptoms are likely to be especially acute if the death has been sudden or violent and in some extreme cases may recur when, for example, the sight of a mutilated body is recalled. The accompanying emotional shock is often described by those who have experienced it as numbness. The event itself can feel unreal and the whole world may seem to be made of cardboard. This sense of being cut off from reality can be frightening but it usually soon passes. It is also

common, at this early stage, for the bereaved person to be unwilling to accept what has happened, even when they have seen the body. This irrational response can be disconcerting to friends and family who may in these circumstances have to take charge of the funeral arrangements. However, they should try, with gentleness and understanding, to involve the mourner so that the practical aspects of funeral ritual will encourage him or her to accept the fact of bereavement.

The anguish of loss

As the shock passes and the bereaved person begins to accept what has happened, they enter a period of intense emotional and often physical pain that surrounds the loss of the loved one. Many therapists feel that this is a very neces-

HELPING THE BEREAVED
- Offer help with practical matters – such as the funeral. The bereaved may feel "numb" immediately after the death.
- Remember that your support will be needed long after the funeral.
- Don't be embarrassed by their grief or your own. Encourage them to show it.
- Be patient. Grief lasts a long time and the bereaved may sometimes seem irrational.

Frequently, this open expression of grief is echoed by other members of the community. This helps the bereaved to start working through their feelings and goes a considerable way toward coping with the strong and conflicting emotions they feel.

Many Western societies, however, are very uncomfortable when it comes to coping with death. We tend to be trained from an early age that it

is wrong to show deep emotion in public. As a result, bereaved people often struggle to hide their feelings. At the same time, friends and relatives are inhibited in their efforts to give comfort. Most of us have experienced loss and sharing a mourner's grief inevitably reawakens our own pain to some degree. We have to be prepared to cope with our pain if we are to help those who mourn.

Sometimes the effect of

death is lessened by creating an illusion of life. The deceased's body is preserved with chemicals and is then clothed and displayed in a way that suggests that he or she is only sleeping. Some psychologists criticize this practice. They believe that maintaining an illusion of life only prolongs the grieving period for the mourner by making it more difficult for them to accept that the person they love is dead.

As the intensity of the grief passes, the bereaved person may be bewildered by their feelings of anger and guilt. These are normal reactions and should not be denied. Expressing them openly can help to make them less disturbing.

sary and helpful part of grieving. We are unlikely to accept the reality of loss until we can allow ourselves to vent our anguish. Most survivors experience intense crying fits, and physical symptoms, such as restlessness, insomnia, poor appetite and weight loss, become noticeable. This is the period of desperate yearning and yet the bereaved is often given little emotional support during this stage. Why is this? One reason may be that the funeral or memorial service can seem, to others, to mark the end of the bereavement. The immediate practical tasks have been completed and people forget about, or do not recognize, the less obvious but equally important sort of help that they can still give. Another reason is that, especially in Western countries, many people find it difficult to cope with or share strong emotion. Friends and relatives should encourage those of us who mourn to cry and even share that crying if they are able. However, many Western men may need to be alone before they can give way enough to weep. This stage can last from a few weeks to a few months and, again, it is important that the mourner should not be alone too much.

Feeling deserted

Our main emotions during the third stage are likely to be anger and guilt. In some cases the anger will be directed toward the deceased "who has abandoned me." Sometimes it will be vented on others, especially family and friends or those who were in some way associated with the death (such as a doctor). People with religious beliefs will probably feel great and bewildered anger with God "for letting this happen." Anger is an emotion that many people, particularly in Western countries, find difficult at any time. As mourners, we may feel very guilty about our anger with the deceased and this sense of shock can be shared by our friends and relatives. We are likely to feel confused and ashamed of ourselves and we may become depressed and withdrawn if we cannot admit and express these feelings openly. Those round us can play an important role in encouraging us to vent our emotions but they should be mindful that they may become objects of our anger themselves. There is a danger that, during this stage, the bereaved may alienate the people they need most. A great deal of understanding and forgiveness can be needed on both sides. It is difficult to predict how long this stage is likely to last as so much depends on how satisfactorily survivors can resolve their strong and ambivalent feelings. If they fail to do this, they will probably sink into a despairing mood of chronic mourning and become unable to cope with day-to-day activities. Should this happen, it is wise to seek professional therapy. However, survivors who work through this stage can progress to the fourth and last stage where reintegration begins.

Recovering from grief

The last stage can be the most difficult of all. The most intense time of grieving is behind us and we begin to feel again the rewards of everyday living. However, each mourner needs to withdraw emotional energy from the past bond to invest it in new ones. At any time in our lives, we risk rejection when we look for emotional comfort in a new relationship. When we have just been bereaved, we are especially easily hurt and may find that the process of forming new bonds takes real courage. In addition, we may feel that new attachments mean that we are being disloyal to the deceased. Family and friends can help by reassuring us that

223

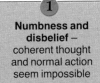

◄ **Anniversaries bring reminders** of the person we have lost. Here a mother remembers her son, the first American to die in the Vietnam War. As grief fades, keeping alive positive memories can give continuance to some of the emotional benefits previously enjoyed.

MOURNING

■ *Mourning is the process through which we incorporate the event and circumstances of bereavement into our day-to-day experience. It is an acknowledgment of loss but in most cases it is also a healing process. Different societies observe the process of mourning in different ways. In some* parts of the world, widows, in particular, dress in black and may even wear veils for many years after their partner's death. Most Western societies no longer indicate mourning so publicly or for so long. The bereaved may wear dark clothing or a black armband for a while. If the deceased is well-known, the national flag may fly at half-mast to show society's sense of loss. However, we must always be aware that a shorter, less public, period of visible mourning does not lessen the time it will take for those of us who are bereaved to work through our grief.

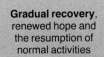

FOUR STAGES OF GRIEF

1 Numbness and disbelief – coherent thought and normal action seem impossible

2 Anguish – great misery and desperate yearning for the dead person

3 Anger and guilt as the reality of loss is accepted

4 Gradual recovery, renewed hope and the resumption of normal activities

such relationships do not mean that we no longer love the person who has died. This stage ends when survivors establish an identity and patterns of behavior independent of the deceased. Family and friends can, understandably, find this transition difficult to accept. They too have suffered a loss. However, their acceptance of the bereaved person's way of adjusting to a new reality is a very real way of showing love and support.

In time, many people who have been bereaved can look back to their days with the deceased and take a great deal of pleasure in remembering the happy and humorous aspects of the relationship. We will feel a sense of loss occasionally, even when new relationships give us joy and comfort: each person is unique and so, inevitably, we lose something irreplaceable when someone that we love dies. But the predominant feelings will be happiness and thankfulness for the times we shared. The reality of the relationship remains.

Bereavement is the most extreme form of loss but it is of course not the only kind. People who undergo other severe losses – such as separation, the loss of a home or the loss of a job – will experience many of the same feelings.

Problems that women face

Bereaved women can have a particular problem of adjustment following their partner's death. Many societies find it more difficult to cope with women who have lost their partners than with men in the same position. A woman whose partner has died can discover that her social status has changed and not for the better. She may receive fewer invitations to social functions and she may, herself, find it more daunting to attend such functions on her own. We can each of us help by re-examining our attitudes on this point. In many societies, couples seem to be more socially acceptable than people on their own. Men on their own are often more welcome than a woman in the same position. This seems to be little more than social convention and it is a convention that lacks insight and understanding of the needs of all bereaved people.

Be kind to yourself

Family and friends give important help to the bereaved. However, when you are bereaved you can help yourself, even in the middle of intense grief. You need to do so in

224

WIDOWS IN SATI

■ *Widows respecting the Indian tradition of sati no longer sacrifice themselves on their husband's funeral pyres, but they withdraw permanently from normal life. Even in countries and social circles where women are regarded as liberated, a widow may have to make special efforts to establish a new and independent social status.*

Keeping a diary of your feelings can help you to face your loss and feel more confident about adjusting to changes in social and financial status. Making new friends and taking on new challenges are important steps in returning to normal.

order to cope with the immense stress of mourning. First, accept that grieving is a long process. Many people who have suffered bereavement report that their grieving lasted two or even three years. During that time, be kind and understanding toward yourself. It is helpful to keep routinely busy but you should not use work or the need to cope with practical matters as a way of blotting out emotional pain. When you feel tired, then rest or sleep. Intense emotion is very draining and you need to make allowance for that. You should remind yourself frequently that powerful, overwhelming feelings will lessen with time. Meanwhile, it is very important to allow yourself to be vulnerable and share your pain with concerned relatives and friends. Most people feel

embarrassed with someone who is bereaved because, however much they sympathize, they are afraid that anything they can say will be inadequate. You should remind yourself of that and reassure those who are giving support. That way, you can also give comfort to them and this will reinforce warm relationships at a time when they are most important to you. Some people find that it is a good idea to keep a diary and write down feelings, conflicts, memories and successes. It will help you to work through your grieving and, as time passes, it can show you that things are gradually improving. You need to avoid living in the past but, if possible, you should also avoid too many major changes in your life: big decisions and rebound relationships will increase your sense of insecurity. Be especially careful to avoid anything addictive, such as alcohol. Finally, it is good to surround yourself with life – plants, animals, friends – and prepare for orderly change by acquiring new interests and new friends.

Can we prepare in advance?

Few of us can ever be fully prepared for the death of a partner, family member or close friend, even when it is expected. (This is especially true for parents who suffer the death of a young child.) How someone is likely to cope with bereavement can usually be predicted from how they cope with the everyday stresses of daily life. If little things, such as losing a handkerchief or burning a cake, really upset us, then the death of a loved one is likely to be a catastrophic shock. In addition, we are better prepared to cope with bereavement if we have a strong social support network. Family, friends and social institutions from whom we can receive comfort can help us to cope with and work through the intense and conflicting emotions aroused by the loss of someone we love. **PMI**

■ **Carrying on alone**. *The death of a partner brings a multiplicity of losses – of companionship, sexual satisfaction and social status, and sometimes of financial security as well. When the domestic roles of the partners have been distinct, especially in a traditional marriage, the survivor may also find that he or she is unprepared to deal with the practical tasks usually performed by the other partner – for example, cooking a meal or fixing a fuse – and the accompanying sense of helplessness adds to the burden of grief. Some people find it helpful to list all their losses, from the most emotionally searing to the most trivial. The enormity of bereavement cannot, of course, be neatly resolved in this way, but analyzing needs can be a prelude to discovering what we can do about them – by learning new skills, perhaps, or developing existing relationships, as this grandparent is doing.*

Managing Guilt

ALL OF US feel guilt sometimes. It is a normal, inborn, human emotion, and, like other emotions, it serves a purpose. Guilt is a way of controlling wild and primitive feelings that would threaten our existence or even that of civilization if we acted on them. The capacity to feel guilty does not vary among different cultures, but each society has its own code of behavior from which the ingredients of guilt arise. As children, we learn about the consequences of behaving against this code and what it is to feel guilty. If we were to feel no guilt, we would not be human, but the extent to which it affects us can range from beneficial to harmful.

What is guilt?

Guilt is a complex feeling that we should atone for something we have either done or thought of doing. It has developed as a force for preserving society by giving humans the means to deal with the constant temptation to put their own interests and immediate gratification before the needs of the community. To be effective, such a force must be very strong, and it is therefore not surprising that guilt is probably the most oppressive of all emotions. However, within limits, it is valuable both to the individual and to society.

Unfortunately, these limits are frequently broken. Some people feel guilty about almost everything they do; their whole lives revolve around a belief in their own wrongdoing, they apologize constantly and they find it impossible to be happy. Others claim not to feel guilty, yet they continually act in a self-defeating manner that reveals their true feelings. A few people have such an intense need to be punished that they repeatedly claim responsibility for crimes they have not committed. Although this last example may seem extreme, a milder form of irrational guilt is a familiar part of many people's sex lives, preventing them from sharing a natural pleasure.

No human relationship is free from guilt. Even in the most open, we imagine obligations toward one another, and we feel guilty about failing to measure up to some mythical ideal of loving perfection or about our inability to achieve everything that we feel is expected of us. As a result, guilty feelings are an important feature in most relationships.

Developing a sense of guilt

Children become aware of goodness and badness as early as their second year of life. At this stage, toddlers begin to realize that "bad" actions displease their parents – usually those involving dirt (rubbing dirty hands on a wall), the destruction of property (tearing up books) and hurting others (taking a toy away from another child). The reactions of parents to these kinds of activities eventually teach children to apply the words "good" and "bad" to things they do.

Guilt itself first appears at around the age of three, when children begin to describe themselves as "naughty." They show signs of emotional upset after misbehaving, and may burst into tears or run away and hide even before anyone has scolded them.

This internal feeling of badness, of not living up to the expectations of parents, makes small children anxious. They may feel that being bad will result in loss of love, physical hurt or even abandonment; moreover, the intensity of parents' own emotional reactions to bad behavior is itself frightening. It is also frustrating to be told "Never do that again," and children channel this into a feeling of anger, which mixes with the fear that they already feel. However, because it is dangerous to feel furious with those we love and, at the same time, afraid of them, children turn their feelings inward, against themselves.

◄ **The reaction of parents** *teaches children from the age of two years to distinguish between right and wrong. The feeling of guilt first appears around the age of three, as children begin to understand the consequences of their actions. They should only be made to feel guilty about specific acts that they can realistically identify as their own, whose consequences they can recognize as undesirable, and for which they can successfully atone.*

The capacity for guilt develops in childhood, and nobody is free from self-blame. Too much guilt can be oppressive but, within limits, it may also have a positive value – teaching us to reconcile our interests with the needs of the community.

This is when guilt occurs: it is a way for children to punish themselves for any real or imagined wrongdoing while avoiding the dangers of violent feelings toward their parents. Thus guilt is inseparable from even the most loving of parent-child relationships.

Young children can tell the difference between violations against moral standards and those against social conventions. If you ask three-year-olds whether hitting someone or taking their possessions would be bad even if there were no rules against it, they are likely to say "Yes." But if you ask the same question about being noisy at the dinner table, these children would probably think this was all right.

Children seem to have an innate sense of morality. Although they are naturally aggressive, the readiness with which they develop an intuitive understanding of morality and other social standards suggests an equally natural tendency toward curbing their aggression.

227

■ **Original sin**, *a feeling that our capacity to do wrong makes us unworthy, is a theme of most religions. However, few have practices that compare to the Catholic confessional* TOP, *in which believers examine their consciences regularly for breaches of religious trust and obligation.* RIGHT *A Hindu woman seeks ritual purification by bathing in the sacred waters of the Ganges River in India. The Christian practice of baptism is similarly a ritual washing away of personal impurity.*

Measuring guilt

Guilt is difficult for psychologists to measure mechanically because, unlike anxiety, it does not cause any obvious physical changes such as an increase in the heart rate or in sweating. "Lie detectors" (polygraphs) are sometimes used, but their reliability is often questioned (see *Ch 21*).

However, psychologists have found ways to measure the amount of guilt felt by children. Normally they tell them an unfinished story about a child who has misbehaved, and then ask them to supply the ending. For example, the story might be about a little boy who has stolen cookies from a jar in the kitchen. A child who is capable of feeling guilt will finish the story in a way that shows that the boy accepts responsibility for his bad behavior and wants to reform himself and/or make reparation, perhaps by confessing his "crime" to his mother and spending his own pocket money to replace the cookies.

Story-finishing tests have shown that girls are likely to give more guilty responses than boys. They are also more apt to produce endings that involve self-punishment, such as the little boy getting a stomachache from eating too many cookies. In general, girls also confess more often to having misbehaved than boys do.

This difference between the sexes continues into adult

SHAME AND GUILT

■ *Shame and guilt are closely related, but there is a clear difference between them.*

With both, we feel bad about ourselves because of something we have done. However, shame occurs when our transgressions are observed by others, whereas guilt, which may involve the same disagreeable emotion, does not need to involve the judgments of others.

The feeling of shame is related to public humiliation or embarrassment about a misdeed or to real or imagined inadequacy in ourselves. For example, in the Far East, concern about "losing face" is a main motive of law-abiding behavior, for wrongdoers are publicly humiliated or ostracized from the group.

Guilt, on the other hand, arises because you have violated someone's trust or confidence in you. For example, successfully stealing from friends without their ever finding out would cause most of us to feel guilty, but if the friends were to discover what we had done, we would feel both shame and guilt.

The 17th-century Puritans provide an extreme example of socially induced guilt: they believed that, since everyone was born with sin, it was the duty of all parents to enforce a strict and austere code of behavior on their children in order to protect their families from moral pollution.

Such rigid religious attitudes may also promote intense guilt feelings about sexual behavior. Studies show that, in some orthodox homes where there is no open discussion about sex, children may infer that it is sinful, immoral and dirty. Reversing these attitudes later in the context of adult married life may be impossible, so that what should be an enjoyable and socially valued relationship is disabled by guilt, causing sexual unresponsiveness or even impotence.

Despite the "sexual revolution," young people often still feel intensely guilty about many aspects of sex. Almost all boys and over 50 percent of girls masturbate, for example, but even today's teenagers feel that masturbation is somehow shameful.

However, the fact that, for many people, masturbation continues to be a guilty secret indicates that changes in cultural beliefs can only partially affect deeply rooted human attitudes.

▲ **Public humiliation** *through denunciation. An accuser gives vent to harsh feelings during the impromptu trial of a suspected Nazi collaborator after the liberation of France in World War II.*

▶ **Shame is external.** *We feel it when the eyes of others are upon us. Guilt is internal.*

GUILT

SHAME

Traumatic experiences too often give the victims feelings of remorse and personal responsibility. We are bewildered when random events harm us. It is as though we have allowed matters to fly out of our control, and we blame ourselves.

life. For example, in psychological questionnaires on issues such as sexuality, hostility and moral conscience, women tend to report more feelings of guilt. The reason probably lies in their psychological makeup.

From infancy onward, females traditionally emphasize attachment and connectedness, while males value individuality and separateness; women stress care and sensitivity to the needs of everyone with whom they are involved, while men see moral issues as matters of individual rights and abstract rules. However, it is not clear whether these sex differences are inborn or learned because it has been found that, today, feminist women show less guilt than their non-feminist counterparts.

Loss of control and self-blame

When something traumatic happens that is completely outside our control, we may still end up filled with guilt and remorse. For example, rape victims commonly show "rape trauma syndrome" immediately after the attack. Typically, they are anxious, vulnerable and filled with guilt and self-blame, and sometimes feel that they are actually partly responsible for the rape because of a lack of good judgment, failing to react properly or a lapse in alertness. Until recently, the judicial system took these painful feelings at face value and, on the basis of them, judges showed leniency toward rapists while failing to offer understanding and support to their victims.

Society is now beginning to recognize that self-blame is a common reaction to the trauma of rape, and that the victims require the same understanding support from the community as anyone else who is enduring a life crisis.

This reaction is not limited to rape victims, however; it has also been found in people who have suffered other sorts of traumatic experiences: concentration-camp victims and war veterans, who feel guilty for having survived while so many perished; child victims of sexual abuse, who may well feel that they caused the sexual activity to occur in the first place; people close to those who have committed suicide, who may experience intense guilt for not having done more to prevent the death. In all these cases, the survivors feel that they have lost control of aspects of their world that were normally under their influence; consequently, in their imaginations they extend this control and thus feel a sense of personal responsibility and guilt.

Depressed people, too, very frequently believe that they are to blame for what has happened to them (see *Ch 28*). However, most of those who become depressed have suffered some upsetting life event such as the loss of a loved one through death or divorce, or a severe financial setback – things that were, again, largely outside their control. Depression is not an inevitable outcome of suffering such an experience: those who feel that they are the unfortunate victims of circumstance are much less likely to become depressed than those who believe that they must bear responsibility for their situation. **AH PF**

▶ **"It wasn't my fault!"** *An accusing finger points to the guilt of someone who is absent. A hand on the heart asserts a blameless part in the incident under investigation.*

▲ **A psychopath feels no guilt.** *Without remorse, Daniel Camargo raped and murdered over 70 adolescent girls in little more than a year in Ecuador. In some people, feelings of interpersonal responsibility fail to occur. On the surface, they may seem friendly and charming,* but they are unable to form any lasting bonds of affection, and may be very good at manipulating situations to their own advantage. And because they feel no guilt, they are able to commit aggressive and brutal crimes without feeling blame. No one really knows what causes psychopathic behavior. It has been suggested that, through brain chemistry, some people are so chronically understimulated that they cannot tolerate boredom and so seek out excitement and danger. The early loss of parents, primarily through family breakup, probably also plays a role: the fear of losing parental love is a crucial feature in developing a sense of guilt, and when this emotional bond is missing, guilt, along with love, may be absent.

COPING POSITIVELY WITH GUILT

■ Guilt in itself is not a bad thing, as long as it is kept under control. The ability to accept our guilt is a sign of concern and love, and it only becomes a problem when we begin to believe that it has wider implications, that it indicates that we are, at bottom, bad or worthless people. This kind of self-judgment often follows the feeling of guilt, and can lead to depression or to self-destructive behavior.

To cope positively with guilt, we must not accept at face value the bad feelings that it causes. Instead, we should examine the underlying reasons that made us decide that we should feel guilty in the first place. To do this, it is important to confront specific issues rather than abstractions. For example, if you feel guilty and worthless, ask yourself what you mean by "worthless," what characteristics or actions you would need to observe in others in order to define them as worthless, and whether any of these apply to you. Then try to discover whether the standards you apply to others are the same as the ones you expect of

yourself. If you treat yourself in a fair and even-handed way, your guilt will remain within manageable proportions.

There are a number of questions that you can ask yourself to prevent guilt from taking control of your life.

"I may have done something bad, but does this mean that I am bad?"

The reasons why we do things are complex, involving our past experience, our understanding of a situation, our feelings at the time and interactions between all these things. Only rarely do we have a chance to analyze a situation before we act; instead, we usually do not think our actions through, and we may not have all the relevant facts before we need to act.

For example, parents sometimes punish their children for things that they later find out were not their fault. In these circumstances, the parents are right to feel guilty, but they must not hate themselves for these blunders. Quite often the situation is as much to blame as the individuals concerned. Money

or health worries, noisy neighbors preventing sleep, having to cope alone all day – any number of reasons may contribute toward producing an emotional outburst. The important thing to remember is not to fall into the trap of self-recrimination or mindless self-blame, which can result in further guilt feelings and depression. Rather, we need to understand the reasons behind our actions; dwelling on the idea that we are valueless or wicked actually prevents us from thinking our problems through.

"Am I being conceited when I feel guilty?"

Most of us easily accept that others have faults and make

▶ Re-establishing control. Many people react to painful experiences with feelings of guilt, remorse and self-blame. War veterans, like rape and concentration-camp victims, may blame themselves for not doing more to prevent what happened. Treatment often centers on "psychological liberation": in this instance, it requires a troubled Vietnam War veteran to hand over his knife.

mistakes but feel that we should be perfect. This is a form of conceit – an unconscious feeling that we are indeed better than others. It is an unattractive trait that everyone should try to avoid – and if we do, we may have the added bonus of feeling

HOW NOT TO MANAGE GUILT

■ Deeply felt guilt is a powerful emotion that many people find difficult to cope with. For some, it is so unbearable that they drink to excess, take drugs or involve themselves in some other form of self-destructive behavior in order to forget whatever it is that arouses their guilt. These activities may be extremely harmful, but the problems they cause often seem to the victim less burdensome than the guilt they are masking.

Business executives who lose most of their money in bad investments turn to drink because they cannot face their inability to provide the luxuries to which their families have

▶ Personal relationships will suffer if you cope with guilt through displacing it – through finding fault with others.

become accustomed. Young women starve themselves to the brink of death – and sometimes beyond – because they feel guilty about not looking like society's absurdly slim ideal. Some men can only experience sexual pleasure when their erotic excitement is mixed with physical punishment.

Trying to achieve perfection is another bad way of dealing with guilt. Some people perceive the world as extremes of

> To prevent guilt taking control of your life, you should examine the reasons behind your original actions and confront specific issues rather than abstractions. Too much self-blame only prevents you from thinking through your problems.

good and evil and strive to be the most productive and moral in their community. However, should they fail in this, their guilt causes them to feel self-hate and anguish.

Others cope with unbearable guilt by accusing and criticizing others, especially those they value most. How this works was shown in an experiment: a researcher hypnotized a girl and then told her that she had stolen some money. When she came out of the hypnotic state, she was very depressed but did not know why; later, she accused the boy sitting next to her of stealing her money.

less guilt about imperfections.

"Am I exaggerating my own importance when I feel guilty?"

Very often we are aware, either consciously or unconsciously, that we wish or intend to do something terrible. Unwelcome thoughts can be quite common, and we usually do not worry about them until something really does happen to that person. Then we may feel responsible for the event, exaggerating our own importance as if we had the power to make things happen just by thinking them – for example, after wishing a parent would die so that you can receive your inheritance sooner, hoping a friend might die so that you can start to have a relationship with the

remaining partner, or wishing ill of a former friend or associate who may have double-crossed you in a business deal. Imagine trying to make the world perfect by wishing it: just as this is not possible, neither can you cause negative events to occur simply because, in a rather emotional moment, you think you would be glad for them to happen.

"Who is being hurt when I blame myself?"

Sometimes we feel anger that is difficult to express because those causing us to feel this way are our loved ones. By blaming and hating ourselves, we get as close to hurting them as we dare, but we feel guilty because we are frightened of telling them how we feel and perhaps risking a quarrel. Our

misery may affect them indirectly, but sometimes they do not even notice. It is easier – and better in the long run – to think about whom the guilt is really protecting, and to figure out a way to stand up to those who make us angry and tell them what we think.

"Am I oversimplifying matters by feeling guilty?"

Guilt can be the result of a tendency to categorize everything into opposite extremes: black or white, immaculate or filthy, saint or sinner. While such opposites are certainly easier to understand than the gray areas, it is important to accept that we are neither the best nor the worst, the biggest nor the smallest, but something quite ordinary in between.

Survival Strategies

EVERYONE has to deal with the normal ups and downs of daily life, and most people take minor setbacks in their stride. Even in the most extreme situations, such as imprisonment or war, the majority prove to have a most remarkable ability to cope. To tackle demanding or stressful situations and feelings such as sadness, anger, fear and confusion, each of us has developed a set of survival strategies. Some of these are quite simple methods of thinking about what has to be done to put things right and then doing it. However, many survival strategies are used automatically – unconsciously – and involve an element of personal self-deception. This may work for us or against us.

Taking direct action

One obvious way of coping with a situation that is very difficult to tolerate is to change it in some way. Taking such direct action is not always possible, but it can often be the best solution. It may be fairly dramatic, such as abandoning an unsatisfactory career by resigning from your job. Alternatively, it can simply involve some minor adjustment to your lifestyle, such as avoiding stress on winter mornings by replacing an unreliable car, expanding a limited social life by finding a babysitter or avoiding the rush hour by arranging to travel to and from work at different hours.

Psychological strategies

Another way of dealing with stress or unpleasantness is to do so indirectly, by changing the way you respond psycho-logically to these situations. This might involve employing a relaxation technique such as meditation or self-hypnosis. You could also try letting off steam through energetic exercise, or obtaining emotional release by screaming loudly in the privacy of your car. Thinking constructively about things that bother you can also be effective. Parents often make a conscious decision to stop resenting their baby for crying, and to concentrate instead on being loving, reminding themselves that infancy only lasts a few years.

These indirect methods of coping are healthy ways of adapting to unpleasant things that you can neither change nor avoid. Other indirect methods may, unfortunately, be less beneficial; although they might help you to cope for a while, they may do harm in the long term. Smoking, drinking, eating junk food and using mood-altering drugs are all good examples – they can be aids toward relaxation at a time of crisis, but as well as being physically harmful, they can also bring about psychological dependence. When this happens, you will find that you cannot tolerate life without these props, and will fail to develop other ways of coping.

■ **Confront the problem or change the way you feel?**
RIGHT When we can, we usually deal with a problem by taking practical action, like this mother studying with her daughter to improve her job skills and earning power. Making yourself forget about problems *ABOVE* is also a strategy. It is a self-defeating one when it involves excessive drinking or when you put symptoms of disease out of your mind because you do not like to go to the doctor. However, refusing to think about

PROTECTING YOURSELF FROM FAILURE

■ *You may find it particularly difficult to cope in "performance situations," such as examinations and interviews. Not only a passing grade or a chance of a job is at stake, but so is your self-esteem, and this can become the decisive concern.*

One strategy that people use to protect their self-esteem in such situations is "self-handicapping." They take some action that will actually endanger their success but will also give a good excuse for failure. This may take the form of getting drunk before an interview, staying awake all night before an examination or getting pregnant in the middle of a college course. Obviously, behavior such as this involves a real risk to success, but for some, it is apparently a price worth paying.

Others do not indulge in such obviously self-damaging behavior but, instead, look for reasons to explain and excuse a possible failure.

Examples are: "I won't get a date because I've got acne on my nose," "I won't pass my driving test because I suffer terribly from nerves," "I won't get the job because it's the first day of my period."

Another related strategy is "defensive pessimism." It is quite common to hear people say, "I'm sure I'm going to fail" before an important test of their skills. However, they may be employing this strategy as a way of raising their anxiety in order to motivate themselves. For instance, after telling everyone that they are going to fail an exam, they may go home, study very hard and perform well.

An obviously good way of dealing with situations that cause you stress is to change them for the better, but often this is not feasible. What are the strategies that make it possible to endure what you cannot like and cannot change?

Among the indirect methods we all use are *defense mechanisms*. These are self-deceiving strategies (see p234). Sometimes they are beneficial, but they can themselves cause problems in our ability to relate to other people and to understand our own behavior. They can also make us less content, and may even have a negative effect on our physical health.

Defense mechanisms

Defense mechanisms may be wholly unconscious or they may be deliberate to some extent. They may come into play to help us come to terms with things in the outside world that we do not know how to deal with, or we may use them to deal with painful feelings, unacceptable urges or internal conflicts.

Some would say that all defenses are bad, but it is doubtful whether we can expect ourselves to do without them and still be able to deal adequately and immediately with all that life throws at us. We could, for instance, spend vast amounts of time thinking about the suffering of the world, to the point where we are unable to do any living at all. Or we could worry continually when our children are out of our sight in case they are in danger. However, the defense of *suppression* – putting things out of our minds – helps us to avoid spending "emotional" energy on matters that we cannot control.

Sometimes, too, defenses make it possible to cope with demanding situations when it would not be very constructive to sit and weep inconsolably. An example is when a friend dies suddenly. While you might be devastated, members of the bereaved family may need your support, and someone to organize the funeral. Your own grief has to take a back seat until there is time and opportunity to express it.

Defense mechanisms can also help us to adapt to new and difficult situations. If we are told that we have a serious illness, most of us would find it difficult to accept this fact immediately. By denying what we have been told, we give

situations that you can really do nothing about is a way of reserving energy and attention for the problems you can solve.

233

Defense mechanisms, although self-deceptive, may help us to cope in a more positive way than we could if we tried to face reality squarely every moment. You may genuinely need the relief you gain by suppressing or denying your problem.

ourselves a chance to adapt to the new reality and to take it in gradually. However, psychological testing has found that people with high self-esteem make less use of defense mechanisms than anxious people. The only exception is that people with high self-esteem are more likely to make a successful use of denial, for example, denying the reality of their own fear when they face danger (see p236).

When defenses work against us

In many situations defense mechanisms are not very useful. Sometimes they may prevent us taking the best course of action. For instance, the best thing to do if you discover something that could be a symptom of cancer – say, a breast lump – is to consult a physician immediately. If you use defenses such as suppression or rationalization and take no action your life might be endangered.

Defense mechanisms can also damage relationships. Displacing anger caused by frustration at work onto a member of the family would be an obvious example of this, although

---

SELF-DEFENSE THROUGH SELF-DECEPTION

■ *"Defense mechanisms" are pieces of self-deception that we all use to help us cope with stressful problems. Here is a list:*
Denial and repression. *One way to deal with things that you cannot cope with is to refuse to admit that they exist, denial, or refuse to think about them, repression. These defense mechanisms usually operate unconsciously to block out un-*

■ **Angry denial** *of reality helps a tennis star cope with the unwelcome consequences of a blunder. Shouting "no" in exasperation can seem pointless, and yet we all do it when we*

make a mistake under pressure: it eases the tension, allowing us to recover our sense of control and carry on.

acceptable desires or feelings or to stop us remembering dreadful occurrences.
Suppression. *You can deliberately choose not to think about something. You may tell yourself that when you have the time or energy you will worry, cry or be angry about whatever it is, but now is not the time. The last words of Scarlett O'Hara in Gone with the Wind are perhaps the most famous example of suppression: "I'll think of it all tomorrow, at Tara. I can stand it then. Tomorrow, I'll think of some way to get him back. After all, tomorrow is another day."*
Rationalization. *You find a nice, neat, rational explanation for your behavior. For example, you are in fact afraid of meeting new people but think that you cannot go to a party because of all the problems involved in finding a babysitter.*
Regression. *You retreat to behavior that is more appropriate in an earlier stage of development. Young children sometimes regress when they are ill – they may want to be cuddled like a baby – or on the arrival of a new baby in the home, when they may begin bedwetting again. Sick adults, too, can regress and behave like children by becoming irrationally demanding. Regression can also be seen in people under emotional stress: bursting into tears at the slightest disappointment or having a temper tantrum are childlike forms of behavior. Behaving like someone younger may not be harmful in itself, and can sometimes*

be fun. However, regression may not bring about the most helpful responses in the adults around us. Sometimes a loved one might be happy to nurture us when we feel like needy children, but if we act like children at work or when a close relationship is under threat, this behavior can be embarrassing.
Projection. *Some people cope with unacceptable aspects of their own makeup by projecting unpleasantness onto someone else. We all have a bad side – eg selfish and aggressive urges – but we do not like to recognize it. It is quite common to see people projecting their own faults onto others – convincing themselves that it is the boss who is being unreasonable (not themselves who are incompetent), or their partner who is constantly fantasizing about having affairs (and not themselves who have a roving eye). Those who do this a great deal are prone to criticizing or blaming others. Sometimes groups of people or even whole nations jointly project negative feelings, such as when one country thinks another wants to start a war.*
Displacement. *This means taking out a negative emotion – usually anger – on someone or something who is not responsible for it. If you feel angry and for some reason cannot show it to the person who makes you angry, you let out your feelings by attacking someone else. The classic example is kicking the cat while angry with your boss.*
Reaction. *When you feel*

234

there are many more subtle ways in which harm can be done. Yet another hazard is that our mental and physical health might be damaged.

Researchers have found that people who do not deal directly with their emotions are more likely to succumb to infections and to medical conditions of many kinds, notably cancer. Women with breast lumps were interviewed before diagnosis. In those found to have a repressed hostility the tumor was then more frequently diagnosed as cancerous. The overuse of defenses may also be a factor in the development of some mental illness.

When to use coping strategies

If we wish to lead healthy lives, we should try to become aware of the way in which we tend to use defenses and try not to resort to them except in emergencies. This involves

**WAYS OF
AVOIDING
THE ISSUE**

Wheel diagram labeled "WHAT PROBLEM?" with segments: Compensation, Reaction, Displacement, Projection, Regression, Rationalization, Suppression, Repression, Denial, Fantasizing, Intellectualizing

attracted to unacceptable behavior, you might turn your feeling on its head by forming an extreme reaction against this behavior. For instance, if you cannot live with your fascination for pornography you may become ardently opposed to pornography. When you have to give up smoking, it helps if you become an enthusiastic campaigner against smoking.
Compensation. This means trying to make up for what you see as your personal deficiencies. You can do this directly, by working hard to overcome the deficiency, or indirectly, by excelling in another area (see Ch 6). It has been suggested, for example, that Napoleon's career was a compensation for his short stature.
Intellectualizing. Some people never express their real feelings, and instead develop all kinds of interesting intellectual theories about their emotions.

The characters in the films of Woody Allen often do this. Sometimes a traumatic event is remembered in detail but none of the feelings that went with it.

Fantasizing. Occasionally we may also withdraw from our feelings by throwing ourselves into energetic activity or by retreating into daydreams and fantasies.

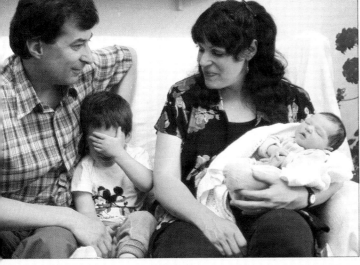

■ **Shutting out the truth** with hands over eyes is the reality-denying strategy of this blundering tennis player ABOVE and this boy LEFT, confronted with the prospect of a rival for his parents' resources and attention. Long-term denial of reality, such as the insistence that smoking will not harm you, is more dangerous.

235

staying in touch with reality and not deceiving ourselves, even though deception may be more comfortable than facing up to the truth. We all have a "coping style," and, in some people, it relies quite heavily on defenses. If this applies to you, you may need to work on widening your repertoire of coping strategies and choosing to use healthier methods.

Talking about your feelings to those who seem to cause them, as and when they arise, is also a good way to avoid overuse of defenses. Learning to express yourself assertively can be a great help when you are trying to do this. A common pattern is the refusal to mention feelings until they explode in a way that may hurt the other person and start a damaging quarrel. After assertiveness training (see *Ch15*), you will find it easier to say such things as "I feel a little angry with you" or "I was terribly jealous when you were talking to that person," instead of making an aggressive, blaming attack. Assertiveness skills help us to inform others about our feelings in the best possible way.

Identifying your own defenses

One of the problems with defense mechanisms is that, because they are often unconscious, it can be hard to know when you are using them. For example, it may be perfectly obvious to a man's friends that he is deceiving himself about the faithfulness of his partner, but if that self-deception is successful, he will not be able to acknowledge the truth himself. Fortunately, however, for those who wish to understand themselves better, there are a number of ways in which defenses can be explored.

Investigating your own defenses and discovering new insights about yourself can be extremely interesting, and eliminating your defenses may be the only way to break out of repeating patterns of behavior that prevent you getting the

► **Failure to deny fear** *when you are faced with a frightening task makes it difficult to perform. Fear is the urge to avoid or escape what frightens you, and this may be contrary to the action that you need somehow to manage.*

DENIAL OF FEAR IN PARACHUTISTS

■ It is difficult to study strong feelings under laboratory conditions, and researchers have found that they can learn a lot by studying people in real situations in which strong emotions are involved. This was certainly true when psychologists carried out a series of studies to investigate responses to parachute jumping as a sport. In these, the reactions of those making their first jumps were compared to those of experienced jumpers.

The levels of stress in both types of parachutists were recorded by measuring heart rate and other indicators. In the beginners, stress levels rose steadily as the time for the jump approached. The experienced jumpers showed quite a different pattern: an initial increase in stress was followed by a fall, so that they were apparently calm when the time came to jump. They had learned how to deny to themselves that they were afraid. The psychologists also followed the progress of a group of beginners, from their first jumps until they had jumped a number of times. The researchers found that the pattern typical of experienced jumpers gradually developed, and the ones who performed best were those who were most calm, and whose stress levels seemed to have come down to near normal just before jumping, a useful adaptation to the situation.

DEFENSE MECHANISMS AND RAPE

■ Rape is one of the most stressful events that it is possible to experience – one in which a woman's body is invaded, and she suffers a massive loss of control over her environment and, worst of all, fears for her life.

Psychologists studied the reactions of 92 women raped in Boston, Massachusetts. They wanted to find out what sorts of survival strategies the women had adopted during their ordeals.

Some women tried to talk the rapist out of it, attempted to defend themselves using self-defense tactics, or they tried to escape. One third felt paralyzed with fear, unable to do anything. This could be the remnant of a defensive technique common in animals in which they freeze or play dead when under threat of attack.

Once the rape was actually taking place, many women reported thinking of something else, such as trying to keep calm, praying, or trying to memorize details of the rapist. Distraction from thinking about what is actually happening represents a kind of defense mechanism. Others reported making a noise, either to release tension, distract the rapist or attract help. Others reported involuntary physical reactions such as vomiting.

Just after the rape, about half were obviously upset. The remainder were "controlled" and presumably employing a defense mechanism such as repression or suppression. Later, all the victims experienced a long period of emotional disorientation, suffering a variety of psychological and physical symptoms.

Since this research was done, women's groups in many cities throughout the world have set up rape crisis counseling groups so that victims of rape can talk through their experiences, to help them deal with the emotional aftermath.

Discovering your own defensive style can be hard work, and learning to cope with emotions that you have kept at bay for years can be painful. But this may be the only way of breaking out of the limits this style has placed on you.

most out of life. However, this can be hard work. For one thing, it can be a painful process getting back in touch with powerful emotions that you have been successfully keeping at bay. Once you have looked at your defenses, you may also feel that you have to take some action, and this, too, can be difficult. However, bottling things up for years, or even just for a few days, results in its own kind of suffering, and the feeling of relief that occurs when this stops can be tremendous.

Overreacting reveals your defenses

The most important sign that defense mechanisms are causing problems in daily behavior is when you overreact to something that, on the face of it, seems quite trivial – for example, if you lose your temper over something insignificant or burst into floods of tears while watching a sad movie. If you want to understand the reason, the first thing to do is not to fight the emotion: let yourself feel it to the full. Then ask yourself whether you felt any other emotion immediately before – for instance, a feeling of hurt often comes before anger. Now ask yourself what caused this first reaction and what it reminds you of. You may then discover that you can trace and feel the original emotion.

Perhaps your child has made you furiously angry by refusing to eat the food you have so lovingly prepared for her. You realize that, before you became angry, you felt hurt and rejected – as if your love, and not the food, was being refused. Then you might remember a time in the past when your loving advances to your mother had been rejected, and re-experience the hurt that you had felt then. Once the root cause of the unexpected outburst has been uncovered, you

may be able to handle the situation differently – that is, not *displacing* the anger you feel toward your mother – the next time your child behaves in the same way. You could say to yourself, "I am being irrational and reacting to this child as if she were my mother pushing me away when I wanted a hug. She is just a child who is not very hungry."

Sometimes it may not be enough simply to identify the origins of your feelings. Even though you may now remember that your mother pushed you away when you needed closeness, the hurt that this caused may remain bottled up. If you still feel angry with your mother (or, for that matter, your father or any other person close to you) for rejecting your love, it can help to take this out on a pillow, a mattress or a pile of cardboard boxes. Really let yourself go and scream and shout if you can. If you feel terribly sad, then you should cry about it.

However, if the hurt felt in childhood was very severe, occurred early or was repeated often or over a long period, it may take quite a time to unbottle your feelings. You may do it quicker with the help of a counselor or therapist, but beginning to understand it is the essential first step.

▼ **Taking it out on a pile of mats** *can be a better alternative than misdirecting your anger toward innocent human victims.*

Displacement of emotion is necessary when you cannot express yourself to the person who has upset you: the person may be a dead parent, a departed lover or an inaccessible employer. It may be you, when you have done something to make you feel guilty or foolish. You can relieve the tension by striking out at another person, but your relationships will benefit if you strike out instead at a pillow or a mattress.

▶ **We can endure almost any ordeal** *if we convince ourselves that it will soon end.*

The pain that you are defending yourself against may, of course, not originate in childhood but in an early stage in adult life. A marriage or any other significant relationship that has broken down can leave you with emotional wounds that have not yet healed. If you are dealing with these wounds by erecting defenses, you will not truly recover. The wounds can very easily cause problems with new relationships. Hurts sustained in adult life are, however, easier to identify and deal with than those left over from early childhood.

Underreacting reveals your defenses

Sometimes people underreact to an event that should upset them. If you crash your car badly but afterward feel calm, controlled, empty or numb, you are repressing the shock, anger, fear and relief that it is natural to feel. These emotions could surface later, perhaps when you do not have immediate demands on your attention such as taking care of an injured passenger or talking to the police.

If your feelings do not emerge within a reasonable time, they are likely to appear later in a distorted way, such as an anxiety attack or severe migraine. If you have unexpectedly felt a lack of feeling about some occurrence that should have upset you, you should make a conscious effort to give yourself the opportunity to feel. You may be able to do this

for yourself by sitting quietly and thinking about it, or you may need to talk with someone who is good at listening.

Unpleasant feelings that keep coming back

A defense mechanism may become apparent if you realize that you often experience the same unpleasant emotion. You might, for example, find that you are very often jealous of your partner when he or she has an innocent

If you notice a surprising lack of feeling about an event that should have upset you, you should make a conscious effort to think about the event or talk about it with a friend, to release your suppressed emotions and allow yourself to feel.

conversation with a member of the opposite sex. Your sensible, rational, adult self knows that you are being silly, but you go on making yourself uncomfortable, and perhaps starting quarrels or behaving in a way that you despise because the jealousy will not go away.

Again, you might be able to trace your feelings back to your earlier life by asking, "What does this remind me of?" You might discover that the intense feelings of jealousy you felt when a baby brother was born lie at the root of your present jealousy, or perhaps your first partner gave you something to be jealous about. Identifying origins of feelings can help you to be more rational about the present.

One way to become more aware of the way in which you use one specific defense mechanism – that is, projecting the unacceptable in yourself onto other people – is to think about a person whom you dislike intensely and try to work out exactly what it is about him or her that causes this reaction in you. Ask yourself if there is a hidden part of yourself that is like this, or whether you wish to have the very qualities that annoy you so much.

An example would be disliking someone at work who treats subordinates in a tough and not particularly fair way. Could it be that, at home, you treat your children in much the same manner? Or perhaps you find it difficult to be assertive and wish to be a bit tougher yourself? Of course, the person could simply be eminently dislikable.

Freudian slips and dreams

One way of uncovering your defenses is to notice and interpret slips of the tongue – so-called "Freudian slips" – by which the workings of our subconscious minds leak into the things we say. If, for instance, a young woman who appears to be looking forward to her wedding says that she is going to be "buried" instead of "married" the following week, you might reasonably suspect that she has some doubts that she is repressing or suppressing. Such revealing slips of the tongue are, however, fairly rare, and although the more common types may give us the occasional flash of insight, they do not provide us with a systematic tool for understanding the subconscious mind.

Another method is to examine your dreams. Keep a pencil and paper beside your bed and write down your dreams as soon as you wake. When you have time, think about what you have recorded and try to interpret it. Some believe that the best way of using dreams is to try to imagine yourself in the role of everything that appears in them. If a dream was about a little girl in a haunted house with a monster chasing her, you would try to imagine yourself as the little girl, as the monster and as the haunted house.

If you keep an open mind, you might be able to identify hidden parts of yourself in the most unexpected places. For example, the little girl running away could represent a fear that you need to come to terms with; the monster might symbolize an unpleasant bullying side to your nature (we all have one); and the haunted house could be your emotional self, full of memories and pain from the past that are affecting the present. There are no right or wrong ways of interpreting your dreams – you can take from them whatever seems useful. **JM**

239

◄ **Suppress your feelings or let them take over?** *TOP A woman in grief is overwhelmed by emotion. BOTTOM Following an earthquake, a subdued family in Chile tries to keep spirits up as they camp in the ruins of their home. During crises you have to suppress the feeling of despair in order to cope with present problems and give attention to the future. It is dangerous, however, to suppress feelings too much. You should find time to give full expression to the anguish of personal loss.*

► **Escaping from reality into fantasy,** *like this woman daydreaming by the fire, may help you to cope better with real problems. Daydreaming is a highly relaxed state from which you are likely to return to practical concerns with a fresher mind. While thinking aimless, relaxed thoughts, you are more likely to stand back from your failures and realize that they can be accepted – this will make it easier to turn your energies in more constructive directions. But it is dangerous to meet all of your needs for stimulation and excitement through mere imagination.*

Happiness and Contentment

RESEARCH finds that the success or failure of our relationships, how much we enjoy our work, and how we spend our leisure time are of particular importance in the achievement of a lasting sense of well-being. By managing these aspects of our lives effectively we can maximize our individual potential for happiness. The degree to which this potential varies from one person to another, because of advantages such as talent, beauty or wealth, is slight.

What is the nature of happiness?

People seem to be reasonably accurate in assessing their own feelings of happiness as well as their feelings of satisfaction or contentment with life as a whole. Whether asked about their typical mood over the previous week, or to respond to the question "How do you feel about your life as a whole?" on a scale ranging from "delighted" to "terrible," people's scores tend to agree with those of independent judges who know them well.

People who claim to be happy on one day are also likely to be happy on another, which suggests happiness is as much a function of the person as it is of circumstances. Some people, because of their constitution, are going to be more or less happy regardless of their circumstances. Happiness is related to personality. Extroverted, impulsive people are more likely to report being happy than those who are introverted.

In contrast, unhappiness is related not to introversion but to emotionality. It is negative emotions that seem to cause unhappiness, not just an absence of positive emotions. Happiness is not the exact opposite of unhappiness. Some-

one who is often intensely happy is also capable of experiencing deep unhappiness. Joy and sadness are controlled by a common mechanism of strong emotion. The more emotional you are, the greater number of different emotions you will experience.

The level of happiness seems to be much the same throughout the world. This is further evidence for a constitutional basis for happiness. In addition, people living in deprived areas seem to remain happy because they compare themselves with others around them and with their own past; this explanation is consistent with the maxim "Happiness is relative."

On what does happiness depend?

Many aspects of our life can contribute to happiness, not just the obvious things like material possessions. Indeed, there is much truth in the old song title "The best things in life are free." In one American survey, over 2,000 people were asked to attach "importance ratings" to the various aspects of their lives. The main sources of satisfaction were summarized as centering around health and family life, followed by friendships and work, with leisure and finance being considered relatively unimportant.

Research has shown that we have a better chance of being happy and contented if we get married, visit friends and relatives, join clubs and societies and make friends with our neighbors and the people with whom we work.

Marriage often brings happiness, even though it is the distress caused by disharmony and divorce that we are most likely to hear about. Surveys indicate that married people as

MEASURING HAPPINESS

■ *Simply asking people to rate how happy or sad they are can be a surprisingly consistent measurement of these moods. Results obtained by various methods tend to agree with one another.*

Two of the most popular methods for measuring happiness are the "faces test" TOP RIGHT and satisfaction scales. The graph BOTTOM RIGHT shows results from a survey using a satisfaction ladder scale.

SATISFACTION SCALES

The graph shows the percentages of people in an American survey who identified their lives as "the worst possible" (1) or the "best possible" (9) or something between (2-8). They were shown a ladder diagram with nine rungs and asked to mark an X on the rung that came closest to their position

THE FACES TEST

Which face comes closest to expressing how you feel about your life as a whole? Nearly half of those tested choose the

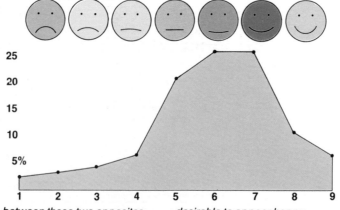

between these two opposites.
In tests such as this, nearly everyone chooses one of the higher rungs. However, perhaps because it is so socially

second most intense smile. Warmth and brightness of color here correspond to the proportions normally choosing each face.

desirable to appear happy, people tend to rate themselves even higher on the faces test than on the ladder scale.

HAPPINESS IN DIFFERENT COUNTRIES

■ *The table below gives examples of comparative rates of happiness and satisfaction reported by people in different countries. Denmark reports the highest. Paradoxically, Denmark also reports the highest suicide rate. This in part reflects inquest practices. Especially in Catholic countries, doubtful cases are less often recorded as suicides.*

	Happiness self-ratings	Satisfaction self-rating
Belgium	2.9	3.2
Denmark	2.9	3.5
France	2.4	2.8
W Germany	2.5	3.0
Ireland	2.8	3.2
Italy	2.0	2.6
Holland	3.0	3.3
UK	2.7	3.1

Happiness is partly a matter of our luck – it may reflect personal advantages and temperament. Other factors can be worked at – we can cultivate relationships and we can be realistic in our goals at work and at leisure.

241

The happiest people are those who form close relationships and have a wide circle of friends. Married couples are happier than single people, and partners who share leisure pursuits are most likely to report being satisfied with marriage.

a group are much happier than those who are single or divorced: in one study, approximately 40 percent of married men and women claimed to be "very happy" compared with about 20 percent of single people and just under 20 percent of divorced people. However, contrary to expectations, it is men who most need marriage: when couples split up, it is the men who are most likely to become depressed and even ill. It has been argued that men get more from marriage (and thus feel its absence more acutely when it breaks down) because women are particularly good at providing social support for themselves and others, including their husbands.

It might be thought that children would enhance a marriage by providing a shared interest. However, it is usually found that couples without children are the happiest, and that the happiness of those that do have them increases when the children finally leave home. Perhaps couples have more time to develop shared interests when children are not a feature in their daily lives, and of course, children can be a source of stress in many families.

Although having a close, long-term, stable relationship with one person is seen by most people to be the basis of true happiness, having a circle of friends – about 25 seems to be the optimum number – is also vital.

Perhaps this is best seen in the effect that a lack of friends can have on mood and mental health. Studies have shown that people are especially vulnerable to depression if they have no close companions – for example, a characteristic of depressed housewives has repeatedly been found to be a lack of friends in whom they can confide. However, mood and the ability to make friends are interrelated: happy people attract friends, who in turn increase happiness; depressed people repel potential friends, which then increases depression.

242

■ **With or without children,** *life can be filled with satisfactions. LEFT Being a mother or father is a fulfillment of role expectations, and parents report that they enjoy the affection and companionship of their offspring. TOP Although it can sometimes be bitterly disappointing to be childless, surveys find that couples without children, including those who chose to be so, or who are planning to start a family later, have greater marital satisfaction. They have greater freedom to enjoy each other's company and share experiences.*

Happy at work and happy at play

There are many ways in which work can contribute to the way we feel. Apart from the satisfaction of doing well and gaining promotion, a job can give a sense of status and purpose as well as an important structure to each day. It may also give individuals something to look forward to – even if it is only a coffee or tea break. In fact, many surveys have shown that job satisfaction and morale can be enhanced simply by the introduction of breaks from work, especially if these entail going to, say, a central coffee lounge.

About half of those who are employed claim to be satisfied with their jobs – approximately one-third say that they would continue to work even if they did not have to. However, for a minority of people, job dissatisfaction is a great source of unhappiness.

Job satisfaction tends to occur in the more technical and/ or highly paid occupations because these are likely to be the more interesting and challenging. The highest ratings of job satisfaction are usually obtained from university teachers, scientists and chemists, followed by farmers, lawyers and managers, with sales staff and clerical and manual workers giving progressively lower ratings. The lowest of all tend to be given by unskilled workers.

The importance of work is reflected by the fact that the unemployed as a group are far from happy. Many symptoms or warning signs of mental illness become apparent following the loss of a job; indeed, work is most appreciated when it is lost. It is clear that the unemployed need a substitute (such as an absorbing hobby) if they are unable to find work.

SMILING AND FRIENDS

■ *Friendship is one of the most important factors associated with happiness. The diagrams* BELOW *reveal that smiling, an index of happiness, is most likely to occur when we are with other people. It does not matter too much whether we have a hit or a miss at bowling or whether it is a sunny or a cloudy day (the examples reported here), since it is the presence of friends that prompts our smiling.*

In the street
% smiling with friends
when sunny **61**
57 when cloudy

% smiling when alone
when sunny **12**
when cloudy **5**

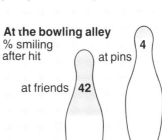

At the bowling alley
% smiling after hit
at pins **4**
at friends **42**

% smiling after miss
at pins **3**
at friends **28**

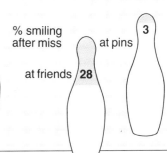

■ **Pleasures of solitude and pleasures of friendship**. *RIGHT Alone with her thoughts, a young woman contemplates an imposing landscape. Solitude is calming, and the opportunities it gives us to reassess our goals may help to unfreeze self-limiting attitudes. Solitude also pleasantly enhances our appetite for the company of the friends to whom we return.* TOP *Three friends consult a guidebook during a holiday. Sharing other people's experiences magnifies our enjoyment, and mattering to someone underpins our self-regard.*

Hobbies are crucial whether we are employed or not. As well as the intrinsic satisfaction that can be gained, many of our needs can be met by what we do in our spare time. We may need to relax and so choose something like painting landscapes or yoga, or we may require stimulation, in which case we might decide to play in a jazz band or go in for parachute jumping. Some people deliberately choose something completely different from their work – a contact sport for an office worker or stamp collecting for a laborer. More often, though, our work spills over into our leisure hours, so that, for example, book editors read books and gardeners tend their own rosebeds in their spare time.

However, it does seem that whatever we do, who we do it with is an important factor. When over 1,000 adults were asked to rate their happiness in various aspects of their lives, family activities were reported to be the most important element in overall quality of life. Evidence from a study of 200 couples also indicates the truth behind the slogan "The family that plays together, stays together." Those pursuing joint or shared activities with their partners expressed a greater degree of marital satisfaction than did those pursuing parallel activities, and worst off were those involved in completely separate activities. Whether this means that

couples with shared interests are going to be happier, or that efforts to cultivate similar interests will enhance a marriage is not clear; there is probably truth in both views.

Do money and beauty bring happiness?

Happiness from relationships, work and leisure is within the reach of most people, but what is the happiness factor of special advantages such as money and beauty? A study carried out in Britain on 191 people who had won huge cash prizes showed that, as expected, they acquired better houses and cars with their winnings, and they took more luxurious holidays. Apart from an increase in headaches, they also seemed to be in better health, but not everything was to their advantage.

Many of them complained of being pestered with requests

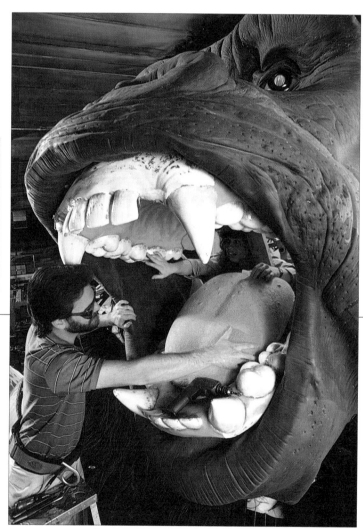

AGE AND JOB SATISFACTION

■ *Evidence that interest in work can increase over the years comes from surveys of job satisfaction at different ages. The graph shows the combined results of several large-scale American surveys. For both men and women, there is an increase in job satisfaction right up to retirement age, when many people are forced to retire.*

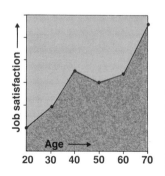

▲ **Creative work is the most satisfying.** *ABOVE Designers at Universal Studios in Hollywood make adjustments to a model for the film "King Kong." University teachers, scientists and laboratory chemists report the* highest levels of job satisfaction. Less interesting and less demanding jobs are rated progressively lower, with unskilled jobs at the bottom.

Job satisfaction increases with age, reaching a peak at retirement. Half of employed people report satisfaction with their jobs and one-third say they would continue to work even if they did not need to earn the money.

for money by charitable and not-so-charitable causes. Those winners who chose to move to a new area were likely to experience loneliness. Complaints about the snobbishness of new neighbors were also common. About 70 percent of the winners decided to give up work, and this too led to an increase in loneliness.

On balance, the researchers concluded that happiness is not increased as a result of coming into money. Similar findings were obtained in a study of 22 winners of large lotteries in the United States: they proved to be no happier than a comparison group of nonwinners.

Surprisingly, people in poor, underdeveloped countries have a high happiness rating despite their poverty. Simple things, like receiving more food, cause them to experience extreme happiness, though their capacity for misery due to

their circumstances is also great. Research into the relationship between beauty and happiness yielded more positive results. When the numerous social advantages that beauty bestows (especially on women) are considered, it is not very surprising that many beautiful women claim to be particularly happy.

In one study, students were asked to rate their happiness, self-esteem and mental health, while independent judges rated them for physical attractiveness. There was a slight but consistent trend for attractive female students to report greater happiness and more positive feelings about themselves, but this finding did not apply to men, perhaps because society places far less value on men's looks.

In addition, attractive couples seem to be happier together. Students were asked to nominate examples of well-adjusted and poorly adjusted couples from among their friends and acquaintances, and these were then visited by interviewers who rated them for physical attractiveness. The results showed a preponderance of attractive people in the well-adjusted group. There was also an indication that the attractiveness of the woman was more important than that of the man: the happy and well-adjusted partners tended to be similar in degree of attractiveness, but where there was a

VACATIONS AND HAPPINESS

■ *It may hardly be surprising to learn that people are happier when on vacation, but researchers have added the weight of their evidence to this*

**% of sufferers reporting
no symptoms on vacation**

Tiredness	65
Irritability	73
Worry and anxiety	74
Loss of interest in sex	50
Digestive problems	62.5
Insomnia	64
Headaches	86

common assumption. For example, when holidaymakers on an island near the Australian Barrier Reef were assessed for such psychologically influenced symptoms as insomnia and headaches, it was found that, after a few days, these ailments tended to disappear. The table LEFT gives similar results from a study carried out in the United States: it can be seen that people's symptoms were more than halved when they were on holiday.

SATISFACTION AND LEISURE ACTIVITIES

Activity	Great satisfaction %
Parenting	79
Intimate relationship	75
Homemaking	40
Religion	34
Being with friends	33
Helping others	33
Reading	32
Being with relatives	27
Making or fixing things	27
Relaxing, sitting around	27
Sports or games	26
Housework	25
Car ownership	25
Cooking	23
Shopping	17
Watching television	17
Clubs	13
Politics	9

■ *The table LEFT gives the percentage of people who, during an extensive American survey, said that they derived "great satisfaction" from a variety of different activities. Family life clearly comes top, followed by social activities, with more mundane pursuits being relatively unpopular. The most frequent leisure activity – watching television – was found to give great satisfaction to only 17 percent of people.*

▶ **Making home and garden what we want them to be** *gives great satisfaction to about 40 percent of us.*

Increasing your happiness may mean leading a more active life, becoming better oriented to the present and setting your sights on more attainable goals. The results are enhanced self-esteem and a more positive outlook.

discrepancy, the woman was likely to be the better looking.

If adjusting well to life is partly based on physical charms, what happens when looks begin to fade? One of the ways in which we assess our current level of happiness is by comparison with what we have experienced in the past. This was examined in a study in which the adjustment of middle-aged people was compared with their attractiveness when young (as rated from college yearbook photographs). Women who were very attractive in their teens and early twenties tended to be less happy and less well adjusted to life by the time they reached the age of 50 than those who were less well endowed by nature. Again, no such relationship was found for men. Plain women may come into their own in the autumn of their lives.

Increasing your happiness

Such activities as listening to cheerful music and watching funny films can enhance our mood and help to make happiness a habit (see *Ch 26*). Other methods of "happiness

■ **Roots of happiness.** *ABOVE LEFT Becoming a millionaire is the dream of many who believe money can buy everything, but research finds that million-dollar lottery winners are not happier after the initial euphoria. ABOVE RIGHT People who lead active lives are usually the happiest. Meeting the challenge of keeping fit gives a sense of achievement as well as improving general well-being. LEFT A sense of meaning in life is essential to anyone's happiness. For some it is a source of profound satisfaction.*

training" include exercise, which works both directly and indirectly to enhance our mood. A direct physiological effect may occur by way of an increase both in adrenaline and in endorphins, the body's own natural painkillers. Increased fitness and health lead indirectly to an improved lifestyle and a consequent increase in happiness and satisfaction with life in general.

Evidence for these beneficial effects comes from a study in which moderately depressed, neurotic patients were assigned either to psychotherapy or to a graduated program of walking, then jogging, then running. Depression declined in most of those in the exercise group – but only in some members of the psychotherapy group – and this was still apparent when the patients' cases were followed up over the next year. Significantly, almost all those in the exercise group continued with their new-found interest in jogging.

A characteristic of depressed, unhappy people is that, as well as perceiving the world in a negative way, they overgeneralize about their own failures, blaming themselves for almost everything that goes wrong.

Based on this observation, techniques of "cognitive therapy" (therapy that changes the way you *think*) have been developed in which people are trained to stop blaming themselves, to lower their aspirations and to become more oriented to the present, no longer dwelling on past mistakes. This type of training to improve one's outlook on life is found to work for most people, and more importantly, it can have long-lasting effects.

One kind of cognitive therapy involves setting realistic goals and then planning to achieve them. The discovery that some goals are attainable can increase self-esteem. Together with the satisfaction inherent in achievement, this can lead to an improved outlook on life and increased satisfaction. Evidence for the benefits of this technique has come from comparisons of its effects with those of other therapies. Even people who are not depressed report feeling happier after goal-setting therapy, which typically is conducted twice a week for several weeks, and this improvement is still apparent six weeks later. Another technique is "anticipation training" (see *Ch 28*).

It is obvious that we should aim to avoid unnecessary distress in life – although this may be easier said than done – and we should try not to set ourselves unrealistically high goals. Aristotle claimed that a person must be virtuous in order to be happy, which illustrates the point that we may need to avoid inner conflict in order to achieve happiness.

Also, we need to find meaning and purpose in life, and perhaps this is most easily achieved through work and leisure. For some people, though, this meaning and purpose is to be found in religion; in fact, compared with the general population, religious people, especially those getting on in years, are happier.

But, we should aim to maximize the pleasure we get from our friendships and other relationships. It is also important to remember that cultivating a positive outlook on life can be as important as the things we do. **DKBN**

▲ **Contentment** *may be a passing mood as you drift across the lake on an afternoon outing or it may be a feeling of satisfac-* *tion with your life in general. It is the central part of a happy life, but is not identical with happiness, which also includes the* *more active pleasures of setting goals and rising to challenges.*

READERS may want information about other aspects of a subject, or detail on particular topics that have aroused their interest. Some generally available books and periodicals suggested for further reading are listed below. The main published sources consulted by the contributors to this book follow the further reading suggestions.

1 Self-Fulfillment

Cirese, S 1977 *Quest: A Search for Self* Holt, Rinehart and Winston, New York; Corey, G 1983 *I Never Knew I Had a Choice* Brooks Cole, Monterey, CA; Maslow, A H 1970 *Towards a Psychology of Being* Van Nostrand, Princeton, NJ; Rogers, C R 1961 *On Becoming a Person* Houghton Mifflin, Boston, IL.

2 Origins of Self-Awareness

Markova, I 1987 *Human Awareness: Its Social Development* Hutchinson, London; Mead, G H 1934 *Mind, Self and Society: From the Standpoint of a Social Behaviorist* University of Chicago Press, Chicago, IL; Piaget, J 1952 *The Origins of Intelligence in Children* Norton, New York.

3 Your Self-Image

Bem, D J 1972 "Self-Perception Theory" in Berkowitz, L (ed) *Advances in Experimental Social Psychology* Academic Press, New York, 6, pp2-62; Gazzaniga, M S 1972 "One Brain – Two Minds?" *American Scientist* 60, pp300-17; Rotter, J B 1966 "Generalized Expectancies for Internal Versus External Control of Reinforcement" *Psychological Monographs* 80, (609); Thigpen, C H and Checkley, H M 1957 *The Three Faces of Eve* McGraw-Hill, New York; Mischel, W 1981 *Introduction to Personality* Holt, Rinehart and Winston, New York.

4 Your Impressions of Others

Archer, D 1980 *How to Expand Your SIQ* Evans, New York; Cook, M 1979 *Perceiving Others* Methuen, London; Cook, M 1984 *Levels of Personality* Holt, London; MacKenzie, D M 1982 *Judging People* McGraw-Hill, London.

5 Self-Presentation

Goffman, E 1959 *The Presentation of Self in Everyday Life* Doubleday, New York; Forgas, J P 1985 *Interpersonal Behaviour: the Psychology of Social Interaction* Pergamon, Oxford.

6 Self-Esteem

Burns, R B 1979 *The Self Concept* Longman, London; Gale, R 1983 *Who Are You?: The Psychology of Being Yourself* Prentice-Hall/Spectrum, Englewood Cliffs, NJ.

7 Individuality and Creativity

Gerard, M 1968 *Dali* Harry N Abrams, New York; Sitwell, E 1971 *English Eccentrics* Penguin, Harmondsworth.

8 Instinct and Human Nature

Daly, M and Wilson, M 1983 2nd edn *Sex, Evolution and Behavior* PWS Publishers, Boston, IL; Dawkins, R 1976 *The Selfish Gene* Oxford University Press, Oxford; Trivers, R 1985 *Social Evolution* Benjamin-Cummings, Menlo Park, CA; Maslow, A H 1970 *Towards a Psychology of Being* Van Nostrand, Princeton.

9 The Psychoanalytic Perspective

Freud, S *An Outline of Psychoanalysis* Penguin, Harmondsworth; Kline, P *Psychology and Freudian Theory* Methuen, London; Eysenck, H J *Decline and Fall of the Freudian Empire* Penguin, Harmondsworth.

FURTHER READING
AND CONTRIBUTORS' SOURCES

10 Personality Types
Cook, M 1984 *Levels of Personality* Holt, Rinehart and Winston, New York; Mischel, W 1987 4th edn *Introduction to Personality* Holt, Rinehart and Winston, New York; Modgil, S and Modgil, C 1986 in Eysenck, H (ed) *Consensus and Controversy*, Falmer Press, New York; Roediger, H L et al 1988 2nd edn *Psychology* Little, Brown, Boston, MA.

11 Expressing Your Personality
Eysenck, H J and Wilson, G 1976 *Know Your Own Personality* Penguin, Harmondsworth; Koestler, A 1964 *The Act of Creation* Hutchinson, London; Morris, D 1982 *The Pocket Guide to Manwatching* Triad, Granada, London; Ziv, A 1964 *Personality and Sense of Humor* Springer, New York.

12 The Roots of Personality
Berch, D B and Bender, B 1987 "Margins of Sexuality" *Psychology Today* December issue, pp54-7; Eysenck, H 1967 *The Biological Basis of Personality* Charles C Thomas, Springfield, IL; Hopson, J L 1987 "Boys Will Be Boys, Girls Will Be..." *Psychology Today* August issue, pp60-4; Mischel, W 1983 *Introduction to Personality* Holt, Rinehart and Winston, New York; Ryschlack, J F 1973 *Introduction to Personality and Psychotherapy* Houghton Mifflin, Boston, IL; Sandstrom, C I 1979 *The Psychology of Childhood and Adolescence* Penguin, Harmondsworth; Thomas, A and Chess, S 1977 *Temperament and Development* Brunner/Mazel, New York.

13 Assessing Your Personality
Eysenck, H J 1954 *The Psychology of Politics* Routledge and Kegan Paul, London; Jung, C G 1963 *Memories, Dreams, Reflections* Routledge and Kegan Paul, London; Kline, P 1984 *Personality Measurement and Theory* Hutchinson, London.

14 Becoming Well Adjusted
Davison G C and Neale, N M 1986 *Abnormal Psychology* Wiley, New York; Fonagy, P and Higgitt, A C 1985 *Personality Theory and Clinical Practice* Methuen, London.

15 Personal Growth
Breuer, J and Freud, S 1980 *Studies in Hysteria* Penguin, Harmondsworth; Corey, G, Corey, M, Callanan, P and Russell, J M 1982 *Group Techniques* Brooks/Cole, Monterey, CA; Williams, R and Long, J 1982 *Toward a Self-Managed Life-Style* Houghton Mifflin, Boston, IL.

16 The World of Your Emotions
Plutchik, R 1980 *Emotion: A Psychoevolutionary Synthesis* Harper and Row, New York; Plutchik, R and Kellerman, H (eds) 1980 *Theories of Emotion* Academic Press, New York, 1; Plutchik, R and Kellerman, H (eds) 1983 *Emotions in Early Development* Academic Press, New York, 2; Plutchik, R and Kellerman, H (eds) 1986 *Biological Foundations of Emotion* Academic Press, New York, 3.

17 Emotional Development
Field, T and Fogel A (eds) 1982 *Emotion and Early Interaction* Erlbaum, Hillsdale, NJ; Giele, J Z (ed) 1982 *Women in the Middle Years: Current Knowledge and Directions for Research and Policy* Wiley, New York; Group for the Advancement of Psychiatry 1968 *Normal Adolescence* Charles Scribner and Sons, New York; Izard, C 1972 *The Face of Emotion* Appleton-Century-Crofts, New York; Osofsky, J D (ed) 1979 *Handbook of Infant Development* Wiley, New York; Strongman, K T 1987 3rd edn *The Psychology of Emotion* Wiley, London.

18 Understanding Your Feelings
Strongman, K T 1987 3rd edn *The Psychology of Emotion* Wiley, London; Schachter, S 1971 *Emotion, Obesity and Crime* Academic Press, New York and London.

19 How Moods Come and Go
Ellis, A and Harper, R A 1975 *A New Guide to Rational Living* Prentice-Hall, Englewood Cliffs, NJ; Harrison, M 1984 *Self Help for Premenstrual Syndrome* Matrix Press, Cambridge, MA; Laws, S, Hey, V and Egan, A 1985 *Seeing Red* Hutchinson, London.

20 Expressing Your Feelings
Izard, C E 1972 *The Face of Emotion* Appleton-Century-Croft, New York; Strongman, K T 1987 3rd edn *The Psychology of Emotion* Wiley, London.

21 Anxiety and Stress
Cousins, N 1984 *The Healing Heart* Norton, New York; Eliot, R S 1979 *Stress and the Major Cardiovascular Disorders* Future, New York; Lykken, D T 1984 "Polygraphic interrogation" *Nature* 307, pp681-4.

22 Facing Life's Crises
Cutter, F 1974 *Coming to Terms With Death: How to Face the Inevitable With Wisdom and Dignity* Nelson-Hall, Chicago, IL.

23 Signs of Stress
Cousins, N 1970 *Anatomy of an Illness* Norton, New York; Selye, H 1976 *Stress Without Distress* New American Library, New York; Selye, H 1956 *The Stress of Life* McGraw-Hill, New York.

24 Emotional Breakdown
Cronin, D 1982 *Anxiety, Depression and Phobias: How to Understand and Deal with Them* Prentice-Hall, Englewood Cliffs, NJ; Greenwald, J A 1980 *Overcoming Loneliness* Ramsey Hall, New York; McGuigan, F J 1981 *Calm Down* Prentice-Hall, Englewood Cliffs, NJ.

25 Learning to Relax
Bernstein, D A and Borkovec, T D 1973 *Progressive Relaxation Training* Chicago Research Press, Chicago, IL; Benson, H 1975 *The Relaxation Response* Morrow, New York; Tavris, C 1982 *Anger: The Misunderstood Emotion* Simon and Schuster, New York.

26 Positive Thinking
Bower, G H 1981 "Mood and Memory" *American Psychologist* 36, pp129-48; Gardner, H 1985 *The Mind's New Science* Basic Books, New York; Solso, R L 1988 *Cognitive Psychology* Allyn and Bacon, Newton, MA; Blakemore, C 1977 *Mechanics of the Mind* Cambridge University Press, Cambridge.

27 Dealing with Fear
Marks, J M *Living with Fear* McGraw-Hill, New York; Mitchell, R 1982 *Phobias* Penguin, Harmondsworth; Rachman, S 1974 *The Meanings of Fear* Penguin, Harmondsworth.

28 Overcoming Depression
Rowe, D 1983 *Depression: The Way Out of Your Prison* Routledge and Kegan Paul, London; Blackburn, I M 1987 *Coping with Depression* Chambers, Edinburgh; Williams, J M G 1984 *The Psychological Treatment of Depression* Croom Helm, Beckenham and Free Press, New York.

29 Coping with Grief
Dykstra, R 1988 *A Passage Through Grief* Bridge Publishers, Los Angeles, CA; Kameraman, J *Death in the Midst of Life* Prentice-Hall, Englewood Cliffs, NJ; Schiff, H 1986 *Living Through Mourning* Viking, New York; Van Der Hart, O 1988 *Coping With Loss* Irvington, New York.

30 Managing Guilt
Freeman, L and Stream, H S 1986 *Guilt: Letting Go* Wiley, New York; Ellis, A and Harper, R A 1975 *A New Guide to Rational Living* Prentice-Hall, Englewood Cliffs, NJ.

31 Survival Strategies
James, M and Jongeward, D 1971 *Born to Win* Addison-Wesley, Reading, MA; Harris, T A 1973 *I'm OK You're OK* Pan, London; Schiffman, M 1971 *Gestalt Self Therapy* Wingbow, Berkeley, CA.

32 Happiness and Contentment
Argyle, M 1987 *The Psychology of Happiness* Methuen, London; Barrow, R 1980 *Happiness* Robertson, Oxford; Campbell, A 1981 *The Sense of Well-Being in America* McGraw-Hill, New York; Warr, P B and Wall, T D 1975 *Work and Well-Being* Penguin, Harmondsworth.

CONTRIBUTORS' SOURCES

1 Self-Fulfillment Jung, C G (ed) 1980 *Man and His Symbols* Picador, London; Maslow, A H 1971 *Motivation and Personality* Viking, New York; Maslow, A H 1971 *The Farther Reaches of Human Nature* Penguin, Harmondsworth; Rogers, C R 1980 *A Way of Being* Houghton Mifflin, Boston, MA; Wells, B W P 1983 *Self Analysis* Alvie, St Andrews.

2 Origins of Self-Awareness Amsterdam, B 1972 "Mirror Self-Image Reaction Before Age Two" *Developmental Psychobiology* 5, pp297-305; Brooks-Gunn, J and Lewis, M 1982 "The Development of Self-Knowledge" in Kopp, C P and Krakow, J (eds) *The Child: Development in a Social Context* Addison-Wesley, Readington, MA; Gallup, G G 1982 "Self-Awareness and the Emergence of Mind in Primates" *American Journal of Primatology* 2, pp237-48; Mahler, M, Pine, F and Bergman, A 1975 *The Psychological Birth of the Human Infant* Basic Books, New York; Masterson, J F 1985 *The Real Self: A Developmental, Self and Object Relations Approach* Bruner/Mazel, New York; Markova, I 1987 *Human Awareness: Its Social Development* Hutchinson, London; Mead, G H 1934 *Mind, Self and Society: From the Standpoint of a Social Behaviorist* University of Chicago Press, Chicago, IL; Olson, G M and Sherman, T 1983 "Attention, Learning and Memory in Infants" in Mussen P H (ed) *Handbook of Child Psychology* 2, Wiley, New York; Piaget, J 1952 *The Origins of Intelligence in Children* Norton, New York.

3 Your Self-Image Eskew, R T and Rice, C V 1982 "Pacing and Locus of Control in Quality Control Inspection" *Human Factors* 24, pp411-15; Eysenck, H J and Nias, D K B 1982 *Astrology: Science or Superstition* Temple-Smith, London; Freedman, J L and Fraser, S C 1966 "Compliance Without Pressure: the Foot-in-the-Door Technique" *J of Personality and Social Psychology* 4, pp195-202; Henry, W E and Sims, J H 1970 "Actors' Search for Self" *Transaction* 7, pp57-62; Jahoda, G 1954 "A Note on Ashanti Names and Their Relationship to Personality" *British Journal of Psychology* 45, pp192-5; Kirchner, P and Vondraek, S 1975 "Perceived Sources of Esteem in Early Childhood" *J of Genetic Psychology* 126, pp169-76; Lieberman, S 1956 "The Effects of Changes in Roles on the Attitude of Role Occupants" *Human Relations* 9, pp385-402; McKennell, A C and Bynner, J M 1969 "Self-Image and Smoking Behaviour Among School Boys" *British Journal of Educational Psychology* 39, pp27-39; Rotter, J B 1966 "Generalized Expectancies for Internal Versus External Control of Reinforcement" *Psychological Monographs* 80,

249

CONTRIBUTORS' SOURCES CONTINUED

pp1-28; Schopler, J and Compere, J S 1971 "Effects of Being Kind or Harsh to Another on Liking" *J of Personality and Social Psychology* 20, pp155-9; Wooster, A and Harris, G 1973 "Concepts of Self in Highly Mobile Service Boys" *Educational Research* 14, pp195-9.

4 Your Impressions of Others Allport, G W 1937 *Personality: a Psychological Interpretation* Holt, Rinehart and Winston, New York; Argyle, M and McHenry, R 1971 "Do Spectacles Really Affect Judgements of Intelligence?" *British Journal of Social and Clinical Psychology* 10, pp27-9; Baron, R A 1983 "Sweet Smell of Success?: the Impact of Pleasant Artificial Scents on Evaluations of Job Applicants" *J of Applied Psychology* 68, pp709-13; Cook, M 1988 *Personnel Selection and Productivity* Wiley, Chichester; Fancher, R E 1969 "Group and Individual Accuracy in Person Perception" *J of Consulting Psychology* 33, p127; Forsythe, S, Drake, M F and Cox, C E 1985 "Influence of Applicant's Dress on Interviewer's Selection Decisions" *J of Applied Psychology* 70, pp374-8; Gifford, R, Ng, C F and Wilkinson, M 1985 "Non-verbal Cues in the Employment Interview: Links Between Applicant Qualities and Interviewer Judgements" *J of Applied Psychology* 70, pp729-36; Hoffman, M L 1977 "Sex Differences in Empathy and Related Behavior" *Psychological Bulletin* 84, pp712-22; Jahoda, G 1954 "A Note on Ashanti Names and Their Relation to Personality" *British Journal of Psychology* 45, pp192-9; Kelley, H H 1950 "The Warm-Cold Variable in First Impressions of Persons" *J of Personality* 18, pp431-9; Wiggins, N, Hoffman, P J and Taber, T 1969 "Types of Judges and Cue Utilisation in Judgements of Intelligence" *J of Personality and Social Psychology* 12, pp52-9.

5 Self-Presentation Christie, R and Geis, F L (eds) 1970 *Studies in Macchiavellianism* Academic Press, New York; Crowne, D P and Marlowe, D 1964 *The Approval Motive* Wiley, New York; Forgas, J P 1979 *Social Episodes: The Study of Interaction Routines* Academic Press, London; Forgas, J P 1985 *Interpersonal Behaviour: The Psychology of Social Interaction* Pergamon, Oxford; Freedman, J L and Fraser, S C 1966 "Compliance Without Pressure: the Foot-in-the-Door Technique" *J of Personality and Social Psychology* 4, pp195-202; Goffman, E 1963 *Behaviour in Public Places* The Free Press, Glencoe; Goffman, E 1959 *The Presentation of Self in Everyday Life* Doubleday, New York; Jones, E E 1964 *Ingratiation* Appleton-Century-Crofts, New York; Schlenker, B 1980 *Impression Management* Brooks Cole, Monterey, CA; Tedeschi, J T (ed) 1981 *Impression Management Theory and Social Research* Academic Press, New York.

6 Self-Esteem Adler, A 1969 *The Science of Living* Anchor Books, New York; Coopersmith, S 1967 *The Antecedents of Self-Esteem* Freeman, San Francisco, CA; Guthrie, E G 1962 *The Psychology of Human Conflict* Beacon, Boston, MA; Kennedy, E 1975 *If You Knew Me Would You Still Like Me?* Argus, Niles, IL; Rogers, C R 1965 *Client-Centered Therapy* Houghton Mifflin, Boston, MA; Stevenson, W 1953 *The Study of Behavior: Q-Sort and Its Methodology* Chicago University Press, Chicago, IL; Wells, B W P 1983 *Body and Personality* Longman, London.

7 Individuality and Creativity Drinkwater, J 1962 *Shakespeare* Collier Books, New York; *Encyclopedia Britannica* 1985 edn Articles on Beethoven, Holderlin, Tesla, Weber, Darwin, Reich, O'Neill, Presley, Piaf; Ellmann, R 1982 *James Joyce* Oxford University Press, New York; Carlyle, T 1895 *On Heroes, Hero-Worship, and the Heroic in History* Carlyle's House Memorial Trust, London; Arieti, S 1974 *Interpretation of Schizophrenia* Basic Books, New York; Weber, M 1968 *The Theory of Social and Economic Organization* Free Press, New York; Sinclair, U 1956 *The Cup of Fury* Hawthorne Books, New York.

8 Instinct and Human Nature Axelrod, R 1984 *The Evolution of Cooperation* Basic Books, New York; Coombs, R H and Kenkel, W F 1966 "Sex Differences in Dating Aspirations and Satisfaction with Computer-Selected Partners" *J of Marriage and the Family* 28, pp62-6; Daly, M and Wilson, M I 1982 "Homicide and Kinship" *American Anthropologist* 84, pp372-8; Daly, M and Wilson, M I 1985 "Child Abuse and Other Risks of Not Living with Both Parents" *Ethology and Sociobiology* 6, pp197-210; Maslow, A H 1971 *Motivation and Personality* Viking, New York; Maslow, A H 1971 *The Farther Reaches of Human Nature* Penguin, Harmondsworth; Rushton, J P 1985 "Differential K Theory: the Sociobiology of Individual and Group Differences" *Personality and Individual Differences* 6, pp441-52; Trivers, R L 1974 "Parent-Offspring Conflict" *American Zoologist* 14, pp249-64; Wilkinson, G S 1984 "Reciprocal Food Sharing in the Vampire Bat" *Nature* 308, pp181-4.

9 The Psychoanalytic Perspective Eysenck, H J 1985 *Decline and Fall of the Freudian Empire* Penguin, Harmondsworth; Freud, A 1946 *The Ego and The Mechanisms of Defence* Hogarth, London; Freud, S 1973 *New Introductory Lectures* Pelican Freud Library 2, Penguin, Harmondsworth; Freud, S 1976 *The Interpretation of Dreams* Pelican Freud Library 4, Penguin, Harmondsworth; Freud, S *Art and Literature* Pelican Freud Library 14, Penguin, Harmondsworth; Kline, P 1979 *Psychometrics and Psychology* Academic Press, London; Kline, P 1981 *Fact and Fantasy in Freudian Theory* Methuen, London.

10 Personality Types Allport, G W 1937 *Pattern and Growth in Personality* Holt, Rinehart and Winston, New York; Allport, G W and Odbert, H S 1936 "Trait-Names: A Psycho-Lexical Study" *Psychological Monographs* 47 (211); Block, J 1981 "Some Enduring and Consequential Structures of Personality" in Rabin, A I et al (eds) *Further Explorations in Personality* Wiley, New York; Epstein, S 1979 "The Stability of Behavior: I" *J of Personality and Social Psychology* 37, pp1097-126; Epstein, S 1980 "The Stability of Behavior: II" *American Psychologist* 35, pp790-806; Eysenck, H J and Eysenck, S B G 1975 *Manual of the EPQ* Educational and Testing Service; Eysenck, M W and Eysenck, H J 1980 "Mischel and the Concept of Personality" *British Journal of Psychology* 71, pp191-204; Hartshore, H and Mav, M A 1928 *Studies in the Nature of Character* 1, Macmillan, London; Mischel, W 1973 "Toward a Cognitive-Social Learning Reconceptualisation of Personality" *Psychological Review* 80, pp252-83; Mischel, W and Peake, P K 1982 "Beyond Déjà vu in the Search for Cross-Situational Consistency" *Psychological Review* 89, pp730-55; Rushton, J P et al 1983 "Behaviour Development and Construct Validity: The Principle of Aggregation" *Psychological Bulletin* 94, pp18-38; Sheldon, W H 1954 *Atlas of Man: A Guide For Somatotyping the Adult Male of All Ages* Harper and Row, New York.

11 Expressing Your Personality Birdwhistell, R L 1970 *Kinesics and Contexts* Philadelphia University Press, Philadelphia, CA; Izzard, C E 1977 *Human Emotions* Plenum, New York; Klinger, E 1981 (ed) *Imagery: Concepts, Results and Applications* Plenum, New York; Lester, D 1981 *The Psychological Basis of Handwriting Analysis* Nelson-Hall, Chicago, IL; Mehrabian, A 1972 *Nonverbal Communication* Aldine-Atherton, Chicago, IL; Miller, G A 1962 *Psychology: the Science of Mental Life* Harper and Row, New York; Morris, D 1977 *Manwatching* Cape, London; Singer, J J 1975 *The Inner World of Daydreaming* Harper and Row, New York; Snyder, M 1987 *Public Appearances, Private Realities: the Psychology of Self-Monitoring* Freeman, New York.

12 The Roots of Personality Bigelow, H J 1850 "Dr Harlow's Case of Recovery From the Passage of an Iron Bar Through the Head" *American Journal of the Medical Sciences* 39, pp2-22; Buchsbaum, M S, Coursey, R D and Murphy, D L 1976 "The Biochemical High-Risk Paradigm: Behavioral and Familial Correlates of Low Platelet Monoamine Oxidase Activity" *Science* 194, pp339-41; Buss, A H and Plomin, R 1984 *Temperament: Early Developing Personality Traits* Erlbaum, Hillsdale, NJ; Eaves, L and Eysenck H 1975 "The Nature of Extraversion: A Genetical Analysis" *J of Personality and Social Psychology* 32, pp102-12; Ellis, L 1986 "Evidence of Neuroandrogenic Etiology of Sex Roles from a Combined Analysis of Human, Nonhuman Primate and Nonprimate Mammalian Studies" *Personality and Individual Differences* 7, pp519-52; Floderus-Myrhed, B, Pederson, N and Rasmuson, S 1980 "Assessment of Heritability for Personality Based on a Short Form of the Eysenck Personality Inventory" *Behavior Genetics* 10, pp153-62; Fulker, D W, Eysenck, S B G and Zuckerman, M 1980 "A Genetic and Environmental Analysis of Sensation Seeking" *J of Research in Personality* 14, pp261-81; Goldsmith, H H 1983 "Genetic Influences on Personality from Infancy to Adulthood" *Child Development* 54, pp331-55; Hinde, R 1988 *The Genesis of Gender* (paper delivered at the Christmas Conference of the British Psychological Society) The University of London; King, R J, Mefford, I N, Wang, C, Murchison, A, Caligari, E and Berger, P A 1986 "CSF Dopamine Levels Correlate with Extraversion in Depressed Patients" *Psychiatry Research* 19, p305; Rushton, J P 1984 "Sociobiology: Toward a Theory of Individual and Group Differences in Personality and Social Behavior" in Royce, J R and Mos, L P (eds) *Annals of Theoretical Psychology* 2, Plenum, New York; Scarr, S and Grajek, S 1982 "Similarities and Differences Among Siblings" in Lamb, M E and Sutton-Smith, B (eds) *Sibling Relationships* Erlbaum, Hillsdale, NJ; Susman, E J 1987 "Hormones, Emotional Dispositions, and Aggressive Attributes in Early Adolescents" *Child Development* 58, pp1114-34; Thomas, A and Chess, S 1977 *Temperament and Development* Brunner/Mazel, New York; Trivers, R L 1985 *Social Evolution* Cummings, Menlo Park, CA; Weissbluth, R 1982 "Plasma Progesterone Levels, Infant Temperament, Arousals from Sleep and Sudden Death Infant Syndrome" *Medical Hypotheses* 9, pp215-22.

13 Assessing Your Personality Bem, S L 1974 "The Measurement of Psychological Androgyny" *J of Consulting and Clinical Psychology* 42, pp155-62; Butler, J M and Haigh, G V 1971 "Changes in the Correlation Between Self-Concepts and Ideal Self Upon Client-Centered Counseling" in Vetter H J and Smith, B D (eds) *Personality Theory: A Source Book* Appleton-Century-Crofts, New York; Cattell, R B and Kline, P 1977 *The Scientific Analysis of Personality and Motivation* Academic Press, New York; Eysenck, H J 1967 *The Biological Basis of Personality* Springer, New York; Freud, S 1940 *An Outline of Psychoanalysis* Hogarth Press, London; Jung, C G 1987 *Dictionary of Analytical Psychology* Ark Paperbacks, London; Zuckerman, M 1974 "The Sensation-Seeking Motive" in Maher, B (ed) *Progress in Experimental Personality Research* 7, Academic Press, New York.

14 Becoming Well Adjusted American Psychiatric Association 1980 3rd edn *Diagnostic and Statistical Manual of Mental Disorders* APA, Washington, DC; Earls, F and Jung, K G 1987 "Temperament and Home Environment Characteristics as Causal Factors in the Early Development of Childhood Psychopathology" *J of the American Academy of Child Psychiatry* 26, pp491-8; Rutter, M 1987 "Temperament, Personality and Personality Disorder" *British Journal of Psychiatry* 150, pp443-58; Shaffer, J W, Graves, P L, Swank, R T and Pearson, T A 1987 "Clustering of Personality Traits in Youth and Subsequent Development of Cancer Among Physicians" *J of Behavioural Medicine* 10, pp441-7; Skolnick, A S 1986 *The Psychology of Human Development* Harcourt Brace Jovanovich, San Diego, CA.

15 Personal Growth Alberti, R E and Emmons, M L 1978 *Your Perfect Right: A Guide to Assertive Behavior* Impact, San Luis Obispo, CA; Bennis, W G 1964 "Patterns and Vicissitudes in T-Group Development" in Bradford, L P, Gibb, J R and Benne K D (eds) *T-Group and Laboratory Method* Wiley, New York; Berland, T 1980 *Rating the Diets* Beekman House, New York; Carnegie, D 1987 *How to Win Friends and Influence People* Cedar Books, Bungay; Marcuse, F L 1982 *Hypnosis: Fact and Fiction* Penguin, Harmondsworth; Rogers, C R 1975 *Encounter Groups* Penguin, Harmondsworth.

16 The World of Your Emotions Plutchik, R 1980 *Emotion: A Psychoevolutionary Synthesis* Harper and Row, New York; Plutchik, R "A Language For the Emotions" *Psychology Today* 13, February issue, pp68-80; Plutchik, R and Kellerman, H (eds) 1980 *Theories of Emotion* 1, Academic Press, New York; Plutchik, R and Kellerman H (eds) 1983 *Emotions in Early Development* 2, Academic Press, New York; Plutchik, R and Kellerman, H (eds) *Biological Foundations of Emotion* 3, Academic Press, New York.

17 Emotional Development Bowlby J 1961 "Separation Anxiety: a Critical Review of Literature" *J of Child Psychology* 15, pp9-52; Bridges, K M B 1932 *The Social and Emotional Development of the Pre-School Child* Routledge and Kegan Paul, London; Entwisle, D R and Doering, S J 1981 *The First Birth: A Family Turning Point* Johns Hopkins University Press, Baltimore, MA; Frank E et al 1988 "Sex Differences in Recurrent Depressions: Are There Any That Are Significant?" *American Journal of*

Psychiatry 145, pp41-5; Gray, J A 1971 *The Psychology of Fear and Stress* Weidenfeld and Nicholson, London; Harlow, H F and Harlow M K 1962 "Social Deprivation in Monkeys" *Science America* 207, pp136-46; Lewis, M and Rosenblum L A (eds) 1978 *The Development of Affect* Plenum, New York; Pietromonaco, P R and Frohart-Lone, K 1984 *Psychological Consequences of Multiple Social Roles* paper presented at the annual meeting of the American Psychological Association; Plutchik, R 1983 "Emotions in Early Development: A Psychoevolutionary Approach" in Plutchik, R and Kellerman, H (eds) *Emotion: Theory, Research and Experience* 2, Academic Press, New York; Sroufe, L A 1979 "Socioemotional Development" in Osofsky, J D (ed) *Handbook of Infant Development* Wiley, New York.

18 Understanding Your Feelings Bersheid, E 1983 "Emotion" in Kelley, H H et al (eds) *Close Relationships* Freeman, New York; Festinger, L 1957 *A Theory of Cognitive Dissonance* Stanford University Press, Stanford, CA; Festinger, L and Carlsmith, J M 1959 "Cognitive Consequences of Forced Compliance" *J of Abnormal and Social Psychology* 58, pp203-10; Schachter, S and Singer, J 1962 "Cognitive, Social and Physiological Determinants of Emotional State" *Psychological Review* 69, pp378-99.

19 How Moods Come and Go Thompson, W A R 1979 *A Change of Air* Adam and Charles Black, London; Mehrabian, A and Russell, J A 1974 *An Approach to Environmental Psychology* MIT Press, Cambridge, MA; Strongman, K T 1987 3rd edn *The Psychology of Emotion* Wiley, Chichester; Reid, R L and Yen, S S 1981 "Premenstrual Syndrome" *American Journal of Obstetrics and Gynecology* 139, pp85-104; Rosenhan, D L and Seligman, M E P 1984 *Abnormal Psychology* Norton, New York; Lewy, A J, Sack, R L and Singer, C M 1985 "Melatonin, Light and Chronobiological Disorders" *Photoperiodism, Melatonin and the Pineal* Pitman, (Ciba Foundation Symposium 117) London.

20 Expressing Your Feelings Davitz, J R 1964 *The Communication of Emotional Meaning* McGraw-Hill, New York; Ekman, P and Friesen, W V 1969 "Nonverbal Leakage and Cues to Deception" *Psychiatry* 32, pp88-106; Grinker Sr, R R and Spiegel, J P 1961 *Men Under Stress* McGraw-Hill, New York; Izard, C E 1977 *Human Emotions* Plenum, New York; Stotland, E 1969 "Exploratory Investigations of Empathy" in Berkowitz, L (ed) *Advances in Experimental Social Psychology* 4, pp271-314.

21 Anxiety and Stress Brown, G W, Harris, T 1978 *Social Origins of Depression: A Study of Psychiatric Disorders in Women* Free Press, New York; Holmes, T H and Rahe, R H 1987 "The Social Readjustment Rating Scale" *J of Psychosomatic Research* 11, pp213-18; Karasek, R, Baker, B, Maryer, F et al 1981 "Job Decision Latitude, Job Demands and Cardiovascular Disease: A Prospective Study of Swedish Men" *American Journal of Public Health* 71, pp694-705; Lazarus, R S and Folkman, S 1984 *Stress, Appraisal and Coping* Springer, New York; Lykken, D T 1984 "Polygraphic Interrogation" *Nature* 307, pp681-4; Melzack, R 1973 *The Puzzle of Pain* Penguin, Harmondsworth; Sklar, L S and Anisman, H 1981 "Stress and Cancer" *Psychological Bulletin* 89, pp369-406; Williams, R B 1986 "Type A Behavior and Coronary Heart Disease: Something Old, Something New" *Annals of Behavioral Medicine* 6, pp29-35; Wolff, S and Wolff, H G 1942 "Evidence on the Genesis of Peptic Ulcer in Men" *J of American Medical Association* 120, pp670-5.

22 Facing Life's Crises Ader, R (ed) *Psychoneuroimmunology* Academic Press, New York; Elder, G H 1974 *Children of the Great Depression: Social Change in Life Experience* University of Chicago Press, Chicago, IL; Farberow, N L (ed) 1980 *The Many Faces of Suicide: Indirect Self-Destructive Behavior* McGraw-Hill, New York; Figley, C R 1985 *Trauma and Its Wake: The Study and Treatment of Post-Traumatic Stress Disorder* Bruner/Mazel, New York; Holmes, T H and Rahe, R H 1967 "The Social Readjustment Rating Scale" *J of Psychosomatic Research* 11, pp213-18; Kiecolt-Blaser, J K, Glaser, R 1987 "Psychosocial Moderators of Immune Function" *Annals of Behavioral medicine* 9, pp16-20; Scrignar, C B 1984 *Post-Traumatic Stress Disorder: Diagnosis, Treatment and Legal Issues* Praeger, New York; Trimble, M R 1981 *Post Traumatic Neurosis* Wiley, Chichester; Wolff, S 1969 *Children Under Stress* Penguin, Baltimore, MA.

23 Signs of Stress Beech, H R, Burns, L E and Sheffield, B F 1982 *A Behavioral Approach to the Management of Stress* Wiley, New York; Cannon, W B 1929 *Bodily Changes in Pain, Hunger, Fear and Rage* Brenford, Boston, MA; French, J R, Caplan, P D and Harrison, R V 1982 *The Mechanisms of Job Stress and Strain* Wiley, New York; Horowitz, M 1976 *Stress Response Syndromes* Aronion, New York; Kasl, S V 1984 "Stress and Health" *Annual Review of Public Health* 5, pp319-41; Rabkin, J E and Struening, E L 1976 "Life Events, Stress and Illness" *Science* 194, pp1013-20.

24 Emotional Breakdown Dryden, W 1984 *Rational Emotive Therapy Fundamentals and Innovations* Croom Helm, London; Faber, B A 1983 *Stress and Burn Out* Pergamon, New York; Kutash, I L and Schlesinger, L B 1980 *Handbook on Stress and Anxiety* Jossey-Bass, San Francisco, CA; Levine, S and Scotch, N A 1970 *Social Stress* Aldine, Chicago, IL; Maslow, A 1976 *The Farther Reaches of Human Nature* Penguin, New York; Newman, F 1980 *Caring: Home Treatment for the Emotionally Disturbed* The Dial Press, New York; Shapiro, D 1965 *Neurotic Styles* Basic Books, New York; Spielberger, C C and Sarason, I G 1978 *Stress and Anxiety* 5, Wiley, New York; Jung, C G 1963 *Memories, Dreams, Reflections* Random House, London; Sutherland, S 1976 *Breakdown* Weidenfeld and Nicolson, London.

25 Learning to Relax Agras, W S, Taylor, C B, Kraemer, H S, Southam, M A and Schneider, J A 1987 "Relaxation Training for Essential Hypertension at the Worksite: II The Poorly Controlled Hypertensive" *Psychosomatic Medicine* 49, pp264-73; Benson, H 1975 *The Relaxation Response* Morrow, New York; Chesney, M, Black, G W, Swan, G E and Ward, M M 1987 "Relaxation Training for Essential Hypertension at the Worksite: I The Untreated Mild Hypertensive" *Psychosomatic Medicine* 49, pp250-63; Friedman, M, Thoresen, C E, Gill, J J, Ulmer, D et al 1986 "Alteration of Type A Behavior and Its Effect on Cardiac Recurrences in Post Myocardial Infarction Patients: Summary Results of the Recurrent Prevention Project" *American Heart Journal* 112, pp653-65; Holmes, D S and McGilley, B M 1987 "Influence of a Brief Aerobic Training Program on Heart Rate and Subjective Response to a Psychologic Stressor" *Psychosomatic Medicine* 49, pp366-76; Peters, R K, Benson, H and Porter, D 1977 "Daily Relaxation Breaks in the Workplace: I Effects on Self Reported Sources of Health, Performance and Well-Being" *American Journal of Public Health* 67, pp946-53; Roth, D L and Holmes, D S 1987 "Influence of Aerobic Exercise Training and Relaxation Training on Physical and Psychologic Health Following Stressful Life Events" *Psychosomatic Medicine* 49, pp355-65; Tavris, C 1982 *Anger: The Misunderstood Emotion* Simon and Schuster, New York.

26 Positive Thinking Loftus, E F 1983 "Misfortunes of Memory" *Philosophical Transactions of the Royal Society, London* 302, pp413-21; Loftus, E F, Miller, D G and Burns, H J 1978 "Semantic Integration of Verbal Information Into a Visual Memory" *J of Experimental Psychology: Human Learning and Memory* 4, pp19-31; Bower, G H 1981 "Mood and Memory" *American Psychologist* 36, pp129-48; Velten, E 1968 "A Laboratory Task for Induction of Mood States" *Behaviour Research and Therapy* 6, pp473-82; Young, R and Crandall, R 1984 "Wilderness Use and Self-Actualization" *J of Leisure Research* 16, pp149-60.

27 Dealing with Fear Myers, J K, Weissman, M M, Tischler, G L, Holzer, C E, Leaf, P J, Orvaschel, H, Anthony, J C, Boyd, J H, Burke, J D, Kramer, M and Stolzman, R 1984 "Six-Month Prevalence of Psychiatric Disorders in Three Communities" *Archives of General Psychiatry* 41, pp959-67; Robins, L N, Helzer, J E, Weissman, M M, Orvaschel, H, Gruenberg, E, Burke, J D and Regier, D J 1984 "Lifetime Prevalence of Specific Psychiatric Disorder in Three Sites" *Archives of General Psychiatry* 41, pp949-58; Rachman, S and Hodgson R 1974 "Synchrony and Desynchrony in Fear and Avoidance" *Behaviour Research and Therapy* 12, pp311-18; Seligman, M E P 1971 "Phobias and Preparedness" *Behavior Therapy* 2, pp307-20; Watson, J B and Rayner, R 1920 "Conditioned Emotional Reactions" *J of Experimental Psychology* 3, pp1-14.

28 Overcoming Depression Kuhl, J and Beckman, J (eds) 1985 *Action Control: From Cognition to Behaviour* Springer-Verlag, New York; Williams, J M G 1984 *The Psychological Treatment of Depression* Croom Helm, Beckenham and Free Press, New York; Willner, P 1985 *Depression: A Psychological Synthesis* Wiley, Chichester.

29 Coping with Grief Carr, A C and Schoenberg, B 1970 "Object-Loss and Somatic Symptom Formation" in Schoenberg, B et al (eds) *Loss and Grief: Psychological Management in Medical Practice* Columbia University Press, New York, pp36-47; Freud, S 1959 "Mourning and Melancholia" *Collected Papers* 4, Basic Books, New York, pp152-70; Gorer, G 1965 *Death, Grief and Mourning in Contemporary Britain* Cresset, London, p112; Weizman, S G and Kamm, P 1985 *About Mourning: Support and Guidance for the Bereaved* Human Sciences Press, New York, pp42-63; Irwin, I, Daniels, D and Weiner, H 1987 "Immune and Neuroendocrine Changes During Bereavement" *Psychiatric Clinics of North America* 10 (3) September issue; Irwin, I, Daniels, D, Bloom, E, Smith, T and Weiner, H 1987 "Life Events, Depressive Symptoms and Immune Function" *American Journal of Psychiatry* 144, pp437-41; Lindemann, E 1944 "Symptomatology and Management of Acute Grief" *American Journal of Psychiatry* 101, pp141-8; Parkes, C M 1973 *Bereavement: Studies of Grief in Adult Life* International Universities Press, New York, p39; Raphael, B 1983 *The Anatomy of Bereavement* Basic Books, New York, pp33-51; Rees, W D and Lutkins, S G 1967 "The Mortality of Bereavement" *British Medical Journal* 4, pp13-16; Selye, H 1976 (rev edn) *The Stress of Life* McGraw-Hill, New York, p36; Worden, J W 1982 *Grief Counseling and Grief Therapy: A Handbook for the Mental Health Practitioner* Springer, New York, pp11-16.

30 Managing Guilt Beck, A T, Rush, A J, Shaw, B F and Emery, G 1979 *Cognitive Therapy of Depression* Guildford Press, New York; Mezey, G C 1985 "Rape: Victiminological and Psychiatric Aspects" *British Journal of Hospital Medicine* 35, pp152-8; Shapiro, S 1987 "Self-Mutilation and Self-Blame in Incest Victims" *American Journal of Psychotherapy* 41, pp46-54; Skolnick, A S 1986 *The Psychology of Human Development* Harcourt Brace Jovanovich, San Diego, CA.

31 Survival Strategies Burgess, A W and Holstrom, L L 1974 "Rape Trauma Syndrome" *American Journal of Psychiatry* 131, p981; Burgess, A W and Holstrom, L L 1976 "Coping Behavior of the Rape Victim" *American Journal of Psychiatry* 133, p413; Fenz, W D 1975 "Strategies for Coping with Stress" in Sarason, I G and Spielberger, C D (eds) *Stress and Anxiety* Hemisphere, New York; Freud, A 1966 (previously 1937) *The Ego and the Mechanisms of Defense* International Universities Press, New York; Harris, R N and Snyder, C R 1986 "The Role of Uncertain Self Esteem in Self-Handicapping" *J of Personality and Social Psychology* 51 (2), pp451-8; Plutchik, R, Kellerman, H and Conte, H R 1979 "A Structural Theory of Ego Defenses and Emotions" in Izard, C E (ed) *Emotions in Personality and Psychopathology* Plenum, New York.

32 Happiness and Contentment Argyle, M 1987 *The Psychology of Happiness* Methuen, London; Barrow, R 1980 *Happiness* Robertson, Oxford; Bradburn, N 1969 *The Structure of Psychological Well-Being* Aldine, New York; Campbell, A 1981 *The Sense of Well-Being in America* McGraw-Hill, New York; Diener, E 1984 "Subjective Well-Being" *Psychological Bulletin* 95, pp542-75; Dion, K et al 1972 "What is Beautiful is Good" *J of Personality and Social Psychology* 24, pp285-90; Kirkpatrick, C and Cotton, J 1951 "Physical Attractiveness, Age and Marital Adjustment" *American Sociological Review* 16, pp81-6; Mathes, E and Kahn, A 1975 "Physical Attractiveness, Happiness, Neuroticism, and Self-Esteem" *J of Psychology* 90, pp27-30; Tolor, A 1978 "Personality Correlates of the Joy of Life" *J of Clinical Psychology* 34, pp671-6; Warr, P B and Wall, T D 1975 *Work and Well-Being* Penguin, Harmondsworth.

PICTURE AGENCIES/SOURCES

AD Art Directors Photo Library.
AP The Associated Press Ltd, London.
APA Ace Photo Agency, London.
AR Ardea, London.
ASp Allsport UK Ltd.
BAL Bridgeman Art Library.
BBC HPL BBC Hulton Picture Library, London.
B/C Blackstar/Colorific.
C Colorific Photo Library Ltd, London, New York.
C/C Colorific/Contact.
CJ Camilla Jessel, Twickenham, Middx.
Fo Fovea.
FSP Frank Spooner Pictures, London.
G/FSP Gamma/Frank Spooner Pictures, London.
H The Hutchison Library, London.
HS Homer Sykes, London.
I Impact Photos, London.
L/FSP Liaison/Frank Spooner Pictures, London.
ME Mary Evans Picture Library, London.
MG Magnum Photos Ltd, London, Paris, New York.

N Network Photographers, London.
P/SGA Photofile/Susan Griggs Agency, London.
PI Pictor International.
PP Picturepoint Ltd, London.
PF Popperfoto, London.
R Rex Features Ltd, London.
RHPL Robert Harding Picture Library Ltd, London.
R/S Rex/Sipa.
SGA Susan Griggs Agency, London.
SPL Science Photo Library, London.
SRG Sally and Richard Greenhill, London.
ST Stockphotos.
T Topham Picture Library, Kent.
TCL Daily Telegraph Colour Library, London.
TIB The Image Bank, London.
TIB/JA TIB/Janeart Ltd.
TSW Tony Stone Photo Library, London.
V Viewfinder Colour Photo Library, Bristol.
VI Vision International, London.
WIL Wellcome Institute Library, London.
WP/C Wheeler Pictures/Colorific.
Z Zefa, London.
Z/S Zefa/Stockmarket.
ZZ Zentralbibliothek Zürich.

KEY TO PHOTOGRAPHERS

AEr Alain Ernoult. **AG** Alain le Garsmeur. **AM** Antonio Martinelli. **AR** Alon Reininger. **AS** Anthea Sieveking. **ASu** Anthony Suau. **AU** Alvis Upitis. **AWe** Alex Webb. **Bl** Blumebild. **Bo** Bourseiller. **BB** Bruno Barbey. **BBa** Bill Bachman. **BBn** Bernard Bakalian. **BGl** Burt Glinn. **BH** Brian Harris. **BHa** B Harlington. **BHb** Bob Hobby. **BL** Barry Lewis. **BPi** B Pierce. **BR** Bernard Régent. **BTh** Bob Thomason. **BWi** Bob Willoughby. **C** Colton. **CB** Catherine Blackie. **CFi** Chuck Fishman. **CSK** Charles S Knight. **CJ** Camilla Jessel. **CLe** Caryn Levy. **CLo** Christophe Loviny. **CLb** Cesare Lombroso. **CM** Costa Manos. **CP/MC** Chris Priest/Mark Clarke. **CSK** Charles S Knight. **CSP** Chris Steele-Perkins. **CV** C Voigt. **DBe** David Beatty. **DB** David Burnett. **DE** Dan Esgro. **DK** Don Klumpp. **DKi** Douglas Kirkland. **DKg** Don King. **DLa** Don Landwehrle. **DMe** Dilip Mehta. **DrM** Dr Mueller. **DR** Dick Rowan. **DW** David Woo. **DWH** David W Hamilton. **EA** Eve Arnold. **EE** Elliott Erwitt. **EH** Eric Hartmann. **ER** Eli Reed. **ERi** Eugene Richards. **ESa** Eric Sander. **FB** F Bouillot. **FF** Frank Fournier. **Ga** Gaywood. **Gu** Gunther. **GD** Gerald Davis. **GGe** G Germany. **GH** Gregory Heisler. **GLQ** Guy Le Querrec. **GMS** G M Smith. **GNo** Gérard Noel. **GP** Gabe Palmer. **GPe** Gilles Peress. **GSo** Gaby Sommer. **HE** Hemsey. **HCB** Henri Cartier Bresson. **HHa** Heather Hancock. **HK/T** Heinz Kluctmuer/Sports Illustrated Time Inc. **HS** Homer Sykes. **HSu** Harald Sund. **HY** H Yamaguchi. **IB** Ian Berry. **JAz** Jose Azel. **JBr** Jack Bradley. **JBl** Jacques Blot. **JoB** Jonathan Blair. **JCa** Julian Calder. **JCF** Jean-Claude Francolon. **JdaC** Jérôme da Cunha. **JDr** John Drysdale. **JF** James Fraser. **JE** John Egan. **JGF** J G Fuller. **JG** Jon Gray. **JGa** Jean Gaumy. **JH** Jim Howard. **JMcC** Joanna McCarthy. **JMe** Joel Meyerowitz. **JN** Jeremy Nicholl. **JNa** James Nachtwey. **JPK** Jesco von Puttkamer. **JS** John Sturrock. **JSc** James Schnepf. **JSm** Jeff

Smith. **JW** Jenny Woodcock. **JY** John Yates. **KBo** Karen Borchers. **KC** Kay Chernush. **KD** Karim Daher. **KE** Karin Elmers. **KL** Katherine Lambert. **KP** Kate Pattullo. **KS** Kyoichi Sawada. **LB** Lee E Battaglia. **LF** Leonard Freed. **LG** Louise Gubb. **LS** Laurie Sparham. **LSh** Les Sheen. **LT** Liba Taylor. **LW** Leslie Woodhead. **Ma** Magubane. **MA** Mike Abrahams. **MBl** Martin Black. **MBo** Michael Boys. **MC** Mark Cator. **MD** Mel Digiacomo. **MFi** Mary Fisher. **MI** Masahiro Iijima. **MMa** Mieke Maas. **MMe** Michael Melford. **MMI** Michael MacIntyre. **MN** Michael Nichols. **M/GN** M/G Noel. **MPe** Mark Perlstein. **MS** Michael Salas. **MY** Mike Yamashita. **N** Nuvoletti. **NB** Nancy Brown. **NBe** Nathan Benn. **NDMcK** Nancy Durrell McKenna. **NJ** Nils Jorgensen. **NL** Norman Lomax. **OPi** Olivier Pighetti. **PAv** Patrick Aventurier. **PB** Paul Brown. **PC** Paul Conklin. **PCo** Peter Correz. **PFu** Paul Fusco. **PI** Peter Ibbotson. **PJG** Philip Jones Griffiths. **PK** P Kasterine. **PM** Peter Marlow. **PMe** Peter Menzel. **PPa** Prasphant Panjiar. **PPo** Paul Popper. **PT** Pennie Tweedie. **PTu** Peter Turnley. **P/W** Pierce/Wheeler pictures. **PZ** Patrick Zachmann. **RBi** Randa Bishop. **RCa** Russ Carmack. **RG** Robert Garvey. **RK** Richard Kalvar. **RKr** Robert Kristofik. **RNe** Robert Nelson. **RPh** Robert Phillips. **RR** Raghu Rai. **RRe** Roger Ressmeyer. **RSt** Richard Steedman. **RWo** R Wollman. **ScM** Scott Morrison. **SBr** Simon Bruty. **SF** Stuart Franklin. **SFe** Sally Fear. **SLo** Sandra Lousada. **SMa** Stanley Matchett. **S/G** Smeal/Galella Ltd. **SMo** Sonia Moskowitz. **SP** Steve Pyke. **SRG** Sally and Richard Greenhill. **ST** Susan Turvey. **T** Torreganu. **TD** Tony Duffy. **TLG** Terence Le Goubin. **TJ** Trevor Jones. **TK** Tom Kasser. **US** Udo Schreiber. **W** Wheeler. **WB** Werner Bokelberg. **WL** Whitney Lane. **WMc** Wally McNamee. **WDMc** Will and Dean McIntyre. **WM** Wayne Miller. **WMc** Will McBride. **WS/V** Wayne Source/Vision. **WY** Wu Yinxian. **YAB** Yann Arthus-Bertrand.

252

Dali, R/S. **66** Einstein (PPo) PF. Pavement artist (AM) Fo/I. **67** Student composer Roxanna Panufnik (CJ) CJ. Snow leopard (MC) I. Picture restoration (WMc) C. **68** Edith Piaf, R. Edith Piaf on stage (JBl) R. Dylan Thomas 1945 (PPo) PF. **69** Metamorphosis of Narcissus (1934), Salvador Dali, The Tate Gallery, London © DEMART PRO ARTE BV/DACS 1988.

8 Instinct and Human Nature
70 Fleeing from bombing (KS) UPI/PF. **70-1** Group on boat (MC) I. **72** A new sister (SRG) SRG. **73** In the snow (MY) C. Rajasthani wedding (RR) MG. **74** Hand-fed chimp (BHb) I. Building a house, (KP). **76** Refugee camp, Somalia (CSP) MG. Anita Roddick receives award from Princess Michael of Kent (PB) R. **77** Mother Teresa, R. 4th of July parade, New Hampshire (PC) C.

9 The Psychoanalytic Perspective
78 Toddlers fighting (CJ) CJ. **79** Drama lesson (HS) HS. Jogging (GMS) TIB. **80** Fat man (BGl) MG. Marines in training (JNa) MG. **81** Mother and son (PZ) MG. Couple at party (DWH) TIB. **82** Winter landscape (DBe) SGA. **82-3** Steps, Greece (HCB) MG. **83** Friends hugging (GLQ) MG. Surgery (BHa) Z/S. **84** Virgin and Child with St Anne by Leonardo da Vinci, Louvre, Paris, BAL. **85** Anatomical drawing, Leonardo da Vinci. Bartolozzi after Leonardo, Windsor Castle, Royal Library © 1988 Her Majesty The Queen.

10 Personality Types
87 Rent-a-butler (BL) N. Jesse Jackson (AWe) MG. Stewardess in plane, Z. President Aquino, Philippines (JNa) MG. **88** Criminal types (CLb) WIL. Woman at table (ST). Woman on death row (HE) L/FSP. L Vitale, G/FSP. Phrenological chart, ME. **89** Swedish relay team (TD) ASp. **90** Lady by window, Alaska (JAz) C. Happy man, New York City (RKr) TIB. **91** Police, New York (AG) I. Wall Street after crash (GPe) MG. **93** Four Humors, ZZ Ms. C 54 f. 34v 36r.

11 Expressing Your Personality
94 Phyllis Diller and D Thomas (S/G) C. **95** Royal Academy summer show (HS) HS. Woman reading, AD. **97** By the pool (JdaC) R. New Year's Eve party (HS) HS. **98** Marilyn Monroe (EA) MG. **98-9** Two men laughing (SMo) R. **99** Traders bargaining, Algeria, H. Woman gesturing (FF) C. **100** Girls and woman laughing (MD) TIB. **101** Two sisters (SRG) SRG. Rice grass mustache (JoB) B/C.

12 The Roots of Personality
102 Babies: easy, slow to warm up, difficult (SRG) SRG. **103** Baby surrounded by family (WM) MG. **104** Twins: Roger Brooks (left), Tony Milasi (right) (MN) MG. **105** The Richmond four (MN) MG. **106** Corrida, PP. **107** Amish people (JMcC) TIB. DNA molecule, SPL. Prague Spartakiad 85 (LT) H. **109** PET scans, by Dr Richard J Hayer, University of California, Irvine. **111** Hang-gliding (AEr) I.

13 Assessing Your Personality
112 Coffee break (GP) APA. **113** Business lunch, P/SGA. Window shopping, TIB/JA. **114** Rorschach inkblot test (WDMc) SPL. **116** Losing weight (C) G/FSP. **117** Adolescent (SP) TCL.

14 Becoming Well Adjusted
118 Feeding toddler (RK) MG. **119** Mother and baby (BBa) C. Orphans, South Vietnam (PT) C. **120** Nun at altar (HS) HS. Chicago Mercantile Exchange (PFu) MG. **121** New York 9th Precinct policewoman (LF) MG. **122** Children at funeral (P/W) C. Philippine children in rubbish tip (CLo) FSP.

123 President and Mrs Roosevelt, PF. **124** Joan Crawford (EA) MG. **125** Edna Gardner Whyte piloting (MPe) B/C. Disabled gardener (PK) TCL.

15 Personal Growth
126 Couple at table, R. **126-7** Couple laughing (N) TCL. **127** Talking about yourself, R/S. **128** Chocoholics weekend (HS) I. **128-9** Japanese bowing (HY) FSP. **129** Business management school, Japan (MMI) H. Touch therapy, California (TK) G/L/FSP. **130** Couple, R. **131** Beach (GD) C. Couple, Soviet Union (PTu) C. Mothers and babies (LT) H.

Part Title Your Emotional Well-Being
132-133 Girl, Lake Tahoe, AD.

16 The World of Your Emotions
134 Woman and chimpanzee (YAB) I. **135** Boris Becker, ASp. Indian boy, Brazil (JPK) H. Woman crying (HS) I. Exuberant crowd, Siena, Italy (RK) MG. **136** Sebastian Coe and father (TD) ASp. **137** Survivor, Herald of Free Enterprise (T) R/S. Little boy in distress (BL) N. **138** Boy crying (NDMcK) H. **139** Nigel Mansell, British Grand Prix, 1986 (SBr) ASp.

17 Emotional Development
140 Father and son (SRG) SRG. Girlfriends (HS) HS. Couple (PJG) MG. **141** Boys hugging (NDMcK) H. **142** Mother and daughter (SRG) SRG. Father and infant, (AS). **143** Country school, Soviet Union (EA) MG. **144** Boys fighting (AS). Girls playing (JF) I. **145** Model trains (JSm) TIB. **146-7** Grandmother and baby (SRG) SRG. **148** Mother and daughter (DWH) TIB. **148-9** Father and daughter (NDMcK) H

18 Understanding Your Feelings
150 Rollercoaster, USA (LB) C. **151** Lunchtime, London (JS) N. Jimmy Swaggart, television preacher (ASu) C. **152** Couple in kitchen (PZ) MG. **153** World's largest pizza, Florida (RNe) C.

19 How Moods Come and Go
154 Girl at window (RPh) TIB. Couple on beach (RBi) C. **155** Spanish dancers, Seville (PMe) C. **156** Drinking (JCa) I. **157** Paris Stock Exchange (JGa) MG. **158** Office workers at night (DE) TIB. Man reading in sunlit room (GH) TIB. **159** Woman at breakfast (KE) TIB.

20 Expressing Your Feelings
160-61 Facial expressions, Andromeda. **161** Tears (CM) MG. **162** Mourning Indira Gandhi's death (DMe) C. Man leaning on bicycle (LT) H. **163** Women grieving, Mexico (AWe) MG. **164** Class reunion (RK) MG. Royal family, Denmark (JCF) G/FSP. **165** Young girl in silver dress (HHa) V. At the airport (PFu) MG. **166** Baseball spectators, Tokyo (BB) MG. **167** Children at Punch and Judy show (SLo) SGA.

21 Anxiety and Stress
168 Security men (ER) MG. **168-9** Maze (HSu) TIB. **169** Lifeboatmen, Australia (RG) C. **170** Commuters, Tokyo (BB) MG. **171** Lie detector, USA (AR) C. **172** Bob Champion riding Aldaniti (BWi) MG. **173** Woman with influenza (KP).

22 Facing Life's Crises
174 At the train station (CSK) R. **174-5** Helicopter accident (GSo) G/FSP. **175** Car bomb, Beirut (KD) G/FSP. **176** Street accident, Los Angeles (BL) N. Unemployed, Japan (SF) MG. **177** Wedding (JW) V. **178** Survivor, Zeebrugge ferry disaster R. **179** Test-tube twins (LG) L/FSP. Zaadi doll (ESa) L/FSP.

23 Signs of Stress
180 Going to work, Waterloo Bridge, London (PM) MG. **180-1** Policewoman (KBo) C. **181** Girl on

fence (EA) MG. **182** Man with two telephones (EH) MG. **183** Businessmen, P/SGA. Woman on telephone (ERi) MG. **184** Fast-food meal (KL) C. Woman hailing taxi P/SGA. **185** Richard Nixon, R. Richard Nixon's signatures, AP. **187** Grand Prix driver (BBn) G/FSP.

24 Emotional Breakdown
188 Emergency, P/SGA. **189** Breaking down (MD) TIB. **190** Working mother (DW) C. Nurses protesting (Ga) G/FSP. **191** Men laughing (RK) MG. **192** Pottery, Pl. **193** Spectators, Wimbledon (NJ) R.

25 Learning to Relax
194 Chocolate dessert (JMe) TIB. **195** In pool (DKi) C. Man and parrot (JDr) C. **196** Woman with headache (JH) C. **197** Yoga (Bl) Z. Woman praying (KC) TIB. **198** Underwater hotel (JAz) C/C. **199** Taxi driver, Rome (MC) I.

26 Positive Thinking
201 Gymnasium (WS/V) C. Shipyard worker (MFi) C. Chatting, New York City (JSc/W) C. **202** Demonstration (BH) I. Hot dogs over Olympic flame (HK/T) C. **203** Girl in telephone booth, Pl. **204** Toddler with earphones, Z. **204** Outdoor aerobics, Paris (BR) H. **205** Canoe in sunset (DLa) TIB.

27 Dealing with Fear
206 Policewoman (EA) MG. **206-7** Pair of eyes (CP/MC) SPL. Don Dulac paints Golden Gate Bridge (RRe) WP/C. **207** Offshore oilfield workers in survival training (HS) I. **208** Woman and snake, (SMa) R. **209** Rush hour (BL) N. Girl at window (MMa) TIB. **210** Flying (AEr) I. **211** Stuntman (MBl) I. Skier (MMe) WP/C. **212** Fear of flying (GNo) G/FSP. Fear of flying (GNo) G/SFP. Girl with horses (DR) SGA. **213** Tarantula, AD.

28 Overcoming Depression
214 Computer executive, Pl. Tito funeral, Yugoslavia (CFi) C. **214-5** Woman in bed, TSW. **216** High-rise housing, Glasgow (JS) N. **217** Couple in new house, Pl. **218** Couple, Z. **219** Sea World, San Diego (BR) H. Couple eating ice cream (JH) C.

29 Coping with Grief
220 Funeral, Northern Ireland (BPi) C/C. Funeral, Ghana, H. **221** Buddhist funeral, Thailand, H. **222** Mrs Ford and picture of son, (PM) MG. **224** Widows of India (PPa) G/FSP. **225** Grandfather and boy (AU) TIB.

30 Managing Guilt
226 Mother and daughter, AS. **227** Confession (WMc) TIB. Bathing in Ganges (IB) MG. **228** French collaborator (HCB) MG. **229** Camargo (OPi) G/FSP. Man with police (GD) C. **230** Couple arguing, Pl. **231** Vietnam veteran (RCa) G/FSP.

31 Survival Strategies
232 Young man at bar (MMa) TIB. **233** Mother and daughter in classroom (LS) N. **234** John McEnroe (NL) I. **235** Pat Cash (CLe) ASp. New arrival in the family (SRG) SRG. **236** Parachuting (Bo) G/FSP. **237** Pillow bashing, T. At the barber (BL) N. **238** Earthquake, Chile (RWo) FSP. Grieving, South Africa (Ma) L/FSP. **239** Girl on couch (EA) MG.

32 Happiness and Contentment
241 Woman (NDMcK) H. **242** Mother and children (FB) TCL. Picnic at Machu Picchu (JGF) H. **243** Three girls (JE) H. Camping, Monument Valley, Arizona (BTh) C. **244** Executive at desk (HS) HS. Designers, Universal Studios, California (RBi) C/C. **245** Roofgarden (MBl) I. **246** Wealth, Dallas, Texas (BL) N. Madge Sharples jogging (MBl) I. Mother Teresa (JCF) G/FSP. **247** Family in boat (PCo) TSW.